The Roman Inquisition
Trying Galileo

THE ROMAN INQUISITION

TRYING GALILEO

Thomas F. Mayer

PENN

UNIVERSITY OF PENNSYLVANIA PRESS

PHILADELPHIA

A volume in the Haney Foundation Series, established in
1961 with the generous support of Dr. John Louis Haney.

Published by
University of Pennsylvania Press
Philadelphia, Pennsylvania 19104-4112
www.upenn.edu/pennpress

Printed in the United States of America on acid-free paper
1 3 5 7 9 10 8 6 4 2

Library of Congress Cataloging-in-Publication Data
ISBN 978-0-8122-4655-1

Ad piam memoriam Frederick Emanuel Mayer († 1954)

CONTENTS

Introduction

As the popular historian Dava Sobel put it without much exaggeration, "no other process in the annals of canon or common law has ricocheted through history with more meanings, more consequences, more conjecture, more regrets" than Galileo's.[1] And as Adriano Prosperi, a dean of historians of the Inquisition, well says that *processo* is "more intricate and problematic" than most historians think.[2] One of the most serious problems in understanding what happened to Galileo is that his trial has almost never been treated as a legal event. Without an understanding of both how the Roman Inquisition worked and how the law it applied was constantly modified, grasping how Galileo came to be condemned is impossible. Building on my earlier work on both points, this book marks the first full-length attempt to study Galileo's trial as such, and one of a handful of any size

Galileo's case resonates far outside academe. Dan Brown's *Angels and Demons*, like his *Da Vinci Code*, spins yarns about the Vatican's inner workings. It also partly concerns Galileo's trial. Although most of what Brown says about both is purely fictional, he agreed about the trial's importance with no less an authority than Stephen Hawking. Like many others, both make Galileo an icon of modern Western culture, the heroic scientist martyred by a reactionary church for daring to claim that the earth moved and the sun did not. Even for those who do not draw the lines so starkly, Galileo stands at the watershed of the divide between science and religion, notably in Wade Rowland's recent *Galileo's Mistake*, a widely reviewed book and almost as fictional as Brown's. To Brown, Hawking, and Rowland, Galileo's trial lacks intrinsic interest. They are as wrong on that score as they are about its significance.

Method

There have been only a handful of previous studies of Galileo's trial.[3] This one differs in a number of ways from them as well as the hundreds (thousands?) about his case or affair.

This books rests on a simple philosophical premise. Humans make history. One of my central objects is to restore agency to all the individual actors involved, above all to Galileo, who has most often been left a passive victim, even in his own view. Thus I have followed a similar prosopographical approach to that used in *The Roman Inquisition*, providing capsule biographies where possible designed to help navigate the complicated world of Roman bureaucracy and courts.[4] These biographies also sometimes contain sufficient detail to allow inferences about motives. That said, I do not dwell on them, preferring to lay out events, rather than contributing to the miasma of speculation about why Urban or Galileo or anyone else did what he did. In order to make such inferences more concrete, I have paid careful attention to detailed chronology, which at least allows the possibility of better guesses based on who was where, when, and doing what. While introducing faction as an element in Galileo's trial certainly pushed its study in the direction of human actors, it has been both over- and underdone. Faction between religious orders, especially Dominicans and Jesuits, has become an almost universally accepted factor, with the two orders reversing positions relative to Galileo over the course of his trial. No doubt this interpretation has much value, but it almost always overlooks the fact that neither order had an agreed position about Galileo (Copernicus may have been another matter), that factions within orders could be as important as battles between them, especially at the origin of Galileo's troubles, and that other orders should come into consideration. Similarly, the analysis of the outcome of Galileo's trial as founded in infighting among the Cardinal Inquisitors has become almost as solid an article of faith, despite the fact that it is supported by precious little evidence, primarily the fact that only seven of ten Inquisitors signed Galileo's sentence.[5]

This book differs most from other studies nominally about Galileo's trial in that it treats his *trial*, not his case, nor his affair. Thus the second important element in my approach is a careful study of the law and procedures involved. For procedure, I draw on *The Roman Inquisition*, while the treatment of the law applied to Galileo is new. In this book I offer a detailed study of the device of the precept, the first since the 1940s, in particular, the Roman Inquisition's jurisprudence and practice in its regard, which has never been given attention despite the precept's centrality to the proceedings against Galileo. The precept given Galileo in 1616 has always been regarded as a singularity. In fact, the Inquisition handed them out quite frequently, along with the companion device of an admonition.

A Theory of the Trial in Context and a Summary of This Book

Galileo's trial can be made simple. Its first phase began in 1616 and ended when he was given a precept utterly to abandon Copernicus's principles. Seventeen years later in its second phase, he was found guilty of having violated that precept by publishing the *Dialogue on the Two Chief World Systems*.

I am the first to admit that this theory is a silly caricature. That said, the "precept interpretation" summarizes most of the case I shall argue. It is chronologically the second interpretation to arise. At the very beginning of Galileo's trial, it had a competitor, the "heresy interpretation."[6] This theory lost out to the second at the end of the trial's first phase and did not reappear, almost evanescently, until its final four months, with terminal consequences for Galileo. The two theories exist in a dialectic that frames the narrative parts of this book. While the first, the heresy interpretation, is replete with drama, the second superficially lacks the contingency of false starts, twists and turns, and plain blundering inherent in any legal process involving as many people, institutions, and ideas as Galileo's did. Thus in most of this book I shall resort to narrative in order to explicate how a great, buzzing confusion became a conviction on simple grounds, if not necessarily clear ones. If that sounds like a paradox, so be it.

Despite extensive prepublication censorship of Galileo's *Sunspot Letters* (1613) by the Inquisition, the work gave Galileo's enemies in Florence an opening to attack him, in both the pulpit and the Inquisition (Chapter 1). The conspiracy against him in Florence had arisen almost as soon as he arrived from Venice in 1610. By 1614 it had moved into high gear, and early the following year two of its Dominican members were ready to denounce Galileo in Rome. The formal proceedings opened on the strength of their claims were aborted early in 1616, probably for lack of evidence, despite the condemnation of two propositions allegedly taken from *Sunspot Letters*. Instead, the Inquisition turned to a familiar device in its extensive arsenal, a precept. Acting with the full authority of the Congregation of the Holy Office and its sole head the pope, Cardinal Roberto Bellarmino first ordered Galileo through a "warning" to stop defending Copernicus's sun-centered theory of the universe. At the same time, Galileo received a precept saying the same thing in even stronger terms. A few days later the Congregation of the Index, the chief Roman censor, suspended publication of Copernicus's own book (Chapter 2).

The precept was a mild outcome. Not for the first nor last time did Galileo get special treatment because of his status as client of the grand duke of Tuscany. The nature and use of precepts especially by the Roman Inquisition are the subject of Chapters 3 and 4. As an interim measure that might also become permanent, a precept could allow for its removal in the future. Galileo had at least three chances to secure that result and thereby avoid condemnation and threw all of them away. The law gave Galileo both gentle treatment and a way to escape its rigors; Galileo failed to understand either point.

The first chance to get out from under the precept came at the beginning of Urban VIII's reign. The new pope had allegedly opposed the censuring of Copernicus in 1616 and admired Galileo. Galileo had merely to tell him about Bellarmino's order, and Urban could probably have made it disappear. Second, the pope might have been able to annul the precept had Galileo admitted its existence when seeking permission to publish the *Dialogue* (this may be why the draft bill of charges in summer 1632 insisted that Galileo had acted "fraudulently" in concealing the precept) (Chapter 5).

Even missing these two opportunitites did not doom Galileo. The particular congregation in summer 1632 that decided that his case had to go to the Inquisition homed in on the precept at the same time as it concluded that there was not all that much wrong with the *Dialogue*. It thereby gave Galileo an opening to negotiate, a tactic the Inquisition commonly used. Instead, Galileo made another key blunder and insisted on formal proceedings. Had he at least consulted a canon lawyer at this point, counsel could have done one or both of two things. He could have encouraged Galileo to negotiate, perhaps in just the way Galileo eventually did when it was too late, by offering to rewrite his book to make clear that he did not defend Copernicus. Or that canonist, moving in the direction of but stopping short of formally reopening Galileo's trial, could have lodged the objection that a precept expired with the death of the man who issued it. Paul V, in whose name both Bellarmino's order and the precept had been issued, died in 1621. Circumstances had changed dramatically by 1633, and legal arguments might not have worked as well then as earlier in Urban's pontificate, but they could have. Galileo had at least two lawyers whom he might have used, his own in-law Giovanfrancesco Buonamici and Niccolò Gherardini, and rejected advice from both of them (Chapter 6).

No doubt but that Urban decided to punish his client Galileo. A lawyer, he chose the law as his instrument, bending it creatively when necessary, following it carefully when convenient. But Urban's very dependence on the law dictated that the precept take center stage. This inadvertently magnified Galileo's chance to escape. Not that Urban did not have powerful resources that in the end proved too much even for Galileo, his many friends in Rome, and his powerful political backers. Urban used the Inquisition against Galileo. After some disagreement about exactly how (or whether) to do that, its key personnel were changed in late 1632, probably for reasons having little to do with Galileo's trial, but nonetheless with the effect of clearing the way to his conviction. The most important figure after the pope was Vincenzo Maculano, the Inquisition's commissary or chief operating officer. Guided by the pope's brother Cardinal Antonio Barberini, Sr., secretary of the Inquisition, and their nephew Cardinal Francesco Barberini, the papal secretary of state, Maculano brilliantly entrapped Galileo with a good deal of help from Galileo himself. He did so via the precept. It therefore figured centrally in the narrative of Galileo's sentence, although it did not appear in the sentence proper. That oversight was remedied in Galileo's abjuration on the same day, 22 June 1633, which began with and turned on the precept. Ideally, the Inquisition under Urban and his brother Antonio's guidance would have done its work more carefully, removing a considerable amount of ambiguity about precisely of what Galileo was convicted (Chapter 6). That it did not should cause no surprise. In sloppiness, creative record-keeping, and inventive jurisprudence the Inquisition treated Galileo no differently than most of the rest of those who underwent trial before it.

How Many Trials?

Now we are in a position to answer one last question. How many trials did Galileo undergo? Most investigators say two, one in 1616, one in 1633, and only the second was serious. This is a mistake, grounded in misunderstanding of the precept. On another level this question is absurd, since, once the Inquisition opened a dossier, all subsequent investigations went into it, thereby creating a single "trial." An ambiguity in Latin and Italian usage that is difficult to capture in English compounds the problem. Both languages have one word for both "dossier" and "trial," *processus* in Latin, *processo* in Italian. Nevertheless, any trial by the Inquisition went through a fairly regular set of phases, as did Galileo's (see the Conclusion). The only apparent difficulty in sorting out Galileo's trial is once more the precept. Sigismondo Scaccia's claim that an emergency, extrajudicial precept—one possible understanding of Galileo's—could initiate process provides legal rather than administrative grounds for speaking of a single trial (see Chapter 4). Alternatively, taking the precept out of the proceedings leaves a straightforward, single trial. Orio Giacchi first put forward this argument in 1942.[7] Building on the synthetic and rather ahistorical work of Pio Fedele on precepts in canon law, Giacchi argued that a precept was an administrative, not a judicial act. and that its effect was therefore not condemnation but suspension of judicial process.[8] Galileo's most crucial blunder was to think his trial had ended in 1616 while, in fact, it had merely been put on hold.[9]

A Note on Key Terms

Originally meaning "meeting" and still used in that sense by the Inquisition, "congregation" had been routinized into the name for the central organs of papal government especially after Sixtus V's reforms of 1585.[10] I shall use it in both senses; with a lower-case "c" it denotes a meeting of the Congregation of the Holy Office, which is always given with an upper-case "C" in order to distinguish the two. A congregation with the pope, always on Thursday, is called a coram. Any congregation without him, usually on Wednesday, is a non-coram. One other kind of congregation is centrally important, a particular congregation. This was an ad hoc body assigned to consider a "particular," or detail, a single point. The Inquisition used them frequently.[11] Inquisitor with a capital "I" means a cardinal of the Congregation; "inquisitor" with a small "i" means any inquisitor not a member of the Congregation. Inquisition with a capital "I" always signifies the Roman Inquisition. Inquisition with a lower case "i" indicates a local tribunal.

CHAPTER I

The Florentine Opposition

The Roman Inquisition showed interest in Galileo several times before formal proceedings began in 1615. His mother may have denounced him to the Holy Office in Florence for calling her names.[1] Next, one of his household servants in Padua denounced him for practicing judicial astrology. The Venetians quashed the proceedings.[2] In 1611 during its protracted investigation of Galileo's Paduan friend the Aristotelian philosopher Cesare Cremonini, the Congregation ordered its archives searched to see what it had against Galileo.[3] The Inquisition's most serious interest came in 1612–1613 when it somewhat unusually subjected Galileo's *Sunspot Letters* to prepublication censorship. It objected most seriously to Galileo's attempt to interpret scripture.[4] As always, Galileo paid the Inquisition's interventions only as much heed as he had to and seems to have taken away nothing whatever by way of a lesson. The pattern for his trial was set.

The Florentine Opposition

Almost as soon as Galileo arrived in Florence from Padua in 1610, opposition arose to him and his ideas. It reached critical mass about eighteen months after the publication in 1613 of *Sunspot Letters*, its target. The conspiracy grew among a tight-knit group of Florentine Dominicans, probably with ramifications to the top of the Florentine social and economic hierarchy. The conspirators used two basic approaches: preaching, the Dominicans' forte; and denunciation to the Inquisition in Rome, an institution they dominated.

Raffaello Delle Colombe

Pride of place in launching the campaign from the pulpit against Galileo has always gone to Tommaso Caccini (see the next chapter), but priority probably belongs to his fellow Florentine Dominican Raffaelo delle Colombe (1563–1627).[5] Luigi Guerrini calls Delle Colombe "the most important Dominican active in Florence in the first two and a half decades of the seventeenth century" as well as "one of the principal collaborators" of Archbishop Alessandro Marzi Medici in both his general efforts to control Florentine culture and more specifically to rein in Galileo.[6] His brother Ludovico delle Colombe, a more obscure figure, has usually been taken as the ringleader of the Florentine cabal.[7] Raffaello Delle Colombe entered the Dominican order on 6 November 1577 at Santa Maria Novella, studying theology in Perugia before preaching there, in Rome, and elsewhere in the Roman province.[8] He authored or contributed to three books, all of them about saints.[9] He probably spent considerable time in Santa Maria Novella before taking up permanent residence in 1612.[10] Elected prior in 1620, he resigned in 1623. The convent's library benefited greatly from monetary donations he arranged from his brothers and the 7,000 books Archbishop Francesco Bonciani of Pisa bequeathed in late 1619.[11]

Between 1613 and 1627, Delle Colombe published five large volumes of sermons, all by the Florentine house of Sermartelli. The first, dedicated to Marzi Medici's nephew, *Delle prediche sopra tutto gli Evangeli dell'anno* (*Sermons on all the Gospels of the Year*), appeared in 1613 (IT\ICCU\RLZE\034354) (2nd ed. 1619; IT\ICCU\UM1E\004084), although its permissions date from 1609 and 1610, including one from Emanuele Ximenes, S.J., a prominent member of the opposition to Galileo, as we shall see in the next chapter.[12] Next came *Prediche della Quaresima* (*Lent Sermons*) (IT\ICCU\BVEE\056825), published in 1615, although all the approvals are of 1613. They are in themselves of interest. The first of 3 July 1613 is by Dominican Michele Arrighi (1567–1634), then prior of Santa Maria Novella and teacher and friend of Giacinto Stefani, the man who would review Galileo's *Dialogo* in Florence.[13] The Jesuit Claudio Seripando's opinion at Archbishop Marzi Medici's request is dated 31 August 1613; the archbishop's own approval "if so it pleases the reverend master father inquisitor" rests on Seripando's.[14] Seripando had been involved with Rodrigo Alidosi during Alidosi's legation to Prague in 1605–1607 and later cooperated with Lelio Medici, the inquisitor of Florence, in a proposed abjuration of one of Alidosi's Bohemian Lutheran clients.[15] Then "by order of the Holy Office," comes an opinion dated 2 September 1613 "del nostro Collegio della Compagnia di Giesù," Emanuele Ximenes again. All in all, a nicely balanced set of licenses. The second edition of 1622 (IT\ICCU\UM1E\004089) was dedicated to Federico Borromeo and included a third volume, *Prediche aggiunte a quella della Quaresima* [*Sermons added to those for Lent*] (IT\ICCU\TO0E\028863), dedicated to Desiderio Scaglia, another Dominican but much more important an Inquisitor. Volume 4, *Prediche sopra le solennità della beatissima madre di Dio* [*Sermons for the Solemnities of the the Most Blessed Mother of God*] (1619; IT\ICCU\CFIE\016595), was dedicated to another Dominican and Inquisitor Agostino Galamini, the man who directed Galileo's prosecution in 1616. These two dedications cannot have been casual. Last came *Dupplicato avvento di prediche* [*Doubled Advent Sermons*, one set for religious, the other for the laity] (1627; IT\ICCU\CFIE\016608).[16]

Delle Colombe's preaching campaign had two phases according to Guerrini. Between 1608 and 1610 when Galileo arrived in Florence, he attacked Copernicans in general.[17] In a sermon dating from before 1613, Delle Colombe broadened his criticism of worldly wisdom into harsh criticism of a long list of fools, ending with "Copernicans":

The[18] men of the world are so far from this humility that there is nothing they study more than to hide than their ignorance nor to show than "science;" and indeed human "science" if it is not tempered with the water of divine wisdom is nothing other than a drunkenness. . . . Pride has disturbed their vision. . . . Thus if whoever drinks the wine of the world's science, if he does not mix some water of which it is written "she . . . will give him the water of wisdom to drink" [Ecclesiasticus 15.3] will give into a delirium and commit insanities. What greater insanity than to deny God as Pythagoras [did] or divine providence as Ibn Rush [did], and similar things? What greater foolishness than to make the soul mortal, as Galen [did]? . . . What [is] more reasonable than to see "You [Yahweh] have made the world, firm, unshakeable" [Ps. 92/3.2] and with all this that the Copernicans [*Copernici*] say that the earth moves and the heavens stay still, because the sun is the center of the earth, for which reason it can be said of these that they have dizziness, "On them Yahweh has poured out a spirit of giddiness . . . as a drunkard slithers in his vomit" [an edited version of Isaiah 19.14]

Beginning in 1612, Delle Colombe's target became Galileo and—as Guerrini notes—specifically his ideas about sunspots.[19] On at least two occasions, Delle Colombe inserted direct criticisms of them into his sermons, one explicit, the other thinly veiled.[20] The first came in a sermon for the second day of the first week of Lent, probably—given the dates of all the permissions for the volume of Lent sermons listed above—26 February 1613, just before *Sunspot Letters* appeared, suggesting a highly organized campaign.[21] The printed version highlighted the target with a heavy-handed marginal reference to "Galileo in *On Sunspots*." The passage comes near the sermon's end, rhetorically its most important section:

> While[22] the world lasts our ignorance also lasts, we know little of others and nothing of our own selves. The time will come that the fabric will be explained, that the development of this heart will be unfolded, the hiding place of this brain will be opened. And as St. Peter Damian said "Everyone's every secret will be revealed."[23] That ingenious Florentine mathematician of ours [Galileo] laughs at the ancients who made the sun the most clear and clean of even the smallest spot, whence they formed the proverb "To seek a spot on the sun."[24] But he, with the instrument called by him telescope makes visible that it has its regular spots, as by observations of days and months he had demonstrated. But this more truly God does, because "The heavens are not of the world in His sight."[25] If spots are found in the suns of the just, do you think that they will be found in the moons of the unjust?[26]

The indirect assault came in a more sensitive context, the Feast of the Immaculate Conception of Mary, probably on 8 December 1615, just as the first phase of Galileo's trial approached its denoument and from a much more prominent pulpit, that of the cathedral of Florence, the first time Delle Colombe preached there.

> It[27] was Seneca's thought that the mirror was invented to allow contemplating the sun. It did not seem a fitting thing that man could not consider the beauty of the greatest light that appears in the theatre of the world. But because the mortal eye, for the weaknesses of its vision, cannot fix its gaze on it for its too great light, at least it can be stared at in a clear crystal behind which

the sun presents to us its beautiful image. Therefore an ingenious
Academic took for his device a mirror in the face of the sun with
the motto "It shows what is received." ["Receptum exhibet."][28] That
means that he had carved in his spirit I do not know what kind of
beloved sun. But what would be better for Mary? Who could fixedly
look at the infinite light of the Divine Sun, were it not for this
virginal mirror, that in itself conceives it [the light] and renders it
to the world? "Born to us, given to us from an intact virgin?"[29] This
is "let what is received be shown." For one who seeks defects where
there are none, is it not to be said to him "he seeks a spot in the
sun?" The sun is without spot, and the mother of the sun without
spot. "From whom Jesus was born."[30]

Yet like Domenico Gori, Delle Colombe was not entirely an old unrecon-
struct. While he often referred to traditional cosmology, he also cited the work
of the Jesuit astronomer Christoph Clavius.[31]

Dominican Science and Theology

That Delle Colombe knew Clavius's work should not surprise us. Florentine
Dominicans enjoyed a deep theological and scientific culture, as Guerrini has
shown in two books devoted to broadening our understanding of that culture
and its role in the opposition to Galileo, especially in the preaching campaign
of Delle Colombe, Caccini, and Niccolò Lorini (the last not much more than
mentioned). Following Eugenio Garin, Guerrini emphasizes the quality of
science available at both San Marco and Santa Maria Novella right through
the early seventeenth century.[32] The key figure in the construction of the Dominicans' distinctive anti-Copernicanism is Giovanni Maria Tolosani who in
his "De veritate sacrae scripturae" (1546) had provided all the ammunition his
confreres needed to attack Copernicus.[33] Guerrini stresses, almost certainly
too much, that Tolosani's work provided "the theoretical basis on which the discourse of the censors (for the most part Dominicans) was developed in the proceeding [against Galileo] of 1616."[34] As Tolosani's work's title suggests, the problem
lay in the contradiction between *De revolutionibus* and scripture.[35]

Niccolò Lorini, Turbulent Priest

As damaging as Delle Colombe's sermons might have been and however important his role in the conspiracy against Galileo, he never took as active a role as two other Florentine Dominicans. The most egregious of them was Tommaso Caccini (see the next two chapters). Lorini had greater stature (ca. 1544–?after 1617).[36] He was much older than Caccini, but age never made him diplomatic. Born to a Florentine noble family probably from Mugello, after entering the Dominican order at San Marco (not Santa Maria Novella as is universally said) in 1561, he next appears in Genoa in 1577, probably preaching against the plague.[37] If so, this was the first of a number of sermons he delivered in his youth, including one for the first Sunday of Advent 1585 in the Sistine Chapel before the pope himself that earned him an appointment as apostolic preacher; he was already a reader and general preacher in the Dominicans' Roman province.[38] The text was published at least twice, originally by the papal printer.[39] This was Lorini's second printed sermon, the first coming the previous year after being preached on All Souls (given the delays of printing possibly 1583) in Santa Maria del Fiore.[40]

Shortly before that Lorini had begun to manifest another facet of his career, stirring up controversy, at first through preaching. In January 1583, the chronicler Giuliano de' Ricci noted that, in the midst of a campaign by the Dominicans to canonize a former prior of Santa Maria Novella, Lorini attacked the Conventual Franciscans, who opposed the canonization, for setting a bad example and not following their rule.[41] He seems to have suffered no consequences, but he did three years later. This time in another fiery sermon de' Ricci heard (describing it as exaggerated "according to his usual"), Lorini had attacked "the many thefts and homicides that had been done in this state [the grand duchy of Tuscany] and the few that were punished," and went on to name names, saying that "Annibale's brother did more damage at present in Tuscany by freeing prisoners than the same Hannibal had done in all of Italy." "[A]ll the people" understood Annibale to mean Annibale da Pescia, and his brother—or at least relative—Lorenzo, secretary of the Florentine criminal magistracy, the Otto di Balìa.[42] This charge, which turned out to be true, led to Lorini being prohibited first from preaching in the cathedral of Florence and then its entire diocese.[43] Lorini took an MA in 1592, but there is no evidence he ever taught.[44]

Now things become really interesting. In 1602, at age fifty-seven, Lorini was banned by the Roman Inquisition from the diocese of Florence for objecting to the Council of Trent's prohibition of public confession.[45] The trouble blew up before 18 May 1602 when the Jesuit general Claudio Acquaviva wrote from Rome that there was to be no response to Lorini's provocation that Acquaviva was addressing "by another road."[46] He sent a more detailed version of this order to the Jesuit rector four days later. The Jesuits were to ignore Lorini's preaching, leaving it to Cardinal Alessandro de' Medici, archbishop of Florence, to take action once his vicar had informed him of the problem.[47] The nuncio seems to have superseded Acquaviva's plan, in the process providing more detail about what happened. Lorini had tried to attack Antonio Santarelli, reader in the Jesuit house, over a sermon considering whether it was possible to confess via letter or messenger. An "ordine" from the archiepiscopal vicar had been put in place preventing him from doing so, which he circumvented by proposing to "read" in his own convent, San Marco, where the vicar had no jurisdiction. He planned to invite people to attend. The nuncio, Ascanio Jacovacci or Giacovazzi, seeing a scandal brewing and the prospect of worse, had issued a precept to both Lorini and Santarelli and to their superiors. The precept's prohibition was remarkably similar to Galileo's (see Chapter 3). It read that "in the future either of them [Lorini and Santarelli] not dare, nor in any way whatsover presume both in preaching and in readings or otherwise to discuss or in another manner treat the article, often brought into controversy by them in recent days by preaching, that is, whether sacramental confession can be done through writing or a messenger." The penalty was excommunication *latae sententiae*.[48] Lorini reacted by complaining publicly about the "prohibitione" and "precetto" and threatening to go to preach in Lucca outside the nuncio's jurisdiction. He also alleged that Galileo's enemy Giovanni de' Medici put the nuncio up to his action.[49] Jacovacci closed by reminding the cardinal's nephew, Pietro Aldobrandini, and Pope Clement VIII that they knew Lorini well and "how freely and imprudently he speaks," suggesting a history of trouble with the ecclesiastical authorities in Rome.[50]

Jacovacci's precept had little effect. On 11 August, he complained that a Jesuit had preached in their house of S. Giovanni about a papal decree on confessors. One of two Dominicans in the audience (Lorini?) had "struck his hands together with a great shout" and walked out, which understandably caused surprise, including to the nuncio who thought matters settled by the pope and by his precept. He summoned the Jesuit rector, who claimed he was merely publishing the papal decree that the Dominicans took as aimed at them. Jacovazzi told him to do no more and also told the priors of Santa Maria Novella and San Marco not to deal with the matter on the following Sunday.[51]

Then the Inquisition took a hand. On 21 August 1602, after hearing complaints from both sides, the Jesuit one about Lorini (for what not said), it ordered Jacovacci and the vicar to investigate.[52] In the following day's meeting with the pope (a coram), the Congregation read the letters again, and the pope issued the proposed order to investigate Lorini and his new Jesuit antagonist.[53] The nuncio's report was delayed until 15 September, but when it was read in another coram on 26 September, the pope ordered the Dominican general "to have removed from the city and diocese of Florence Fra Niccolò Lorini and order (*praecipiat*) him not to speak or treat of this matter ("ut removere faciat a civitate ac diocesi Florentiae fratrem Nicolaum Lorinum, eique praecipiat ne loquatur, ne tractet de hac materia").[54] The nuncio had to defend himself for allegedly having begun judicial process in the case, although Lorini was not specifically mentioned. In fact, he disappears from the record, suggesting that he had indeed finally accepted the Inquisition's precept and gone into exile.

Lorini's "exile" did not prevent him from serving as prior of S. Domenico, Pistoia, from at least 9 February 1604; he was replaced by 22 January 1606.[55] In the fall of 1605 (and possibly the following year as well), Lorini preached at least one more set of Advent sermons in Rome. The sermons were published in 1615 with a dedication to the Florentine Cardinal Luigi Capponi, new legate of Bologna, another home of Galileo's enemies, suspiciously dated the day after Caccini's reading.[56] In the preface Lorini claimed that he would bring out the "moral sense, and the points addressed to the soul will all be taken from the proper bowels of the letter" ("il senso morale, e gl'avvertimenti nell'anima saranno tolti tutti di peso dalle proprie viscere della lettera"); in other words, he rooted his preaching in the literal sense of scripture. Interestingly enough, the first sermon has a lot to say about the sun and the heavens in both a natural and metaphorical sense. Preaching on one of the prescribed texts for 1 Advent "There will be signs in the sun and moon and stars" (Luke 21.25), he told his hearers that they well knew "that really in these bodies and globes and celestial planets will be caused many unusual things, which will multiply so much, the noises and crashes, that it will appear that the same bodies and celestial globes, that is, the stars, fall down and disappear or do not appear because of the thick fogs or darkest clouds, it will be exactly as if they had fallen, losing especially their usual influence" ("che realmente in questi corpi, e globi, e Pianeti celesti faranno cagionate molte cose disusate, a talche tanto si multiplicaranno, i rumori, e fracassi, che egli parrà, che gli stessi corpi, e globi celesti, cioe le stelle caschino, e sparendo, o non si appalesando per rispetto alle nebbie folte, o oscurissime nugole sarà proprio, come se fossero cadute, mancando massimo da loro consueti influssi").

The regular motions of "the celestial orders" would be altered such that the end would come. But not because the heaven's intrinsic motion given it by God had failed, which by its nature it never could, but because of that same God's extrinsic action to stop that motion.[57] Although the apocalyptic and astrological overtones and content are clear, Lorini's point was that Christian philosophers and theologians offered the same explanation of these phenomena, as did astrologers and physicians, no matter how their language might differ.[58] The absence of astronomers, whom Lorini would have called mathematicians, might have struck his audience.

In several sermons of another collection published two years later, *Elogii delle più principali sante donne del sagro calendario* [*Praises of all the Principal Sainted Women of the Sacred Calendar*], dedicated to the grand duke's wife and proclaiming Lorini his preacher on the title page, the now seventy-three-year-old Dominican often came closer than he had in 1605 to leveling criticisms as Caccini had of "mathematicians" and on one occasion in a sermon perhaps given to his fellow Dominicans (the audience is addressed as "fratelli") explicitly faulted Copernicus for saying the earth moved.[59] The dedication helped explain why such ideas were so dangerous. Lorini told the grand duchess that he often thought about why Jesus likened the church to the heaven and concluded that it was because "just as the aforesaid heaven for His greater beauty and our greater utility has been by nature, not wanderingly (*errante*) so egregiously adorned with planets or masculine and feminine names and by so many other splendid lights, so His church by Him in resemblance to these lights of the heaven should have been adorned by His Divine Majesty with most select men and most prefect women, lights no less resplendent than those" ("si come il predetto Cielo per maggior bellezza di lui, e utilità di noi, è stato dalla Natura, non errante, tanto egregiamente adornato di Pianeti, di nome maschile, e femminile, e di tant'altri splendentissimi lumi, così la sua Chiesa di lui a somiglianza di essi lumi del Cielo, sia stata di S. D. M. adornata d'huomini sceltissimi, e di perfettisime donne, lumi non meno risplendenti di quelli").[60]

Lorini spun out another long metaphor in a sermon for the feast of Sant'Agnese, 21 January. This time he raised the seemingly threatening possibility that the worthless, lowly earth might compete with "the heaven, the firmament and the pavement of God's feet" and the heaven agree to comparison with the earth in certain respects. The stars in the heaven were like flames on earth, and both were full of flowers.[61] The sun, "the queen of heaven," was like a carbuncle (the gem, not a sore) on earth:[62]

Much proportion is found between virtues and jewels, since
jewels are nothing other than vapor and a dry exhalation from the
earth, frozen, or petrified by the cold by virtue of the heaven and
operation of the sun and reduced by them to the highest digestion,
from which the heaven and the sun receive the variety of colors and
beauties and various properties and virtues; because finding [them]
in the earth they are however generated by the goodness and virtue
of heaven, as virtues are on earth in saintly souls, by God's gift."[63]

Lorini closed with what seems a veiled criticism of the Copernicans. The stars
served to show human weakness "that could not rise to accomplish the tiniest
thing in the starry heaven."[64]

Lorini's sermon on St. Ursula and her 11,000 virgins began with a metaphor promising more reflections on the relations between heaven and earth.
Likening Ursula's legendary battle with the Huns under the walls of Cologne
to conflict or war between inanimate objects and "flowers of that great garden
of the firmament," he described the stars assembled into troops, then into
battle array, and finally an army that naturally defeated the enemy. They did
this without leaving their "order." Lorini cited the examples of the combats
between St. Michael and the dragon and the angels and Pharoah, as well as the
Exodus, before observing "that the stars, standing firm, without leaving the
firmament, should have battled, this is completely unheard of" ("che le stelle,
stando ferme, senza partirsi del firmamento abbiano battagliato, questo è al
tutto inaudito").[65] He amplified the point by comparing the stars to Ursula's
virgins, calling them "stars of the ecclesiastical firmament" ("stelle del firmamento ecclesiastico").

Sometime after giving these sermons, Lorini returned from exile, reenter-
ing the convent of San Marco, where Caccini lived and the house the Medici
particularly favored. He was also made preacher to Grand Duke Cosimo II
(ruled 1609–1621) and allegedly reader in ecclesiastical history at the fledgling
University of Florence.[66] Lorini had good reason to regard sermons as his best
weapon. Relying on it ten years after his banning, he tried exactly the same
gambit as Caccini, attacking Galileo from the pulpit; his sermon has been
lost.[67] Later that same year Galileo called Lorini out and forced him to apologize for raising objections in conversation (or just possibly in another sermon)
to "Ipernicus, or whatever his name is."[68] If Lorini really did not know Copernicus's name, this suggests that he may not yet have been cooperating closely
with Caccini, or that Caccini had not yet imbibed his anti-Copernican views,

or some combination of the two. It is worth noting that, as of 1612, Galileo's position was strong enough to force Lorini to crawl to him. Not that Lorini went quietly. The last sentence of his letter with its dark mutterings about "the Companies of Piano and Ghighnoni" suppressed long ago and its perhaps ironic assurance "that all our [Florentine] nobility is optimally catholic" made a barely implicit threat.[69]

Whatever Lorini may have said on "la mattina dei Morti" (probably 1 November 1612), and even if the points in his sermons were not directed, even implicitly, at Copernicus, and certainly not at Galileo, given the sermons' early date, they serve to explain how Lorini could become violently opposed to both men's ideas. He soon had help from Caccini.

CHAPTER 2

Formal Proceedings Begin
(late 1614–mid-February 1616)

Brother Thomas's Stupidities

Tommaso Caccini (26 April 1574–1648) entered the Order of Preachers at San Marco in Florence at fifteen, changing his name from Cosimo to Tommaso after Thomas Aquinas.[1] An ambitious, possibly unstable man, Caccini made a perfect cat's paw for what even his brother and chief sponsor Matteo called the "pigeons," the conspiracy Galileo called the "pigeon league," detailed in the previous chapter, aided and abetted by the man who had put Niccolò Lorini up to attacking the Jesuits in 1602, Giovanni de' Medici.[2] Luigi Guerrini goes as far as to claim that everything in Caccini's testimony against Galileo came from Raffaelo Delle Colombe and that he at least "favored" if not "promoted" Caccini's anti-Galilean preaching.[3]

Caccini may have been among the first to preach against Galileo, including in Bologna during Lent 1611. This could have been the occasion when he literally had the police (*birri*) called on him by the legate of Bologna, Cardinal Benedetto Giustiniani, who forced him to recant after an "escapade."[4] The opportunity to attack Galileo arose again in late 1614, and this time Caccini enjoyed greater success. On the fourth Sunday of Advent 1614, 21 December, in the church of Santa Maria Novella in Florence Caccini delivered a rousing reading on the book of Joshua 10.[5] (The friars themselves seem not to have been impressed; they did not record the reading, and four years later when criticizing Caccini for preaching too freely, the Dominican general referred to his sermons in Bologna, not to this reading.)[6] He focused especially on verses 12 and 13, "'Sun, stand still over Gibeon, and moon, you also, over the Vale of Aijalon.' And the sun stood still, and the moon halted, till the people had vengeance on their enemies." Punning on Acts 1:11, Caccini converted the original addressees, "you inhabitants of Galilee," into "Galileans," meaning followers of Galileo, and supposedly thundered, "why stand you staring up into the heavens?"[7] His audience could not miss the point of his play on the words Jesus had originally directed to "you men of Galilee." Without quite putting his finger directly on the point, Caccini noted that a "similar opinion" to the sun's movement as taught by Copernicus "had been held by the most serious authors to be dissonant from the Catholic faith." This was a subtle turn of phrase that does not accord well with Caccini's reputation for hot-headedness. Neither does his possible expectation that the more educated among his hearers might have remembered the anti-Copernican views put forward by another Dominican of Santa Maria Novella, Giovanni Maria Tolosani. Caccini later lectured on at least part of Tolosani's book.[8] What was wrong with Copernicus's ideas according to Tolosani? They offended against scripture. This was exactly Caccini's point.

With his lecture still smoking in his hand, Caccini set out for Rome on 14 or 15 February 1615 to try to nail down a prestigious teaching post, the bachelorate, at the Dominican "university" at Santa Maria sopra Minerva.[9] The appointment became a tangled affair, and Caccini apparently never got the office, despite his claim to the title in his deposition against Galileo.[10] (The significance of Caccini's mistaken claim to the office remains to be worked out. In common law, a mistake in a deponent's "extension," or legal description of his or her status, might be enough to void his or her testimony. If the same holds true in civil law systems, this makes another point where Galileo hurt himself by refusing to engage an advocate in his defense.) Seizing the opportunity presented by Tommaso's upcoming trip to Rome (his brother and manager Matteo had promised Cardinal [and Inquisitor] Agostino Galamini on 7 February that he would come "as soon as possible and immediately" ["quanto prima et subito"]), Caccini's fellow conspirator Niccolò Lorini now hit on a more subtle gambit against Galileo and his followers than a public lecture, one much more likely to work.[11] Caccini was only too glad to help, despite strong criticism of his lecture by his brother and others and warnings to keep his head down.[12] Lorini gave Caccini two documents, a letter and its enclosure, to deliver to Cardinal Paolo Emilio Sfondrato. The letter served mainly to cover the enclosure that Lorini assured Sfondrato "runs here [Florence] in the hands of all these that are called Galileisti" and in which in "the judgment of these our fathers of the most religious convent of San Marco

there are many propositions that appear either suspect or temerarious" especially for their treatment of the Bible.[13] The fact that such ideas were "being
sown throughout our city" scandalized Lorini even more.[14]

As the first sentence of his letter with its reference to Dominicans as "the
white and black dogs of the Holy Office" suggests, Lorini probably chose
Sfondrato because he was the most senior Inquisitor, appointed in 1591.[15] It
may not have hurt that he was also the head of the Congregation of the Index,
but Lorini made no mention of that fact. Sfondrato would have appealed to
Lorini in addition as a major benefactor of the Dominicans, to whom in 1608
he donated one of the churches dependent on his cardinal's church in Rome,
Santa Cecilia in Trastevere. Lorini may not have cared that Sfondrato, Gregory
XIV's cardinal nephew, had sunk a huge amount of money into Santa Cecilia.
His investment jumped out especially in Stefano Maderno's one masterpiece,
an utterly realistic sculpture of the dead saint displaying the three wounds at
the base of her neck through which she bled to death after a botched attempt
to behead her. It sat directly above Sfondrato's burial vault.

Nevertheless, Lorini's choice was not an entirely obvious one, nor may
it have been the best possible. He could have written other men in Rome,
beginning with his fellow Dominican Agostino Galamini, recently general
of the order, appointed cardinal and Inquisitor almost simultaneously three
years earlier.[16] Pope Paul V lavished favors on Galamini despite his professed
reluctance to accept them.[17] Lorini probably did not need to write the Dominican cardinal because he was already in Caccini's corner, pushing hard for
his appointment at Santa Maria sopra Minerva as we have seen. He certainly
cooperated in Lorini's scheme in other ways, or it may have been that he or-
chestrated it.[18] Sfondrato far outranked Galamini, but not on the list of the
pope's favorite people. Lorini could not have known that the headstrong Sfondrato had lately crossed swords repeatedly with the pope.[19] Paul had walked
out on him in one consistory (a regular, usually once weekly formal meeting
between the pope and cardinals) when Sfondrato refused to stop criticizing
papal policy, and in another when Sfondrato had dared to object to the pope's
expenditures on the Quirinal palace, Paul had replied faulting Sfondrato for
being absent from Rome for whole years at a time.

This was not quite fair. Sfondrato had resided in his bishopric of Cremona
as the rules of Trent required him to do. Many cardinals were also bishops and
therefore under the same obligation; in fact, popes regularly used it as a way
to get rid of inconvenient cardinals. During his time in Cremona, Sfondrato
cooperated unusually closely with its inquisitor, Lorini's fellow Dominican

Michelangelo Seghizzi, on the point of becoming the Inquisition commissary.[20] Sfondrato and Seghizzi made an effective team in the effort to bring the former notary of Cremona's inquisition to justice, a marked contrast to Seghizzi's always strained relationship with Sfondrato's predecessor. Instead of the usual wrangling over jurisdiction between inquisitor and bishop, Seghizzi gladly added some of Sfondrato's most important officials to his panel of experts. It looks as if someone was coordinating the attack on Galileo by moving it to Rome just when both Sfondrato and Seghizzi would be in place to take action. Sfondrato's ruthless piety may also have attracted Lorini. Shortly before Sfondrato had come back to Rome in 1610, he had ordered a number of shops around Cremona's cathedral torn down and the proceeds used to pay for a monastery he had founded.[21]

However well he had worked with Seghizzi, Sfondrato was undoubtedly spoiling for a fight, and on just Lorini's grounds. He was frustrated by the Index's ineffectiveness in the face of the Inquisition's already great and constantly increasing power and was about to ask for permission to retire from Rome to his new suburban bishopric of Albano.[22] Sfondrato's ultimate appeal to Lorini was the deniability the cardinal could give him. As ranking member of both Index and Inquisition, Sfondrato could decide for himself whether to accept Lorini's insistence that he did not want his letter taken as a "judicial deposition" against Galileo and instead as "a loving piece of news (*avviso*)."[23] In choosing this form of words, it seems likely that Lorini had in the back of his mind the contrast between a legal proceeding and the much milder "charitable admonition."[24] The Congregation of the Index, unlike the Inquisition, had no judicial powers; all it could do was prohibit books, not punish their authors or those who read them. Given Sfondrato's annoyance with the toothless Index, Lorini virtually goaded him into pursuing the first option. Lorini pushed Sfondrato further in the direction of a legal remedy by providing written evidence, the enclosure in his letter, which he had also shown Caccini. This was a copy of Galileo's letter to his favorite pupil, Benedetto Castelli. Lorini set the letter in a false context by claiming it had been written in reaction to Caccini's sermon when in fact it dated from exactly a year earlier. This was a stupid thing to do, since the copy had the correct date of 21 December 1613.

Galileo's Letter to Castelli

Lorini had good reason to think the "Letter" might cause Galileo trouble. In it Galileo offered his most extended discussion of the relations between Copernicus's ideas and scripture and, unlike in the case of his correspondence with Piero Dini, did so in a more or less public way, even if not in the medium of print.

The "Letter" arose out of a debate in the grand duke's presence between Castelli, the grand duchess mother, the grand duke's wife, and a few other members of their court. Reasonably subtly, Galileo sent Castelli more arguments he could (or should) have used in reply to objections the two women had made "especially about the verse in Joshua [10.12–13] proposed against the mobility of the earth and the stability of the Sun."[25] His first point concerned the inerrancy of scripture. While agreeing with Castelli that scripture could never be wrong, Galileo maintained that "nonetheless *its interpreters and expositors* can err *in various ways*, among which would be a most serious and frequent one when they would want always to stop at *the pure literal sense*." Galileo may have thought this a simple point, but, as we have seen, the literal sense was precisely where Galileo's opponents thought they stopped, no matter how quickly they moved to metaphorical interpretation. Many things in scripture seemed not only contradictory but heretical and blasphemous when read at that level. "Therefore, since *in the scripture there are many false propositions as far as the plain sense* of the words*, but which have been expressed in that manner in order to accommodate the incapacity of the many common people,* thus for those few who deserve to be separated from the dull common people it is necessary that wise expositors of scripture extrapolate the true senses and add the particular reasons why such meanings are expressed in such words."[26] Galileo drew the conclusion that "Since, therefore, sacred scripture in many places is not only susceptible of, but necessarily in need of expositions varying from the apparent sense of the words, *it seems to me that in discussions of natural [philosophy] it ought to be reserved to the last place.*" From its interpreters to the text of scripture evidently seemed a short step to Galileo, but falsity in the first case connoted mere human error, whereas in the second it could only mean a breakdown in the communication of the divine word and, worse, dethronement of what his opponents regarded as the most direct form of that communication.

Scripture had to give way to nature because there was only one truth, and nature, unlike scripture, "is inexorable and immutable and does not care at all that its hidden reasons and means of proceeding may be or may not be fit for men's capacity." Then Galileo introduced his famous two-pronged mode of discerning nature's intent, "sensory experience" (*esperienza*, which also means "experiment" in Italian) and "necessary [logical] demonstrations."[27] The rigor of this approach combined with nature's law-governed behavior meant that any passages in scripture that appeared to contradict a natural effect should never be allowed to raise questions about it. Galileo pushed the point into increasingly dangerous territory, drawing another corollary about scripture: "Indeed, if only for this reason, to accommodate the incapacity of the people, *scripture has not abstained from perverting some of its most principal dogmas, attributing to God Himself conditions very far from and contrary to His essence.*" Thus "wise expositors" had to find meaning in scripture that agreed with "those natural [philosophical] conclusions of which first the plain sense or general, indeed necessary, demonstrations have made us certain and sure." First nature, then the Bible. Therefore, no interpreter should be forced to maintain a proposition drawn from the Bible that "those natural conclusions" do not support.

Then Galileo drew a distinction between kinds of biblical content. Articles about the faith had such "firmness" that there was no danger of contradicting them; therefore nothing should be added to them "unnecessarily." Scripture existed solely to persuade humans "that those articles and propositions that, being necessary for their salvation and surpassing any human discourse, could not have made themselves believable by any other science nor any other means than by the mouth of the Holy Spirit itself." Interpreters of the Bible could not be trusted, since one never knew whether they spoke by divine inspiration. Contrariwise, Galileo did not think God meant to deny humans the use of their senses in the investigation of natural phenomena, especially since the Bible contained almost nothing about them, "such as precisely is astronomy" (52). Repeating his claim that two truths could not contradict one another, Galileo concluded that those who had the right to investigate nature—meaning philosophers—should not be forced by threats to concede to those who could not avoid presenting sophistical and false arguments (53).

In order to demonstrate his point, Galileo turned to Joshua. Like his "adversary," Galileo proposed to begin from the text's literal sense. But he drew the opposite conclusion, "that this verse shows clearly the falsity and impossibility of the Aristotelian and Ptolemaic world system, and by contrast fits the Copernican very well." True to his own method described earlier, Galileo immediately ignored the Bible and instead carefully constructed an argument grounded in sensory experience and necessary demonstrations. How many movements does the sun have, he asked? Two, annual and daily. Of these, only the first "belonged" to it; the Primum Mobile transmitted the second to it, which produced day and night. Galileo concluded rhetorically that prolonging a day meant stopping the Primum Mobile, not the sun. Indeed, stopping the sun would shorten the day. This was a clever sally against Ptolemaic and Aristotelian astronomers, unhorsing them, as Galileo might have said, with one of their own central concepts. Either Ptolemy was wrong about the Primum Mobile, or the literal sense of the scripture was in saying sun instead of Primum Mobile. Nor could God have stopped the sun alone, since that would have caused unnecessary disruption of "the entire course of nature," that law-governed behavior on which Galileo had earlier insisted.

Instead Galileo offered in a few lines a simple Copernican solution. Since the sun gave movement to the earth, to stop the earth one had only to stop the sun, just as the Bible said (55). And that was that.

The matter was not so simple to Galileo's opponents. Although we have no direct response to the "Letter" from any of them, we can infer from the underlining in the copy in Galileo's dossier that Galileo's science, including his alternative explanation of the text of Joshua, interested them not at all. Instead, his handling of scripture drew all their attention.

And quickly. Not ten days after Lorini's letter, Galileo knew that a copy of the "Letter to Castelli" was circulating among his enemies, apparently including in Rome, who found "many heresies" in it and used it to "open a new field to injure me."[28] Writing to Dini, whom he thought to be one of his closest allies in Rome, Galileo also casually, perhaps too casually, suggested that "whoever transcribed it [the 'Letter to Castelli']" had "inadvertently changed some words," which, together with "a little disposition to censures, could make things appear much different from my intention." He had also heard that Caccini had gone to Rome "to make some other attempt" against him. (Whatever he knew about Lorini's actions, chronology makes it seem certain that Caccini's departure triggered Galileo's letter. The two events came at most two days apart.) As a prophylactic, Galileo enclosed a copy "in the right manner that I have written it." He hoped Dini would show the correct version to the Jesuit mathematician Christoph Grienberger, Galileo's "greatest friend and patron," and, even better, Cardinal Roberto Bellarmino, "to whom these Dominican fathers have let it be understood that they intend to rally around" ("al quale questi Padri Domenicani si son lasciati intendere di voler far capo"). While it is not terribly surprising that Galileo knew Lorini had a copy, it does raise eyebrows that he thought it necessary to distribute others. Since one of the recipients was to be Bellarmino, an Inquisitor, and Galileo feared that Lorini was headed to the Inquisition, why worry about getting a copy directly to the cardinal? Did Galileo really fear that Lorini had altered the text, a charge nearly all historians have made? The letter exists in multiple versions, and the one Lorini sent differs in several significant ways from what Galileo claimed as his authentic text.[29] It may be coincidence, but the Inquisition's anonymous expert assigned to read the letter singled out three of these differences in his report on the possible heresy in the document. This fact may seem to incriminate Lorini, but Galileo's strategy for dissemination instead almost has to mean that Galileo and not Lorini altered the text. Thus Galileo told his first big lie and blamed it on Lorini. He did that a great deal.

In most of his letter, Galileo indulged in one of his specialties, giving at least as good as he got. Galileo complained about a verbal assault by the bishop of Fiesole, Baccio Gherardini, in front of some of his friends. Galileo fired back one of his best shots (in his eyes), accusing his enemy of thinking that he, Galileo, had written *On the Revolutions of the Spheres*. Besides, Galileo had defended its real author Copernicus on the extrinsic grounds that he was "not only a Catholic man, but a religious and a [cathedral] canon" ("uomo non pur cattolico, ma religioso e canonico").

It may be that Galileo was right about what "the Dominican fathers" had planned and that Lorini was using Sfondrato as a conduit to his real target, Bellarmino, the recipient of Sfondrato's complaint about the Index's lack of power. Lorini may have thought it diplomatically inadvisable for a Dominican to approach a Jesuit directly in the wake of their orders' violent and still unresolved dispute over the role of grace in salvation, not to mention his own difficulties with them in 1602. He may have known that Sfondrato had been among those trying to make Bellarmino pope in 1605.[30] He must have known that Bellarmino had severe doubts about Copernicus. Galileo's friend and patron, Federico Cesi, founder of the Academy of the Lynxes, certainly was aware of Bellarmino's views and made sure Galileo knew them. In the context of Caccini's reading, Cesi wrote Galileo that Bellarmino had told him Copernicus's ideas were heretical and the "motion of the earth without any doubt is against scripture." Cesi added that, if the Index considered Copernicus's book, it would be banned.[31] He urged Galileo to proceed very carefully indeed in responding to Caccini and warned that the most Galileo could hope for was a private censure of the friar. Cesi knew what he was talking about and so did Bellarmino. He was in a position to consult some of the best scientists at the Jesuits' Collegio Romano, as he did on several occasions. But not now. He had no need.

Bellarmino was not a scientist, but he already had his mind made up on the burning scientific question of the constitution of the universe before Lorini and Caccini hatched their plot.[32] Even if he ever had, he no longer had the slightest interest in matters of science. No, his thoughts had turned all to his own mortality. Just before Caccini's sermon, Bellarmino finished *Ascent of the Soul to God*.[33] As the title makes plain, this is an intensely mystical work. Not even the command of theology on which Bellarmino had once prided himself mattered any more.

The key point for Bellarmino, as for Caccini, was the role of scripture and its interpreters. It looks at first blush as if he changed his mind on this point right in the midst of things in March 1615. On 7 March, Dini passed to Galileo what amounted to an invitation from Bellarmino to lay out his interpretation of how scripture fit his case.[34] Bellarmino had carefully pointed out that any republication of Copernicus's book would require a note added to it that his system was intended merely "to save the appearances," that is, it was a theory, no more. Then came the implicit invitation. Bellarmino suggested that only one scripture verse caused trouble, and it was not the one in Joshua Caccini had used. Instead, Bellarmino pointed to Psalm 19.4–5: "[Yet] their voice goes out through all the earth, and their message to the end of the world. High above, he pitched a tent for the sun, who comes out of his pavilion like a bridegroom, exulting like a hero to run his race." The problem to Bellarmino was that this passage appeared to say the sun had been permanently fixed in that "tent." (Neither he nor Galileo seems to have had any problem with the verse representing the sun as a person.) Galileo, who had already risen to similar bait in his "Letter to Castelli," seized the invitation and barely two weeks later fired off by express a much more succinct letter to Dini, responding directly and bluntly to the invitation.[35] Meanwhile, Bellarmino changed his mind, again in a talk with Dini, but reported at second hand by another of Galileo's circle, Giovanni Ciampoli, that Galileo should *not* meddle in scripture because he lacked the proper qualifications as a theologian, more or less Cardinal Maffeo Barberini's opinion, as Ciampoli summed up.[36] Did Bellarmino really change his mind, or does what he said depend on who reported it, especially since it could be that Ciampoli was describing the same conversation as Dini had earlier? If Bellarmino's change of mind is real, the "Letter to Castelli" was precisely what changed it. In the version Lorini sent via Caccini, Bellarmino and five other Inquisitors—not including Sfondrato—had discussed it on 25

February in a meeting at his palazzo, Palazzo Gabrielli in via del Seminario at the end next to Piazza Macuto.[37] The day before Ciampoli's letter, Caccini had testified before the Inquisition, although Bellarmino probably did not learn the content of his deposition until it was reported in the secret part of a congregation of 2 April, Sfondrato this time in attendance.[38] In that context, Galileo's letter to Dini looked like more provocation, and in consultation with Cesi Dini decided to suppress it.[39]

Even with Bellarmino's expected support, Lorini still did not have easy sledding, as his conspiracy began to mesh with the independent and more important "motor" of developments in Rome.[40] Galileo had powerful defenders there as he did in Florence. To begin with, a faction in Santa Maria Novella—home of the "moderate" Domenico Gori (see below)—opposed Lorini and Caccini and, unlike them, already had an agent in Rome, general preacher Luigi Maraffi. Maraffi was an old friend of Galileo and, even better, well enough placed to become an expert consultant to the Index in 1616, although not until after it had condemned Copernicus.[41] Maraffi thus served as an excellent conduit for the latest news from Rome and might have been able to help Galileo especially well, that is, unless he was acting as a double agent. Even before Galileo wrote to warn him of it, Maraffi already had news of Caccini's lecture, as well as of efforts to prevent it.[42] Galileo could also hope for help from Caccini's own family. Caccini's reading horrified his brother Matteo, manager of its social-climbing operation in Rome, who blasted him for having acted like "a pigeon, testicle (coglione, i.e., with vulgar stupidity), or certain doves."[43] Much more important, Cardinal Andrea Giustiniani was still angry with Caccini, and Matteo feared Caccini's behavior would likely cost him his chance to bring his brother into the service of Cardinal Pompeo Arrigoni, former secretary of the Inquisition, now in residence in his archbishopric of Benevento.[44] Matteo Caccini, who held high office in Arrigoni's household, put his brother forward as the cardinal's theologian.[45]

For all Maraffi's encouragement to Galileo, his letter contained one worrying piece of news. The latest book of Galileo's old Paduan friend, the Aristotelian philosopher Cesare Cremonini, had run into serious trouble. Galileo had talked about it to Maraffi at length (but, then, Galileo talked about everything at length). Maraffi was indeed a well-placed source, since the Inquisition's records contain little about Cremonini at precisely this time. But in October 1614 just before Caccini's lecture, there had been a burst of activity directed by Pope Paul against his De coelo.[46] When the Venetians tried to defend Cremonini in Rome, they met a flat condemnation from Arrigoni's successor as secretary of the Inquisition, Cardinal Giovanni Garzia Millini. Cremonini offended by putting forward the Aristotelian doctrine of the soul's mortality. The danger this idea posed to the Christian notion of salvation does not need emphasis. Cremonini and Galileo had been linked once before in the Roman Inquisition's records when Pope Paul in 1611 ordered a search through them to see whether Galileo's name appeared in Cremonini's interminable case.[47] The Inquisition in Padua had jointly investigated the two men in 1604. Worse, Cremonini's case had opened in 1598 with exactly the same treatment it would shortly give Galileo, a precept not to teach a particular doctrine. When it heated up again in late April, Cremonini's file fell into first Bellarmino's hands and then those of Caccini's patron Galamini, the second of whom was specifically asked to consider the impact of the precept on Cremonini's failure to observe it both in general and in the particular case of refusing to revise his book as ordered. Put in these terms, Cremonini faced exactly the same situation as Galileo would in 1632.

Trouble for one thus almost inevitably meant trouble for the other. Did Galileo miss a nudge and wink from Rome?

In this crisis Galileo relied most heavily not on Maraffi but on Dini, a man like Maraffi of the third tier in Rome, a professional lawyer but nowhere near the top of the legal heap. It is important to the story that Galileo did not read his carefully worded letters closely. Dini had been nominated by the grand duke for the Florentine slot on the Rota, the papal supreme court. Cardinal Nephew Scipione Borghese's candidate landed the job instead, and Dini wound up with the ordinary consolation prize of "referendary of both signatures," appointed to practice in the Courts (Signatures) of Grace and Justice, a notch below the Rota.[48] He was involved with Francesco Ingoli, one of Galileo's sparring partners, and Cardinal Bonifazio Caetani in the translation of Ptolemy's *Tetrabiblos*.[49] He was also one of Galileo's numerous supporters in the Academy of the Crusca, the Italian equivalent of the Académie Française, the central agency in the invention of modern Italian.[50] More even than their work together in the increasingly successful Florentine offensive to dominate Italian culture, what really attracted Galileo to Dini was his family. He was the nephew of another Florentine, Cardinal Ottavio Bandini. In his garden on the Quirinal, Bandini had hosted the most important of the parties in Rome in 1611 at which Galileo had demonstrated his telescope and talked about sunspots, the phenomenon that was about to get him in serious trouble.[51] Bandini was also Cardinal Giustiniani's brother-in-law. Although not yet an Inquisitor or quasi-papal nephew, as he would be under Paul's successor Gregory XV,

Bandini represented money in the bank, and his nephew automatically became a VIP in Rome. Dini's official status scarcely mattered. He had entrée.

Galileo called up other soldiers of the Florentine mafia, including Michelangelo's grand nephew.[52] Much more important than Dini in the long term was Ciampoli, author of some of the most fawning letters Galileo ever got, which is saying a lot. Galileo ordered him and Dini to coordinate their efforts and decide jointly who else should get the "Letter to Castelli."[53] Like Dini and Ciampoli, most of the rest of the Florentine establishment rallied strongly behind Galileo. This may not have been quite as good a thing as it sounds. For one, it produced a steady stream of reports, especially from Ciampoli in Rome and Castelli in Pisa, that Galileo had nothing to worry about. For another, its most powerful members, the cardinals who were in or close to a position to decide his case, were prepared to defend Galileo only within largely political limits, and not on the issues. If a theological argument could be made against him, politics would have to give way. In other words, if forced to choose between loyalty to the grand duke and to the pope, these men would choose the pope. One of them, Cardinal Francesco Del Monte, inherited his support of Galileo from his brother Guidobaldo who had gotten Galileo his first job; the cardinal had been among Galileo's protectors in Rome in 1611.[54] He gladly hosted Galileo's team of Dini, Ciampoli, and Maraffi.

Far the most potent backer beyond Bellarmino that Ciampoli tried to enlist was another Florentine cardinal, Maffeo Barberini, the third main protagonist of this tale as Pope Urban VIII, elected in 1623. He was a patron of choice, including of Ciampoli; Matteo Caccini had tried to attach Tommaso to his service.[55] Barberini may have lacked social cachet, his merchant family having recently arrived in the metropolis from the Florentine outback, but they had moved fast. Maffeo's uncle Francesco, using the same platform as Dini, referendary of the Signatures, had built up a large fortune and cleared the way for Maffeo's rapid ascent by buying him offices, opening doors, and making him his heir.[56] Uncles backing nephews (including when they were actually sons) is true nepotism, the way Rome worked. Rome also worked increasingly by the law, and that is what Maffeo studied, that is, after he had received his basic education from the Jesuits in both Florence and the Collegio Romano and made a start on writing poetry.[57] Among a vast output, Barberini wrote a poem praising Galileo's astronomical discoveries. His career in papal service had gone swimmingly, including a highly successful legation to France that left him with a permanent case of Francophilia. That made him an odd man out in strongly pro-Spanish Florence. Paul V rewarded him with a cardinalate. He had then succeeded Cardinal Giustiniani as legate in Bologna, as well as holding one bishopric *in partibus infidelium* (the archdiocese of Nazareth, in Turkish hands) and the real see of Spoleto where he had made a show of implementing Trent's decree about visiting his diocese to see what needed correction. When Ciampoli first spoke to him, Barberini, like Cesi, urged caution lest "physical or mathematical limits" be exceeded.[58] This remained his line. Galileo did not pay much attention, even after Barberini later told Dini that the matter would likely come before either the Index or the Inquisition.[59]

Galileo's begging letter to Dini arrived in Rome at almost the same time as Caccini. Galileo had also written Ciampoli, questioning the depth of his devotion, which Ciampoli took pains to demonstrate, calling Galileo among other things "infallible oracle."[60] He, Dini, and Maraffi had been hard at work on Galileo's behalf, and he assured Galileo that no one was making anything of the denunciations. Unfortunately for Galileo, Ciampoli was not the best-informed man in Rome, to put it mildly. His reports were often not quite right. For example, although he should have been keeping his ear as close to the Inquisition's ground as possible and had at least a couple of times seen Inquisitor Bellarmino, he did not know the elementary fact that the Inquisition met at least twice a week, not once a month, a mistake he made after spending the entire day, so he claimed, with Maraffi who must surely have known better.[61]

That was a comparatively trivial mistake. When Ciampoli told Galileo all was well, he was dead wrong. Three days before he wrote, the Congregation of the Inquisition met in the *palazzo* of the most senior Inquisitor, Bellarmino. Millini, Galamini, and four other cardinals, but not Sfondrato (he usually avoided meetings at Bellarmino's residence), considered Lorini's letter, together with a report on the "Letter to Castelli."[62] The six Inquisitors present judged the second letter to contain "erroneous propositions about the meaning and interpreters of sacred scripture" and ordered the archbishop and inquisitor of Pisa to get Galileo's original from Castelli and send it to Rome.[63]

Ordering was one thing, but producing the letter proved to be quite another. As far as the records say, the inquisitor of Pisa never did anything more than acknowledge the order; in this, he was running true to the form of the rest of his career, as we shall see after he moved to Florence in a few months.[64] The archbishop, Francesco Bonciani, did better. He was an exceptionally smooth character even in an age full of them. He did not make the mistake of summoning Castelli to his presence. Instead, he waited until Castelli got back to Pisa and came to make the necessary courtesy visit. The archbishop smothered Castelli in kindness in an attempt to persuade him to abandon heliocentrism for his (and Galileo's) own good. At one point, he took Castelli for a ride in his carriage. Eventually the archbishop said the idea that the earth moved was foolish, and Castelli replied in knee-jerk fashion that, no, the idea that it did not was. The archbishop naturally raised the level of his reply, saying that the belief in the earth's movement needed to be condemned. Calming down, he finally asked Castelli for the "Letter." Castelli replied that he had sent it back to Galileo.[65] The archbishop tried again a week later, attempting to win Castelli's confidence by telling him that the cathedral preacher in Pisa had criticized Caccini's "brutto termine" (displeasing, dangerous, or inopportune conclusion).[66] While that information may have been true, it failed to secure Castelli's cooperation, so the archbishop tried a direct order. Castelli insisted he did not have the "Letter."[67] The Inquisitors never got the original, nor do we have it now. The smoking gun disappeared.

The cathedral preacher was Domenico Gori (1571–1620), Bonciani's theologian, confessor, and *uomo di fiducia*, and also friar of Santa Maria Novella and its prior in 1618.[68] His position alone makes his criticism of Caccini important. A famous preacher and commentator on the Bible, he had a position like Lorini's as both general preacher in his order and a favorite of the Medici court.[69] The grand duke visited him on his deathbed.[70] Granted an MA in 1598, he taught at Santa Maria sopra Minerva and in other Dominican convents and was a friend of at least two Inquisitors (Giovanni Battista Bonsi and Galamini) and of another principal in Galileo's case, Cardinal Alessandro Orsini.[71] Large numbers of his sermons and readings (*lezioni*) on scripture survive.[72] Guerrini finds in them "an attempt at compromise and partial conciliation with the Galilean 'party'" despite Gori's firm allegiance to traditional biblical cosmology.[73] Guerrini rests his conclusion in part on Gori's intervention against Caccini, which impressed Castelli. He had nothing but kind words for Gori in his next week's letter to Galileo. He had visited him and found him in private a person *di molto garbo* (roughly "a very clever fellow") and praised his sermons as "the word of God," which he would never fail to attend. Nevertheless, Castelli had not wanted to bring up Caccini on this first visit. It seems he never did.[74] If nothing else, Gori provides more evidence that the Dominican order was not a monolith and had no official position on Galileo's ideas.

Foscarini's *Letter on the*
Opinion of the Pythagoreans and Copernicus

With impressively bad timing, just at this moment the Carmelite friar Paolo
Antonio Foscarini published his *Letter on the Opinion of the Pythagoreans and
Copernicus* (Naples: Lazzaro Scorrigio, 1615). Foscarini suffered from the same
kind of ambitions as Caccini. He changed his name from Scarini to make it
appear that he belonged to a Venetian noble family instead of coming from
an undistinguished one in the kingdom of Naples.[75] Like Caccini, he tried to
make his career in part through preaching, which he was doing in Rome about
the time his book appeared, as well as offering to debate all and sundry.[76] It
might seem from the fact that it was the only book outright condemned the
next year that he was a committed Copernican. He was not. His book represented a recent and incomplete conversion. Yes, it defended Copernicus, but
Foscarini knew little of mathematics and less of recent astronomy.[77] Galileo
and even more Castelli had serious reservations about how much use he could
be to them, despite Foscarini's determined efforts to curry favor with both.[78]

Bellarmino had no doubts at all about the potential dangers in Foscarini's
book. He chose a subtle means of making his point. He wrote the author a
letter in April 1615 in which he praised him for treating the Copernican system
as merely the best hypothesis, a position to which Bellarmino stuck, while
remaining certain that if taken as fact it was heretical.[79] Foscarini, who did
not treat Copernicus as merely the best available theory, got the letter, but
not the point. He replied to Bellarmino supporting himself and Copernicus
on scriptural grounds, just the territory Bellarmino was determined to defend
to the death.[80] Foscarini was not the only one to miss the point. Galileo also
failed to get it.

Acting with its usual secrecy, the Inquisition's machine continued to grind
away. Among the results was a very tiny explosion in the form of an anonymous
consultor's opinion on the "Letter to Castelli."[81] The consultor failed to find
much cause for complaint. The best he could do was to object mildly to three
of Galileo's statements: (1) although the claim that scripture contained many
false propositions according to the "bare sense of the words" could be taken in
a good sense, it was still not wise to bandy the label "false" in connection with
scripture; (2) using "abstain" and "pervert" relative to scripture "sounds bad";
and (3) the treatment of Joshua could also "sound bad," although once again it
could also be well interpreted—otherwise, no complaints. This was not much,
and it is almost surprising to find this short document near the beginning of

Galileo's dossier. The order to the consultor does not appear in the record, nor is there any sign of an official reaction to his report.[82]

Caccini's Deposition

The Inquisitors did not need either the opinion or the "Letter to Castelli." They had something better: Caccini's live testimony. Massimo Bucciantini argues that Caccini's deposition combined with Foscarini's *Letter* "determined" the decree of 5 March suspending *De Revolutionibus*. He therefore suggests reading Caccini's testimony "with great caution" and not 'rationally,' dividing what is true from what is false or not yet sufficiently proved." According to Bucciantini, Caccini went beyond a judicial act and attempted to "delineate the heterodox character contained in the philosophical and scientific conceptions sustained by the group of 'sectarians' led by the Tuscan scientist." The deposition moved on two fronts: (1) the relation between "Copernicanism" and scripture depended on an analysis of Galileo's writings, especially his "Letter to Castelli"; and (2) an effort to make Galileo a heresiarch founded on more circumstantial evidence, also perhaps on misinterpretations of that same "Letter."[83] The deposition was carefully constructed, as one might expect of a witness like Caccini. Most people did not give evidence to the Inquisition on the recommendation of one of the Inquisitors. Caccini did.[84] His patron was his fellow Dominican Galamini.[85] Unlike many of the characters in this drama, Galamini came from humble origins. He still profited from nepotism, since his maternal uncle had been general of the Dominicans, the order Galamini entered at a typically young age. After education at the *studio* in Bologna and in Naples, he followed a typical career as an inquisitor, beginning first in the provinces, Brescia, Genoa, then Milan. With on-the-job training typical of what most inquisitors got, Galamini left them behind when he was summoned to Rome to become commissary in 1604. After an atypically short three years in that post, he made another reasonably typical move up, to master of the sacred palace, chief papal censor. As such he continued to attend Inquisition meetings, but only for a few months. Paul V had other plans for him, having the Dominicans elect him their general in 1608. When in Rome, he continued to attend the Inquisition. He was an active general and frequently absent from Rome, including on an extended visit to the Dominicans of France at royal request. This helped cement a political allegiance to France like Barberini's. That made them members of the same faction in Rome. Once he became an Inquisitor, Galamini was among the most regular attenders at meetings including many occasions on which he was one of only two or three cardinals present. The other was often the secretary, Cardinal Millini who almost had to attend.[86]

This was a typical career for a Dominican Inquisitor. Galamini's intensity and zeal for religion were anything but typical, even in the overheated piety of baroque Rome. The commentators agreed unanimously in praising his sincerity and goodness, at the same time as they stressed his lack of concern for ordinary human considerations. They used on him the same adjective once used to describe the dreaded warrior pope Julius II: *terribile*, literally terrifying. They also called him "hard" and "courageous." And rigid.[87] Such was Caccini's new patron, stepping in for the ailing and absent Arrigoni, who nevertheless continued to cooperate with Galamini. The second took complete charge of Caccini's move to Rome, orchestrating every step.[88] Galamini ordered Caccini there by coincidence—or perhaps his plan all along—just when Caccini already intended to do that. Galamini lobbied hard for him, on one occasion talking to "more than fifteen cardinals" on his behalf.[89] Even when it appeared that his competitor, backed by the cardinal nephew, had beaten him for the teaching post at the Minerva, Galamini did not give up.[90] Caccini's testimony against Galileo came right in the middle of Galamini's scheme to promote him.

On 20 March, the day immediately after Galamini reported that Caccini had information about Galileo's errors and Pope Paul ordered him examined, "he appeared spontaneously" before the Inquisition's new commissary, Seghizzi, and one of its notaries, perhaps even the chief, Andrea Pettini.[91] The interrogation took place in the Palazzo del Sant'Uffizio, immediately south of St. Peter's where it still is. A new building was or would soon be under construction, but Caccini probably appeared in the old one "in the great hall of examinations." He began by saying that Galamini had told him yesterday that he had no choice but to "depose judicially" against Galileo. Then he reported an edited version of his scriptural reading without its confrontational opening, skipping straight to the exposition of Joshua "first in the literal sense and then in the spiritual meaning for the salvation of souls," sanctimoniously adding that he had spoken "with that modesty that is proper to the office [of reader in Scripture] that I held." Before going on to say that he had cited other Bible verses as interpreted by all the fathers of the church, Caccini made one of the two most important points in his deposition. Somebody had coached him on exactly how to spin his testimony in legal terms. Often the commissary had to

ask a witness about one of the key elements in what we would call the indictment, the "public reputation" or "public rumor" (*publica fama*) about an accused.[92] Caccini spared Seghizzi the trouble by immediately saying that it was
"most publicly known" (*publichissima fama*) in Florence that Galileo "held
and taught" Copernicus's opinion. Holding and teaching were two separate
offenses. Held was bad, taught worse. How did Caccini know what was wrong
with Galileo? Because he had read Nicholaus Serrarius, who had declared Copernicus's views "contrary to the common opinion of almost all philosophers,
all scholastic theologians and all the holy fathers." Serrarius had added that
"that doctrine could not be other than heretical."[93] Poor Serrarius (who had
recently died) has been mangled in scholarship, identified as Spanish, Italian,
about anything other than what he really was, a German Jesuit.[94] The great
church historian Cesare Baronio called him "the light of the church in Germany," and his Bible commentaries were popular. But was he also attractive as
a Jesuit when Caccini knew Bellarmino would see his evidence?

Caccini described his reading's force as "a loving admonition" (*caritativa
ammonitione*).[95] As a friar used to seeing that disciplinary tool applied to his
fellows, he had to know that the talk could have been no such thing, since that
kind of warning depended on secrecy to give the sinner a chance to amend his
ways before more serious (and more public) measures were taken against him
(see Chapter 4 below). Caccini aimed to demonstrate how nobly he had acted
in the face of Galileo's "disciples," who had asked the official preacher of the
cathedral of Florence, Santa Maria del Fiore, to reply to Caccini, who in his
turn had complained to Inquisitor Lelio Marzari. At this point, Caccini did
not say whether anything came of either action. Later he admitted that the cathedral preacher, a Neapolitan Jesuit whose name he claimed not to know, had
been talked out of attacking him by another Jesuit, Emanuele Ximenes (see
previous chapter).[96] Ximenes was probably a member of a wealthy Marrano
banking family transferred to Florence in the fifteenth century, many of whose
members opposed Galileo.[97] By labeling his talk an "admonition," Caccini also
set the stage for the next step after it failed, as this one clearly had, a precept.
Once again, somebody had to have coached Caccini in just how to put his
testimony in legal terms. Now Caccini named his first witness against Galileo,
Ferdinando Ximenes, shortly to be Arrighi's official substitute as Dominican
provincial and probably some kind of cousin of Emanuele, whom Caccini said
would testify that the Galileisti held three propositions, two of them about
God: that it was not a substance but an accident (almost equivalent to saying God did not really exist) and that it was "sensitive," apparently meaning

that it had senses like humans, only divine; and that miracles done by saints were false.[98] After noting that Lorini had shown him a copy of the "Letter to Castelli," Caccini ended his "spontaneous" testimony by noting once more Galileo's "public reputation" and his two dangerous propositions. There was nothing spontaneous about his performance. It was a speech carefully crafted according to the rules of rhetoric, designed to persuade its audience (however small) to take action on the facts alleged.

Seghizzi began his questioning by asking how Caccini knew about Galileo's propositions. Caccini, never one to use subtlety where a sledge hammer would work, trotted out Galileo's reputation for the third time, and then named names. The bishop of Cortona, Filippo Bardi dei Verni, had warned him twice about Galileo, first when they were together in Cortona in 1611 and then again in Florence.[99] The bishop would have been a dangerous witness since he and his brothers were among the cultural kingpins of Florence, yet he was never called to testify. Then Caccini adduced a friendly witness, a "sectarian" of Galileo, one Attavanti, the man he had surprised and silenced in Santa Maria Novella, although without knowing exactly who he was.[100] This unsubtle move also implicitly labeled Galileo as the worst kind of heretic, a founder of a sect and therefore an inventor of heresies, a heresiarch. Caccini had also read Galileo's *Sunspot Letters*, which Ferdinando Ximenes had lent him. In other words, Caccini knew what he was talking about. Next Seghizzi asked how Galileo was regarded in Florence. Caccini had to reply that many thought him a good Catholic, before hurrying on with a completely gratuitous accusation that could have ruined Galileo no matter what he thought about cosmology or astronomy or anything else. Caccini said that "others" (who turned out to be Lorini) had severe doubts because he was known as a friend of "that Fra Paolo, Servite, so notorious in Venice for his impieties," with whom Galileo still exchanged letters.[101] This of course is Paolo Sarpi, whom Paul V would gladly have assassinated.[102] This specific accusation was not pursued, any more than the similar one of association with Cremonini, but in both cases the damage had been done. Caccini also vaguely noted that Ferdinando Ximenes thought ill of Galileo. "Oh, yes," added Caccini again spontaneously, Galileo belongs to the Academy of the Lynxes and writes letters to Germany about sunspots, naturally if only by implication, to Lutheran heretics. Whatever the truth value of the rest of Caccini's testimony, this point was false since the dedicatee of the *Sunspot Letters*, Mark Welser, was not only a city father of the thoroughly Catholic Augsburg but also an informer for the Roman Inquisition.[103]

Then, as often happened, the examination began to go in circles, the interrogator returning to the same central points from several different directions. How did Ximenes know what he had told Caccini? Attavanti told him. Where did Ximenes talk to Attavanti? In Santa Maria Novella, replied Caccini. Finally, Seghizzi got around to asking whether Caccini had "enmity" against Galileo or any of his disciples. Caccini piously replied indeed not, in fact, he prayed for them. Seghizzi had to ask and Caccini had to answer because, under Inquisition rules, the testimony of mortal enemies was inadmissible or at least severely discounted.[104] With Caccini safely, if to our eyes rather oddly, qualified as neutral, all was well. Again because the rules said he had to, Seghizzi asked Caccini for details about Galileo. Not only could he not have recognized Galileo on the street, but Caccini thought he was more than sixty (instead of barely fifty), had no idea whether he taught, and although alleging that he had so many followers they had a name (the Galileisti, on whom he may have punned at the beginning of his lecture), the only one he ever produced was the semi-anonymous Attavanti. Caccini's testimony, at least after his opening mini-sermon, was less than compelling. Nevertheless, when his deposition was read in the Inquisition's meeting of 2 April, Paul ordered a copy immediately dispatched to Florence for further investigation. The packet went off two days later.[105]

The pressure stayed on in Rome. Only Dini seems to have noticed. He continued to write Galileo regularly, almost always reporting his intention to see Bellarmino as soon as possible. Alas, Dini had come down with life-threatening laryngitis and never did quite get to the cardinal.[106] Somehow he managed to talk just fine to Cesi, Ciampoli, and at least several other people whom he named to Galileo. He, Cesi, and Ciampoli had more or less agreed, if likely for different reasons, that there was no reason to mount a defense.[107] In Dini, Galileo was relying on a cautious man, the kind of courtier who could go far and one to whom he would have been well advised to listen. It is odd that, despite Galileo's rampant paranoia, he paid more attention to the pollyanna Ciampoli than either of the worrywarts Dini and Cesi.

Cardinal Millini and Paul V

By the end of April the situation in Rome seemed to have improved markedly. Dini wrote Galileo that Grienberger's *compagno* (perhaps meaning official substitute) had told him on the way to mass how happy he was that Galileo's case was "accommodated."[108] Galileo himself seems to have developed a measure of discretion. He drafted, but for a change did not fire off, a reply to Bellarmino's letter to Foscarini.[109] He did write Foscarini, and so should have been glad to hear the news that he, now under Cardinal Millini's protection, was thinking of reprinting his book.[110] Millini's position as secretary of the Inquisition by itself indicates the extent of this cardinal's power.[111] Millini was physically striking, tall and graceful, with a big head and nose, wide forehead, long, thin arms, hands, and fingers, a pale complexion, and chestnut hair. A native Roman noble, he was born in Florence where his father had been exiled. His mother was a cousin of the short-lived Urban VII, who when still a cardinal had taught Millini law. He had gotten his start in Rome in 1591 as an auditor of the Rota, the position Dini failed to get.[112] As soon as he left that job in 1607, he was almost immediately made cardinal and, with dizzying speed, four days later appeared as an Inquisitor, before again, almost as immediately, leaving on a diplomatic mission to Germany. Like Barberini in France just a little earlier, Millini met with great success.

On his return, Millini became Arrigoni's assistant as secretary of the Inquisition, before quickly but briefly serving as bishop of the bandit country of Imola (where he cooperated with the legate Giustiniani and was peripherally involved in Rodrigo Alidosi's case [see *SI*, Chapter 5]). On his return, the pope made Millini vicar of Rome, his personal representative in the government of the bishopric, as well as adding him to numerous particular congregations. Right from the first, Millini was numbered among Paul's most trusted advisors. Except for the cardinal nephew, no one was more powerful in Rome. There was also no one harder to read, as even his admiring nephew had to admit in the authorized biography. Thus Millini's blunt speech about the evils in Cremonini's book should have carried double weight, and Galileo should have been doubly warned by his friend's example. Although some complained that Millini moved slowly, he was a hard worker, in the habit of holding lengthy meetings of the Inquisition in his palace in Piazza Navona (now engulfed by the Brazilian embassy) in the heat of August to clear its docket. Since there were no manuals from which he could learn how to be Inquisition secretary, he taught himself by studying its files. What theology he knew, he picked up from Bellarmino in the congregations on which both served, in the same way Bellarmino got law from Millini such that they "made a beautiful *concerto*," as the official biography put it.

There can be no doubt that anything Millini said, the pope said. So how could Paul have protected Foscarini by proxy at the same time that Bellarmino unsubtly warned him to watch his step? The answer is simple. The papal government was a sprawling, disjointed institution; especially at the top, differences of direction frequently arose, even among cardinals as close to one another as Millini and Bellarmino. As between the two, Bellarmino was the more likely to make policy, Millini to execute it. Chance cannot be overlooked as a factor, either. Given how quickly opinions changed, a cardinal missing one key meeting (as Millini would that deciding the ban on Foscarini) could have enormous consequences.

Millini's master, Paul V, is a difficult pope to come to grips with.[113] Anyone who has ever seen the monumental inscription on the façade of St Peter's or the only slightly smaller one on the new fountain he built on top of the Janiculum in Rome knows Paul had a big ego. His portraits, especially his funeral monument, on the other hand, make him look almost embarrassingly kindly, playing down his height and regal bearing, which a goatee also helped to offset. He had a slightly different family background from other recent popes. He came from a legal dynasty and was himself a lawyer, but his father, Marcantonio Borghese, had distinguished himself not in papal service as an Inquisitor, for example, but as a high-profile defense attorney. Among his clients was Cardinal Giovanni Morone, one of the Inquisition's most important sixteenth-century targets.[114] Marcantonio had moved the family from Siena to Rome, making them arrivistes and explaining the gigantic "Romanus" after Paul's name on St. Peter's. Camillo Borghese, as he then was, rejected his father's ladder to success and instead worked his way up the other side of the legal hierarchy in Rome until he became secretary of the Congregation of the Holy Office, an excellent springboard to pope.

Paul and even more his nephew Scipione Caffarelli who took the name Borghese were together about as grasping as any papal family ever. Scipione had no less than four palaces all to himself, the smallest and least grand of which was the spectacular one now known as Giraud-Torlonia in via della Conciliazione between St. Peter's and the Tiber. The Villa Borghese, one of Rome's most important museums, was intended to be even larger than the grand duke's nearby establishment at Trinità dei Monti and contained even more art. Scipione also built nearly from scratch a huge villa at Frascati, surrounded by even more extensive grounds than the Villa Borghese.[115] Paul also undertook a gargantuan building project at the Quirinal Palace, which he almost entirely rebuilt and vastly enlarged, the one to which Sfondrato objected.[116] The family defined conspicuous consumption.

After these outward clues to Paul's character, things become more difficult.

The Tuscan ambassador, probably for reasons of his own, made the pope out to be an ignoramus.[117] That he was not. A glance into his funeral chapel in Santa Maria Maggiore will knock that notion on the head.[118] If one looks a little harder, one will also see that Paul was very much up to date. Not only did he bring in the best artists to decorate his chapel, among them Galileo's close friend Ludovico Cigoli, but he also let Cigoli pay homage to Galileo's telescopic discoveries by painting in its cupola a moon with blemishes.[119] Paul had a great deal of work done on the church, including erecting a small plaque in honor of St. Francis, which almost appears to be a joke in light of Francis's notorious insistence on apostolic poverty. Beyond these hints from his patronage, just how Paul used his brain poses more problems. He was not as lucky as Urban VIII in having a relatively factual official biography in eight massive volumes. Instead, he got a sprawling puff piece almost as long and almost completely useless.[120] The official printed biography by Dominican historian Abraham Bzowski at least contains information, but it is so suffocatingly pious as to tell us next to nothing about Paul the man.[121] Nor does the comparison to other popes numbered V help much!

Bzowski does say two things of great interest. First, no one was harder than Paul on heretical books—as Bzowski should have known since his own continuation of Cardinal Baronio's history of the church had encountered difficulties with the Inquisition. Second, the pope never did anything without carefully taking advice. Other commentators agree in making caution Paul's defining characteristic. That makes sense for a lawyer, but it happens not to be true. Paul was perfectly prepared to shoot from the hip, whether by airily ordering an entire new street to be built because his carriage had been forced to take a small detour or—much more important—without consulting anyone at all, slapping the interdict on Venice in 1606 that just about wrecked the papacy.[122] He acted in much the same hasty fashion in Galileo's case. He is alleged never to have taken any step without calculating its political impact, especially when it came to the grand duke, to whom he owed a big leg up into the papal chair. His handling of Galileo's case raises doubts about this claim, too. He was not a man to be pushed around.

Florence Gets a New Inquisitor

Despite Paul's prodding, the investigation into Galileo in Florence was not making much headway. Its inquisitor, Cornelio Priatoni, reported on 11 May that he could not question Ximenes since he was still in Milan, and Priatoni thought it best not to talk to anyone else first.[123] Since the inquisitor in Milan reported soon after that Ximenes had returned to Florence, one or the other inquisitor may have been passing the buck.[124] Priatoni never did manage to interview Ximenes. (Meanwhile the inquisitor of the frontier post at Belluno was asked to look for the "Letter to Castelli" on a rumor that its dean had a copy of one of Galileo's writings, which one not specified. The Inquisition could be both incredibly thorough and incredibly sloppy.)[125] Priatoni found himself in an almost impossible situation.[126] Immediately after Caccini's lecture, he tried to resign. Rome refused to let him step down until the middle of 1615 on the face-saving pretext of ill health.

Lelio Marzari, the inquisitor of Pisa, wound up replacing Priatoni.[127] Marzari's arrival at this precise moment cannot be coincidence. Priatoni's foot-dragging may well have been meant to help Galileo, who was probably being leaked information about the progress of his case.[128] Marzari's arrival therefore looked doubly menacing. Galileo ignored the signals and wrote a more inflammatory letter than the one to Castelli. This time he addressed himself directly to the grand duke's mother, Grand Duchess Christina.[129] His central point was that scientists should not start their investigations from the Bible. Whether he meant this as a defense of separate spheres for science and religion or to save the Bible from possible attack by less devout scientists—or a number of other possibilities—the danger arose in his liberal citation of scripture to support his argument, as well as trotting out an arsenal of citations from the fathers of the church. Not that Galileo had suddenly developed expertise in patristics. Instead, he probably got the whole set of texts from the Bible commentary of Spanish Jesuit Benito Pereyra that an unknown monk, probably a Barnabite (possibly Pomponio Tartaglia, who knew Castelli in Pisa), had sent him.[130]

On new orders from Rome, Marzari rummaged around in the files and found the earlier instructions to Priatoni and, on 13 November, finally interviewed Ximenes, who had probably returned to Florence no later than early July.[131] Ximenes had recently arrived there from Portugal, perhaps following his brother, a canon of its cathedral.[132] He would sing the mass in 1629 in Rome for the canonization of the Florentine saint Andrea Corsini.[133] Conveniently enough, the Florentine inquisition sat in Ximenes's own convent of Santa Maria Novella, so he need not leave the building. Marzari asked questions, and the Florentine inquisition's chancellor took down the answers. As always happened, the first question to Ximenes was whether he knew the cause of his summons.[134] No, Ximenes said, possibly a little disingenuously since the next question was whether he knew Galileo. Marzari did not waste time getting to the point. No, answered Ximenes again, nor could I recognize him, but I do hear rumors that he thinks the earth moves and "the heaven" stands still, and such belief is "diametrically opposed to true theology and philosophy." Why? prodded Marzari. A. I heard some of his students say that "the heaven" does not move, that God is an accident and has no substance, that everything is a quantity made of a vacuum, that God laughs and cries. But I do not know whether this is just their opinion or whether Galileo believes all this, too. Q. Did you hear anyone say Galileo thought miracles were not really miracles, pressed Marzari. No, responded Ximenes. Q. From whom did you hear these things? A. From Giannozzo Attavanti, parish priest of Castel-fiorentino, in the presence of Ridolfi, a knight of St. Stephen (the noble order founded by Cosimo I).[135] It happened in my room last year, many times, but I cannot give the month, much less the day, and in addition to Ridolfi there were sometimes friars in attendance—but Ximenes could not remember who. Ximenes's testimony was becoming dangerously vague, and it got worse. Marzari: can you conjecture whether Attavanti was speaking as if he believed these things? Ximenes: I do not think so; he was putting an argument and referred all to the Church's judgment. Q. What else do you know about him? A. He has no training in theology or philosophy and does not have a degree, but he has some experience with both and was probably expressing Galileo's views rather than his own. The question arose while we were discussing cases of conscience (in other words, while Ximenes was training Attavanti how to hear confessions). Some of Caccini's readings came up, especially about Joshua and the sun.[136] I reprimanded Attavanti harshly, Ximenes asserted piously. Then came the standard closing question about whether he was an enemy of either Galileo or Attavanti. Ximenes repeated that he could not pick Galileo out of a lineup if he had to and at worst was Attavanti's friend. Ximenes was sworn to silence and signed his deposition, and the interview ended.

The next day Marzari deposed Attavanti.[137] He was described as "a noble Florentine, thirty-three years old" and in minor orders (very minor; he had no more than the tonsure, the initial sign of clerical status).[138] After the usual opening question, Marzari asked whether Attavanti had studied "letters" in Florence. Yes, under two Dominicans whom Attavanti named, then two more teachers (possibly also Dominicans), as well as with Ximenes who taught him cases of conscience. Q. Did you study with Galileo? A. No, I discussed philosophy with him as I do with all learned men. Then Marzari made a huge blunder, just what we would expect given his checkered career. He asked a leading question. If there was one rule on which the Roman Inquisition constantly harped, it was under no circumstances, ever, ever, feed the witness his lines.[139] In his day the Inquisition had not quite figured out that learning on the job without much (or any) supervision was not the best imaginable way to prepare inquisitors. Only later did it begin circulating once a year copies of its general decrees and bringing inquisitors to Rome for short, total immersion courses during which they sat in on parts of the Congregation's sessions.[140] So Marzari did his best. Did you ever hear Galileo say anything "repugnant" to scripture or the faith? No, I did not, huffed Attavanti. I only heard him say, following Copernicus, that the earth moved, as he wrote in his *Sunspot Letters*, to which I refer you. Marzari kept on leading Attavanti. Did Galileo ever interpret scripture, "maybe badly?" A. He interpreted Joshua, but Attavanti ignored the rest of the question. Then Marzari turned to the more solid evidence Ximenes had given. Attavanti gave a much more precise answer about his discussions with his former teacher than Ximenes had, volunteering the circumstances including Caccini's presence (his cell was next door), while insisting that the whole thing was a disputation that Caccini might have misunderstood. That was probably what happened on another occasion when Caccini had interrupted to condemn heliocentrism as heretical. About miracles, Attavanti knew nothing and about God's nature only what Aquinas taught. Marzari's next question went over the same ground, asking about the circumstances under which Attavanti had gained his information. Attavanti could not resist pointing out that he had already testified to them. What is your opinion about Galileo, asked Marzari? I think him a very good Catholic, otherwise he would not be in the grand duke's service, rejoindered Attavanti. Then Marzari asked another odd question, about Attavanti's "enmity" not with Galileo but with Caccini. Attavanti contradicted himself by saying he did not even know Caccini's name, after having given it twice before. And that was it.

With commendable speed, Marzari expressed the transcripts to Rome. Just ten days later, meeting in Sfondrato's palace in the Via Giulia (the present Palazzo Sacchetti, one of the grandest in Rome, which shortly afterward sold for the colossal sum of 55,000 *scudi*), the Inquisition ordered *Sunspot Letters* examined but took no other action.[141] Now, after all this rush, nothing happened until February 1616, that is, except for Galileo's decision to go to Rome.

Galileo Goes to Rome

It may be coincidence, but, within a week of the Inquisition's decree on 25 November 1615 calling for review of his *Sunspot Letters*, Galileo was collecting letters of recommendation and preparing to leave for the eternal city.[142] It seems likely that his principal concern remained the effect his "Letter to Castelli" was having, although the proximate trigger may well have been the Florentine depositions in his case, about which Attavanti likely told him.[143] It may also be that continuing echoes of Lorini's letter motivated his trip.[144] Galileo probably reached Rome on or about 11 December.[145] He stayed at the Villa Medici, rather than in the Tuscan embassy in Palazzo Firenze. That would have been more convenient but much less pleasant. His visit did not please the Tuscan ambassador, Piero Guicciardini. As soon as he got wind of Galileo's proposed trip, he fired off a long letter to the secretary of state complaining that he had not been consulted, which was true if irrelevant, and that the visit was a really bad idea.[146] About the second point he may well have been right. He was not the only one to make it. Bellarmino told Guicciardini more or less the same thing, warning him that, if Galileo overstayed his (short) welcome, action would have to be taken about Copernicus. Of course, that was just what Galileo wanted. Guicciardini did not. He added ominously that he thought Bellarmino had heard something objectionable, perhaps even in the ambassador's residence, and that influential Dominican Inquisitors did not care for Galileo at all. As we have seen, this is certainly true at least in Cardinal Galamini's case.

Speaking of influential Dominicans, there was still Caccini to contend with. Galileo took care to try to neutralize him, enlisting the aid of the *balìa*, the chief executive of the city government of Florence, to write the highest-placed member of the Caccini family asking him to keep Tommaso under control while Galileo justified himself to Tommaso's fellows.[147] Matteo, with Cardinal Arrigoni in Naples, lamented Tommaso's involvement and suggested that he get Lorini to cease and desist, too.[148] Galileo, as usual when he had chosen to take action, exuded confidence, that is, when he was not muttering darkly about the enemies who laid traps for him everywhere.[149] He even thought Lorini had come to Rome because his denunciation had run into difficulties. The friar had not, but he had been to see the grand duchess, which was almost as bad, even if the secretary of state, eavesdropping, thought they had spoken about another matter.[150]

Paranoia might have suited Galileo better than cockiness, both because discretion would have served his purposes well and because there were good reasons for worry, including Lorini's continued efforts. Galileo found himself in early January forced to combat a bruit in Rome that he had been disgraced at home.[151] In a city that worked as much by rumor as by reality, there was plenty of danger reflected in a report sent about the same time by one of his friends from Paduan days, Antonio Querenghi, and mirrored back to Galileo by his Venetian intimate Giovanni Sagredo.[152] Querenghi was considered cardinal material a bit earlier in Paul's reign, so he would have had a pretty good idea what was going on or rumored to be going on in Rome. He wrote his employer that Galileo had not come to Rome voluntarily and would be called to account for his notions "completely contrary to holy scripture." Galileo did not see fit to keep his head down, instead making the rounds of Roman salons arguing the truth of Copernicus's ideas, as Querenghi regularly reported. Galileo called it breaking lances, as if he were one of the knights in his beloved *Orlando Furioso*.[153] Among those he disputed was Francesco Ingoli, a client of Cardinal Caetani, one of Galileo's potentially most important backers, another well-placed and wealthy Roman.[154] The debate took place before Cardinal Barberini's right-hand man.[155] Annoying Ingoli in that context did not represent a victory.[156]

Yet, as January wore on, the worrying rumors began to die down. Almost as soon as he arrived, Galileo heard that his stay might be cut short on the strength of "a few words" that could be taken as orders to return and asked for reassurance that he had not been recalled. No, no, everything is fine, replied the secretary of state.[157] On some days it was. Querenghi made light of Galileo's facility with words and gradually sent more and more cheerful (and funny) reports of his derring-do, taking on fifteen or twenty opponents and making monkeys of all of them.[158] But he still failed to convince them. By the end of the month even Querenghi was half-persuaded, enough so to pass on Galileo's offer to come to Modena to prove his propositions.[159]

Despite his gallivanting around Rome unhorsing his opponents, Galileo knew the battle would be won in back rooms where he had to go carefully. It frustrated him both that he was forced to put his case in "dead writings" instead of in "live voice" and also that he could not deal directly with the people he needed to see because that would embarrass an unnamed friend and those people in turn could not approach him without "incurring the most severe censures."[160] In order to reach the right people, he had to work through third parties who tried to bring his case up casually, as if the decision makers had thought of it themselves. He meant men at least close to if not in

the Inquisition. Despite setbacks, he remained certain that he could convince
"those on whom the decision depends" not least because God was on his side.
But did Galileo really think Ingoli and others who dealt with those very men
(and their God) on a daily basis could not and did not talk to them more
easily and with more authority than he did? What friend could trump them?
The supporters Galileo had collected in 1611 in Rome were mostly still there,
including Maraffi at the Minerva and Cardinal Bandini, but neither was in
quite the right position to help.

The man Galileo did single out to represent him in the papal court seems
an odd choice. This was Ciampoli's original recruit, Alessandro Orsini, the
almost ridiculously young, twenty-three-year-old, brand-new cardinal, just
given the right to vote on 11 January 1616.[161] Not that Orsini did not have a
glittering lineage as a member of one of the oldest Roman baronial families,
the son of the duke of Bracciano, the grand duke's most southerly vassal, and
a bulwark against the papal states.[162] He was still a politically questionable
choice for Galileo, since, after Alessandro's father's unexpected death in September 1615, his brother, the new duke, had broken with Florence and tried to
strike an alliance with France.[163] As a result, the grand duke almost withdrew
Orsini's nomination as cardinal. Possibly as a quid pro quo for saving it, the
new duke promised his full protection to Galileo.[164] That may have patched
things up in Florence; it did nothing to defuse a tense situation in Rome.
The Orsini, like many such families, were in difficult financial straits and had
pulled off a marriage alliance with Paul V's fabulously wealthy family.[165] The
Borghese were after a real noble title (not the ones Paul had invented for them)
and were happy to part with some real estate to sweeten the deal. They were,
however, considerably less than excited by the bride's wish to become a nun.
Cardinal Alessandro had the same problem, having to be talked out of entering the Jesuits once already and eventually succumbing to the temptation of
the religious life.[166] At this moment he temporarily behaved as a new cardinal
should, making the rounds of banquets, including with Cardinal Caetani,
going hunting, leading parades, and, oh yes, being seen at mass in St. Peter's.[167]
A little less typically, he also became Galileo's protégé, the addressee of his
most dangerously Copernican work yet, "The Discourse on the Flux and Reflux of the Tides," sent (or handed) to him on 8 January 1616; it allegedly arose
from conversations in Rome between the two.[168] By that act, Galileo anointed
Orsini his official champion.

By the end of January Galileo had become so confident in his success
that, in addition to dismissing Caccini as a continuing threat, he generously

offered to intercede to protect his accuser from punishment for his denunciations.[169] On 6 February, Galileo announced to Florence that the people in
charge assured him "my business is completely wound up as far as my person
is concerned," since they had seen both his innocence and the "malignity" of
his enemies. He could go home.[170] This may sound like the end of a letter; in
fact, it is only the first sentence. This is the second time we have seen Galileo's
"business" finished. It was not the first time in early 1615, nor was it now. Why
not? Because Galileo had no idea how to leave well enough alone. He rushed
on to demand not only that he be cleared but also that all other followers of
Copernicus had to be, too, and heliocentrism accepted as true. Getting that
job done was wearing him out, but, as "a zealous and Catholic Christian"
pursuing a "just and religious end," he was determined to overthrow those
who for their own selfish reasons opposed the truth. It is typical of Galileo as
a man of the seventeenth century to trivialize and personalize his opponents.
Manifesting contempt for one's opponents is never a compelling persuasive
tactic, and it did not work well for Galileo, either, not if we consider that all
this is the prologue to a report on a lengthy meeting with Caccini that Galileo
was forced to admit left the Dominican completely unconvinced.

On 5 February, one month before Copernicus's book would be suspended,
Caccini came to visit Galileo.[171] They began by spending half an hour alone.
Caccini begged Galileo to believe that he had not "been the motor of that
other noise here [in Rome, in addition to his reading in Florence]." Then five
other people, most of them Florentines, showed up, two of them dependents
of one of the Inquisitors to whom Galileo later claimed to have talked during
this visit, Giovanni Battista Bonsi: his favored nephew Domenico Bonsi and
his auditor Francesco Venturi.[172] All three were lawyers. The Florentine Cardinal Bonsi had spent much of his career in France before coming to Rome
in mid-1615 to represent French interests.[173] He became an Inquisitor on 21
July 1615 and later served as deputy secretary, although there is little sign of
his impact as such or as a representative of Florence. The appearance of two of
Bonsi's familiars in Galileo's room was no accident. They had come to witness
Caccini's submission to Galileo in case evidence was needed in the future.
Bonsi has to have been one of the men on whom Galileo relied. If so, he
did not help much. It is a great irony that Galileo or his backers tried to give
Caccini exactly the same treatment he would himself receive shortly. Caccini
probably had the last laugh. It is likely that he was spying on Galileo and
gleefully reported finding him as determined as ever to defend Copernicus.

Galileo closed his report with one of the most accurate things he said throughout this episode: "Now the discussion has become more open, considering it in a certain way a public matter, even if in respect to the other courts this one [the Inquisition], including in these actions, is very secretive."[174] Since things were going so well, Galileo had decided to present the grand duke's recommendation to Cardinal Nephew Borghese on the following Tuesday, 9 February. He also decided to activate Orsini, first of all as his means of access to Borghese. Borghese effusively promised full support.[175] Orsini was jumping up and down with excitement at the important job he had been given. Just in case, Galileo asked for another recommendation from the grand duke to him.[176] It was dispatched as soon as Galileo's letter reached Florence, despite the distractions of Carnival, including the rehearsal of an equestrian ballet that was proving difficult because there was so much ice.[177] Borghese's interest was great news. Orsini's was not.

A week later Galileo sent another letter to Florence.[178] This time a passage he may have meant as rhetorical exaggeration came, unbeknownst to him, even closer to the truth than his last letter. Now he wrote that his three principal enemies, "ignorance, envy, and impiety" ("ignoranza, invidia et impietà," a nice piece of assonance in Italian), wanted to "annihilate" the Copernicans. He could not have been more right.

Probably about this time one of Galileo's oddest backers weighed in.[179] The Dominican Tommaso Campanella had been imprisoned for almost twenty years in Naples (and had more than another decade to go before being released), yet Cardinal Caetani thought it worth asking him for an opinion about Copernicus and Galileo.[180] Caetani was a member of the Index, not the Inquisition, so his move may be another instance of one hand not knowing what the other was doing. It is hard to believe that Caetani knew how much Paul V hated Campanella. Campanella's little *Apologia pro Galileo* would probably not have been much help, even if it had arrived in time. It did not really defend Galileo, since Campanella did not accept heliocentrism, nor was he comfortable with the moral implications of Galileo's proposed divorce between science and religion (despite all Galileo's protestations of loyalty to holy mother church).[181] Campanella took up Caetani's invitation for two reasons: to defend "the liberty of philosophizing" for all philosophers, not just Galileo, and to make a case, not unlike Galileo's, against the continued blending of Aristotle and Christian theology. While Campanella was writing, Caccini's leader, Cardinal Galamini, was reviewing one of Campanella's prides and joys, "Atheismus triumphatus" (Atheism conquered) written a decade earlier against Niccolò Machiavelli; Galamini was still working on the book a decade later—the Inquisition could drag its feet with the best of them.[182] Galamini's opinion was then highly valued, and in May 1616 he would get Cremonini's most recent publication to critique.[183] Alas, we do not know what if anything Galamini said about Campanella's book. A review by the Inquisition was not necessarily the kiss of death, but it was rarely a good thing. Given the Inquisition's tendency to rely heavily on guilt by association, trouble for Campanella (and Cremonini) was likely to spill over onto Galileo and vice versa.

"Not without my prior information": The Approach to the Precept

After a lull of about three weeks, matters came to a head. At this point, it was still only a rumor that the Holy Office had summoned Galileo, but it was about to. The crisis began around February 20, when Galileo reported to Florence that he had given Orsini the second recommendation from the grand duke and that the young cardinal could not wait to talk to Cardinal Borghese and the pope himself about "the public case."[184] Galileo had primed Orsini about its importance and how much he needed to find "an extraordinary authority" against those who were trying to trick "the superiors." Galileo devoutly asserted that God was still on his side and would prevent "any scandal for holy church." Although he found himself alone against his enemies' skullduggery, he had no fear of putting everything in writing, unlike his sneaky opponents who worked by whisper and innuendo. This is classic Galileo. He had also changed his mind about Caccini, whom he now once again thought not only completely ignorant but also "full of poison and empty of charity," a man to stay well away from. Of course, he hurried on to write, there are plenty of "good" Dominicans. Then he said something strange, at least for him: "I am in Rome where the air [the weather] is constantly changing, just as the negotiations are always fluctuating." Maybe this pessimistic judgment arose from a bad turn in his health, or maybe this time, when he said he could not put anything more in writing, he knew how bad things were becoming. The same packet to Florence included an ominously gushing letter from Orsini to the grand duke about his eagerness to help Galileo.[185]

The day before, 19 February, the Inquisition's theologian experts received copies of *Sunspot Letters*.[186] Now the pace picks up. In the early morning of 23 February, they held a meeting at which they tabled two propositions "to be censured": "that the sun is the center of the world and consequently immovable by local motion" and "that the earth is not the center of the world nor immovable, but that it moves by itself, including by a daily motion." Those two propositions were identified as coming from the book, first, in the *summarium* drawn up near the end of Galileo's trial and on which his sentence rested and then unsurprisingly in the sentence itself.[187] Paul V's order of 25 February 1616 to silence Galileo also identified the two propositions as Galileo's, without giving their precise source.[188] It is nevertheless well known that the propositions as quoted do not appear in *Sunspot Letters*. The closest passage I have found in any of Galileo's writing comes from a letter of 16 July 1611 to Gallanzone Gallanzoni, *maestro di camera* to Cardinal François de Joyeuse, the man who had mediated the end of the Interdict crisis with Venice, where Galileo wrote that "the earth moves with two motions . . . that is the diurnal in itself around its own center . . . and the annual motion."[189] I am unable to suggest how this letter could have reached the Inquisition or Galileo's enemies in Florence.[190] It is often suggested that the propositions came from Caccini's deposition, but it is worth raising the possibility that they really arose from the censoring of Galileo's book and that Caccini got his evidence from his sponsors in the Inquisition, not from Ximenes.[191]

Even had they met straight through until the next day, the consultors did not take long over their decision. They had help moving as fast as they did. Before they made their judgment, Orsini had taken up the cudgels for Galileo. With the enthusiasm of the raw youth given his first big assignment, he barged into the consistory of Wednesday 24 February, stoutly defending Galileo, perhaps even waving around "Discourse on the Tides."[192] Paul replied that it would be well for Orsini to tell Galileo to give up his opinion. Orsini persisted and Paul, visibly annoyed, snapped back, chopping off further discussion (as the Tuscan ambassador put it) by bluntly saying the matter had been turned over to the Inquisition. After Orsini left, Paul summoned Bellarmino, and together the two of them (again, according to the ambassador) decided Galileo's opinion was "erroneous and heretical." Of course, the pope should not have done that, even in consultation with Bellarmino, and probably he did not. Nevertheless, things moved with as much speed as if done by a single man. Would Paul have acted so quickly—by himself, with Bellarmino, or through the Inquisition—if Orsini, on Galileo's instructions, had not egged him on?[193]

The theologians handed down their brief opinion on 24 February.[194] To the first point "everybody said the aforesaid proposition was foolish and absurd in philosophy and formally heretical, in that it expressly contradicts the opinions of Holy Scripture in many places according to the proper sense of the words and the common exposition and sense of the holy fathers and doctors of theology" ("Omnes dixerunt dictam propositionem esse stultam et absurdam in philosophia et formaliter haereticam, quatenus contradicit expresse sententiis Sacrae Scripturae in multis locis secundum proprietatem verborum et secundum communem expositionem et sensum Sanctorum Patrum et theologorum doctorum"). Number 2 ("2.a Terra non est centrum mundi nec immobilis, sed secundum se totam movetur, etiam motu diurno") fared little better. Again unanimously, the theologians decided that it had the same philosophical status as no. 1 and theologically was "at least erroneous." Eleven experts signed the opinion. They have usually been dismissed as dunderheads. No generalization could be further from the truth. No, they did not know much about arithmetic, but they knew plenty about theology.

They were the following:[195]

(1) Peter Lombard, the archbishop of Armagh and primate of Ireland (not to be confused as incredibly enough has sometimes happened with his twelfth-century namesake, one of the inventors of scholastic theology), a prolific writer and almost as well regarded as a theologian in Rome as Bellarmino, his comrade-in-arms against James I of England;[196]

(2) Giacinto Petronio, Dominican, master of the sacred palace, chief papal censor, later Urban VIII's point man in the effort to force the Roman Inquisition on the Spanish kingdom of Naples, one of the irritants in the background of the second phase of Galileo's trial;[197]

(3) the Aragonese Raphael Riphoz, the number-three man in the Dominican hierarchy on the cardinal nephew's recommendation;[198]

(4) Seghizzi;[199]

(5) Girolamo da Casalmaggiore (whose surname was apparently Cappello), Conventual Franciscan, appointed consultor of the Holy Office just about a year earlier;[200]

(6) Tomás de Lemos, O.P., one of the most distinguished Spanish theologians of the early seventeenth century and a major figure in the dispute about grace between the Dominicans and the Jesuits;[201]

(7) the Portuguese Augustinian Gregorio Nuñez Coronel, another member of the papal commission about grace and a consultor by this time for almost twenty years;

(8) Benedetto Giustiniani, S.J., a protégé but perhaps not a relative of Cardinal Giustiniani and once Caetani's theologian, as well as Bandini's teacher at the Collegio Romano, deeply involved with Bellarmino in responding to Venetian attacks on the Interdict in 1606;[202]

(9) Raphael Rastellius, Theatine, doctor of theology, about whom little is known before this moment and who would later lose his job as consultor and have other troubles with the Inquisition over his books;[203]

(10) Michele da Napoli, a member of Castelli's order of Cassinese Benedictines and the most obscure of the lot;[204] and

(11) Jacopo Tinto, Seghizzi's *socius* and his relative, who went on to have a distinguished career as a provincial inquisitor, including in their hometown of Lodi.[205]

It is hard to miss the Inquisition's dominance of this panel, seven of whose members also served it as consultors, experts who attended nearly all its meetings. Five were Dominicans, all but one of the total a member of a religious order. The panel was probably carefully chosen to represent a broad range of opinion to make its decision that much more solid. The Inquisition had its grounds for silencing Galileo. The fact that two witnesses agreed about Galileo's Copernican allegiance, that both propositions documenting it were condemned, and yet the Inquisition still decided *noli prosequi* confirms that Copernicanism was not the real issue and was instead a smokescreen, intended to deflect the more serious charge of interpreting scripture.[206]

CHAPTER 3

The Precept of 26 February 1616

Once the consultors finished their work, the stage was set for the Inquisition to move against Galileo. On 26 February 1616, he had a meeting with Inquisitor Roberto Bellarmino. What happened has generated controversy almost from that moment forward.[1] The discussion in this chapter and the next about precepts, and that in particular issued to Galileo in 1616, is long and complicated. This is necessary because so much past controversy over Galileo's treatment and his trial has been conditioned by misunderstandings of the legal role of precepts, and the English language used in translations. In this chapter I shall deal with the textual evidence allowing a reconstruction of the event, and in the next with its legal meaning. I shall argue that Galileo received a precept that in all likelihood ordered him utterly to abandon Copernican ideas. Given improving knowledge of how the Inquisition worked, including how it produced and preserved its records, it becomes possible to create a consistent account of what happened in 1616.[2] A point of terminology: I have chosen to use the term "precept" instead of "injunction" because it comes closer to *praeceptum* (Latin) or *precetto* (Italian) and also avoids confusion with an injunction in common law, which it only partly resembles. The key difference is that a competent court must issue an injunction, while in canon law any superior with the proper authority (including private) may give a precept.[3]

Six documents bear directly on the episode in Bellarmino's palazzo at San Macuto (the present via del Seminario No. 120). All are in the Inquisition's files, four of them in Galileo's dossier. The first three as minutes have the greatest authority:

No. 1. Paul V's order on 25 February to Bellarmino and Commissary Michelangelo Seghizzi transmitted via the Inquisition's secretary Cardinal Giovanni Garzia Millini (hereafter "Paul's order");[4]

No. 2. A precept dated the next day; there is also an abbreviated (and irrelevant) eighteenth-century copy of both 1 and 2 ("the precept minute");[5]
No. 3. The report of a meeting of the Congregation of the Inquisition on 3 March 1616 found in the decree register of that year ("the *decretum*").[6]

The other three texts probably descend from No. 2 and therefore say less about the events of 1616:

No. 4. Part of the particular congregation's report of September 1632;[7]
No. 5. The "Summary" (*Summarium*) prepared by the Inquisition's assessor near the end of Galileo's trial in 1633, and the basis on which the Inquisitors passed sentence;[8]
No. 6. Galileo's sentence.[9]

Most scholars have thought that the minute of 26 February recording the administration of the precept (No. 2) makes the most trouble. This is not the case. That honor instead belongs to the same kind of note of the Inquisition's meeting a week later (the *decretum* of 3 March, No. 3). Nearly all commentators treat a seventh text, an affidavit (*fede*) from Bellarmino requested by Galileo and dated 26 May 1616 ("Bellarmino's affidavit"), as if it is most important. In fact, it says nothing directly about what happened on 26 February and is largely insignificant.[10]

I shall save one final piece of evidence for separate treatment, Galileo's deposition of 12 April 1633, mainly because it is the only one of these texts that offers a slanted view of what happened. Despite many interpreters' deep suspicions, it is much more likely that Galileo fudged the truth in his testimony than that any of the other documents were falsified or otherwise manipulated. When carefully read, Galileo's testimony agrees well with the interpretation argued here.

It is as well to admit immediately that any reconstruction will never meet the standards of legal proof. Not only did the Inquisition both generate and manage its records in ways guaranteed to produce problems, it was an institution run by men only some of whom were fully qualified. Some of the least well credentialed, the notaries, had the greatest impact on the quality of its records.[11] Nevertheless, it was their intervention alone that made an act authentic, as medieval legal commentators had long argued.[12] Many of the rest of the Inquisition's personnel were lawyers who one might hope would do their job with precision. They too often did not. As one basic albeit largely insignificant indication, they failed to settle on a stable text of the strongest form of the precept even when allegedly quoting it directly.[13]

The *Decretum* of 3 March

The only serious discrepancy about what happened on 26 February 1616 arises from document No. 3 (the *decretum*). It has Bellarmino on 3 March report to the Congregation simply that Galileo had "agreed" to "abandon" heliocentrism after being "warned" to do so.[14] This statement has often been taken to mean both that Galileo received *only* a warning and, more important, that Commissary Michelangelo Seghizzi never issued the precept. The other texts disagree. Paul's order (No. 1), the one found in Galileo's dossier but not the *decreta*, read that Seghizzi should proceed to the precept if Galileo "refused" to agree to the "warning." It gave the text of the precept as ordering Galileo "to abandon completely teaching, defending or treating this doctrine [of the earth's movement and the sun's fixity]," which is almost identical to the wording of No. 2. No. 4 read that Galileo could "in no manner whatever hold, teach or defend [Copernicus's ideas], in word or in writing" or he would be proceeded against, and that he promised to obey. No. 5 combines all these texts, perhaps sloppily, perhaps maliciously, and makes Bellarmino alone give Galileo the precept in its strongest form. To bring confusion full circle, No. 6, Galileo's sentence, contains the most detailed account, having Bellarmino warn Galileo "benignly" before Seghizzi gave him the strongest form of the precept.[15]

Thus, except for the *decretum* of 3 March, all the texts agree that Galileo got the precept in full form, leaving a little unclear only from whom, a point that may be irrelevant. We are left with one crucial fact: No. 3 stands alone both in its content and, more important, in its status and location. The second point is vital to the second phase of Galileo's trial. Since it was not in his dossier, the Inquisition staff in 1632–1633 could not have been expected to know about it unless someone had ordered them to search all the Inquisition's voluminous and poorly indexed records.[16] The absence of an order for such a search might mean that it was never handed down and that No. 3, therefore, never came into evidence[17]—hence the near-perfect consistency between the other two documents of 1616, the "Summary" and the sentence.

The *decretum* of 3 March might seem the most authoritative text since it records what happened at the Inquisition's Thursday meeting with the pope, when it made its most important decisions.[18] Inclusion in the *decreta* converted the act into a precedent, on which the Inquisition relied nearly as much as common lawyers do.[19] Although both points have significance, neither bears as much weight as might at first appear. Above all, the *decreta* were frequently sloppily kept.[20] The minute of Paul's order (No. 1), recording a direct if informal command from the pope via the Inquisition's secretary to the two heads of its permanent staff, is a good example of the many notes in the decree registers scrawled in the margin or crammed in at the end of a meeting.[21] Since it had not gone through the Congregation, the pope's order need not have been recorded there at all, although more than a few similar acts were. As just one example, take the informational note exactly like No. 1 saying that Secretary Gian Garzia Millini "told me, the assessor, that the pope had ordered" that the Inquisition not accept recommendations, letters offering protection to suspects.[22]

Next, the way the Inquisition noted its decisions produced an important weakness in its records bearing directly on the status of No. 3, the only one of these documents explicitly to identify itself as a second-hand summary. The notary said he had transcribed a text given to him by the assessor, the permanent head of the Inquisition staff, who had jotted down what Bellarmino had said during the secret part of the Inquisition meeting from which the notary was barred.[23] Quite apart from the strong suspicion that in some cases the assessor did no more than hand the notary the meeting agenda, perhaps with notes of action taken, perhaps in its original, unannotated form, so far as we know there was no procedure in place by which to check the accuracy of either the assessor's jottings or the notary's transcriptions of them.[24] In this case, we need look no farther than the next clause of the same document for evidence of the confusion this clumsy second-hand recording could produce. In it the same notary, again allegedly working from the assessor's notes, entered the Congregation of the Index's order that Copernicus's *De Revolutionibus* and two other books had been "prohibited and suspended, respectively" and then reversed the sequence of those words followed again by "respectively" at the end of the note. By also listing the books incorrectly relative to which was prohibited or suspended, the assessor/notary created an insoluble mess.[25] There is every reason to think he/they did the same in No. 2, the precept minute. Besides, as its context shows, the decree of 3 March did not primarily concern Galileo, who appeared in it only as advance recipient of the Index's action, so the notary (and maybe Bellarmino himself) worried less about getting what happened to him right. As Sergio Pagano also observes, Bellarmino was under no obligation in the first place to report in detail what had happened.[26]

The Precept Minute: A Forgery?

From the moment serious study of Galileo's trial began in the late 1860s, document No. 2 has been the object of determined efforts to get rid of it because it does the most damage to Galileo.[27] It posed an even greater danger than previously realized. Incredibly enough two words in it, *et constituto*, that would by themselves have settled once and for all what happened have been overlooked.[28] They appear in the phrase recording Seghizzi's action, "and afterward and *incontinenti*, in my and witnesses' [presence], etc., still being then present the same illustrious lord cardinal [Roberto Bellarmino], the abovesaid father commissary [Seghizzi] ordered and ordered [*sic*] the aforesaid Galileo, still present *et constituto*" ("et successive ac incontinenti, in mei etc. et testium etc., praesenti etiam adhuc eodem illustrissimo Domino cardinali, supradictus Pater Commissarius praedicto Galileo adhuc ibidem praesenti et constituto praecepit et ordinavit") to abandon his Copernican beliefs. *Constitutus*, literally "constituted," is the vital term. It regularly appears at the beginning of a deposition or interrogation before the Inquisition and other courts and led to records of them being known as *constituta*. Galileo's contemporary Sigismondo Scaccia unhelpfully said that definition arose because *constitutus* was their first word.[29] It also appears frequently in canon law in several senses. One of the most common occurs in the phrase *in nostra [the pope's] praesentia constitutus*, which probably comes close to the sense it has in the precept and cannot mean simply "present," unless "present in our presence" makes any kind of sense.[30] The precept's text similarly couples *praesenti* to *constitutus*. The papal chancery might have filled its documents with unneccessary rhetorical flourishes, but the Inquisition did not. The use in the precept of two words (*praecipere* and *ordinare*) that both must be translated into English as "order" does not provide a counter-example. Legal commentators gave exhaustive treatment to a whole range of related terms for "to order," all of which they apparently thought denoted or connoted slightly different meanings.[31]

Another common sense of *constitutus* in canon law helps explain the first meaning. This is the phrase *in minoribus ordinibus constitutus* ("*constitutus* in minor orders") or the like, for example, *in tua et Tolosana ecclesia est archidiaconus constitutus* ("*constitutus* archdeacon in your church [cathedral] of Toulouse"), where the word signifies that a person holds an office. That sense becomes much clearer by the time Francisco Peña uses it several times in his commentary on Nicolau Eymeric's *Directorium Inquisitorum* to refer to an inquisitor's or his vicar's establishment in power.[32] The fact that other of the Inquisition's judicial acts, including several of Galileo's (for example, the interrogation of 12 April 1633 or his "defense" of 10 May [*DV*, nos. 37 and 40]), begin instead with *vocatus* may provide another clue to the meaning of *constitutus*. According to Francesco Beretta, *vocatus* signified that the suspect or witness had received the *citatio verbalis*, while *constitutus* meant more or less the same thing, that he or she had the required citation and had responded to it by making him- or herself available to the court. Above all, Beretta concluded, *constitutus* indicated that the act had taken place in a notary's presence and was therefore both authentic and legally valid. He cites a passage in Francisco Peña's "Introductio" setting *constituuntur* parallel to *interrogantur*.[33] Thus *consitutus* and *vocatus* mean nearly the same thing. The support Beretta offered for this conclusion may be a little thin, but it at least indicates the functional equivalence of the two terms as indicating that a person had become involved in a legal proceeding.

In order to incorporate this range of meanings, I suggest that *constitutus* is best translated as "established," which has the advantage of being a plausible extension of its classical sense of "to cause to stand."[34] In a legal document, then, it indicates a person's change in status qua legal subject (but apparently usually stopping short of his transformation into witness or deponent, which happened only after taking the appropriate oath) and thereby indicates the legal nature of the proceeding. Its predicate in this phrase of the precept is Galileo and in tandem with *adhuc ibidem praesenti*, the key word being the adverb *adhuc* ("still"), it signifies that at least the notary regarded both Bellarmino's and Seghizzi's actions as part of the same legal proceeding. Furthermore, those two words exclude the possibility of a charitable admonition, an act that by design never had legal significance. This problem will receive more attention below and in the next chapter.

The attack on the precept minute followed two lines, advanced most influentially by Emil Wohlwill.[35] He maintained that it was a forgery and, even if not, legally illegitimate. Both criticisms turned on a key point, the lack of the witnesses' signatures. Although the forgery thesis proved popular for a long time, only two historians still seriously entertain it, Francesco Beretta and Vittorio Frajese, the first much better informed than the second and oddly the man who has done most to demonstrate the unlikelihood of his contention. His case depends on neither palaeographical nor codicological grounds but on an argument lifted from Wohlwill without acknowledgment about the contradiction between No. 3 and No. 1, leading to the slippage between No. 2's two actions. Beretta calls the "material authenticity" of its second half "very problematic," before concluding that it was forged in 1632 in order to extricate from trouble the man who had licensed the *Dialogue*.[36]

Beretta admits that the palaeographical and codicological evidence is against him. Thus, all of No. 2 "appears" to be in the hand of Andrea Pettini, the chief notary in 1616.[37] Furthermore, he concludes on formal grounds that the first half of the precept minute is authentic, and does not criticize the second in these terms.[38] He also disproves the theory that the document was interpolated into the dossier at a later date.[39] Finally, Beretta shows that witnesses' signatures would not have been expected on a document like No. 2, an *imbreviatura* or minute.[40] Its authenticity derived not from those signatures but from the notary's, which Beretta claims normally occurred only once per dossier, at the bottom of the front cover.[41] Galileo's file lacks such a signature. Beretta rather tendentiously maintains that either Pettini never signed it or his signature had already been torn off before Galileo was sentenced, making the outcome illegal. This point signifies little, since it is impossible to say when the damage occurred.[42] Nor, given the loss of nearly all the Inquisition's *processi*, can Beretta cite evidence for his description of normal practice in cases like Galileo's. He seems instead to base himself on the files in Trinity College Dublin, MS 1232.[43] This comparison may not hold up, since these dossiers (1) concern suspects who appeared spontaneously before the Inquisition and, therefore, merited substantially different treatment from other accuseds, which may well mean that their records were handled differently; and (2) include multiple proceedings, not one.[44] Nor even on these dossiers is the (same) notary's practice uniform. Some signatures appear to be autograph for example, fo. 1r), others fair copies probably written by a substitute notary (for example, fo. 9r). In short, neither the signatures of the witnesses—which would not have been expected—nor the notary's—which, unlike the witnesses's, may really be missing—effect No. 2's authenticity.

Monitio caritativa or Fraternal Correction?

Many commentators read No. 1 as ordering a two-phase proceeding, a "warning" by Bellarmino, followed by a precept from Seghizzi. No one before Beretta had tried to explain that "warning." He identified it as a *caritativa monitio*
recorded in the authentic part of No. 2. Bellarmino did not take even the
next step, a *denunciatio evangelica*, much less administer or countenance the
administration of a precept.[45] This assertion drives Beretta's case for forgery.

As little as has been said about precepts in connection with Galileo's trial,
until Beretta's thesis almost nothing had been entered into evidence about either admonition or "evangelical denunciation" (*denunciatio evangelica*).[46] His
discussion draws mainly on three works, Sigismondo Scaccia's *Tractatus de
iudiciis*, Francisco Peña's unpublished "Introductio, sive Praxis Inquisitorum,"
and Prospero Farinacci's *Tractatus de haeresi*. All are roughly contemporary
with the beginning of Galileo's trial, and all constitute reasonably weighty
sources. The author of the first had experience as inquisitor of Malta, and
Peña had sat for years as a consultor to the Roman Inquisition in his capacity
as dean of the Rota.[47] Farinacci had never had any position in the Inquisition,
but he had been for a long time the fiscal general (roughly chief prosecutor)
for the city of Rome; his book was dedicated to the Congregation of the Inquisition, and he claimed that Bellarmino had read it.[48] All three agreed that
the essence of a *monitio caritativa* was secrecy in order to protect the sinner;
for just that reason, it preceded the *denunciatio*. They also all agreed that heresy did not require such a *monitio* because it was a public crime.[49] Beretta
saves what looks like an unpromising situation by noting that prior to such
an admonition ignorance excused misdeeds, but not afterward. Thus Galileo,
charitably warned, amended his ways especially by protesting at the beginning of his *Dialogue on the Two Chief World Systems* that he always intended
to submit to the Church's judgment. Had he persisted in error after such an
admonition, that would have constituted pertinacy that became heresy.[50] Thus
by implication since Galileo got only an admonition, he could not have been
accused (even tacitly) of heresy, and the entire proceeding was extrajudicial.

Unfortunately, Beretta is unlikely to be correct about Bellarmino's action.
As we shall see in the next chapter, the Inquisition used *monitiones* in exactly
the way I think Bellarmino did, not out of charity but as a means to suspend
or to conclude process, and therefore in almost exactly the same way it used
precepts; by contrast, I have not found a single *monitio* in the decree registers
qualified as charitable. Again in the next chapter we shall see that, while the

jurists' commentary on the use and nature of admonitions is nothing like as extensive as in the case of precepts (unsurprising, since they were not a legal device), there is more than enough to demonstrate against Beretta that what happened to Galileo was not a "charitable admonition," and that in fact the kind of "warning" he got is virtually indistinguishable from a precept.

At more or less the same time as Beretta, Matthias Dorn, a geologist, also undertook to demonstrate that the precept minute, No. 2, had been forged.[51] In addition to repeating Wohlwill's twin claims (again, without acknowledgment), Dorn offered a quasi-scientific criticism based on observations by an apparently professional document examiner, G. Schöneberg.[52] Almost certainly working at second hand from photographs supplied by Dorn, Schöneberg identified four differences in the hand of the first and second parts of the minute: (1) in the form of characters, especially "d"; (2) in the ductus, the general way in which a particular writer forms characters, especially *Oberlängenverzierungen*, which I take to mean serifs on the ascenders; (3) in the size of the characters; and (4) in the ligature between magiscule "T" and "e."[53] These results are all open to serious question. Above all, small, sometimes very small details best distinguish one hand from another, especially in the case of scripts as highly formalized as papal chancery hand. Many such will be hard to see in photographs. I have not been able to see the originals, but, on the basis not of the tiny prints reproduced in Dorn's book but of Henri de L'Épinois's much clearer (in part because more than a century older) photographic reproductions and the strength of professional training in palaeography and thirty years practice and teaching of it, I reject all Schöneberg's points.[54] Neither of the most solid-looking ones, 1 and 4, is true. Any alleged difference in the characters' size could easily be explained by the fact that the first half of the text is written into a smallish space at the bottom of a mostly full page, while the second half is at the top of a new, otherwise blank one. Schöneberg did not perform the surest test to distinguish two hands, including their ductus, the measurement of the characters' slant. I do not detect any variation in slant from either set of plates. The second surest measure, differences in infrequently written characters, is impossible since there are none to compare.[55]

Annibale Fantoli offers a number of extrinsic criticisms of Beretta's forgery thesis. One of the best involves the witnesses' names. How would a forger in 1632 have known them?[56] This objection has a possible answer. An especially clever man could have found them in a biography of Bellarmino published in 1624 and again in 1631. The first, the Cypriot Badino or Bandino de Nores, served as *maestro di camera* to both Cesare Baronio and Bellarmino.[57] The second, Agostino Mongardo, served Bellarmino as one of Nores's subordinates (*cubiculi administer*).[58] In a note, Fantoli speculated that the public version of No. 2 is missing because it went into the now mostly lost series of *Libri extensorum*.[59] Fantoli adopts Beretta's description of this formerly extensive set of volumes as "the registers of acts emitted in public form by the notary."[60] Once again, Beretta painted a bit broadly on the basis of limited evidence. One of the few surviving such volumes I examined, ACDFSO, St.st.LL-5-g, contains no public instruments. Finally, like Guido Morpurgo-Tagliabue, Fantoli pointed to the seeming contradiction between Nos. 1 and 2 to support the second's authenticity, arguing that a forger would have tried to make his work agree with an authentic document.[61] And one might add, especially since he had taken care to unearth the real witnesses.

Most recently, Frajese has revisited the precept leading to a rejoinder from Pagano who also criticizes other work from Wohlwill forward, both men recycling a number of earlier arguments, both adding a few original points.[62] Frajese's argument rests on a distinction between a "private and extrajudicial admonition" given by Bellarmino and Seghizzi's "judicial precept."[63] Instead of demonstrating the nature of Bellarmino's action, Frajese rests his case on the claim that the precept minute is a forgery. In addition to most of the timeworn arguments dating back to Wohlwill, especially the allegation that the precept minute is an unicum, contradicting all the other documents, and that the putative original should have been signed by Galileo and the witnesses—a claim constantly repeated, even though, given the lack of any original precepts, one necessarily without evidence—he bases his conclusion on more or less original codicological and palaeographical grounds.[64] First, the minute is in an odd place, beginning on the verso of one sheet and continuing on the recto of another, the reverse of what should have happened according to the papal chancery's customs.[65] The minute began in that spot because the notary Pettini had to work around a date already entered, which Frajese thinks was that of the presentation to the pope of the theologian consultors' opinion condemning two propositions allegedly drawn from Galileo's *Sunspot Letters*.[66] Instead of entering the pope's decision about the opinion (because he took none), Pettini began the precept minute following Seghizzi's orders.[67] Second, Frajese makes a great deal of changes in the hand over the course of the minute's text. Although constantly qualifying the point with phrases like "if we are dealing with him," Frajese seems to agree with Beretta that the whole of the minute is in Pettini's hand, the only time it occurs in Galileo's dossier.[68] Based on a change in the size of the text on the initial verso, he theorizes that the minute was not written continuously but in three separate blocks. He thinks it highly significant that the hand begins to shrink as it approaches the word *successive* and becomes smaller thereafter, a point once more adapted from Wohlwill. Therefore the text must originally have ended with the word "deserat." After the interruption, the notary resumed with another pen or ink. Frajese concludes that Seghizzi ordered Pettini to enter the precept minute instead of leaving the two sheets blank; Bellarmino's extrajudicial action should have left no record.[69] Third, a point about the document's form. While allowing that the text is an *imbreviatura*, that fact deprives it of legal validity since such documents were intended only for internal use and in the absence of the proper signatures (again) lacked legal validity.[70] Finally, an argument from content. Frajese alleges that the precept minute was modeled—with suitable alterations to the truth—on the the text of Paul's order located immediately before it in Galileo's dossier.[71] The notary had no choice but to do that, since he had "no real referent" (that is, a legitimate precept) to follow. From this, Frajese concludes that no original precept ever existed.[72] The blame for all this falls on Seghizzi.[73]

Pagano has disposed of most of Frajese's points, while operating within the same undemonstrated opposition between an "admonition" and a "formal precept."[74] Like Frajese, he makes assumptions about the Inquisition's record-keeping practices, especially that it was normal for its notaries to write up documents later. This point happens to be true, but Pagano infers it from a couple of sixteenth-century examples of Holy Office officials visiting suspects at their houses.[75] He further alleges without evidence that the Inquisition often used the resulting minute (which following Beretta he calls an *imbreviatura* or *matrix seu originale instrumentum*) during an informative process, a point he then contradicts by incorrectly claiming that Galileo did not undergo such an investigation in 1615–1616.[76] More substantial criticisms of Frajese follow. First, Pagano easily disproves Frajese's largest codicological claim. The precept minute's location is not unusual: Pagano cites a number of instances of documents in Galileo's dossier beginning on the reverse of sheets and in the middle of the page.[77] Next, he almost as easily quashes Frajese's palaeographical evidence. Pagano sees no change in the hand's size on the initial verso, calling the allegation "unconvincing" and the supposed change in the ink as due to the degradation of oak gall ink over time.[78] The abbreviations Pettini used and to which Frajese pointed as evidence of the writing's compression are also found throughout the dossier and are those usually found in documents generated by the papal bureaucracy.[79] Thus Pagano sees no evidence of any interruption.

Nevertheless, he thinks it "very possible" that Seghizzi directed Pettini, while absolving the commissary of malicious intent.[80] Pagano also makes at least one large mistake in his criticism of Frajese. He alleges that Paul's order of 25 February is not found in the decree register because no actions taken in the secret part of corams were recorded there. This is not true.[81]

Bellarmino's "Certificate" and Evidence from the Second Phase of Galileo's Trial in 1633

In his reports on what happened, Galileo failed altogether to refer to the precept.[82] Since he also made light of the Index's decree of 5 March against Copernicus, it might seem that Galileo took neither event seriously.[83] Indeed he did, especially when he learned of rumors that he had been forced to abjure.[84] Those rumors gave rise to the seventh document. Galileo asked Bellarmino for an affidavit (*fede*) that he had not abjured or suffered other punishment.[85] The cardinal, apparently acting as a member of the Index rather than as an Inquisitor, agreed. He wrote at least one draft of his text before settling on the final form.

The *fede* is dated 26 May 1616 and reads as follows:

> We, Roberto Cardinal Bellarmino, having understood that Signor
> Galileo Galilei is being slandered or accused of having abjured in
> our hands, and also of being "penanced" [punished] for this with
> salutary penances, and having been sought out about the truth,
> we say that the said Signor Galileo has not abjured in our hands
> nor in those of others in Rome, nor anywhere else that we know,
> any opinion or doctrine, nor even more has he received salutary
> penances nor of any other sort, but has only had announced to him
> the declaration made by Our Lord [the pope] and published by the
> Sacred Congregation of the Index, in which is contained that the
> doctrine ascribed to Copernicus that the earth moves around the
> sun and the sun is at the center of the world without moving from
> east to west is contrary to Holy Scripture and therefore cannot be
> defended nor held. And in testimony of this we have written and
> signed this document with our own hand.[86]

The text manifests Bellarmino's skill as a rhetorician. While carefully avoiding assigning responsibility for the precept, he also smoothly, almost casually noted the warning specifically to Galileo not to defend or hold either of the two condemned propositions. And he changed the draft's link between its first and second sections to take away some of the force of what he was about to say, or perhaps he was trying to keep the Inquisition's action secret by deflecting attention from it. Instead of the original "of any other sort *ma si bene,*" which literally means "but although," he switched to "ma solo" ("but only or merely").[87] So, condemned in terms of the Index decree, or maybe not, Bellarmino left it to the reader to decide. Galileo read the text in one way, his judges in 1633 in another. Galileo perhaps naturally enough concentrated on those two little words "ma solo," whereas his judges looked past them to Bellarmino's statement that Galileo knew all about the Index decree, whatever else Bellarmino and Seghizzi might have ordered him to do. Galileo's judges in 1633 took this passage as further incriminating him. In doing so, they forced the sense of Bellarmino's *fede* in the opposite direction that many modern historians do. Neither can safely draw on it, since it says nothing directly about the event of 26 February.[88]

The last piece of evidence is Galileo's deposition of 12 April 1633, on which those same historians have often relied almost as heavily as on Bellarmino's document, and even more unwisely. None have allowed for its obvious nature as a self-interested statement. Even without such an allowance, as Pagano and I more clearly have demonstrated, Galileo's testimony supports the reconstruction argued here.[89]

After an opening that may have been meant to steer his interrogator away from the precept, Galileo quickly produced a copy of Bellarmino's *fede.*[90] Even as he did so, he tried to change its meaning by glossing it in light of Bellarmino's letter of 12 April 1615 to Paolo Antonio Foscarini. While the *fede* drawing on the consultors' opinion correctly said that Copernicus's ideas were "contrary to Holy Scripture and therefore cannot be defended nor held," the earlier letter read instead that Foscarini could safely defend Copernicus only hypothetically. Galileo alleged that was also what Bellarmino had told him in 1616.[91] Introducing Bellarmino's *fede* and thereby contradicting his testimony proved to be a serious mistake. "In any manner whatsoever" (as the precept minute reads) almost becomes redundant.[92]

Galileo's interrogator continued with a series of questions about the interview with Bellarmino. Asked whether anyone else had been present and whether they or anyone else had also given him a precept, he replied, "It could be that some precept was given to me that I not hold nor defend the said opinion, but I do not remember because this is a matter of some years ago."[93]

Damaging as this admission was, Galileo quickly made his situation worse in his reply to a question whether he would remember the precept's content were it read to him: "I do not claim not to have broken that precept in any way." After having been told what the precept said, he once more exacerbated matters by saying, "I remember that the precept was that I could not hold nor defend, and it could be that there was also nor teach. I also do not remember that there was that detail, in any fashion, but it could be that it was there." In short, he admitted that he might have received the precept in the strongest wording including *quovis modo*. The "Summary" (No. 5) recorded Galileo's statement with scrupulous accuracy: "he confesses the precept."[94]

In his brief defense of 10 May, Galileo first denied that he had received a precept (twice called a *comandamento*) and then claimed to have an oral order from Bellarmino that did not contain "in any manner whatsoever," in both cases relying again on Bellarmino's *fede*. He concluded that "when the said two details [teach, and *quovis modo*] are removed, and only the two noted in the present affidavit are retained [that is, not defended or held], there is no point in doubting that the command given in it *is the same precept given in the Sacred Congregation of the Index's decree*."[95] But as Pagano points out, in between Galileo made another damaging admission, or at least accepted without demur a serious point his interrogator had made. The "command" had been "given to me and registered."[96] That last word can only refer to the precept minute, which, of course, contains the strongest form of the order to Galileo. In his last interrogation on 21 June he spoke of "that precept" he had received as the watershed in his intellectual life, after which he scrupulously and sincerely adhered only to Ptolemy's cosmology, as he continued to maintain throughout the balance of this interrogation he had always done.[97] Galileo's sentence the next day brims with the charge that he had violated the precept. so it is no surprise that he confessed to doing so in his abjuration the same day, saying that he had been properly condemned for having published the *Dialogue* "after having been judicially warned with a precept by the same [Holy Office] that I was completely to leave the false opinion that the sun is the center of the world and immobile and that the earth is not the center of the world and moves, and that I could not hold, defend nor teach in any way whatsoever, orally or in writing, the said false doctrine."[98]

Thus, except in his defense of 10 May, Galileo admitted that he received a precept, probably from Bellarmino, and at least left open the possibility that it took the strong form. Galileo's own testimony isolates document No. 3 all the more.

Successive ac incontinenti

Now that the precept minute has been established as authentic, one phrase in it demands careful attention, mainly because it has been taken to mean that Seghizzi violated his instructions to give Galileo a chance to accept whatever Bellarmino had said, going on *successive ac incontinenti*.

The words "successive ac incontinenti" are linked by "et" to the last word in the warning Bellarmino gave, "deserat" ("abandon"). Right from the first, the phrase has been translated as linking the two actions without any temporal interval between them whatsoever. Wohlwill, while translating the phrase in various ways, "und darauf folgend und sofort" ("and thereafter and immediately"), "ohne ihm [Galileo] zur Antwort Zeit zu lassen" or "ohne Pause" ("without giving Galileo time to reply" or "without a break"), and "unmittelbar darauf" ("immediately thereafter"), never allowed it to include even an extra moment.[99] Wohlwill's contemporary and competitor Karl von Gebler similarly rendered it as "gleich darauf ohne Unterbrechung" ("immediately thereafter without interruption").[100] It has usually been translated into English as "immediately thereafter." Fantoli gives the most elaborate translation-cum-gloss: "an intervention that immediately followed Bellarmine's warning, apparently without Galileo having had time to display his acquiescence."[101] The conclusion from such translations follows that Seghizzi violated the contingency in Paul V's instructions that he was to act only if Galileo "refused to obey" ("recusaverit parere").

Neither Wohlwill nor von Gebler tried to establish what *successive ac incontinenti* might have meant in the seventeenth century. Several of their contemporaries did better, including Philippe Gilbert and Franz Reusch. Both turned to inquisitorial manuals, Gilbert to the *Repertorium Inquisitorum* (1575) and Reusch to Eliseo Masini's widely used text for provincial inquisitors, *Sacro arsenale* (first edition 1621 and frequently reprinted). Quintiliano Mandosio added a note to a passage in the *Repertorium* that left *incontinenti* almost without limits as to how much time was meant.[102] Masini gave instances of actions linked by *successive ac incontinenti*, as well as more with only the first word.[103] In one with the whole phrase, Masini paralleled it to *immediatamente*, a word seemingly as strong as its modern English cognate.[104] Yet this cannot be what Masini meant, since he joined two actions that could never occur strictly "immediately" after one another: fetching a suspect from prison (even if in the same building) in order to confront another suspect. Thus on Masini's evidence *successive* can signify no more than "after," perhaps "as soon as possible after" or better "directly" in both a temporal and procedural sense. This comes close to Beretta's gloss of "in continuity with the previous event," that is, part of the same legal proceedings, even if he continues to use the temporal meaning of "immediately."[105]

Uses found in Peña's "Introductio" (written before his death in 1612), as well as in inquisition records, support the same meaning. Thus, Peña once wrote of asking the same questions "*successive* in the same or another examination."[106] At least three times it has the simple meaning "after" in the Holy Office's own records, including indicating a prison visitation that must have begun sometime later than the first event indicated.[107] It also occurs in the records of peripheral tribunals. In Naples, we find it several times in Tommaso Campanella's *processo*, for example, twice to link the examination of two witnesses, once to introduce the swearing in of another after an interval.[108] Likewise, it occurs in Romagna in a similar sense a number of times in the records of Rodrigo Alidosi's trial when witnesses *successive* "appeared."[109] The two words and the joint phrase were also known in the governor of Rome's court.[110]

The entry in Du Cange makes *successive* seem a fifteenth-century neologism since it cites only a letter of Pius II of 1459.[111] Most dictionaries have equally thin entries for it. The only other textual citation in any yet found, Andreas Stübelius's *Thesaurus latinitatis*, quotes a bad reading from Aelius Spartianus on Caracalla taken from Robert Constantin's *Supplementum linguae latinae*, which should be emended to *successisse*.[112] The full title of Constantin's work underscores the word's rarity: *Supplementum linguae Latinae, seu dictionarium abstrusorum vocabulorum*.[113] Johann Matthias Gesner cited the same passage without correction in his slightly later *Novus Linguae et Eruditionis Romanae Thesaurus*.[114] Although certainly rare, a number of uses of the word come up in a search of the *Patrologia latina* database covering patristic and medieval writing before 1215.[115] The interval between then and the seventeenth century still needs investigation, but, by the later period, the word appears fairly frequently, for example, two or three times in Melchior Adam, *Vitae Germanorum iureconsultorum et politicorum*.[116] Since *successive* need not mean much more than "after," by itself it says nothing about whether Galileo had a chance to respond.

Perhaps because they found its meaning obvious, *successive* did not interest the jurists, unlike its mate *incontinenti*. While still far from a common word, the second has a substantially richer history. Along with the then more usual *ex continenti*, it appeared a number of times in Justinian's Code with such a variety of possible meanings as to generate a substantial amount of jurisprudential commentary.[117] Alberico da Rosate (ca. 1290–1360) offered one of the most detailed discussions in his *Dictionarium iuris tam civilis, quam canonici*, which went through many editions.[118] He gave an almost bewildering number of definitions, most in the temporal sense from *statim* onward, and a number of cognates (all meaning at first glance "immediately"), extending all the way to three days as the time limit for revoking an attorney's errors (citing C. 2. 9 and his own discussion in *Commentariorum iuris utriusque summi practici Domini Alberici de Rosate Bergomensis pars prima super codice*).[119] His gloss on *confestim*, one of the synonyms he suggested for *incontinenti*, defined it again as sometimes *statim*, but sometimes ten days. The word also had nontemporal meanings, especially *continuus*, without any "extraneous acts." In this case, the time period might be left entirely undefined; Alberico again suggested the figure of ten days. In his third entry he gave the example of merchants going off in search of a notary or a celebratory drink at the conclusion of a deal, both (especially the second) denoting a possibly protracted interval of time. Other commentators often cited Alberico's three days in the case of a man who died that long after being wounded.[120] Others stretched the time indefinitely, for example, the great late fifteenth-century canonist Felino Sandeo, who left it up to the judge's decision how long an heir had to prove his claim *incontinenti*.[121] The eminent late sixteenth- or early seventeenth-century jurist Giacomo Menochio did the same in his most popular work, throwing out "one day," "three days" or "two months" as possibilities.[122] He also offered almost exactly the same definition as Beretta, citing Bartolo Da Sassoferrato: "before it [the trial] can be diverted to extraneous acts" ("antequam ad actus extraneos divertatur").[123] The exhaustive note in *Repertorium Inquisitorum* said virtually the same thing, although in the specific case of ratification of a confession given under torture it was much more restrictive, saying *incontinenti* meant "intra diem," "within a day."[124] In short, the general opinion was that the word "receives a varying interpretation according to the matter . . . and we [in this case Bernabé Brisson, but it could be any of a number of commentators] interpret it with some modest space of time."[125] German commentators introduced a distinctive subtlety, saying the term should not be interpreted literally but instead *civiliter, moraliter* leaving its precise temporal component to the judge's discretion, as Sandeo and Menochio had thought.[126]

An Elegant but Wrong Solution

In 1987, Thomas Kurig, now an intellectual property lawyer, proposed a radically new translation as a solution to the problem. His argument depended on two grammatical points. "Immediately" ("gleich darauf" in German) is mistaken and ignores "ac incontinenti." "Successive" should be translated not in a temporal sense but as "following thereon (expressing the papal will)," while "ac incontinenti" is a causal dative modifying "Galileo" and the phrase should therefore be rendered as "since Galileo was unwilling" or "being impudent."[127] The first of these at least raises a question about the usual translation. No doubt because of the incorrect linkage to "incontinenti," "successive" lost its simple meaning of "after" with no necessary implication of "right after." Kurig's second point appears even more vital, if not as original as he claims; it had been made if not published already in 1964.[128] By almost literally translating "si recusaverit" of No. 1, "incontinenti" would remove the most important contradiction between it and No. 2. That contradiction has been overdrawn even without the correct translation of "incontinenti," because "recusaverit" need not mean "refuse." "Recusare" principally means "to object," but it also has the sense "to be reluctant" or "unwilling." I do not need to belabor the point that this last meaning agrees exactly with "incontinenti" as translated by Kurig. Thus Galileo would not have had to do anything more than hesitate to obey or give some sign of annoyance, and Seghizzi would have thought himself within his rights to give the precept.

Unfortunately, Kurig's elegant solution is wrong. I have found no other instances of *incontinenti* used in the way he suggests, in a search of the *Patrologia latina* database, a less systematic survey of other medieval and early modern writing, or, most important, among lawyers. Nowhere in their extensive attention to the word is a definition like Kurig's so much as hinted at. More curiously yet, none of the commentators I have checked discuss the phrase *successive ac incontinenti*.

Thus we know much more about the meaning of *incontinenti* than of *successive*. Unfortunately, we know least of all about the phrase *successive ac incontinenti*. Wohlwill correctly identified *successive ac incontinenti* as a "formula" that he translated in a number of ways.[129] As far as anyone now knows, it appears for the first time in the precept minute and might therefore have been invented specially for Galileo.[130] (I hasten to add that I make this point facetiously to underscore another crucial gap in our knowledge.) The only evidence I have found in sources generated by the Roman Inquisition comes from Trinity College, Dublin, MS 1232, which postdates Galileo's trial.[131] Unlike most of these volumes, it is composed of case files rather than sentences. Beretta looked it over, but confined himself to the two instances of *successive ac incontinenti*, ignoring other terms used in similar ways that may help to define the phrase. The first of the two occurrences he did discuss is much like the one in Masini in which a prisoner confronted another prisoner; that is, some indeterminate interval of time must have intervened between two acts. The phrase follows the accused's signature at the end of a *verbale* with the note that he was returned to prison and *successive ac incontinenti* searched.[132] The other case is even less help, except that there are two other phrases on the same page that appear to serve the same function. The passage begins with "successive et immediate ubi coram S. fuit ei dictum per Dominum an velit repeti testes examinatos in presenti causa quia dabuntur, etc." ("*successive ac immediate* where in the presence of his Holiness the lord [cardinal] said to him whether he wished the witnesses examined in the present case to be reexamined"), to which the accused replied in the negative: "Successive et incontinenti supradictus D. fuit ipsi (?) assignatus terminus decem dierum ad faciendum suas defensiones" (*successive et incontinenti* the abovementioned lord [cardinal] had assigned him [the suspect] a term of ten days to making his defenses), which he also declined: "Deinde mandavit dominus reponi ad locum suum" ("Then the lord [cardinal] ordered him put back in his place").[133] Thus we have *incontinenti* parallel to *immediate* but also to *deinde*, which simply means thereafter, almost the same thing as *successive*. There are many cases where *deinde* or even more basically *tunc* (then) do the work that *successive ac incontinenti* sometimes do.[134] In an intensive and extensive search in other sources, I have found all of three occurrences in addition to the three just cited. One instance, missing any conjunction, comes between the end of one deposition and the beginning of the next in a *processo* in Archivio di Stato, Venice, Santo Uffizio, b. 71, an unnumbered and unfoliated piece dated 4 October 1651 at the head. The other two have a conjunction, in the first case of 1630 in the middle of the conferral of a laurea in philosophy at La Sapienza, the second between the first and second questions of the suitability hearing of an auditor of the Rota dating from 1632.[135] In short, the translation of *successive ac incontinenti* as "immediately thereafter" is open to doubt.

Seghizzi's Career and Its Reflection on
His Administration of Galileo's Precept

The legal impropriety hypothesis demands as a corollary that Seghizzi acted illegally and to say the least incautiously. None of those who defend this thesis have investigated Seghizzi's tenure as commissary or the rest of his career.[136] His tombstone in the cathedral of Lodi encapsulates his success as an inquisitor, calling him "hammer of heretics." Of course, a hammer can be wielded in any number of ways, including by a homicidal maniac. This was not Seghizzi's style. Quite the contrary. He was a stickler for proper procedure, of which he had a good deal of experience, beginning as *socio* of the commissary in Rome from 1601 to 1603.[137] Then he was made inquisitor of Cremona and six years later promoted to the the Roman Inquisition's highest-ranking provincial tribunal, Milan.[138] While there, he engaged in a similar procedure to giving a precept (see the next chapter) and was ordered to "gravely warn" ("graviter monere") a Cassinese Benedictine monk in 1612.[139] In both places he peppered the Congregation with questions, many of which led to the elaboration of general principles.[140] However that may be, they demonstrated his pronounced caution. The Congregation evidently wanted such a man as commissary, which he became just about a year before he gave Galileo his precept.[141] Commissary was an important post that often led to higher office, and it would be natural to think that Seghizzi had the kind of ambition that many other of its holders displayed. While he did not have much experience by early 1616, it seems likely that he would have been inclined to handle Galileo's case with extreme care, especially in Bellarmino's presence, lest he damage his prospects. Besides, acting in the reckless fashion often attributed to him would be completely out of line with his previous career.

Not long after Seghizzi gave Galileo his precept, an odd thing happened. Negotiations began for his return to his birthplace of Lodi as its bishop. The holder was allowed to resign on 22 May, and Seghizzi underwent the examination required of a prospective bishop two days later.[142] He was "elected" on 25 May and provided by the pope on 13 June.[143] The process went remarkably quickly. Unfortunately, Seghizzi died shortly after taking up his new post, making it difficult to interpret the move. It might seem that he had been rusticated for violating orders in Galileo's case (a point the legal impropriety theorists have never made). Two other interpretations seem much more likely: (1) he went home to acquire seasoning for further promotion, a bishopric often coming in the cursus honorum of an Inquisitor; or (2) he was forced out to make way for his more highly favored successor, Desiderio Scaglia. The second possibility is supported by the fact that Scaglia's *socio*, Deodato Seghizzi da Lodi, had already taken office on 7 September.[144] Since he almost had to have been Seghizzi's relative, this looks like a quid pro quo. Even better for Seghizzi, his own *socio*, Jacopo Tinti, became inquisitor of Casale in August 1616, whence he quickly moved to Como.[145] Since ordinarily it seems that the commissary named his own *socio*, the fact that Scaglia did not, together with Tinti's appointment and Seghizzi's own to his hometown see, makes it look as if these were bribes intended to induce him to make way for Scaglia.[146]

The Precept of 26 February 1616

With a better understanding of the documents recording the event and of the role and character of the Roman Inquisition's principal agent on that day, we are in a position to make better sense of what happened when Galileo met Cardinal Bellarmino and Commissary Seghizzi on 26 February 1616.

Seghizzi received his orders indirectly from Paul V on 25 February.

> The[147] Most Illustrious Lord Cardinal [Gian Garzia] Millini [secretary of the Inquisition] notified the Reverend Fathers Assessor [Paolo Emilio Filonardi] and Commissary of the Holy Office [Seghizzi] that the censure of the Father theologians on the propositions of Galileo, mathematician, having been reported, that the sun is the center of the world and immobile by local motion and [that] the earth moves even with a daily motion, His Holiness ordered the Most Illustrious Lord Cardinal [Roberto] Bellarmino to summon to his presence the said Galileo and warn him to abandon[148] the said opinion; and if he refused[149] to obey, the Father Commissary, in the presence of a notary and witnesses, should give him a precept that he completely abstain from teaching or defending this sort of doctrine and opinion, or dealing with it; if indeed he should not agree, he will be imprisoned.

The next day, summoned to Bellarmino's palazzo, Galileo was probably brought into the cardinal's innermost public chamber on the *piano nobile*, the second floor. Bellarmino, Seghizzi, and probably some Dominican friars awaited him, along with a notary. Bellarmino first "warned" Galileo. Galileo

objected in some way, perhaps in so mild a fashion as looking grumpy. That
"refusal" authorized Seghizzi to take the second action in Paul's order, and he
duly gave Galileo a precept "completely" to abandon Copernicus's ideas and
never again to deal with them in any way, shape or form. Or as the record in
Galileo's dossier has it:

> In[150] the palace, the said Most Illustrious Lord Cardinal Bellarmino's
> usual residence and in his lordship's rooms, the same lord cardinal,
> the above-mentioned Galileo having been summoned, and the
> same being in the said cardinal's house, in the presence of the
> Very Reverend Father Brother Michelangelo Seghizzi of Lodi,
> Order of Preachers, Commissary general of the Holy Office,
> warned the aforesaid Galileo of the error of the abovesaid opinion
> [Copernicus's] and that he should abandon it; and thereafter and
> immediately, in my [presence], etc. and of witnesses, etc. the
> same lord cardinal still besides being present, the abovesaid Father
> Commissary, the aforesaid Galileo still also present and established,
> enjoined and ordered him in His Holiness the pope's own name and
> of the whole Congregation of the Holy Office that he completely
> give up the abovesaid opinion that the sun is the center of the
> universe and immobile and that the earth moves, nor hold, teach
> or defend the same otherwise in any manner in word or writing;
> otherwise, he will be proceeded against in the Holy Office. To
> which precept the same Galileo agreed and promised to obey. Above
> which, etc. Done at Rome as above, the Reverend Badino Nores
> of Nicosia in the kingdom of Cyprus and Agostino Mongardo of
> the place of the abbey of Rosa in the diocese of Montepulciano,
> familiars of the said lord cardinal being present, witnesses, etc.

In short, Galileo received both a warning and a precept, a common combination as we shall see in the next chapter, and agreed to the second, which was
administered and recorded in the proper form. He was completely to abandon
his belief in Copernicus's core beliefs, which he had publicly made his own in
Sunspot Letters of 1613, and under no circumstances teach, defend, or deal with
them. If he did, he would be imprisoned or proceeded against by the Holy
Office, two more or less equivalent threats (see the next chapter). Galileo the
Copernican had been silenced.

The Aftermath

Bellarmino stayed busy the next week. First, again on Paul's orders, he put three books before the Index, Foscarini's, Copernicus's, and Diego Zuñiga's *Commentary on Job* (1584).[151] Foscarini's book, despite Millini's protection of its author, was to be condemned and the other two suspended.[152] All of them got into trouble because of Galileo, including the relatively obscure Zuñiga whom Galileo had cited in his "Letter to Christina." That Millini, one of the two most powerful cardinals in Rome, could not protect his client Foscarini emphasizes how poorly advised Galileo had been to rely on Alessandro Orsini. Millini missed this critical meeting altogether, maybe taken by surprise, since there is no sign the Index had previously considered any of these books.[153] The discussion may have been quite lively, since two of Galileo's most powerful backers, Cardinals Maffeo Barberini and Bonifazio Caetani, allegedly tried to prevent the banning of Copernicus.[154] Their resistance may have led to his book's being only implicitly labeled heretical and to its suspension "pending correction." It may be that Galileo's victim Francesco Ingoli, although not yet a consultor of the Index, advised his long-time patron Caetani to go easy on Copernicus.[155] Not too far into the future, Ingoli would be assigned to revise Copernicus's book, which he argued was useful to mathematicians.[156] No matter how violent or lengthy or careful the debate, the important part of the final draft decree is almost identical to the original proposal. Then that same day, Thursday 3 March, Bellarmino announced to the Inquisition and the pope both what he had done to Galileo and almost in the same breath (both items appear in the same entry in the decree register) the Index's proposed decree.[157] Six other cardinals attended, including Millini, Agostino Galamini, and Ferdinando Taverna, but, as on nearly all previous important occasions, neither Paolo Emilio Sfondrato nor, perhaps more important to Galileo, Giovanni Battista Bonsi. Unlike Sfondrato, Bonsi usually attended regularly, including on the last occasion of significance to Galileo when his *Sunspot Letters* had been sent to the censor; Bonsi may have been sulking after he had been frozen out when Millini originally delivered the order to Bellarmino a week earlier. After Bellarmino reported, Paul ordered the master of the sacred palace to issue the decree as drafted.

The next day, Tuscan ambassador Piero Guicciardini reported on all this activity.[158] Despite his bias against Galileo, he at first made the situation appear much more favorable than it was. He opened his letter by saying that he, Cardinal Francesco del Monte, and "more, the cardinals of the Holy Office" had "persuaded" Galileo to quiet down and keep his opinion to himself lest it appear that he had come to Rome "to be scarred." The ambassador did not think that Galileo would suffer personally "because as a prudent man he will want and believe what holy church wants and believes." Guicciardini did not really believe that. Instead, he stressed how dangerous Rome was for Galileo, especially under a pope "who abhors learning and these clever men and cannot stand to listen to these novelties and subtleties." Everybody tried to accommodate his ideas to the pope's and, if he had any brains, say the opposite of what he thought. Galileo in particular faced a number of friars who were constantly intriguing to destroy him. Galileo should therefore immediately cut short his stay in Rome. Then the ambassador implicitly threatened the grand duke, reminding him obscurely about what had happened in similar Florentine cases of interest to the Inquisition in the past. One of those was surely Rodrigo Alidosi's, which was still running, although it had nothing whatsoever to do with ideas.[159] I see no reason to run such risk, harped Guicciardini, merely to satisfy Galileo. His "passion" threatened to bring down anyone who supported him. Guicciardini meant the new Cardinal Carlo de' Medici, about to come to Rome. It would do incalculable damage if he failed to endorse the proceedings of the Inquisition, "the foundation and base of religion and the most important congregation in Rome." Guicciardini then revealed the depth of his own ignorance—as well as his negative attitude to "clever men"—by warning that anybody who dabbled in matters "astrological or philosophical" would get into big trouble, again because Paul was such an anti-intellectual blockhead and everybody tried to imitate him. Neither Guicciardini's characterization of the pope nor that of his court came anywhere near reality. True, the books stuffing the pope's new apartments in the Quirinal Palace may have been about the law, but they were still books. And all those cardinals hosting Galileo's extravaganzas were hardly trying to act like "fat-headed ignoramuses," in Guicciardini's crude phrase. Nevertheless, his point sank in, and the letters from Florence took on a much more cautious tone.

Gucciardini sent his dispatch just a moment too soon. The next day, Saturday 5 March, the Index publicly handed down its judgment against Copernicus.[160] This directly violated Paul's order of 3 March that the master of the sacred palace issue the decree. That official did not even sign it. Instead it bore the signatures of Sfondrato in almost his last appearance in the congregation's records, together with that of the Index's brand-new secretary. Perhaps as a result of the rivalry between secretary and master (as well as Sfondrato's indifference), the text of the decree of 5 March looks as if it were put together during a boxing match. Its syntax leaves in doubt the fate of the other two books bracketed with Foscarini's. The only certainty came at his expense, a point driven home when his printer was chased down by the Inquisition a few months later.[161]

Otherwise, there was a great deal of confusion over who had done the deed and what deed it was. Most people decided the Inquisition had issued both the order to Galileo (right) and the decree banning Copernicus (wrong), and quite a few collapsed one into the other (also wrong).[162] Again, what mattered was perception; on that ground putting the Inquisition in charge and making its principal target Galileo was exactly accurate. Antonio Querenghi offered one of the most graphic accounts of what happened, writing that Galileo's ideas had gone up in "the smoke of alchemy" in the face of the "infallible dogmas" expressed in the Index decree.[163] Everyone whose heads had been set spinning by the controversy could relax and no longer worry about being "so many ants on a big ball going through the air." Galileo had once written satire with Querenghi, and it shows in his friend's sarcasm now. Galileo's original attacker Niccolò Lorini copied out the decree and triumphantly waved it around Florence. His leader Ludovico Delle Colombe gleefully put out the same news.[164] Yet at the same time Galileo and his supporters brushed off what happened.[165] In a letter the day after the Index acted, Galileo blithely ignored his interview with Bellarmino and Seghizzi, offhandedly telling the Florentine secretary of state that he had not put a letter into the last weekly post because there was nothing to report![166] Instead, Galileo crowed that Tommaso Caccini had suffered another defeat. None of this has anything to do with me, he added. Galileo was always good at seeing things his way, but this interpretation is nothing short of weird. He must have begun to worry his handlers in Florence, since he continued that he was expecting Cardinal de' Medici's arrival to clear everything up. With transparent alarm, the secretary of state replied by ordering Galileo back home.[167] The Florentine authorities could be forgiven if they began to wonder just what their men in Rome were drinking when two of their cardinals, Orsini and del Monte, both reported that Galileo had triumphed unreservedly.[168]

Five days later Galileo went to see the pope.[169] He told Paul the story of his coming to Rome, complete with juicy details of his enemies' plotting. He acted worried. Paul assured him that neither he nor "the whole congregation [of the Inquisition]" believed a word of those allegations. The pope guaranteed Galileo that he would be safe as long as he, Paul, lived, repeating this "consolation" several times. In case the pope was not good enough, Galileo also noted that Federico Cesi favored him. What parallel universe had Galileo moved into? Since there is no other evidence of his meeting with the pope, it is not impossible that he at the very least heavily embroidered it if he did not invent it. And how he could think that Cesi, a mere marquess albeit a smart one, could in any way be on the same level as the pope beggars the imagination. Ten days later Galileo serenely pronounced the matter closed, expecting the quick republication of the revised Copernicus.[170] He may have got this news from the man charged with correcting the book, Caetani, who may have been suffering from a lower grade form of the same optimistic psychosis as Galileo. In actual fact it was four years before the revision was ready, and a new edition was never published. Shortly after Galileo's letter, back in the real world, the Index cranked out letters to all Inquisitors ordering them to publish the decree, and Bellarmino published another book that made crystal clear where his thoughts were.[171] It was called *De aeterna sanctorum felicitate* (*On the Eternal Salvation of the Saints*).[172] Together with *On the Mind's Ascent to God*, it could not be more obvious that Bellarmino was concentrating all his energies on heaven as the reward of the just, not as an astronomical phenomenon.

And what of Caccini? His brother Matteo, last seen being terrified that Tommaso would ruin the family's prospects, now vaunted the great reputation he had made by besting Galileo.[173] Matteo probably got this assessment straight from Tommaso, but he did check carefully with others about the extent of his brother's success. It included at least one tangible reward. By late summer Cardinal Nephew Scipione Borghese had got him the job of penitentiary of Santa Maria Maggiore, the church on which Paul V lavished particular attention and of which Millini was archpriest.[174] The post paid 400 *scudi* a year (about half what Galileo got as the grand duke's mathematician). Tommaso was also in good odor with the Dominican general.

Caccini had not finished with Galileo. In October 1616 Matteo feared that Caccini meant to publish a book, possibly about the stars.[175] In early 1619 the news or at least rumor was worse. Under guise of a preaching assignment, Caccini had actually resurrected his "intrigues" against Galileo, as another Florentine friar told Matteo.[176] A few months later Matteo thought Caccini meant to return to Florence in order to "terrebbe qualche persona più a segno," which odd phrase Antonio Ricci-Riccardi interpreted as keeping surveillance on Galileo.[177] The last we hear of Caccini "persecuting" Galileo is in a letter from Benedetto Castelli condoling with Galileo over the news that Caccini was going about saying Galileo had escaped only because of the protection of princes.[178] Although he would never be a second Aquinas (to put it mildly), Caccini eventually became a client of Urban VIII's cardinal nephew, Francesco, one of the key actors in the second phase of Galileo's trial. He also published several books, mostly pastiches of other authors' work, including *Storia del primo concilio niceno* (*History of the First Nicene Council*) (Lucca: Pellegrino Bidelli, 1637) that he sent Barberini.[179]

CHAPTER 4

The Legal Meaning of 1616: The Jurisprudence and Use of Admonitions and Precepts

While the controversy over what if anything happened to Galileo on 26 February 1616 careens into eternity, the legal meaning of that event has received next to no attention.[1] I argued in the last chapter that Galileo received a strongly worded precept, not a charitable admonition, and in this chapter I explain what that imports. Unfortunately, the Roman Inquisition's understanding of both admonition and precept must be constructed from its practice; there is almost no jurisprudence like that about its trial process.[2] This chapter first establishes the background of the related concepts of admonition and precept in canon law and then lays out how the Inquisition used them, paying particular attention to those of most relevance to Galileo.

Admonitions

As in the case of precepts, there is a trajectory to the history of *monitiones*. A device that had originally provided strong protection to a defendant gradually became weaker and weaker. Canonists frequently cited two passages in the *Decretum* C.2.q.1.c.19 ("Si peccaverit") and C.12.q.2.c.21 ("Indigne"), but not until the Decretals, especially those originating with Innocent III, did both *monitio* and various cognates (for example, *commonitio* and *admonitio*) and *denunciatio evangelica* receive extensive attention. It is repeated constantly that a *monitio* had to be given three times before any further legal action could be taken as C.5.q.2.c.2 had laid down.[3] Enrico Da Susa (Hostiensis, † 1271) specified that each occasion required a proportionate number of witnesses.[4] Innocent IV systematized the position that *monitio* in some form was always required.[5] By the middle of the fourteenth century, the number of times the *monitio* had to be repeated had been reduced to one, except in the case of inferiors admonishing superiors, in which case the rule of three still obtained.[6] The fourteenth-century canonist Antonio da Budrio († 1408) still usually held out for three no matter what.[7] The issue of number of repetitions is not of much importance to Galileo. Another point of general agreement was that *monitio* was equivalent to a citation; the reason it had to be repeated was to be sure the accused knew he was on the point of being charged.[8] Right from the first in notorious cases, it was not required at all, and a judge could always act solely on the basis of reputation, *publica fama*. Anyone with knowledge of the fact was obliged to report it to the court. A private warning ceased to be an option once the deed became public.[9]

Monitio and denunciation were closely connected. There were four kinds of denunciation, as Domenico da San Gimignano (ca. 1375–1424) summarized the views of Giovanni d'Andrea: evangelical, judicial, canonical, and "regular."[10] The first, the kind of interest here, pertained to a prelate in the first instance, but anyone could do it and to anyone. The only witness needed was the person being warned.[11] That obviously guaranteed (or nearly so) secrecy. Notorious cases, on the other hand, required *denunciatio judicialis* instead.[12] Antonio da Budrio wrote one of the most detailed discussions of evangelical denunciation in his commentary on Innocent III's decretal *Novit* [X.2.1.13], *De denunciatione evangelica* (On evangelical denunciation) as the rubric called it, to which other lawyers frequently referred. *Novit* laid down that "manifest" crimes required denunciation to a judge followed by regular process. Such a denunciation demanded a precedent *monitio*. Da Budrio followed D'Andrea's quadripartite division of denunciation.[13] The first three—judicial, canonical, regular—were relatively straightforward and applied respectively if roughly, to anyone (but especially the laity), to the clergy, and to those under religious obedience (monks, nuns, friars, and the like). The last, which Da Budrio assimilated to *fraterna correctio*, was the least lawlike and consquently hardest to understand. The biggest issue was whether denunciation involved an order also called a precept or involved a counsel instead, a less binding piece of advice. Da Budrio took the position that any precept from a prelate to his subordinate was ipso facto an order if not necessarily a matter of sin, although violating it was, a point of great importance to Galileo. This rather positivist move helped him to collapse the first three kinds of denunciation. It also made

the last more complicated. He noted three cases when *fraterna correctio* could
be omitted: when the merits of the case allowed it, when it was charitable to
do so, and, most interesting, when the prelate feared worse. Evangelical denunciation dealt with hidden sins, since once they became public there was
no point in warning the perpetrator—he had fallen into the hands of the
law. Heresy especially was not subject to this procedure unless it was certain
that using it would produce instant amendment. Besides, given the imminent
danger posed by heresy, there was usually no time for the two *monitiones* or
warnings absolutely required by *Novit* before proceeding to evangelical denunciation. If they had not been given, the case—except for heresy—could
not proceed to further remedies of any kind.

The rules were different when evangelical denunciation was applied. The
first warning was proved merely by the act itself, while the second needed at
least one witness in addition to the person being warned. That witness could
be anyone not a criminal. The whole point of an evangelical denunciation was
to keep the offense secret and induce penance in the offender. Its nearest relative, a canonical denunciation, by contrast, despite also requiring warnings,
was meant to force correction. Therefore an evangelical denunciation, unlike
the other three, should not lead to judicial proceedings. Judicial denunciation differed from evangelical in that, while both aimed to correct sin, any of
the three judicial kinds also demanded restitution. Were that distinction lost,
secular jurisdiction would disappear. Da Budrio noted that there were those
who said that an evangelical denunciation could have no place where a legal
remedy existed.

Relying on the well-established principle that the church did not deal
with hidden acts, Da Budrio argued that secrecy was of the essence of an evangelical admonition. Ergo, it should not (but might?) lead to a sentence, since
it was not a judicial act. But a charitable admonition was not the only private
kind.[14] A judicial one could also be given in that way. A charitable *monitio* had
as its sole object the correction of sin, while a private judicial admonition went
farther and demanded restitution. Thus arose another distinction. While both
led to denial of the sacraments, a judicial (or canonical) admonition did so
through excommunication and the force of law, while a charitable admonition
took effect only through a sort of shunning. Evangelical admonition had no
precise judicial form, since it was "as if in the penitential forum" ("cum sit fori
poenitentialis"), while a judicial admonition necessarily gave rise to legal process. Any kind of sin could be subject to evangelical admonition, while only
certain ones (Da Budrio meant crimes, public sins) could fall under judicial

admonition. If a judge administered such, then his act could serve as a citation depending on the circumstances.[15]

Da Budrio's fellow fourteenth-century jurist Henri de Bohic had gone further, coming close to collapsing any distinction between an admonition and a precept. He observed that some thought that *correctio charitativa* was both an act of charity and of correction; the second also made it an act of justice. If a prelate denounced a crime "charitably," his act became a precept. If a layman did so, then it was only a nonbinding counsel. But Bohic did not ultimately accept this view, following Da Susa and Uguccio to conclude that *any* admonition, no matter by whom administered, constituted a precept, with coercive force. The great fifteenth-century civilian Paolo Da Castro in several places assimilated a judge's *monitio* to a precept.[16] Even better, in the parlance of the papal secretariat of breves in Galileo's day, *monitio* and *praeceptum* were synonymous.[17]

A popular manual summarized the situation at the end of the fifteenth century.[18] The *Repertorium inquisitorum* maintained that an *evangelica monitio* should always precede any denunciation (citing "Si peccaverit" and "Novit") except in public cases or those posing an imminent danger. Two notes added by one of the later editors are more interesting. The first said "a judge must give a charitable admonition to the accused [*denuncianti (sic)*]" and the second after a slew of classical citations about *monitio* as an act of persuasion drew the conclusion that "a simple admonition does not obligate the person warned."[19] Thus it could under no circumstances give rise to judicial process.

The key fact in interpreting any *monitio* is whether the act to which it applied had remained private or whether it had become public, "notorious" (less significant was whether it was corrigible). The procedure Francesco Beretta thinks was applied in Galileo's case, *denunciatio evangelica*, was strictly private. Had there been any doubt up to the point when Tommaso Caccini—along with a number of other Dominicans—denounced Galileo publicly in Florence, thereafter it became notorious that he held Copernican ideas. In the wake of Caccini's actions, a "charitable admonition" leading to a *denunciatio evangelica* would have served no purpose, even if his fellow Dominican Niccolò Lorini claimed that was all he wanted when he also reported Galileo privately to one of the senior Inquisitors.[20] But both Caccini in testimony to the Inquisition in Rome and Lorini in his letter stressed Galileo's *mala fama*. An evangelical denunciation at that point would indeed have represented especially kind treatment, but it would have made legal nonsense and been completely useless in any subsequent proceedings. Nor does the preface to the

Dialogue on the Two Chief World Systems alleged by Beretta prove that Galileo received a *monitio*. As the sequel in 1633 shows, Galileo needed to maintain the purity of his intention as "witness of pure truth" to escape the possibility of conviction on one of the more severe grades of heresy. Besides, according to Sigismondo Scaccia, "customarily" (*de consuetudine*) evangelical denunciation had passed out of usage, since all Christians were bound to denounce heresy.[21] Furthermore, of the nearly five hundred *monitiones* recorded in the Inquisition's decree registers, none are qualified as "charitable."

The case could be made out on these grounds, together with Da Budrio's observation that a single citation in person had the effect of a threefold one by edict "to the church or [suspect's] house" ("ad ecclesiam vel domum"), that is, a broadcast citation, that the Inquisition had designed a procedure to leave Galileo no wiggle room.[22] Since he had been personally cited by either *monitio* or precept or both, he could not possibly pretend ignorance. Any subsequent mention of Copernicus would ipso facto condemn him. Thus it seems unlikely that Galileo got only a "charitable admonition" or, if he did, that the majority of jurists were prepared to make that nearly equivalent to a judicial order, the precept he also received.

One final argument precludes the possibility that Galileo received only a charitable admonition. It turns on a single word in the minute of his precept, *constitutus*. It indicates a similar change in the legal status of the person being given the precept as that a witness underwent when being sworn in, which in turn means the proceeding was judicial, not even extrajudicial, certainly not prejudicial.[23]

The principle that a trial had to begin with a formal citation including the charges did not extend to the Inquisition, which never informed a suspect of the accusations against him or her.[24] It also had much looser rules than other courts about what constituted a citation. It could take the form of a verbal invitation or—more important for us—a precept.[25] By seeing that Galileo got both a warning and a precept, Paul V took no chances that he could wriggle out of papal clutches. Roberto Bellarmino gladly helped, acting on behalf of both pope and Inquisition in summoning Galileo. Paul and Bellarmino could be excused if they were somewhat confused about exactly what to do. The lawyers had not achieved much more clarity. But it does appear that Bellarmino had already opened formal proceedings against Galileo before the precept was delivered. One way or the other, Galileo was, and remained, in trouble.

The Jurisprudence of Precepts Among the Medieval Civilians

We must start with a conceptual clarification. In a wild oversimplification, precept in canon law has two basic meanings that have a vague family resemblance, but neither of which does much to clarify the other. On the one hand, there is *praeceptum* as commandment, the term used in Latin for the Decalogue, a permanent element of divine law. On the other hand, there is precept in the sense of a procedural device, which may or may not be or become a permanent order. While the second has elements, sometimes strong elements, of the first, the first may have nothing at all to do with the second. That precepts have in modern canon law become almost (but not quite) exclusively penal, a permanent sentence handed down in the wake of an infraction, further helps set up the expectation that they always meant more nearly commandment than a possibly temporary maneuver without moral content. Precept belongs in a complicated conceptual field, stretching from mandates to sentences, from citation to monitions, the meanings of which shift depending where and in what kind of process they appear. In order to understand Galileo's precept, we shall have to try to define it as well as may be in a constantly changing relationship to these ideas and others. It helps to conceive of precept as a dialectical term, stretching from permanent to temporary and from utterly authoritative command to mere procedural device.

Although precepts of various kinds and with various meanings appear fairly frequently in one of the principal sources of canon law, Justinian's Code, Roman jurists and their medieval civilian successors never gave much systematic attention to them. The most important postglossators, especially Azo and Accursius, said nothing, and their later medieval successors barely mentioned them. A survey of the commentaries of three representative and, in their day, highly regarded civilians, Bartolo Da Sassoferrato (1313–1357), Paolo Da Castro († 1441), and Giason Del Maino (about a half-century later) produces almost no results. Of the approximately eighty-five places in the Digest and Code on which the three might have seized, Bartolo discussed by far the most, while Paolo and Giason commented on only three or four each.[26] All three treated precepts as a procedural issue, reducing them almost entirely to those issued by trial judges. For our purposes, Bartolo's most important passage draws on his contemporary Cino da Pistoia (1270–1336/37) who, according to Pietro D'Ancarano, created an important distinction between "a precept, a decree, and a definitive or interlocutory sentence." The first was implicitly parallel to the last and came before a case proceeded to *litis contestatio*, the formal laying of claim and counterclaim in a civil suit or of charges in a criminal trial. Pietro further defined an interlocutory sentence as one made by a judge ex officio and incidental to a case.[27] Bartolo agreed, calling such a precept an "interlocutory sentence," that is, a temporary, procedural, or administrative move.[28] Bartolo also maintained that a judge's precept lasted until he was removed from office unless it was against public utility; two *additiones* possibly misinterpreted Bartolo as arguing against the opinion that assimilated such a precept to a mandate that expired with the mandater's death and therefore implicitly said he thought a judge's precept was permanent. In support, the author of the second *additio* cited the canonist Panormitanus (Niccolò De' Tudeschi).[29] Bartolo argued that a precept issued without regard to due process (*ordo iudiciarius*), especially *causa cognitionis* and citation, could be revoked.[30] He also raised the possibility that a precept "has the force of a certain citation," although he appeared to reject it in the case of an order to pay issued before sentence.[31] Lanfranco Da Oriano († 1488), a professor at Padua, agreed, asking whether a precept was valid "without a precedent citation" (*nulla praecedente citatione*) and replied that it was not, citing as proof God's citation of Adam.[32]

Paolo and Giason largely agreed with Bartolo, usually likening a judge's precept to an interlocutory sentence. As Paolo put the point succinctly, "a judge's precept is not a definitive but [rather] interlocutory sentence."[33] They also tried on the one hand to distinguish them from citations, *consilia* (advice or legal opinions) and other judicial actions, and on the other to assimilate them to concepts like mandate.[34] In fact, Paolo defined a mandate issued by a superior "with power" as a precept.[35] Paolo nearly followed Bartolo when he argued that a precept, specifically to pay, could not initiate ordinary judicial process.[36] Giason in addition discussed precepts as expressing a testator's wishes, probably the most common use in Justinian's law book but irrelevant here. The only significant point in his discussion is that he [mis]quoted a canonist, Francesco Zabarella, on a precept's binding force while correctly citing Guido de Baysio's triad of consilium-mandatum-praeceptum (see below).[37] Although it is impossible to predict where a given legist or canonist might choose to comment on a particular term and I cannot pretend to have read all twenty volumes of these two commentaries, that the canonists picked up this handful of citations but little else from either author suggests that this is the sum total of what they said.[38]

For the civilians, a precept remained an unusual concept, not much discussed relative to the vast bulk of commentary on some closely related terms, especially mandate and sentence. Precept hovered uncertainly between on the one hand statute (*statutum*) or law (*lex*) in which case it became permanent, obligatory, and almost synonymous with commandment, and on the other hand counsel, which made it almost ephemeral and of little or no binding force. This liminal status brought it close to sentence, which does not help much, since there were numerous kinds of sentences (interlocutory, definitive, and so on) and consequently much difference of opinion about them.

Among the Medieval Canonists

At least one canonist fully agreed with the civilians about a precept's temporary status, although he also thought that a precept was never any kind of sentence. Domenico da San Gimignano, one of only a handful of jurists whose names appear in Inquisition cases, commenting on C. 2 part 1 d.a.c.1 *Quod autem*, began by saying like Bartolo that, in cases where the judge did not observe proper process, a precept could not even be called a precept, much less an interlocutory or definitive sentence.[39] When the judge did follow the *ordo iudiciarius* and proceeded through *causae cognitio*, the formal opening of a trial, and cited the defendant, such a precept was also not a sentence, although Domenico added that it could be called an interlocutory sentence. He concluded by endorsing a "magisterial" judgment that "a precept properly speaking is not a sentence."[40] His contemporary Pietro d'Ancarano said virtually the same thing.[41]

The canonists' attention to precepts took a while to reach critical mass. Gratian's *Decretum*, the first widely influential compilation of canon law drawn up in the mid-twelfth century, used the term about sixty times. In most instances, it meant in the first broad sense to refer to God's orders, or the apostles or the pope's, all of which were immutable. Gratian included another text that helped establish a broad principle accepted by many other commentators, both civilian and canonist. It distinguished a counsel (*consilium*) from a precept by the fact that "what is commanded is ordered." This sounds silly in English, but the Latin parallels the verb *precipere* to the much more powerful *inperare* (both in Gratian's spelling), which conveyed the right to punish a transgressor and therefore conferred necessity on a precept, while obedience to a counsel was a matter of choice.[42] In another place he quoted a pope defining a precept in a particular case as "a law handed down by the emperor" and then stretching the definition to cover any ecclesiastical or secular law.[43]

Sometimes the *Decretum* appeared to say like the civilians that precepts were temporary. For example, D. 18 d.a.c 1 seemed implicitly to draw a distinction between a precept and a constitution, an episcopal synod being able only to demand observation of the first.[44] In fact, those precepts were permanent laws or commandments, whether laid down by the apostles or the popes; the words were synonyms.[45] This meaning of precept as commandment is far the most common found in the *Decretum*. Some of those commands nevertheless had to have been in a sense temporary, for example, the bishop's order to a priest to "sign" a child (D. 95 C. 11).

Like the first generations of commentators on the rediscovered Roman law, those who commented on the *Decretum*, known as Decretists, apparently had little to say about precepts with one exception, Guido Da Baysio († 1313), called the Archdeacon. He both defined precept and also considered its permanence. Building on Gratian, he constructed a continuum from counsel through mandate to precept, in ascending order of force. Like most canonists, he was more interested in mandates than either of the other two, so his first definition of precept depended from that of mandate: "a mandate stands between a counsel and a precept. For it is beyond a counsel and this side of a precept. A mandate therefore compels just like a precept and one sins if it is not fulfilled."[46] Toward the end of this entry, Guido also addressed the question of a precept's duration, again by comparison to a mandate's. His imaginary interlocutor maintained "that a precept or an order (*iussio*) is not ended by the death of him who ordered (*precipit*)." Guido instead held the opposite, deciding the question on the basis of the words contained in the precept. If an emperor, a pope "or another superior should commit [a task] to an inferior and say 'we order, we command as an order and precept' he imposes necessity," that is, the order is ineluctable. If, on the other hand, the superior says only *mando* (command, again), then his order expired with the death of the mandater. The same held true of a precept, at least in the case of one issued by a judge with delegated jurisdiction, and Guido concluded that "a precept does not oblige forever and ever."[47] In addition to this reasonably lucid discussion, Guido also offered a free-standing, more or less etymologically grounded definition of precept. "Precepts are what they teach either to do or not to do. To order (*precipere*) is to command (*imperare*), or occupy the place to order (*iubere*) and precept is composed of 'pre' and 'capio' ['pre' and 'to take'], to order (*iussio*)," citing the Roman jurist Papinian. Guido continued "or to speak more plainly, precept is said from *precipio*, which is to take others, because precepts must take others from doing what a man holds them to do." Thus a precept came from the issuer's power to make others behave, "not because a precept obliges forever and ever."[48]

Willy Onclin and Pio Fedele

Guido may have been a lonely albeit influential voice. It was far otherwise with his successors the Decretalists, whose subject matter was the corpus of papal legislation that began to accrete in the early thirteenth century. Fortunately, in the wake of the first code of canon law issued in 1917, the continuing obscurity of the nature of precepts gave rise to two dissertations, the first by Willy Onclin at Louvain (published in full) and the second by Pio Fedele (which appeared as an article).[49] Fedele's article is more important than Onclin's book for our purposes because Orio Giacchi used it as the basis for his study of Galileo's trial published in 1942, still the only such by a practicing canonist. Both Fedele and Onclin made extensive use of the Decretalists. Onclin dealt only in passing with precepts since his subject was the territoriality and personality of law, but in so doing he surveyed a massive amount of canonist and theological literature through the nineteenth century. Fedele focused directly on precepts and somewhat more narrowly than Onclin on the canonists while doing a similarly impressive amount of research, concentrating heavily on medieval lawyers. To judge from the burden of much of the commentary, those who apparently used it most, as is still the case in modern canon law, were superiors of religious houses.[50]

Definitions of precept usually took dyadic form, beginning with general and particular, distinguished either according to whether they applied to a group or an individual or by the breadth of the principle laid down or negative and positive. A general precept came very close to a statute and received much more attention. Following a distinction introduced by one of the most eminent medieval canonists, Da Susa (Hostiensis; † 1271), a precept issued "in the fashion of a canon" (*in modum canonis*) had nearly the force of a statute and, consequently, lost most of its peculiar status.[51] A general sentence or precept thus approached a law in breadth of coverage. According to both Onclin and Fedele, the key difference between precept and law remained permanence. Precepts of either kind but certainly particular ones were always assumed to be temporary, laws perpetual. Why this was so attracted much attention, the usual opinion being that, since a precept was an individual man's act, it required his will to keep it in being. When he died, both will and precept expired. Statute by contrast, even when made by a single individual, affected the entire community and thus became independent of his will. Other crucial differences arose between law and precept, including the fact that only a legislator could make law, while anyone with the proper authority, not necessarily formal jurisdiction, could issue a precept that could be either private or public based on that distinction. Furthermore, and more important to Galileo, although a statute in canon law governed exclusively future matters, either kind of precept could apply to either past or future. Yet much the most common opinion was that particular precepts were solely retrospective. This no doubt led to their common—and now almost exclusive—identification as penal, levying a punishment for some past infraction.[52] It also no doubt helped that it was universally thought that negative precepts bound "always and forever more," as Juan de Torquemada predictably put into the strongest form a concept that originally came from Guido de Baysio.[53] The discussion of negative precepts also moved much closer to the meaning of *praeceptum* as one of the Ten Commandments, which of course gave them extra force.[54]

Both Onclin and Fedele relied a little too much on Galileo's contemporary (and fellow victim of the Inquisition and the Index), the Jesuit philosopher-theologian Francisco Suarez as one of their star witnesses. Suarez could not have been clearer about the impermanence of precepts. Although insisting that there was almost no difference between a statute and a general precept, one thing still separated them: a precept was always temporary.[55] In somewhat round-about fashion Suarez explained that a man who could make a law could certainly give a general precept and equally if he could give a general precept, he could give a particular. While it might therefore appear that a particular or a general precept had the same durability as law, in fact, since they depended from the will of an individual, they could not be permanent.[56] Simply put, a permanent precept *was* a law.[57] Suarez also distinguished a precept from custom (which was nearly as universal and binding as law) on the grounds that precepts could "easily be changed."[58]

Fedele distinguished precept from law much more sharply than Onclin, beginning from the distinction Onclin had made between the power to legislate and the power of jurisdiction (*potestas jurisdictionis*), which he regarded as the same as the power to administer (*potestas administrationis*). Precepts arose solely from the second, making them administrative measures, not legal ones at all.[59] Fedele relied heavily on one of several discussions by the early sixteenth-century canonist Filippo Decio, who following in Guido's footsteps distinguished a precept from *consilium, mandatum,* and *adhortatio* because a precept contained *imperium* (a command or order).[60] Thus "a precept in itself has necessity" (*praeceptum in se habet necessitatem*).[61] Fedele was in part arguing against the 1917 code's reduction of precepts to penal status, so he was at pains to demonstrate that they could be used for other purposes.[62] Although he did not discuss their temporal referent in doing so, he elsewhere agreed with Onclin that, beginning with the *Glossa ordinaria* to Gratian, most canonists thought that precepts were temporary, whatever their effect.[63] As for Suarez, the reason was usually because the individual issuer's death ended the force of his will. Fedele took as representative the views of Antonio Da Budrio, albeit writing about special sentences, not precepts. Distinguishing between statutes and special sentences, Da Budrio did indeed conclude that the second expired, while also insisting that they could only be retrospective.[64] Decio, because of his emphasis on the role of command, appeared to agree with Da Budrio.[65] Fedele used Decio (and two of the sources he cited, Giovanni Nicoletti Da Imola—far the more important of the two—and Giovanni Calderini) to represent what Fedele called "the more diffused opinion" that precepts expired when the issuer lost the will to keep the precept in being for whatever reason, death being an excellent one.[66] Unfortunately, Fedele read neither Da Budrio nor Decio nor their sources accurately, nor was he wise to treat special sentences and precepts as equivalent.

Granted, Decio's discussion was dense and a precept's durability came up only in passing as he considered the much more important question of when judicial mandates expired. In his comment on X.1.29.19 (*Relatum*, X, *De officio et potestate iudicis delegati*), the passage of which Fedele quoted a tiny snippet, Decio first cited Niccolò De' Tudeschi as saying that the prolongation of a judicial mandate required only the first step in a trial, citation, the usual canonist position. He also reported De' Tudeschi's view that precepts when issued by a delegate representing the person of the delegater were perpetual, as was not the case with mandates.[67] Then Decio made a crucial move that Fedele missed. He turned to De' Tudeschi's "second conclusion" that it mattered not to duration whether an order took the form of a precept or a "simple commission." Decio cited Nicoletti as saying that mandates expired with death under some conditions precisely because they differed from precepts in that only some of them contained a *iussus* and only those did not expire, whereas *all* precepts did and therefore lasted until revoked. True, Decio did cite Calderini, a less important canonist than either De' Tudeschi or Nicoletti, who did indeed say that both mandate and precept expired with the issuer's death. But as his next citation made clear, Decio nearly ignored Calderini's assimilation of the two and used him only to support the general claim about *iussus*. Decio adduced as his final witness Goffredo da Trani († 1245) (to whom we shall return) as quoted "expressly" by Zabarella to say that the mere issuing of a precept by a superior with power made it permanent.[68] Decio had reservations, but still concluded that Goffredo's argument "seems truer in law" (*de iure verius vide-tur*) if the only question was whether the issuer had the requisite power.[69]

In a note Fedele began to concede that the dominant position among "the old writers" had been that a precept was permanent almost without qualification, saying that "they *seem* to maintain that the precept does not expire 'resoluto iure praecipientis'," referring to Guillaume Durand, the Speculator.[70] Durand laid down the nearly universal opinion that precepts did *not* expire with the death of the issuer in distinction to mandates that did.[71] (Since Fedele also quoted the seventeenth-century canonist Prospero Fagnani as holding the same opinion, he pretty thoroughly undercut his original argument.) Two of the other sources Decio used, the near-contemporaries De' Tudeschi and Zabarella, made the point clearly. One of the most frequent loci classici was the one Decio had chosen, X.1.29.19, *Relatum*, X, *De officio et potestate iudicis delegati*. Almost casually De' Tudeschi generalized to precepts the civilians' principle that a mandate did not expire with death if the matter had gone to *lis contestata*: "one receiving a precept is held to fulfil it, the preceptor's [*precip-ientis*] death notwithstanding."[72] Zabarella's discussion took off from another locus classicus, *Quoniam abbas* (X.1.29.14), and was both longer and more subtle than Panormitanus's. Nevertheless, he made the same point. Zabarella dismissed Da Susa's distinction between precepts against which exceptions could be entered (in the phase of a trial between citation and the presentation of *libelli*, the evidence alleged before witnesses were heard) and those that could not. Any precept "legitimately made" was to be executed no matter whether either the issuer or the person to whom the order had been given had died. The reason was that precepts had to do with jurisdiction, so the issue came back to whether the issuer had it. If so, the precept was permanently valid.[73] Zabarella's older contemporary—and Fedele's star witness—Antonio da Budrio put the basis of their position clearly, once more commenting on *Relatum*. Precepts, in distinction to mandates, did not depend on will and therefore were in and of themselves necessary (*ex necessitate*). In order to make his point, he had both to bend the Speculator's words a little but not much and also implicitly draw on Goffredo to add the vitally important second principle.[74] De' Tudeschi reached the same conclusion by inference from the capitulum *Mandatum*. "A mandate does not necessitate, but a precept does" (*mandatum non necessitat sed preceptum sic*).[75] In the context of a discussion of religious obedience elsewhere, De' Tudeschi put the point even more strongly. If a superior "intends to order (*precipere*), it is certain that it [the law] ties a contravenor to a mortal sin," and again, "if it is spoken through preceptive words, then the contravenor is tied to a mortal sin."[76] A superior exercising his office need not even express the cause of his precept.[77] Da Budrio also brushed aside a distinction sometimes drawn between a precept given in an individual's name and one in the name of an office, saying that all precepts "passed to the successor," in other words, were permanent.[78] Finally, he laid down the principle that, in cases of doubt whether an order were a precept, a precept should be assumed, "because a precept is imperative."[79]

Much of the discussion of a precept's necessity, encased in sometimes almost impenetrable legalese, is a little misleading. Necessity arose in the context of obedience, not as an abstract issue about the nature of precepts. Goffredo's discussion immediately made this clear.[80] "Precept" was the last of three attributes of obedience, the others being *reverentia* (reverence) and *iuditium* (judgment).[81] In this passage Goffredo used precept as synonymous with mandate.[82] Even more significant, his discussion concerned a clergyman's obedience to his superior. The rest of the commentary (including Decio's) on the binding force of precepts assumed when it did not make explicit the same context. Precepts were a device to control religious and members of the clergy. Raymond de Peñafort, the great thirteenth-century systematizer of the Decretals, quoted Goffredo (without attribution) in his manual for religious, *Summa de Poenitentia*.[83] One of the more prolific and often-cited late fifteenth-century canonists, Felino Sandeo, neatly summed up the discussion. He explained that the "necessity" of a precept lay in its matter, not the will of the issuer, even if he appears to have contradicted himself in one of his *consilia*.[84] This meant that it came into force immediately on being issued and its force never (*numquam*) of itself passed away under any conditions.[85] He was also perhaps the most careful in distinguishing precept from related concepts.[86] He began from Guido De Baisio's triad stretching from the weakest form of command, counsel, through mandate to the strongest, precept.[87] As the lawyers often did, he put Guido's words to his own purposes, since, as we have seen, the Archdeacon had raised some of the sharpest doubts both about how permanent precepts were and how binding.[88] Sandeo aimed instead to emphasize both permanence and obligatory force.

Appeal Against a Precept?

Once the canonists had enshrined the twin principles of necessity and permanence, the only remaining question was what recourse the subject might have if he doubted a precept's legitimacy or legality. High on the list and in many cases almost the only valid reason to refuse obedience was again whether the issuer had the requisite authority. This point exercised the canonists much more than the question of duration. Most of them held that, if the issuer had the proper authority, then any precept he gave was ipso facto valid and probably permanent. Innocent IV laid down the basic terms of the discussion in the early thirteenth century. Likening a precept to a sentence of excommunication, as was fairly commonly done, the law professor and future pope gave an inferior what appeared to be a stark choice: obey or appeal.[89] In the case of the pope, who had no superior, a subject at first glance seemed to have absolutely no choice.[90] In fact, the situation was and remained more complicated. Innocent raised two highly important qualifications, both of which would have helped Galileo. First, even the pope had to follow the course of the law. Innocent made the point bluntly in the case of any lesser judge: "A sentence laid down by a judge who did not follow the necessary counsel never holds."[91] This restriction proved to be the entering wedge of the much more important second qualification. If the pope's order contained heresy, it was not to be obeyed. How did a subject know? Conscience. As Innocent put this—among the most cherished fundamental principles of medieval canonist jurisprudence—"One must suffer every evil rather than act against conscience [and fall into] mortal sin." Innocent went on that an evil or unjust mandate did not deserve the name. Nevertheless, it was still better to obey while attempting to induce one's superior to rescind the order or, when refusing obedience, to suffer excommunication patiently. Innocent added one more important qualification on the score of duration, which, together with his views about appeal, gave his successors a way to attenuate a precept's strength. A precept issued before *litis contestatio* lasted no longer than the judge's jurisdiction. These became known as extrajudicial precepts, which Innocent allegedly said a judge could not properly issue at all, since he could only give a precept after *causae cognitio*.[92] Once that point had been passed, a precept became "perpetual."[93]

Later jurists found Innocent's discussion so compelling that many of them did little more than paraphrase it, Da Budrio, for example. Yet there was a great deal of latitude to change the emphasis within it. Innocent's contemporary Da Susa began by trying his best to emphasize obedience but concluded that even an erroneous conscience *could* be followed into disobedience, though obedience was still the safer course.[94] Giovanni D'Andrea, for his part, quoted Da Susa in order to agree with him at one point, although he later stressed the necessity of obeying a papal order, even an unjust one, but not if it would disturb the state of the church in the future, in which case obedience became mortal sin.[95] Likewise, De' Tudeschi at first insisted that disobedience meant damnation, before conceding that unjust orders might not be obeyed.[96] Disobedience had to be founded on good reasons. Following Innocent, De' Tudeschi thought that a subject could disobey a pope if his mandate contained heresy "or is vehemently presumed to disturb the church's state, or have some other bad outcome." Nevertheless, he concluded this passage by saying that a superior exercising his office need not give reasons for his *precipere*, laying the burden of proof that the order was dangerous on the appellant.[97]

More important yet, a number of Innocent's successors built on his discussion of appeal to draw a distinction of direct relevance to Galileo's situation. Baldo Degli Ubaldi, the great fourteenth-century canonist, endorsed Innocent's distinction between judicial precepts that demanded legal process and extrajudicial ones that did not. A precept given at any point before *causae cognitio* could safely be contradicted even without appeal.[98] Baldo's contemporary Da Budrio probably pressed the point furthest and came closest to describing the situation facing Galileo. An order given by a prelate (a bishop or an abbot) acting without his fellows (the cathedral chapter, the rest of his monks) could be no more than an extrajudicial precept that could not become *res iudicata*; in other words, it could not initiate process that led to a sentence.[99] In a long, careful discussion, Da Budrio made it clear that extrajudicial precepts had almost no binding force, or at least were hedged about with so many cautions and qualifications as hardly to be worth the trouble. He had no doubt that a subject was not bound to obey them and need not even appeal in order to be safe.[100] Even De' Tudeschi, who had started from one of the most hard-nosed positions about unconditional obedience, sounded almost like Da Budrio when it came to extrajudicial precepts.[101] Unsurprisingly, he was quoting Innocent.

Early Seventeenth-Century Commentary

Despite the preponderance of canonist opinion in favor of a precept's permanence, as late as the early seventeenth century at least one such lawyer still had doubts. He was Prospero Fagnani, perhaps the most important canonist of the seventeenth century.[102] Although his work did not appear until 1661, he had been centrally involved in papal government in Rome since early in the century, most significantly as secretary of the congregation for the Council of Trent from 1610–1625 and as framer of Gregory XV's important reform of the rules of conclave (1621). Fagnani put his opposition to the majority view that precepts were permanent most pointedly in his comment on X.5.39.21 (*A nobis, De sententia excommunicationis*) about a dean and chapter's powers to excommunicate during an episcopal sede vacante.[103] He took it as read that the chapter had all the bishop's jurisdiction after his death and before his successor's election, but for how long did its orders in the form of precepts last? Did they expire as soon as a new bishop had been elected? He first made Zabarella speak for the majority that they did not, although he thought Federico Petrucci had offered the most famous statement of Zabarella's position. In one of his *consilia*, Petrucci, who had been among Baldo's teachers at Perugia, stated bluntly that any statute the dean and chapter made continued in force precisely because it was a statute.[104] Fagnani disagreed, correctly claiming that the matter was hotly controverted and many others also disagreed (he did not name them). According to Fagnani, the chapter had acted not *per modum statuti* but *per modum sententiae vel interdicti*, in which case their action expired. Going back to the Gloss to defend his position, he made it turn crucially on the distinction between a statute and a sentence. Fagnani further distinguished between sentences with time clauses and those without. His principal concern was what impact this had on legal process. Even though the first endured perpetually, just like statutes, the removal of the judge ended the effect of the sentence. Thus any conditional sentence expired with the removal of the judge by death or otherwise.

At the same time, the divide between civilians and canonists over the issue of a precept's duration continued in force. The civilian tradition about precepts was represented by Giacomo Menochio, whose frequently reprinted ten volumes of professional opinions, *consilia*, were among the most imposing ever and had few competitors in his day, the golden age of legal consulting. Menochio was also on the other side of the political fence from the papal lawyer Fagnani. A native of Pavia and therefore a subject of the Spanish dependency of Milan, Menochio had taught in various law schools including probably the most prestigious in Europe, Padua, before returning home covered with honors to become president of the Magistrato delle reali e ducali entrate straordinarie, the second most important post to which a lawyer in the duchy might aspire.[105] This did not prevent him from falling foul of both the Inquisition and the Index in a case that ran for at least ten years.[106] The Inquisition gave Menochio the same treatment it later gave Galileo, that is, a precept not to publish, and then checked over his work with the same instrument it used on Galileo in 1632, a special (or particular) congregation.[107] After battling Galileo's principal opponent in 1616, Cardinal Bellarmino, Menochio eventually knuckled under and emended two cases in one of his most popular works, *De arbitrariis judicum* (first edition 1569) as well as two of five *consilia* the inquisitior of Milan had singled out of a thousand (!) as needing expurgation, to which he grudgingly agreed, doctoring one and excising the other.[108] He did not back down on probably the most important point, his very last published consilium, no. 1000, which recapitulated the case for the submission of the clergy to secular legislation *pro bono publico*.[109]

In *De praesumptionibus*, Menochio began with his consistent position that "a mandate expires with the death of the mandator," supporting himself with citations to Sebastiano Vanzi and Carlo Ruini, and extended this point in *De arbitrariis*, perhaps his most important work, to "a superior's precept."[110] He had tortured more than one of his sources to get them to agree, perhaps especially Decio, but he left no doubt about the strength of his opinion.[111] Perhaps Menochio's most interesting move was to change the context. Instead of paralleling precepts and mandates, in *De praesumptionibus* he set precepts next to *beneplacita* (acts of grace). Then he raised a series of objections, the first of which was the standard one that neither mandate nor precept expired if the case had not been concluded, *res non integra*. Again, as he had in *De arbitrariis*, Menochio moved into the context of acts of grace, using them as *objections* to his claim. This transit was not original to him, dating back at least as far as Da Susa, who had argued that letters conferring a benefice "either warning or ordering them [those with power to confer the benefice]" (*monendo eos sive pracipiendo*) did not expire with the issuer's death, since the mere request for them had the effect of citation.[112] Florentine jurist Lapo da Castiglionchio, one of Menochio's sources, argued the same point.[113] Thus Menochio's second objection was that a mandate did not expire if it concerned "a pious cause" (*piam causam*). He again cited Vanzi and the Rota to support the point. The seventh objection concerned the case of a papal grace, which, rather like most lawyers' view of precepts, was in itself complete. Menochio trotted out his usual pile of citations, among them Lapo and Domenico da San Gimignano on *Si super gratia*, but also Filippo Franchi (twice), Pierre Rebuffi, Diego Covarruvias, Sandeo, Giason, Decio, and Pietro D'Ancarano, as well as a decision of the Rota.[114] Of most direct relevance to Galileo's problem was objection eight: that a gracious mandate automatically passed to any prelate's successor in his dignity "because the church never dies." Neither, of course, did the Congregation of the Inquisition. Nevertheless, Menochio's stress on the durability of *gracious* mandates reinforced his vociferous insistence on the temporary force of precepts, precisely because they were not issued for the recipient's benefit. True, the point of any precept was to save a soul, but that was not the same kind of tangible good, particularly a piece of real property, that Menochio had in mind.

Although both his status and that of his work is unclear, the discussion of precepts by one last lawyer, Menochio's contemporary Sigismondo Scaccia, may reflect some of the Inquisition's understanding.[115] As he explained, there was much confusion in criminal cases about the document known as a *monitorio*. It could contain three kinds of penal precepts. The first is both directly relevant in Galileo's case and also comes close to the modern distinction between a prospective warning (*monitio*) and a post facto penal precept. This was a penal precept intended to avert "future and imminent evil." Most important, while the other two kinds (intended to discover the truth or control a delinquent) could not initiate process, this one could. "Because when there is danger in delay, we withdraw from the common rules of law and can proceed extrajudicially" (*Quia ubi periculum est in mora, recedimus a regulis iuris communis, & procedi potest extraiudicialiter*). Judges were bound to proceed thus in emergencies in order to keep the law intact from the first rather than remedy a problem later.[116] The third kind of criminal precept could also have applied to Galileo. Its relation to further proceedings depended on whether it was issued before or after an *inquisitio*. If before, a further distinction arose: whether it was preceded by suspicion. If not, then it could not begin a case "because a process cannot be initiated from precepts and comminations" (*quia processus non potest initiari a praeceptis & comminationibus*). If there was prior suspicion, however, all was well. A precept could be issued either before or after an *inquisitio*, but those before were invented by "bad judges" even though tolerated by custom. A precept remained valid even if it merely cited the accused to reply to the *inquisitio*. Although Scaccia included a section on "De praecepto . . . in causis haeresis," it says little about precepts. This was because heresy cases could go ahead on much less evidence than criminal ones, nor did they require *monitio evangelica*.[117]

In the second volume of his magnum opus, *Tractatus de sententia et re judicata*, Scaccia returned to precepts, sketching their meaning in civilian jurisprudence. Thus he implicitly set a precept parallel to a mandate and briefly raised its equivalence to an interlocutory sentence. Then he turned to the specific case of an accused summoned to appear by a precept (*praeceptato*) who failed to do so. Did that precept then "remain firm as does a definitive sentence and become a judgment?" Yes, according to statute law, "the precept remains firm, and consequently the accused [is] warned, and as a contumacious person is condemned according to the *monitorio*" (*praeceptum remanet firmum, & consequenter reus monitus, & contumax condemnatur ad contenta in monitorio*). Scaccia specified that it became a judgment after ten days. The same held true in the *ius comune* until the judge revoked the precept.[118] Thus Scaccia blurred most of the carefully constructed distinctions in both canonist and civilian jurisprudence.

The Roman Inquisition's Use of Admonitions

To judge from the 489 *monitiones* the Inquisition issued between 1597 and mid-1633, an average of 13.6 per year or more than one every month for about thirty-six years, admonition was a concept it understood well. None are classified in the decree registers as *caritativa*. The closest we come are the twenty-seven qualified as extrajudicial.[119] Had the Inquisition meant to give Galileo a weak admonition, contingent or not, it is almost certain that one of the six versions of events in 1616 would have borne that second label. Besides, as the discussion of monitions and precepts by medieval and early modern commentators has already suggested, too much weight should not be placed on important distinctions between them. Quintiliano Mandosio's attempt to distinguish a precept as coming only after *causae cognitio* and a *monitio* before and therefore equivalent to simple citation founders on his own recognition that both did the same things, as well as his explicit statement that neither a mandate nor a precept to appear was "equivalent" to a citation.[120]

In forty-one instances the Inquisition combined a *monitio* and a precept, usually in the sequence *monitio* followed by precept just as happened to Galileo.[121] Thus, on 2 January 1608, a Theatine was ordered under both not to discuss another man's case.[122] In 1616 a consultor of the Holy Office in Pavia was allowed to return there under an admonition and a judicial precept not to talk about his trial.[123] A case of men pretending to be ministers of the Holy Office and therefore claiming exemption from secular jurisdiction was expedited "with a sharp admonition and a precept."[124] A singer of obscene songs in Monopoli also had his case expedited with both.[125] The same happened in a trial for blasphemy in 1619.[126] Sometimes other kinds of threats were added as well. A case in 1616 was sentenced under both an admonition and a precept, plus a bond.[127] A beating was added to the sentence of a case of superstitious curing.[128] And so forth. There seem to be no obvious clues about which kinds of cases demanded these extra penalties.

The Roman Inquisition's Use of Precepts

Historians have implicitly assumed that the Inquisition acted in unusual fashion when it gave Galileo his precept. Nothing could be further from the truth. The first precept issued by the institution thus far located dates from 1569, twenty-eight years after its founding.[129] Thereafter the Inquisition regularly and often used precepts, if not quite as frequently as it did admonitions. Raw statistics drawn almost entirely from the decree registers, and therefore certainly an undercount, demonstrate the point.[130] Between late 1597 and roughly the time of Galileo's condemnation, the Inquisition issued more than 450 precepts, an average of 12.5 per year. There is also a pronounced rhythm to its issuance of precepts. From 1598 until 1619, with the exception of 1605 when the number is skewed by one case containing thirty-three precepts, the Holy Office never handed down more than a dozen precepts in any single year. The last two full years of Paul V's pontificate saw new highs of twenty-two and twenty-one precepts, before falling back somewhat in the next four years. Almost from the beginning of Urban VIII's pontificate the numbers increase substantially, hitting a record thirty-nine in 1629 and totaling 212 (23.5 p.a.) in the nine years from 1624 through 1632 or not much short of half the total in my sample. I have no good explanation for the origin of this sea change, but it seems clear that once the precept's utility was demonstrated, it became popular with Urban's Congregation. The reason could well be the appearance as secretary in 1629 of the disciplinarian and former religious Antonio Barberini, Sr. As the numbers do not indicate, the Inquisition used both devices for a wide variety of purposes, from orders to maintain secrecy, to appear in court, to dispose of a convict including by sending him to prison or the galleys, or to exile him, for a wide range of offenses with blasphemy and gaming heading the list, and as both interlocutory and definitive sentences (see Appendix on Frequency of Precepts). In so doing, it drew on both streams of jurisprudence, civil and canon.

Precepts were well enough known that even a suspect might demand one. Tommaso Campanella did just that. After replying in 1595 or 1598 to the Inquisition's censures of his "De sensu rerum," he later claimed to have asked its "governors" "to bind me either with reasons or a precept that I ought not to maintain such an opinion" about the world's rational soul.[131]

Precepts and the Control of Religious

It is worth emphasis that whichever device Bellarmino and Seghizzi used, either *monitio* or precept, it was originally designed to apply to those under religious obedience. The Inquisition issued thirty-nine precepts for this purpose. One of the very first found ordered the Jesuit Carlo Mastrilli not to preach about propositions under investigation.[132] Another prohibited a Conventual Minim from leaving his "dignities and statuses" in the order.[133] The Capuchins seem to have been unusually fractious, although their confrere Antonio Barberini's appearance as secretary made little difference. Precepts to them give a good idea of the range of monastic behaviors that the Inquisition tried to control via precept. The first Capuchin found in the registers, Celestino da Verona, possibly the same man involved in Giordano Bruno's case, had read to him earlier precepts as well as having renewed a precept of keeping secrecy.[134] As often, those earlier precepts are not to be found in the decree registers.[135] A Neapolitan Capuchin preacher was given a precept not to deal with predestination, justification, or grace in his sermons.[136] Lorenzo da Novara, whose case had been expedited in 1623, was ordered in 1627 not to leave the bounds of his mission, since he had attended heretics' sermons outside them.[137] On 30 October 1630, a Capuchin imprisoned for contravening a precept not to write about St. Francis's habit was released under another to the same effect.[138] In September 1631, a brother was ordered to cease to have visions and to eat what the rest of his fellows did.[139] Two precepts arose from a case involving a goldsmith and a Capuchin, the first of whom the Holy Office ordered not to make medals; the second was to receive a similar precept from his general.[140]

Superiors of orders were not immune, including abbots and generals, especially the Jesuits and Dominicans during their interminable feud over grace.[141] A Vallombrosan prior convicted of false testimony was given a precept by the inquisitor of Florence on the Congregation's orders to appear before the bishop of Perugia.[142] One of the principals in the first phase of Galileo's trial, the Dominican Lorini, first received a precept of banishment from the nuncio in Florence and then in turn a precept from the Holy Office to cease to raise objections about modes of confession.[143] Omobono da Cremona, a Dominican imprisoned in Cremona, received a precept not to defame his accusers. He earned imprisonment by violating it and was not rehabilitated to his convent for seven years.[144] Precepts were frequently used to control suspects' movements, for example, the Brescian Capuchin Ippolito Averoldo, or the rector of a Jesuit college who got a penal precept to appear in Rome.[145]

Often *rei* were relegated to a particular place under precept not to leave it (forty-one instances).

Precepts and the Press

More important, several Capuchins drew attention as authors, among thirteen instances in which the Inquisition used precepts to control the press. One Capuchin was ordered imprisoned, apparently under precept, until he told what he knew about *Libro de praedestinatione quondam fratris Angeli da Chio Capuccini.*[146] Averoldo was ordered via precept not to print a book. The pope meant this precept to be permanent, since he added to it that Averoldo was not to bother him or the Inquisition in the future.[147] Averoldo's fellow Capuchin Giacinto da Casale had both founded a new congregation in Perugia and written a book that he was at first inhibited from publishing including through a papal decree to the order's general. Instead, he passed out manuscript copies.[148] Eventually he received a precept "neither to print nor spread manuscripts, nor deal with [his congregation] or propose novelties unless the matter had first been communicated to the Sacred Congregation." He was also exiled from Perugia.[149] Then it was the turn of the man who had approved the book who was ordered to Rome under precept.[150] One of the more recalcitrant publishing religious was the Dominican Pietro Giuseppe, whose surname was probably Mari.[151] The inquisitor of Genoa, Eliseo Masini, reported him at the end of 1610 for having contravened a precept by publishing "a little book titled *Orationi et devotissime meditationi pro confessari etc.*" with a changed "inscription." The errors found in 1609 were ordered noted.[152] Masini further reported in March 1611 that not only had Mari printed the book, he had taken copies to Rome. The Dominican vicar general was to retain him and collect copies, while the master of the sacred palace's report on errors was sought.[153] Six weeks later, workhorse censor Bellarmino related the errors in both the editio princeps published in Genoa and another printing at Tortona. The book was to be suspended "until corrected" and the author asked for any copies he had.[154] At the end of May, the inquisitor of Tortona confirmed that Mari had published "contra praeceptum," when the Dominican vicar general was again ordered to act.[155] In an odd conclusion, the case was ordered expedited on 3 June, with the note that it was "well expedited, although he had been dealt with kindly enough."[156] His punishment is not recorded.

In mid-1614, another Dominican, Ambrogio de Hortenocio, was implicated in the unlicensed printing in tandem with Roberto de Roberto or Roberti, bishop of Tricarico, of books about Suor Francesca Vacchini da Viterbo, among them *Modo utilissimo di santamente recevere et dobessimente (?) frequentare il S.mo. Sacramento dell'altare insegnato dall'Angelo alla B. Sor Francesca da Viterbo* (Macerata: Sebastiano Martinelli).[157] He received a precept "under penalties at the Congregation's will" to surrender all the books within a month.[158] De Roberto, examined about Francesca's miracles in February in Secretary Gian Garzia Millini's house, was "warned" in a congregation two days after Ambrogio.[159] Ten years later an Observant Franciscan got a precept not only to cease to write or deal with a prohibited topic "in any way" (*omnino*; the same word appears in Galileo's precept) but also imprisoning him in a convent in Rome where he was to limit himself solely to "manual exercises."[160] The Jesuit general was ordered (*praecipiat*) 31 July 1603 to give a decree personally to Suarez not to publish without the Holy Office's approval.[161] The Servite mathematician Filippo de Ferrariis had his request to print additions to Cesare Baronio's martyrology brusquely rejected in the form of a precept "that he not in any way whatsoever print the additions."[162]

Even official propagandists might find themselves in trouble with the Inquisition's censorship and threatened with precepts. Such a fate befell the continuator of Baronio's *Annales ecclesiastici*, the Polish Dominican Abraham Bzowski, along with two other of the most learned historians in Rome, the Cassinese Benedictine Abbot Costantino Gaetani, and Niccolò Alemanno, custodian of the Vatican Library.[163] As a pendent to a general decree that all writers had to seek approval from the master of the sacred palace, in theory the chief papal censor, before publication, these three and "others staying in the apostolic palace or having from the holy see the job of writing particularly under pain of excommunication a precept under other penalties at the will [of the Congregation]" specifically received a stricter form of the same order adding that the master had to consult the Inquisition. Finally, Bzowski was warned personally not to publish without permission, objections having been raised to his life of Amadeo da Savoia, the antipope Felix V.[164]

The larger issue had arisen in the first place as part of Rome's continuing and largely unsuccessful efforts to control publishing in the empire by means of the nuncio and inquisitor of Cologne.[165] The Inquisition's specific focus was Bzowski's treatment of Eugenius IV's pontificate at one of the worst moments of the conciliar movement in the as yet unpublished volume 17 of his continuation of Baronio, as well as a published earlier volume, variously numbered 16 or 2 of the second edition or plain 2.[166] The inquisitor complied with the order to suspend publication.[167] In early 1626, he reported that some folios treating the Council of Basel had been removed from volume 16.[168] Finally, on 12 February 1626, Urban allowed its publication, allegedly already out "in the vernacular" (*in vulgari*) after the expurgation of Basel and Amadeo, without allowing another publication "so altered." The inquisitor was ordered to foster publication as rapidly as possible and to send exemplars of both editions of volume 16.[169] The Inquisition continued to peer over Bzowski's shoulder at least as late as 1630.[170]

Bzowski's situation was not unlike Galileo's in 1616 relative to other defenders of Copernicus, that is, both were subject to a general as well as a specific order. Another precept similar to Galileo's went to the Sicilian Giuseppe Balle in 1626. His request to be told "more openly" what was wrong with his book about transubstantiation was met with a precept "under penalties at [the Congregation's] will" to surrender all his writings about the subject, further spelling out that he was not "to deal in word or writing with any of this kind of material" as well as to name his accomplices ("et non tractet verbo aut scripto cum aliquo de huiusmodi materia, et revelet S. Off.o an dictam (?) doctrinam alicui communicaverit, vel in ea habet complices").[171]

Shortly after Balle's precept, the Carmelite Sebastiano "de Alexandro" was sentenced in a case about his preaching on the immaculate conception of Mary, a theological issue almost as neuralgic as grace. He received both "a serious warning" (*gravi monitione*) and a precept to preach approved doctrine "according to [Paul V's] papal decrees" and, should he think of publishing his sermons, show them to the episcopal vicar of Catanzaro first.[172] We have already seen the case of a Capuchin receiving a precept about publication in 1630, to which can be added one to a Conventual Franciscan imprisoned for contravening a precept not to write against the Capuchins.[173]

Except for Bzowski, none of these authors are well known or probably important. One who received at least two precepts about his writings is both: Cesare Cremonini, Galileo's friend and colleague and one of the most important Aristotelian philosophers of the seventeenth century.[174] Twenty years separate his precepts, neither of which is to be found in its original form in the decree registers. The first, the missing one, came in 1598 or 1599 and apparently ordered Cremonini not to interpret Aristotle's *De Anima* against the teachings of church councils. The source for this alleged precept calls it a *monitio*.[175] Five years later the Inquisition ordered the precept either "resummarized" or "resumed" (*ut reassumat praeceptum*), probably the second, together with a report on Cremonini's "inobservance" of it.[176] The Venetians quashed further investigation. The second precept is referred to obliquely in a letter from Inquisitor Agostino Galamini, weighing in in 1619 on the question of how to handle Cremonini's *Apologia* for *De coelo*, about the second of which Galamini thought Cremonini had received a precept ordering its correction and the confutation of Aristotle's views according to the strictures of the Fifth Lateran Council.[177] Neither precept had much effect, other than to generate lots of traffic between Rome, Venice, and Padua. Cremonini made some effort to comply with Rome's orders, but not much. As a client of the Venetian state, although a subject of the pope, he remained entirely safe from the Inquisition's censorship.

The last case of a precept to control the press concerns Cremonini's colleague at Padua, the ex-Jesuit Paolo Beni († 1625). The book was *Qua tandem ratione dirimi possit controversia quae in praesens de efficaci Dei auxilio et libero arbitrio agitatur* (Padua: Lorenzo Pasquati, 1603).[178] The day after the Inquisition took notice of the book, on 13 May 1604 it ordered the inquisitor of Padua to give a precept to Beni and the two men who had approved the book, Girolamo Zacchi, archpriest of Padua, and Fra Cesare da Narnia, almost certainly the vicar of its inquisition under a mistaken name, to appear before the Holy Office.[179] The master of the sacred palace was to sit in in order to publish the book's prohibition in Rome.[180] The bishop and inquisitor of Padua reported on 23 May that they had given the precept to Beni and Zacchi.[181] On 2 June the second reviser, now called "Fra Cesare Lippi da Mondavio," was given "a similar precept."[182] On 24 June, the Congregation ordered Beni's original sent to Rome and Zacchi examined, the book to go to both the congregation *de auxiliis* and the Jesuit general for censure.[183] In late June, Beni appeared before the Holy Office in Rome, which ordered its secretary Camillo Borghese to protect Beni's financial interests.[184] Zacchi, too, came to Rome. His interrogation on 2 July led the pope to order censures on Beni's book on 22 July.[185] A month later censures were again sought; their production would allow the case's expedition.[186] Zacchi was dismissed from office on 2 September and "warned" the next day.[187]

Zacchi had no chance to negotiate with the Inquisition, but Beni did. Five days after Zacchi was punished the Congregation heard Beni, and his responses went to the consultors who were to propose censures.[188] (It is not entirely clear whether Beni both testified and submitted written responses.) On 23 September, Clement VIII decided that Beni had dealt with condemned propositions in his testimony. Therefore penances were imposed on him and his book was ordered burnt. Mordano or Lippi, who had also approved it, was "sharply rebuked" and deprived of his powers to issue imprimaturs.[189] Unfortunately, what is probably the note of Beni's sentence on 30 September is illegible.[190] The case ended with the nuncio's report from Prague of the burning of a German edition of Beni's book allegedly published in Frankfurt by "Valentino Ceuctio."[191]

Precepts to Appear

Of the forty-nine precepts to appear before it or another tribunal issued by the Roman Inquisition, those like the one Galileo received in 1632 citing him to Rome are of greatest interest. These twenty-one or so precepts come in a variety of forms, some with threats as in Galileo's case, some without. One of the first of these in the decree registers concerns the case of a Venetian subject, Aurelio Vergerio of Capodistria, that ran off and on for at least forty-six years. He was apparently the nephew of the notorious heretic Pier Paolo Vergerio il giovane and son of Niccolò who had abjured in Venice in 1556 after the nuncio had failed to have him extradited.[192] The Venetian inquisition imprisoned him again in 1582, when he received many recommendations including from the king of France; despite efforts to secure his extradition, the Congregation settled for ordering his case expedited after having seen a copy of his *processo*.[193] The decree registers note his sentencing in April 1587.[194] Aurelio di Niccolò Vergerio di Capodistria appears in the prison visitations in Rome of 22 December 1593, 4 April and 20 December 1594, 23 December 1597 (when his memo was read without result), and 16 March 1598 when his request for rehabilitation to Rome was denied.[195] He was still in Rome as of 8 February 1600 when he was denied a license to return home for a year.[196] As usual, the Congregation tried to help with a convict's finances, in this case after seeking information from the inquisitor granting on 11 October 1600 Vergerio's request of 2 August to sell an investment because of reduced revenues.[197] On 28 February 1601, Vergerio was heard in a congregation, granted a license to go home to arrange "his domestic affairs" on paying security of 1,000 *scudi*, and ordered to return to Rome within eight months.[198] After a report from the diocesan vicar general of 19 September, the Congregation on 4 October granted Vergerio a prorogation of unspecified length.[199] By 7 March 1602 the Congregation had lost patience, writing the inquisitor to ask for information about him and to order his return to Rome and proceedings against his guarantors.[200] On 12 July 1602, his revenues were sequestered (meaning he must have been at least nominally a clergyman), and a response was awaited from the inquisitor about what was now called Vergerio's precept to return to Rome. Less than a month later, on 9 August, when the Congregation was often in effect in recess, it gave Vergerio until the end of September to appear and threatened him with imprisonment by the inquisitor in case of failure.[201] He came to Rome a little late sometime in October, and on 23 December the Congregation allowed him to return home under a caution of 500 *scudi* and the obligation to appear before the local inquisitor once a month.[202] Vergerio thus managed to spin out his final trip to Rome considerably longer than Galileo did.

One of the more interesting cases of precepts about which unfortunately little is known concerns Sebastiano Petronio, perhaps a relative of Giacinto Petronio, master of the sacred palace and minister of the Holy Office in Naples. Sebastiano was an advocate of the Holy Office in Foligno and dean of its cathedral. On 31 October 1624, he was given the short term of ten days to appear in Rome under precept.[203] Once there, on 27 November he received another precept not to leave, one of the comparatively rare instances of multiple precepts in a single *processo*.[204]

Precepts to appear were sometimes coupled with explicit threats. At least three times the threat was further proceedings.[205] Precepts also contained more serious threats, including in the event of contravention. Imprisonment and the galleys—in both cases distinct from them as punishment—were the most frequent. Thus a preacher from Ancona was ordered to abstain and, if he contravened the precept, he would be imprisoned.[206] A case of exorcism and curing by a priest from Sant'Angelo that had originally resulted in a precept the contravention of which had already led to imprisonment saw the precept renewed with the rather meaningless threat of continued imprisonment.[207] In three instances, the galleys were threatened in the event of contravention, one for seven years, two forever.[208] Finally, a case of curing from Tortona in which the convict contravened a precept under threat of a fine and beating saw both duly administered, the fine being either doubled or tripled (the reading is obscure) from 50 *scudi*.[209] But it was also at least theoretically possible to appeal against an alleged contravention, as Fr. Luis Gil did one imposed by the inquisitor of Barcelona, with what result is unknown.[210]

One of the oddest instances of contravention concerned a case of pretensed sanctity. On 19 January 1618, Maria Madalena Belga (she was later called both "Hollandum [*sic*]" and "Hollandam," meaning she was from the Netherlands) was found to have violated an earlier precept under pain of

beating not to wear the habit of a tertiary, nor act like a saint in Rome, nor
show false letters attesting to her miracles. The threatened punishment was
ordered to be carried out and her precept renewed.[211] Seven years later on a
denunciation from a parish priest, she was ordered to depose judicially.[212] A
month later on the report of Secretary Millini, who may have been acting as
vicar of Rome, the Congregation ordered her dismissed if nothing was found
in the archives against her.[213] Nothing was, but, unfortunately for Maria, then
imprisoned in Tor di Nona, Millini as vicar claimed that she had once abjured
and been confined to a monastery. This information was to be investigated
at the same time as evidence was to be sought whether she had relapsed.[214] It
seems no such evidence turned up, since on 14 May 1625 the Congregation
decreed "for now nothing shall be done" other than the renewal of the precept
under penalty of beating.[215] Her case ends pathetically with two entries in
September and October 1625, the first claiming she was dying of hunger, the
second asking release because of her old age.[216] It should come as no surprise
by now that the Inquisition could not find the abjuration in its own records.
Since her deposition is also undocumented, Maria Madalena's case appears to
involve a precept issued without process or sentence.

Finally, we have two cases of precepts given to bishops, the second of
which closely resembles Galileo's precept of 1616. The first concerns the bishop
of Catanzaro, Fabrizio Caracciolo.[217] Despite the fact that his bishopric was
in the kingdom of Naples and that even Urban VIII complained about the
way the case was handled, there seem to have been no jurisdictional disputes
about the Caracciolo's *processo*.[218] After an informative process conducted by
a special commissary of the Inquisition, Caracciolo was brought to Rome by
16 July 1625, and his diocese in effect left in receivership to the commissary.[219]
Urban quickly objected to the investigation *per viam inquisitionis* without a
denunciation.[220] That defect was remedied by the episcopal vicar of Catanzaro,
Benedetto Clementini, early the next year, denouncing the bishop for inter-
fering in the administration of justice, extortion, and other crimes.[221] Urban
rewarded Clementini—who had sent yet more denunciations—by appointing
him apostolic vicar in Catanzaro with orders to report on the situation to the
Congregation.[222] Despite a large extra payment to Clementini in November,
in December Urban halted proceedings, again complaining about the lack
of denunciations.[223] The situation remained fraught until 10 June 1627 when
Caracciolo, held in Rome under a verbal precept not to leave it, petitioned to
be allowed to return to his residence in order to feed himself. Urban granted
the bishop the grace of returning to Naples, this time with a judicially given

precept "under the most serious penalties" not to leave the city. Against a repe-
tition of the same decree in the register there is a note that the second precept
was duly given judicially on 15 June.[224] Caracciolo does not seem to have suffered much, since when he resigned Catanzaro in 1629 he was translated to to
Oppido, where he died before 19 January 1632.[225]

The second case offers an almost exact analogue to Galileo's precept including the singularity of a complete transcript of the precept issued. It involved
another Neapolitan, Lorenzo Mongiogo or Mongiò, bishop of Pozzuoli.[226] His
processo opened on 8 September 1627 with a denunciation by the former fiscal
of the episcopal curia. Urban VIII ordered Giacinto Petronio, minister of the
Holy Office in Naples, to investigate "extrajudicially and in secret."[227] By the
middle of the following month, the pope decided that the case merited judicial pursuit, although he still cautioned Petronio to act "with diligence, and
circumspection and most secretly" so that the bishop would not learn what
was afoot at the same time as he was summoned to Rome![228] Another month
later Urban agreed to Petronio's plan to collect evidence after the bishop left.[229]
On 8 February 1628, Petronio reported that Mongiogo intended to make his
ad limen visit to Rome by proxy. On the strength of the evidence Petronio had
seen against the bishop, he was ordered to make the visit in person instead.[230]
In early March, Petronio reported difficulty investigating the bishop while he
was in residence, and the nuncio in Naples, Cesare Monti. was ordered to get
the bishop out of his see somehow.[231] Two weeks later the usual jurisdictional
dispute first appeared when the viceroy proposed that Mongiogo exchange
Pozzuoli for Gallipoli. Urban ordered Monti written secretly to tell the viceroy
that the translation was not allowed because of the *processo* in being, and the
viceroy was warned to keep quiet.[232] On 13 April, after seeing evidence collected by Petronio and Monti, Urban ordered a search while Mongiogo was
in Naples for Easter and his arrest and extradition to Rome.[233] A further two
weeks later, Urban ordered the archbishop to send Mongiogo to Rome under
bond and the formal opening of his *processo*.[234] On 20 May Petronio wrote
that Mongiogo refused to exchange bishoprics or leave, pretending to be ill, or
go to Naples despite an order from the archbishop on visitation executing the
Congregation's order about his imprisonment. Meanwhile the apostolic vicar
was making an informative process. Urban ordered the archbishop to find
proof and help the vicar, and Petronio to take over the informative process
and send the writings found in a search of the bishop's house as well as in his
hometown of San Pietro in Galatina.[235] The entry for this meeting ends with
a note that

on the aforesaid day at the nineteenth hour the assessor ordered a
decree of the following tenor to be noted: the arrival of the bishop
of Pozzuoli in Rome having been reported, the pope ordered him
to be imprisoned in Castel Sant'Angelo, and ordered (*praecipit*) me,
the assessor, that in execution I transfer myself to the boat landing
and lead him in secret to the said Castel and consign him to the
viceprefect of the said Castel, which was done. And he [the pope]
ordered the same man to be carefully kept, well treated, and his
servants be assigned to him with the usual oath, who might serve
him.[236]

Mongiogo's imprisonment did not last long, since on 5 July he was "rehabilitated" to "the hall next to his residence," apparently a more spacious room
in Castel Sant'Angelo, since he was not released from that prison for almost a
year.[237] Urban continued to treat the bishop well, allowing a visit from a Neapolitan physician on 13 July.[238] Two weeks later the pope allowed him to confess, although apparently not to hear mass.[239] Two *avvisi* of 3 June 1628 provide
circumstantial detail of Mongiogo's crime, calling him a coiner (*monetario*)
and a seeker of hidden treasure.[240] The second added the details that he was
"of the Greek nation," that is, of Albanian extraction, and was eighty years old.

Then, out of the blue on 22 February, Mongiogo abjured. The text of the
entry reads as follows:

Reverend father lord "Tedeschus" [*sic?*] Lorenzo, Observant
Franciscan, formerly archbishop of Lanciano, now bishop of
Pozzuoli, established [*constitutus*] and having kneeled in the
presence of his most holy lordship the pope, physically touching
the most holy Gospels of God, has abjured, damned and detested
the heresies of which he is judged vehemently suspected, etc., and
others as more broadly [seen] in the notes of his sentence through
abjuration, etc., as in the book of sentences.[241]

His punishment including a precept came on 8 March:

On 8 March 1629 the present reverend father commissary reported
that his most holiness ordered the bishop of Pozzuoli to be
relegated to the monastery of Santa Prassede of the monks of the
Vallombrosan order next to Santa Maria Maggiore. In execution

of which order the same present reverend father commissary along
with me, the notary, etc., led the aforesaid bishop to the aforesaid
monastery *super Rheda* where in my presence, the notary, and of
the below written witnesses notified the same bishop of the pope's
order, and ordered (*praecipit*; the register text probably reads
praecepto) that he not leave the aforesaid monastery under penalties
at the judgment of his most holiness, and after (*successiveque*)
commended him to the abbot of the said monastery. About which
etc., done at Rome in the aforesaid monastery in the rooms of the
titular cardinal [Marcello Lante] in the presence of Angelo Finati,
Otranto diocese, and Anello de Isanto, priest of Pozzuoli diocese,
witnesses.[242]

An *avviso* reported that Mongiogo was relegated for ten years.[243]

While the pursuit of Mongiogo's accomplices continued, we also finally
implicitly learn Mongiogo's offense according to the Holy Office in August
1629, when his proctor sought the return of his books "except those of natural
and chemical matters."[244] During the rest of the year and into 1630, Mongiogo's confinement was gradually relaxed, although he was not allowed to
go home. As late as August 1631 Monti was still negotiating with the viceroy
about him, by which time he may have been dead (the entries are badly damaged). Mongiogo's ultimate fate is obscure.[245]

Form and Types of Precepts

Mongiogo's is one of only two instances of the full text of a precept I have
found in the decree registers. The other comes shortly after his and involved
two precepts, one to the guilty party and another to his religious superiors, the
one being administered:

> On 3 July 1629 the present reverend father commissary general
> of the Holy Office reported, etc., that his most holiness ordered
> that Fr. Antonio Maria de Occiminiano [province of Torino],
> of the order of Observant Franciscans, not be molested by his
> superiors for pretensed apostasy and other crimes as it is presumed
> were committed by him at other times, who remains under the
> precept of the Holy Office under penalties at the judgment of

his most holiness. On the said day the present aforesaid reverend
father commissary in execution of the aforesaid command ordered
(*mandavit*) summoned to his presence Reverend Father Vincenzo
Stefanello, Roman, commissary of the Observant Franciscans
in the Curia, to whom thus summoned and in the presence of
his paternity [Stefanello] and in mine [the notary's] personally
established (*constituto*) the present reverend [father commissary]
notified and told the aforesaid precept of his holiness, etc., [and]
he promised to obey, and also promised to notify this kind of
precept to other superiors of the same order about which etc. Done
at Rome in the Palazzo del Sant'Uffizio in the rooms of the same
present reverend father commissary, etc.[246]

Except for the lack of witnesses, the form is nearly identical in both cases and
closely resembles Galileo's precept, including in all three cases the key term
"constitutus." The similarities between all three precept minutes suggest that
they had a common form. If so, legal commentators failed to discuss it, Fedele
correctly asserting that nothing was said about formal requirements before
the 1917 code when they took on significance only for penal precepts.[247] He
also alleged that only "solemn" precepts, recorded in a "legitimate document"
issued in the presence of two witnesses, were independent of the issuer's existence, that is, took on permanence.[248] If he is correct in this assertion, then the
question of form is simultaneously vital and ignored.

The Holy Office may have borrowed that common form from other
branches of the Roman bureaucracy, including the secretariat of breves. A
check of ASV, Indice 761 to the breve registers, produced five documents identified as or involving precepts. The most interesting is not itself a precept,
but rather concerned one issued by the Jesuit general Claudio Acquaviva. His
precept—apparently to appear—had been given in both public and private
letters and therefore took the form of a written document. Paul V suspended
it and absolved the Jesuit in question from the punishments threatened.[249]
The other four precepts involved finances, a common usage in Roman and
civil law and one well known in the Rota's jurisprudence.[250] One decision laid
down that a precept to pay money was an interlocutory sentence and therefore
need not be written out anywhere other than in the acta.[251] A judge's precept,
much discussed by medieval commentators, also commonly appeared in Rota
decisions.[252]

The secretariat of state also knew all about precepts. The nuncio's banishment of Lorini from Florence in 1602, mentioned above, was accomplished by a precept that survives. The initiative came from the nuncio who proposed to stop a dispute between Lorini and the Jesuit Antonio Santarelli over proper modes of confession by giving them and their superiors precepts.[253]

> The famous and reverend lord apostolic nuncio for just and
> necessary causes moving his spirit and by the force of any of his
> apostolic faculties and every better manner committed a precept to
> be given.
>
> To Reverend Father Niccolò Lorini of the Order of Preachers,
> presently staying in the convent of San Marco in Florence and
> Reverend Father Antonio Santarelli, reader, of the Order or Society
> of Jesuits, presently staying in the convent or house of San Giovanni
> Evangelista of Florence, that in the future neither of them dare nor
> in any manner presume in sermons, as in readings, nor otherwise,
> to discuss, or in any manner deal with the article, many times by
> them in recent days [brought] into controversy in preaching, that is,
> whether sacramental confession can be done in writing or through
> a messenger, under the penalty of automatic excommunication, and
> this until our most holy lord should have ordered otherwise.

Their superiors received precepts not to allow any preaching or reading about the matter.[254] When Lorini and a Jesuit ignored the precept, the Holy Office opened proceedings, but not for contravention of the precepts, no doubt because it had not issued them, leading the pope to "order" (*praecipiat*) his general to command Lorini to cease and desist and the Jesuit to be brought to Rome.[255] In November, the secretary of state reported *monitiones* to both men.[256] This case thus also provides an example of the papal diplomatic apparatus ultimately bowing to the Inquisition's orders.

A case of murder in Florence in late 1611 further demonstrates the secretariat of state's familiarity with precepts. On 3 January 1612. the nuncio reported that. despite a *precetto* from the secular authorities, he had found and taken a murderer from Santa Maria Novella.[257] Nine days later he issued two *precetti* of his own, one to "Orsello" and another to the bargello. They refused to take copies, but the nuncio's chancellor told them no matter since they had read the text.[258]

Working by induction, we can say that the Inquisition operated with at least three kinds of precepts: judicial (3), penal (11), and neither, the vast majority.[259] Unfortunately, the numbers are too small to allow any useful distinctions between them. Thus a penal precept might demand appearance, prohibit a polygamist from seeing his second wife or a priest from soliciting women in the confessional, be added to earlier precepts in a case of contravention (and interference by the Inquisition in property rights), or exile pretensed "witches" or deny them the use of their curative powers, all crimes that commonly received plain precepts.

Administration of Precepts

One might conclude from Galileo's precept of 1616 that all precepts were given in person. This is not the case. In fact, we know more about those that were not. Thus, we have a decree of 1612 collected by Cardinal Girolamo Casanate spelling out that "inquisitors should have precepts and citations of the Holy Office presented by cursitors and *mandatarii* [agents under orders]."[260] The record of Marcantonio De Dominiis's trial gives ample evidence about the public administration of citations, and it is worth remembering that the decree of 1612 in line with earlier jurisprudence seems to have treated them as equivalent to precepts.[261] A draft citation before the Inquisition drawn up during Paul V's pontificate contains the phrase "we [the Inquisitors] require, warn and ordering (*praecipiendo*) strictly order you . . . these presents having been received" to appear, no matter how the suspects had been notified.[262]

This citation presupposes a written summons containing a precept. Galileo did not receive a copy of his precept, perhaps because giving him one would have violated the Inquisition's secrecy. In only one case in the decree registers was a precept explicitly ordered to be given in writing, which reinforces Galileo's experience that this was not usual practice.[263] But it also seems that a purely verbal precept was unusual enough to be worth noting. I have found only one such, that given to Bishop Caracciolo discussed above. The Holy Office kept "original" precepts, as suggested by a decree granting the proctor of prisons access to one such.[264] It seems likely that more "original" precepts have not been found because, like sentences, they were kept separately and suffered the same fate as the sentence registers.

Legal commentators seem not to have discussed the requisites of a precept's proper administration, but they did mention at least one mode of doing so. De' Tudeschi, for example, in the course of discussing the differences between a mandate and a precept, spoke of the first as issued in "monitory letters" and the second in "preceptory letters."[265] He also noted that some people thought these two had the same force as "executory" letters. The early sixteenth-century canonist Giovanni Francesco Della Ripa followed De' Tudeschi, adding that the equal force of all three arose from their identical form, together with a punning example from Baldo reading "we give a precept and a mandate and we order in ordering (*mandamus in praecipiendo*)."[266] The Inquisition used at least one "preceptory breve."[267]

As in the case of a precept's form, we can turn to other papal bureaucracies for help in understanding how precepts were administered. The clearest instance arose when the papacy used the secretariat of state with the help of that of breves to prevent Rodrigo Alidosi from selling his fief of Castel del Rio.[268] In order to block the sale, the cardinal secretary of state, Scipione Borghese, instructed the legate of Romagna, Domenico Rivarola, to give Alidosi "in person . . . a precept not to sell" ("ella di faccia fare un precetto che non venga a venditione"). Rivarola also received instructions about how to administer the precept, by "affixing" (in certain public locations, usually ecclesiastical) or "personally," two of the possibilities for the issuing of a citation.[269] The nuncio in Florence was also empowered to act on the strength of two breves as was Rivarola, one of 26 May, the other of 31 June 1618.[270] The official version of the transaction by Felice Contelori calls the orders "mandates."[271] The breve of 16 [*sic*] June 1618 to Rivarola reads that "we [the pope] enjoin you through these presents that by our authority you order (*praecipias, et mandes*) [Alidosi] under [threat of] our wrath and that of the holy see" not to sell without permission, "giving you full and free faculty to warn (*monendi*) the aforesaid Rodrigo" by affixing "the warning or precept" (*monitionis seu praecepti*) on the doors of the palace of the Curia in Ravenna or elsewhere.[272] On 30 May 1618 Borghese wrote Rivarola emphasizing that, if he had no time to consult, he should use the breve "and issue the said precept acting according to the writing in the said letter of 26 May ("et faccia fare il precetto suddetto regolandosi nel resto con lo scritto in dette lettere").[273] On 2 June, Rivarola acknowledged receipt of the "contingent breve to give the precept to Alidosi" ("breve facoltativo per fare il precetto all'Alidosio").

A week later the secretary of state acknowledged Rivarola's of 2 June containing the news that the legate had the breve "to precept" (*precettare*) Alidosi.[274] The procedure of giving a precept was evidently common enough for a neologistic verb to have been invented to describe it.[275] On 4 July, Borghese wrote that Paul wanted to strengthen the penalties in the breve about the *precetto* but still left it up to Rivarola whether to administer it.[276] A week later Rivarola acknowledged the new, beefed-up breve.[277] On 21 July, Borghese wrote Rivarola to "supersede in the execution of the precept . . . pending new advice" ("soprasedere nell'essecutione del precetto. . .sino a nuovo aviso").[278] Rivarola announced his compliance on 29 July.[279] Then, all goes quiet until 24 March 1619, when Rivarola reported a deal with the grand duke.[280] In response, Borghese asked the legate's opinion about the *precetto*.[281] The last we know, Borghese (and the pope) decided not to proceed to *precettare*.[282] The records of Alidosi's voluminous *processo* contain many other precepts, including some involving the Holy Office that do not, alas, help with mode of administration.[283]

Galileo's summons to Rome in 1632, long the only instance of a precept known other than his of 1616, again involved the secretary of state in providing instructions about how to administer a precept. This time the situation is more tangled since the Inquisition also passed on orders about the summons. The principals were Francesco Barberini and Secretary Antonio Barberini, Sr. The Congregation called Galileo to Rome on 23 September by a decree that ended by telling the Florentine inquisitor "to receive from him [Galileo] a promise to obey this precept which should be given to him in the presence of witnesses who in case he [Galileo] would not accept it [the precept] and not promise to obey could testify to the fact if need be."[284] Antonio Barberini's letter incorporating the decree renders its substance in fairly straightforward fashion:

> But your lordship [the inquisitor] should summon him [Galileo] to a place where witnesses and the notary should be present, without indicating to the said Galileo why the aforesaid were present and order him to come to Rome before the end of October. . .and if he agrees to come, your lordship will induce him to make an affidavit of what you have told him and of what he has promised and if he does so, your lordship, after his departure, will procure that the witnesses and the notary, who will have been present, attest to the fact that the aforesaid affidavit had been written and signed by the same Galileo; but if he refuses to do what has been said, in that case, you will give him a precept in the presence of the notary and the witnesses and then draw up this act, that he should appear in Rome.[285]

The only discrepancy between decree and letter is that the first called the original summons a precept, while the second said a precept would be given only if Galileo refused the summons.

This difference is comparatively minor when set beside the disaster Francesco Barberini and his experienced clerk Pietro Benessa managed to make out of two instructions to the nuncio. The minute of the first letter of 25 September is an exceptional mess.[286] The passages about the precept had to be reworked at least twice and possibly three times.[287] The final version read that Galileo was to be given a precept by the pope's order and asked to obey it in the presence of witnesses so that in case he refused he could still be "examined."[288] In the second letter of the same date but possibly not enciphered for a few days, Francesco came closer to the pope's original order, adding both that Galileo was not to be told why the witnesses were there and that they were to authenticate his document only after he had left. After these two departures from the *decretum* and from Cardinal Antonio's instructions, Francesco ended by agreeing with his uncle that Galileo would be given a precept only if he refused to obey the summons to Rome.[289] The nuncio, Giorgio Bolognetti, perhaps understandably confused, concluded that he should act only if Galileo were on the point of publishing a new work![290]

Thus we have evidence of mode of administration from five or six precepts, depending on how one counts: Galileo's two (or three), Mongiogo's, Antonio Maria's, and Alidosi's. Fortunately, we can again work by induction beginning with the valuable information contained in the three minutes of precepts discussed above. In three of the six cases, the principal actor was the commissary, seconded by the notary. Another three cases—two overlapping with the first three—also involved witnesses. In two of the three minutes but none of the other cases, the person receiving the precept promised to obey it. Since the notary's action created the authentic record, his presence was essential. The same seems to have been true in the use of precepts given by secular authorities. Menochio, acting as president of the Extraordinary Council of Milan, made sure to "prepare" a notary before giving a precept to an envoy from Rome not to visit a convent that Menochio considered exempt from such visitation.[291] However given, these six cases, together one assumes with the rest of the precepts in the registers, demonstrate that the point of the exercise was to make the suspect aware of his or her precept.

The End of the Legal Impropriety Thesis as Far as the Precept

The evidence just presented about how little we know about the proper administration of precepts together with that earlier in this chapter about *monitiones* and their combination with precepts, as well as that in the last chapter about the meaning of the phrase *successive ac incontinenti* in the precept minute and Commissary Seghizzi's cautious career, amount to more than enough to do away with what has been called the legal impropriety thesis.[292] It rested on two basic claims, both to do with Seghizzi and his action: that he violated his instructions by not giving Galileo a chance to respond to Bellarmino's *monitio* and that he also illegitimately administered the precept. This second point arose from a comparison to the precept of 1632 ordering Galileo to Rome, a thin corpus of evidence that has been superseded by the documentation assembled here. It shows that Seghizzi's actions were both legal and legitimate and consequently so was Galileo's precept.

Léon Garzend's Disciplinary Heresy

In 1912 the French abbot Léon Garzend, making extensive use of inquisitorial manuals, argued that the Inquisition, the fourth "organ" of the faith, developed two concepts of heresy, doctrinal and disciplinary or inquisitorial.[293] The second was much broader than the first, offered only provisional definitions of belief because it substituted doctrine for faith, could be preventive, and defined heretics in a "purely juridical and 'a-doctrinal'" fashion. All decrees embodying this notion of heresy had only a "particular" character, that is, lacked universal application.[294] According to Garzend, refusing a precept (he called it a "monition") like Galileo's ipso facto made one guilty of heresy "in the inquisitorial court," especially when the "monition" had been issued in the pope's name.[295] Galileo's judges in 1633 understood this, even if they had trouble coming up with a theological definition of his heresy.[296]

Beretta has criticized Garzend's thesis, bluntly rejecting his distinction between theological and disciplinary heresy, which Beretta claimed arose from a deficient grasp of Inquisition procedure.[297] Beretta's former teacher Bruno Neveu, along with Pierre-Noël Mayaud, had tried to turn the tables by using Garzend to attack Beretta.[298] Most recently Adriano Prosperi revisited Garzend's interpretation, without endorsing it.[299] He was right to bring the Frenchman's work back into discussion. Garzend may have caused himself a good deal of trouble by overlooking the device of the precept, but he provided an imposing interpretive context for it. He was wrong only in that the Roman Inquisition's disciplinary actions involved any kind of judgment of heresy.

Two Oddities About Galileo's Precept

We are now in a position to make full sense of Galileo's precept, especially its most significant difference from the vast majority of those issued by the Congregation, the moment it came in his proceedings. Most precepts appear at the end of a *processo*, including 119 in definitive sentences, explicitly identified as such or containing standard phraseology, for example, "opinions heard" or expedited, not as his did at an earlier moment of a trial. Not that such cases are unknown. A contingent dismissal in 1625 contained a precept to appear, which must therefore have been an interlocutory sentence.[300] More significant Cremonini's missing precept of 1598 was probably an interlocutory sentence that functioned in his *processo* almost exactly as Galileo's did in his.[301] The location of Galileo's precept makes it an interlocutory sentence, as many jurists had thought all precepts were, a temporary move often assimilated to a judge's act outside the proper course of a trial. This fits with Giacchi's argument that Galileo's precept was a purely administrative device issued by a superior demanding obedience.[302] Giacchi more or less agreed with the burden of opinion reviewed above that such administrative precepts could not serve to initiate process, since he took it to mean that the process opened with Lorini's complaint had been abandoned.[303] Galileo's precept certainly was not a citation, nor did the Inquisition treat it as such, since it cited him to appear in October 1632, which would not have been necessary if he had already been under a citation dating from 1616.

One final element in Galileo's precept supports the interpretation of it as an interlocutory sentence. Although many of the Inquisition's records are in virtual shorthand, the note of Paul's original order to Galileo is exceptionally dense and cuts a number of corners that can be understood only now in the wake of full access to the Congregation's surviving archives. Above all, the penalty clause is unusually worded, appearing to make a threat that has been misinterpreted. It reads, "if indeed he should not agree, he will be imprisoned" ("si vero non acquieverit, carceretur").[304] The imprisonment laconically tossed off at the end is not what it appears to be, an arbitrary exercise of the Inquisition's supreme power. Instead, it is parallel to the formulation at the end of the text of the precept found in the precept minute that reads "otherwise [if he refuses to obey], he will be proceeded against in the Holy Office." In other words, this clause guaranteed Galileo the best of what then was thought to be due process in the event he should contravene the precept. Imprisonment in this context meant the beginning of a proper trial. Giacchi agreed.[305] It is worth emphasis that, even though the number of cases is small, the Inquisition understood contravention of a precept as an offense, but one that did not entail a judgment of heresy. Contravention of a precept would become the most important of the two theories of Galileo's case that the Inquisition entertained.

This chapter has clarified the technical terminology of one particular inquisition procedure and its documentation, the precept. It criticizes some false deductions from the use of English translations of key Latin or Italian words including "precept," "admonition," "injunction," "proceed extrajudicially," and "expedite," because such misleading deductions have produced serious false judgments about the legitimacy of Galileo's trial and documents involved. These criticisms should lay to rest any arguments that documentation was being forged in 1632.

CHAPTER 5

The Beginning of the End

Galileo Ignores the Precept and Publishes His *Dialogue*

The beginning of the end came in 1630 when Galileo sought permission, called an imprimatur ("it may [or shall] be printed"), to have his *Dialogue on the Two Chief World Systems* published. The original plan called for publication in Rome under Lincean auspices.[1] Among other promising signs, the man who had given the copious opinion supporting publication of *The Assayer* in 1623, Niccolò Riccardi, had recently become master of the sacred palace, chief papal censor for Rome.[2] Galileo's twin agents, Benedetto Castelli and Giovanni Ciampoli, both assured him that Riccardi had praised and encouraged Galileo and could be completely relied on, promising among other things to "adjust everything." Both encouraged him to come to Rome.[3] Another even greater reason for optimism was the third-hand report that Urban VIII had told Tommaso Campanella, his semi-official court astrologer and Galileo's long-time backer, that, if it had been up to him, the decree of 1616 against Copernicus would never have been issued.[4]

Niccolò Riccardi

Riccardi (1585–1639) was known as "Padre Mostro" (Father Monster) for his large size and prodigious learning.[5] From Genoa, he seems to have had relatives all over northern Italy, including Florence. Ambassador Francesco Niccolini's wife Caterina, a key actor in the *Dialogue*'s licensing, was his cousin.[6] Other likely relatives include Pietro Martire Riccardi, with whom Niccolò was probably confused as *socius* of the Roman Inquisition's commissary, although it is also possible that Pietro Martire succeeded Niccolò in that office.[7] Probably the same man as Pietro Martire de Acquanegra, this P. M. Riccardi may have been Commissary Ippolito Lanci's nephew. The skein is twisted but reasonably strong. The *socius* almost certainly moved up from that post to inquisitor of Reggio nell'Emilia on 16 July 1625; the toponymic was attached to his surname when a complaint against him as inquisitor was dismissed two years later.[8] By 31 May 1632 he had transferred to the tribunal at Cremona, when he was licensed to come to Rome to assist Lanci, "his uncle," and again in 1634 when called Pietro Martire de Acquanegra.[9] Lanci was from Acquanegra Cremonese. For what it is worth, an *avviso* of 1 January 1633 confidently reported that Riccardi would be brought down "because he is related to [Niccolò] Ridolfi and Acquanegra [Lanci] ("poiche è congionto al Ridolfi, et ad Acquanegra").[10] In Rome's nepotistic world, Niccolò Riccardi may have assisted Francesco Riccardi to become subnotary of the Holy Office.[11]

The Dominican Riccardi studied at Valladolid under Tomas de Lemos, long-time consultor of the Roman Inquisition before teaching at Salamanca beginning in 1613.[12] In 1618 Riccardi became a consultor of the Roman Inquisition, a fact known from Galileo's missing letter of congratulations to him.[13] By 1621 he was teaching at Santa Maria sopra Minerva in Rome, where he soon gained the post Tommaso Caccini had held briefly of "first regent."[14] He met Galileo on his 1624 visit to Rome. Johannes Faber reported to Federico Cesi on 1 June 1624 on a meeting at Cardinal Zollern's of Galileo, Riccardi, and Kaspar Schoppe, adding that Riccardi, although "much for us" ("molto per noi"), did not think the time right to reopen the question of Copernicus.[15] In a letter to Cesi of 8 June that lacks manuscript authority, Galileo said that Riccardi, although lacking proper expertise in astronomy, nevertheless thought Copernicus's ideas "not a matter of faith" ("non sia materia di fede") and had invented his own position, neither Tychonian nor Copernican.[16] A few years later in the context of the continuing controversy between Galileo and the Jesuit Orazio Grassi that he had helped fuel, Riccardi is alleged to have crowed "You have won, Galileo."[17] In retrospect, Riccardi's assurance to Galileo via Castelli that (1) Galileo's opinions did not involve the faith and (2) as a "qualifier" of the Holy Office, he would defend Galileo on "every occasion" on which that institution threatened to "bore" him becomes a little ominous, especially since Riccardi added that his fellow Dominicans had caused trouble for him over Galileo.[18]

However much Riccardi may have helped Galileo during the 1620s, he had two much bigger projects on his hands. The first was the interminable

censoring of Campanella's works in which he cooperated closely with Desiderio Scaglia, Urban's favorite Inquisitor. Riccardi with ten other consultors joined a commission constituted in January 1627 to censor Campanella's
"Atheismus triumphatus" but which only began to meet in November.[19] Riccardi's biographer claims he missed all the most important meetings; even
if true, Campanella still regarded him as among his worst enemies and later
played tit-for-tat with harsh criticisms of Riccardi's book on the Marian litany
as well as some of his sermons.[20] Riccardi is supposed to have treated Campanella's book the same way as he did Galileo's, first approving it and then
ordering its seizure.[21] Meantime, according to Campanella, he had joined in a
plot to get his fellow Dominican into trouble with Urban VIII through publication of an unauthorized edition of his *Astrologia* (Lyon, 1629) that recounted
in detail the astrological measures Campanella had undertaken to protect the
pope.[22] Ten years later Riccardi protested to Campanella that he had never
wished him ill and it was not his fault Campanella was silenced.[23]

Riccardi's other project was to have been the official reply to Paolo Sarpi's
Istoria del concilio di Trento. Riccardi produced a massive work, of which only
a tiny epitome ever saw publication.[24] For research, he was allowed access
to the Inquisition's records.[25] His method involved long quotations in Latin
translated from Sarpi's Italian (which vary in their accuracy) followed by detailed and often sarcastic rebuttals; most of Riccardi's original material appeared in extensive marginalia. Riccardi cast himself as a historian out to teach
Sarpi his craft. For example, he lectured Sarpi that "if you write history . . . you
should report deeds, compose true ones, digest certain ones and collect absolutely everything that pertains to that synod [Trent]. . .and [that] pertains to
your art, because you promise in your title the desired history" ("Si scribebas
[Sarpi] historiam . . . oportebat te gesta referre, vera componere, certa digerere,
et omnia omnium ad eam Synodum pertinentia congregare . . . ad artem tuam
pertinet, quod expetitam historiam in titulo polliceris").[26] Riccardi's definition
of history led directly to an unambiguous statement of his position on the
question of scriptural infallibility: "We have believed in the history of the
sacred Genesis, nor is there any ambiguity about the divine text of the Bible,
and we know every single point is true from the senses by which they are
surrounded, however much [?although; *quamvis*] we may think this or that
[point] drawn where infallible authority or indubtable meaning [*significatio*]
do not outrun the liberty of interpretation [*opinandi libertatem*]."[27] Elsewhere
he enunciated a principle dear to the heart of all strict constructionists: devi-
ating from "the intention [*mente*] of the original author loses all the utility of

testimony."[28] Riccardi was still working on his rebuttal to Sarpi in November 1638 when he noted that it had come under attack (he did not say why) and blamed the delay in its completion on his "small talent" in assembling the masses of material he had found even after he thought the book completed.[29]

In addition to ten volumes of sermons (BAV, Barb. lat. 2942–51), including some in Spanish, Riccardi left in manuscript at least thirteen other works. They are Barb. lat. 2952–56 (including what may be censures written as a qualifier, as well as scriptural commentaries), 1093–94, 1107–10, and 1123 (theological lectures and commentaries on Thomas Aquinas), and 6518, a short sheaf of "academic readings." His only substantial printed work is *Ragionamenti sopra le letanie di Nostra Signora* (Venice: Cristoforo Tomasini, 1626), the manuscript of which is probably BAV, Barb. lat. 2941. Perhaps in part as a reward for his hard work on so many fronts, in 1629 Riccardi ascended to the office of master of the sacred palace, whereafter he continued to sit as an Inquisition consultor ex officio. He took the oath 6 June 1629.[30] Although he remained master until his death, when he was replaced by his archenemy and Galileo's nemesis Vincenzo Maculano, and continued to work hard the whole time, he appears to have lost much of Urban's favor.[31] Melchior Inchofer, the Jesuit who both as unofficial consultor to the Inquisition contributed the most detailed criticism of the *Dialogue* and also wrote the official defense of Galileo's condemnation, preached Riccardi's funeral eulogy.[32]

Whatever Riccardi's attitude, as always in Rome the signals were mixed. At the same time as his positive reports about Riccardi and Urban, Castelli also told his former teacher of discussions with Cardinal Nephew Francesco Barberini about Galileo's theory that the earth's motion caused the tides. Barberini objected that such motion made the earth a star, which would go against "theological truths." Galileo had better be able to prove his point, the cardinal said bluntly. Castelli, missing some of the force of those words, replied that of course Galileo can prove that the earth is not a star, just as he can that the moon is the moon.[33] Castelli's sarcastic rejoinder captures the Galilean lobby's optimism, just as it underestimates the difficulties they faced. Ciampoli more soberly advised Galileo that he should be sure to have the grand duke's backing when he came to Rome.[34]

Galileo in Rome

Bearing his fat manuscript and the recommended endorsement, Galileo arrived unexpectedly in Rome on 3 May 1630.[35] According to Giovanfrancesco Buonamici, Galileo gave his book to Urban, who passed it to Riccardi after crossing out the title "De fluxu et refluxu maris."[36]

At the moment of Galileo's arrival, the pope was in a particularly fragile mood, barricading himself in the papal retreat at Castel Gandolfo high on the slope of a huge extinct volcano above Lago Albano, so tightly that even close servants and important courtiers could not get past the guards.[37] His motive was fear partly of eclipses, partly of Spanish plots, at least if we believe the *avvisi*. The second was not good news for Galileo since the grand dukes owed their power to Spain.

Neither was the first. Campanella, Urban's protector, had also predicted that the pope would die not later than August.[38] Worse, so had Galileo, again, if we believe the *avvisi*. As unlikely as that prediction might seem, on his arrival in Rome a newsletter writer accurately enough announced that "Galileo is here, who is a famous mathematician and astrologer, who is attempting to print a book which calls into question many opinions that are sustained by the Jesuits." He had also allegedly predicted that Anna Barberini would have a son to continue the house of Barberini, that there would be peace in Italy, and that shortly afterward both the pope and his nephew Taddeo, Anna's husband, would die. As proof, the writer adduced two similar prognostications, including Campanella's.[39] All this about Galileo was almost certainly invented, perhaps maliciously, but Galileo did associate closely with one of the most famous astrologers in Rome, Orazio Morandi, abbot of Santa Prassede and master of a notorious library from which those with access could borrow just about anything, even the antichrist Machiavelli's books.[40] Among those who met Galileo at dinner at Santa Prassede was Raffaele Visconti, *compagno* (official substitute) of the papal censor Riccardi, another astrologer and even better the man to whom Riccardi had just assigned the censure of the *Dialogue*, as well as Ludovico Corbuzio, former inquisitor of Florence and consultor of the Inquisition.[41] Campanella claimed that Riccardi chose Visconti as his associate because he wanted lessons in astrology.[42] More, Galileo had once practiced judicial astrology, the kind that might predict deaths, making a fair amount of money out of it.[43] The newsletter's plausible charge worried him enough to enlist Cardinal Francesco to make it go away. Typically for him, Galileo assumed that his fellow Lincean would help, even though he knew Barberini's doubts about the earth's motion. Despite them, Barberini did chip in, brushing aside the bulletin's attempt to equate mathematicians and astrologers and interpreting it as an attack on himself. The anonymous troublemaker was unmasked, but we do not know his name.[44]

Whoever he was, he had the right idea. Urban was addicted to astrology.[45] Could the pope have wanted to add Galileo's alleged expertise to that he already had from Campanella?

There is no doubt about what Galileo wanted from Urban. We do not know when Galileo turned over his manuscript, but only two weeks after his arrival in Rome Ambassador Niccolini feared Riccardi would make trouble.[46] Galileo proposed to go around the master of the sacred palace to Visconti.[47] Visconti quickly agreed to help with the thorny problem of Urban's objection to Galileo's theory of the tides.[48] (The authorities in Florence took this glitch seriously enough to correspond with Galileo about it via *staffetta*, expensive express courier.)[49] That difficulty may have been cleared up by 8 June, although the "cicalata" (gossip?) to which Galileo's supporter Gino Bocchineri referred may have indicated another problem.[50] Eight days later Visconti wrote Galileo directly that Riccardi liked the book. There were still some small problems, and he would have to speak to the pope about the "frontispiece" the next day.[51] When it and the others were cleared up, Riccardi would give Urban the book.[52] Ten days later Galileo left Rome "with compete satisfaction and the matter entirely taken care of" ("con intera sua satisfatione e con la speditione intera").[53] As it turns out, Niccolini had got ahead of things.

Niccolini (1584–1650), son of an earlier ambassador to Rome, was originally intended for the church.[54] After taking a law degree at Pisa in 1604, he obtained his first bureaucratic office from Paul V two years later. When his father died in 1611, he became secretary to the new ambassador Piero Guicciardini. His brother having failed to produce heirs, in 1618 Niccolini married Riccardi's cousin Caterina. Three years later he became Florentine ambassador to Rome, a post he held until 1644. Despite almost universal condemnation, especially for his handling of Galileo's case, not much is known of his activity as ambassador; this chapter and the next contribute a little on that score. Otherwise, we have only crumbs. No doubt because of his office, he received a copy of *Sunspot Letters*, now at Chatsworth,[55] from Cesi's brother Angelo. He also several times received licenses to read prohibited books.[56] Finally, his palace in Rome in which he entertained Galileo may have been in via del Banco del Santo Spirito.[57]

Most unfortunately for Galileo, barely a month after his approach to

Riccardi Prince Cesi died, and the plan to publish in Rome had to be abandoned.[58] This represented a terrible blow. Not only did Galileo lose the wealthy Cesi's contribution to the publication costs of the lavishly illustrated, long, and expensive *Dialogue*, more important he had to do without the prince's excellent editorial skills and, most important of all, his discretion. Cesi and others had heavily modified Galileo's *Assayer*, getting rid of much of its more offensive and dangerous content.[59] This now could and did not happen in the case of the *Dialogue*. As Cesi lay dying, Galileo cast about for alternative printers, taking it as read that the imprimatur had been granted, as Niccolini had done. Florence was out because it had neither the right "characters [in type] nor compositors good for anything," so Galileo thought of Venice or even Genoa.[60] Castelli wrote on 24 August that the book had to be printed in Florence (for various reasons he could not put in writing) and "as soon as possible" ("quanto prima"). Visconti had assured him there would be no problem.[61] Galileo must have put the new plan in train immediately. The Florentine inquisitor's imprimatur is dated 11 September, the grand ducal censor's the next day.

It appears that Galileo neglected to tell Riccardi of the change of plan until it had been executed, or maybe not even then. He wrote Riccardi a missing letter in late September, to which the master replied via Castelli that he thought his agreement with Galileo was still in force, stipulating that he should return to Rome to "adjust certain little things [*coselle*]" in the work's preface and body. Since the plague prevented such a trip, Galileo should send the book to "adjust" it as necessary with Ciampoli's help, and then it could be licensed for publication in Florence or elsewhere. (Riccardi apparently did not mean that he would issue such a license, since his jurisdiction covered only Rome and its environs.) The censor later claimed that he issued the license only after Ciampoli had given him a letter from Urban commanding him to do so, leaving the clear implication that Ciampoli forged it.[62] Castelli judged it "absolutely necessary" that Galileo send the copy, and he, Ciampoli, and Visconti would take care of it.[63]

Processo Morandi

Serious trouble arose before Galileo could comply. Shortly after he left Rome, the pope ordered the arrest of his dinner-party host Abbot Morandi and more than a dozen others on charges of practicing judicial astrology. Morandi was imprisoned on 13 July.[64] In an amusing irony, among the other suspects was the agent of Cardinal Agostino Galamini, the man who had managed Galileo's original prosecution.[65] Urban was almost beside himself. Morandi's alleged offense was to have sent many writings to Florence predicting the pope's death. According to an *avviso*, Urban used the Inquisition against the abbot, two named others, their copyists, and a dozen other astrologers; Commissary Ippolito Lanci had to be summoned back urgently from Perugia to take charge of the investigation.[66] The pope then changed his mind and illegally assigned Morandi's case to the governor of Rome.

It deserves emphasis that Morandi's trial was probably illegal, at the least highly irregular. By Sixtus V's bull *Coeli et terrae*, the prosecution of astrologers fell to the usual ecclesiastical authorities, "both bishops and prelates, superiors and other ordinaries of places as well as Inquisitors of heretical depravity deputed throughout the world [that is, the Congregation of the Holy Office]," not to secular courts.[67] It is not yet clear whether Urban's remedy for the governor's lack of authority over Morandi's case—the pope's personal order on a chirograph, nothing more—was sufficient or, again, even legal. Urban began and ended the trial in that manner. On 13 July 1630, he gave the governor's criminal lieutenant, Antonio Fido, all the governor's powers by his mere signature "although it may not be registered" ("benche non sia registrato"), that is, properly recorded, and on 15 March 1631 he signed another chirograph approving all the lieutenant's actions to date and suspending proceedings, even though he had already issued that order in the Congregation.[68] Of considerable importance to Galileo, the governor's lieutenant was assisted by his fiscal general Pietro Paolo Febei, soon to become the Inquisition's assessor.[69]

Visconti's name figured prominently in Morandi's interrogation by Fido and Febei on 21 July. The abbot first apparently tried to defend Visconti by saying they had often talked about the deficiencies in Ptolemy, before seriously incriminating him by admitting that he had discussed Urban's geniture only with him and Francesco Bracciolini, formerly Antonio Barberini, Sr.'s secretary and perhaps already subsecretary of the Roman Inquisition under him.[70] In late September Visconti was arrested.[71] According to Campanella, he had predicted that Urban would die in February 1630 and had become Ludovico Ludovisi's darling as a result. Ludovisi, former cardinal nephew of the short-lived Gregory XV and vice-chancellor of the Church until his death in late 1632, headed a powerful faction in Rome, many of the members of which, not just Visconti, Urban would destroy over the next two years with diastrous consequences for Galileo. At this moment, things already looked bad enough. In his first interrogation Visconti was asked to identify Morandi's handwriting. He admitted to having seen it once or twice when Morandi had Galileo to dinner and he (Visconti) was reviewing the *Dialogue*.[72] His gratuitous testimony could hardly have been more damaging to Galileo. At a minimum, his detention cannot have increased Riccardi's confidence in the value of his report on Galileo's book.[73] Some even thought Riccardi had inspired the prosecution.[74]

Throughout the summer and into the winter, Morandi's stock fluctuated and with it Galileo's chances of getting his imprimatur. Early on, the Spanish and then the Tuscan ambassador tried to protect the abbot.[75] Despite this support, Morandi remained in prison. Among the charges was writing nasty satires. His defenders facetiously pointed out that, if this were a criminal offense, it would make half of Rome guilty. Urban retorted in deadly seriousness that he would certainly execute Morandi.[76]

Caterina Riccardi Niccolini Takes a Hand

Meanwhile, nothing further happened with Galileo's Roman imprimatur. Trying a different tack, he enlisted the help of Riccardi's cousin and Niccolini's wife, Caterina. Not only that, but Galileo had sent her correspondence intended for Castelli and also asked her to find a mysterious "cassetta."[77] She had been given the leading role in the negotiations with Riccardi, and she continued to play it through at least mid-November. A week after her first letter, she wrote Galileo that Riccardi wanted Ignazio del Nente to censor his book in Florence, or Galileo could choose another Florentine Dominican "who usually reviews books and is assigned to that purpose by the superiors [either the archbishop or the Holy Office] of the said city" ("il quale sia solito di riveder libri et adoperato a quest'effetto da' superiori di cotesta città").[78] Del Nente had been and may perhaps still have been a consultor of the Florentine inquisition, but his speciality was mysticism, not astronomy.[79] Among numerous other such publications, he edited the life and works of the fourteenth-century Dominican mystic (and Luther's favorite) Heinrich Suess. Del Nente was virtually a second Bellarmino, the founder of a confraternity preparing boys (!) for death when the world shortly ended. No surprise then that Galileo countered with Giacinto Stefani, whom Riccardi accepted after Riccardi Niccolini proposed his name. The possible relationship is important since Giacinto Stefani may have been the source of the crucially important

caricature of Galileo's *Dialogue* that reached the pope.[80] Riccardi again demanded that Galileo send "the preface and the end" after which he would send
a few instructions. (Although perhaps written up in final form by Riccardi, the
preface and conclusion came from Urban who demanded that both frame the
Dialogue's treatment of Copernicus's ideas as hypothetical.)[81] Riccardi Niccolini did not think it a good idea to give the copy of the preface Galileo had sent
her to Castelli for revision.[82]

Just as the negotiations over the Florentine review of the *Dialogue* appeared to have been concluded, Morandi died in prison on 7 November, probably of natural causes, and that very day Urban ordered his *processo* sealed
and archived.[83] That was still not the end; at least an *avviso* of 23 November
reported at length that in a coram two days earlier, after hearing the *summarium* of Morandi's case, the cardinals discussed four charges against Morandi as
if the case were proceeding to sentence.[84]

Once again Riccardi had apparently not done as he had said he would.
Castelli told Galileo that Riccardi had promised "many times" to "expedite"
the imprimatur and commit the *Dialogue*'s review to Stefani, but Castelli did
not know whether he had. The same paragraph began ominously with the
news that "our Father Visconti is in trouble for I know not what astrological
writings."[85] By coincidence, the same day as Castelli's letter, Visconti, who
seems to have been under house arrest, wrote Febei that he had been given
three days to mount his defense. Since he had only tried to expose astrological
nonsense on the strength of Ptolemaic cosmology, he would offer nothing
further.[86] Unsurprisingly, this sally failed. An *avviso* reported in December
that Visconti faced a capital case because of his love of astrology and friendship with Morandi, many of whose writings Visconti had. Visconti wound up
exiled to Viterbo, probably already in December, although Castelli did not
send Galileo the news until March, attributing Visconti's rustication "rather to
hatred of judicial astrology than to anything they had against them [Visconti
and another defendant]" ("più presto in odio dell'astrologia giudiziaria che per
cosa che si habbia contro di loro").[87]

Inscrutabilis

The stakes for all astrologers went up as Urban's bull against them and mathematicians in particular, *Inscrutabilis*, slowly wound its way toward promul-
gation.[88] Whatever Francesco Barberini may have thought about the equation

of astrologers and mathematicians, Urban made it an article of law. The bull's opening sentence almost reads like Urban's conversation with Galileo about divine omnipotence (see Chapter 7). "The unfathomable height of God's judgments does not suffer that the human intellect, trapped in the body's dark prison, stretching itself beyond the stars with damned curiosity not only explores the secrets hidden in the divine bosom and unknown even to the blessed spirits but having explored them in contempt of God, disturbance of the commonwealth and danger of princes, setting an arrogant and dangerous example, presumes to sell them." Urban parodied Sixtus V's *Coeli et terrae* against "astrologers once called mathematicians" (Urban left out the "once") and extended it to other innovators who dared to predict princes' health and added that any mathematician "or anyone else practicing judicial astrology," even a duke, who forecast the death of a pope or any of his relatives to the third degree, even if he did not make the death certain, became guilty of treason and deserved death.

Books of astrology had principally concerned Sixtus whose bull ended with a generic order to bishops and inquisitors to go after those possessing them. The astrologer-mathematicians themselves instead worried Urban, and he also changed the manner of proceeding. Of most importance to our tale, in Rome the vicar, governor, or auditor of the Apostolic Chamber could take cognizance of cases. The first of these was a normal move, since the pope was bishop of Rome, and a bishop's vicar almost always did his judicial business for him. The other two provisions are much more unusual and reflect Urban's determination to control these cases himself. Everywhere else, bishops and inquisitors could continue to chase down astrologers except those Urban assigned to his special agents. No one of whatever rank could interfere in these papal cases. One place not easily included in that "everywhere" was Venice.

Urban's inveterate fear of astrology was not the only thing higher on the pope's list of priorities than Galileo's book. In addition to the usual family squabbles (his nephews Cardinals Francesco and Antonio, Jr., Barberini never got along) and failed peace negotiations with Spain that had seemed on the point of success, the pope got himself into another shouting match with the Spanish ambassador Cardinal Gaspar Borja y de Velasco, who was also an Inquisitor.[89] The issue came up in a coram on 19 December and involved Borja's backing of the Franciscan Fra Innocenzo at San Pietro in Montorio.[90] Borja supported Innocenzo in part because his popularity brought in lots of alms. When Borja tried to defend him, Urban, smilingly told the cardinal that he knew Borja often went to hear Innocenzo's "oracles." Upset, Borja retorted that they were "much better than the counsels and thoughts of Father Campanella." His outburst allegedly cost Borja an order not to see Innocenzo again under pain of excommunication.[91] Innocenzo was already under a precept not to see anyone at all.[92] Urban's action was said to have arisen from Innocenzo's prediction of his death, possibly on astrological grounds.[93]

Next the Florentines made trouble, perhaps taking advantage of a vacancy in the nunciature. In January 1631, a jurisdictional dispute blew up between grand ducal and archipiscopal officials about the measures the former took against the plague.[94] Secular authorities commandeered ecclesiastical places, especially a Theatine convent, first as plague houses and then as billets for soldiers. The grand duke ordered the Theatines to obey.[95] One of the theologians called to consult told the secretary of the nunciature in strict confidence that the first would result in censures by the Florentine Holy Office, citing Paolo Sarpi's example.[96] Perhaps as a direct challenge, the soldiers were to be quartered in the Holy Office's headquarters at S.ta Croce, an action the secretary expected to lead to an investigation by the Holy Office since it violated the bull *In coena Domini*.[97] Inquisitor Berlinghiero Gessi seems to have had charge of the case, but there is no record of any of this in the decree registers.[98] Between astrologers, the Spanish in general (Borja in particular), and tensions in Florence, Galileo and his book would have had to fade into the background. By the same token, all three difficulties might well have tainted the atmosphere in Rome around both.

New Pressure on Riccardi

Right in the middle of this, Galileo decided to renew harassment of Riccardi via the grand duke. He planned to go to Florence on 6 March to have a talk with Secretary Andrea Cioli, but illness had prevented him. Instead, the next day Galileo wrote him a long letter summarizing efforts to get the imprimatur. For the first time, Galileo explicitly claimed to have left Rome with Riccardi's autograph license to publish. He also claimed to have written Riccardi and told him of the plan to publish in Florence and of the licenses obtained there. Riccardi replied through "madame ambassadress," Caterina Riccardi Niccolini, that he wished to see the book again. Cioli had told Galileo it was impossible to send such a large volume because of the anti-plague measures. A deal was struck to send the preface and conclusion and have the rest reviewed in Florence. Stefani had done so "with extreme accuracy and severity," noting minutiae that even Galileo's worst enemy might not have and crying over the many passages in which "with such humility and reverent submission I put myself under the superiors' authority." To top things off, Stefani observed that Galileo should have been asked to write the book, rather than having obstacles put in his way. He closed by asking that the grand duke write Niccolini to settle things with Riccardi.[99]

Galileo got his wish the next day when the grand duke ordered Cioli to send a copy of Galileo's letter to Niccolini, who was to press Riccardi for a resolution.[100] Niccolini handed the chore to his wife (her douceur was to be a telescope from Galileo, but the plague prevented its delivery) before reporting a week later that the delay arose from Riccardi's insistence on Del Nente, not Stefani, as the reviewer.[101] A week later Cioli told Niccolini that the grand duke "eagerly awaits the resolution" of the imprimatur.[102] He was still eagerly awaiting it toward the end of April when in a pair of letters Niccolini recounted his and his wife's difficult negotiations with Riccardi.[103] Niccolini reported on 19 April how they had "fought" Riccardi at length the previous Monday (14 April) before finally reaching an agreement that the master would order the book printed under certain conditions that he would put in writing—as Niccolini also wished "in order not to embarrass my conscience and reputation." Niccolini was still hoping to have these conditions, delayed by the events of Holy Week, before sealing his dispatch.[104]

Niccolini still did not have them on 25 April when Riccardi wrote him a long letter of justification. It began with a brief summary of the original terms Riccardi had laid down: publication in Rome after revision in tandem with Ciampoli. Then began a more detailed account of the delays. Visconti had reviewed the book "judiciously," but since he did not know the pope's wishes could not give the approval. That was up to Riccardi, tacitly admitting that the final say rested with Urban. Riccardi moved cautiously not to cause "displeasure" ("disgusto") to either Galileo or him should Galileo's enemies ("emuli") find anything that contravened the agreement. Insisting that he had no greater object than serving the grand duke, "my lord," Riccardi said that meant being certain that none of his clients should suffer damage to their "reputation." Since he could not issue an imprimatur for Florence (the first time anyone made this point), he could protect Galileo only by assuring that the book adhered to the "rule." If Galileo sent the preface and conclusion, Riccardi could write the inquisitor of Florence spelling out what "I had been commanded," another implicit reference to Urban's role. He closed by assuring Niccolini that he had talked to no one alive except "Galileo's and my common friends," again deftly implicitly including Urban.[105]

Two days later, perhaps time taken up with making a copy to protect himself, Niccolini forwarded Riccardi's letter to Cioli, which the secretary passed on to Galileo (apparently the original).[106] Galileo reacted on 3 May, indignantly accusing Riccardi of trying to spin things out with the grand duke as he already had for a year.[107] Riccardi's letter contained nothing new except further delays and demands, all of which Galileo had already disposed of. Galileo proposed that the grand duke convene a body consisting of Cioli and Orso d'Elci (the grand duke's *maestro di camera* who blew hot and cold on Galileo), a consultor of Cioli's choice, the inquisitor of Florence (Clemente Egidi) and Stefani, before whom Galileo would appear with his book as corrected by Visconti. A quick look at it would immediately lead the inquisitor to realize "how inconsequential the things were that had been noted [in the book]" ("quanto leggieri cose siano quelle che venivano notate") and that all had been fixed. (Galileo changed his tune here, since he had earlier insisted that both Stefani and Visconti had provided harsh reviews. Despite Galileo's later claim that the reviewers had gone over his book minutely, both Visconti's and his Florentine opposite number's opinions had to have been purely pro forma, since even a mathematician more highly skilled than Visconti would have needed much more time to digest the *Dialogue*.) Thereafter, all would also realize Galileo's piety and that he "had never had in this matter another opinion or intention than the most holy and venerable fathers and doctors of holy church had" ("haver mai hauto in questa materia altra opinione e intenzione, che quella che hanno i più santi e venerabili Padri e dottori di S.ta Chiesa"), specifying Augustine and Thomas Aquinas.[108]

We do not know whether this assembly ever took place, nor do we have any further orders to Niccolini until he acknowledged one along with two letters from Galileo on 17 May. He promised to try again with Riccardi, taking him the preface and conclusion.[109] On 20 May the ambassador spoke to Riccardi. Perhaps becoming a bit weary of Galileo's constant pestering—he emphasized how busy he had been for three weeks and apologized at length (or facetiously?) for not having answered Galileo's two letters—Niccolini did not send news of the conversation until the following Sunday, his usual day to correspond with Florence. He had finally won the argument with Riccardi by playing the trump card of the grand duke. Riccardi would send Egidi the necessary instructions, as Galileo could see he had in a quick note Niccolini sent Cioli the previous evening (missing).[110] True to his word, Riccardi wrote Egidi on 24 May about Galileo's "On the Flux and Reflux of the Tides." After a summary of developments, Riccardi gave Egidi the right to use his authority "to expedite or not expedite the book without any other dependence on my review," keeping in mind that the pope wanted the title changed to reflect clearly that the book concerned Copernicus's mathematics "absolutely," such that "God's revelation removed and holy learning [*dottrina*], appearances could be saved" about the earth's movement. The book might dispose of any objection based on experience or "peripatetic philosophy," but the result could be no more than "hypothetical and [in accord] with the scriptures on this opinion." Galileo also had to make clear that he was only showing the reasons for the Copernican interpretation while referring in preface and conclusion to the ban on Copernicus's ideas of 1616.[111] Egidi acknowledged the delegation—which Riccardi had sent via the grand duke—a week later, adding that he had turned the manuscript over to Stefani for review.[112] Thus the effort Galileo put about now into a compilation of documents probably designed to force Riccardi's hand proved unnecessary.[113] He pronounced himself *sodisfatissimo* on 13 June.[114]

Scheiner Versus Galileo

One reason for the delay in finishing the *Dialogue* was Galileo's habit of writing and rewriting while a book was in press.[115] One reason he had to write more was the appearance of the Jesuit Christoph Scheiner's intemperate attack on him called *Rosa Ursina*.[116] Scheiner, who would almost burst a blood vessel when he saw the *Dialogue*, called Galileo out, manifesting increasing Jesuit hostility at a particularly delicate moment. Scheiner accused Galileo of having "laid violent hands on [my] *Rosa Ursina*," and the Jesuit had also written a strongly worded critique of the *Dialogue*.[117] (His Society prevented him from publishing the book until 1651.) Francesco Barberini's librarian, the French libertine Gabriel Naudé, agreed about Scheiner's importance, blaming Galileo's citation to Rome on him and other Jesuits.[118] Castelli judged *Rosa Ursina* so venomous that it "needed correction with other than ink."[119] The usually excitable Ciampoli more sensibly advised Galileo to ignore it and somewhat surprisingly for the moment he did.[120] After Galileo saw a copy in September, he added a section about sunspots to the *Dialogue*.[121] He also probably most unwisely parodied Christoph Clavius (as well as the pope) in the book's conclusion.[122]

The *Dialogue* Is Printed and the Imprimatur Arrives

By then the *Dialogue*'s printing had already begun, perhaps a week or so ear-lier.[123] Castelli congratulated Galileo on 20 June 1631 that printing was un-derway.[124] He was on the point of leaving Rome to join Cardinal Antonio Barberini, Jr., on legation during which he would teach him "something" ("qualche cosa").[125] Originally with Roman publication in the offing, in order to speed publication, the printed sheets were to go one by one to Riccardi for review to be sure Galileo had complied with Riccardi's restrictions.[126] This did not happen in the case of the Florentine edition, and Niccolini later much regretted that fact as he did the entire printing in Florence.[127] Completing the press run of 1,000 copies proved a protracted process. Riccardi did not send the preface until 19 July. Although addressed to Egidi, Niccolini sent Riccardi's letter unsealed to Galileo. His covering letter added that Riccardi deserved sympathy because. just when was Niccolini pressuring him, he also suffered "rather great displeasures and humiliations" ("disgusti assai grandi e mortifi-cationi") over other books he had licensed both recently and in the past.[128] Galileo did not bother to acknowledge Niccolini's good news; then again, he seems to have written no one in Rome for at least two months.[129]

Riccardi had finally held up his end of the bargain. Galileo complied with the letter of Riccardi's demands, including changing the title, with an ill grace.[130] But he failed to bargain in entirely good faith. Although the draft pref-ace probably in the form sent to Galileo made implicit reference to the precept of 1616, Galileo never officially told Riccardi of it. The text of the preface read, "I was then [in 1616] in Rome. I had not only audiences, but also praises from the most eminent prelates of that Court, nor did the publication of that decree [suspending Copernicus's book] follow without my previous information." This phrase has been taken to refer to the precept, which raises a problem.[131] If it did, that must mean the preface's author, either Urban or Riccardi, knew of the precept this early, unless Galileo himself added that point. In the first case, at least one of the two would be complicit in the "fraud" of concealing the precept from Riccardi of which Galileo was later accused; in the second, Galileo himself would have admitted the precept's existence long before that admission was dragged out of him in his first interrogation on 12 April 1633. It seems much more likely that Galileo had in mind Roberto Bellarmino's *fede* to him of 26 May 1616 on which he relied constantly throughout the second phase of his trial. Whatever Galileo meant, he certainly kept Riccardi in the dark, as did the Inquisition by failing to tell him of its ongoing suspicion of

Galileo.[132] Both, but especially Galileo, put the master of the sacred palace in an almost impossible position.

On 21 February 1632, the printing of the *Dialogue* ended, and Galileo presented the book to the grand duke the next day.[133] Galileo waited a while to send copies to Rome, deterred by the continuing plague, which made sending such a large package difficult since each page had to be separately (if point-lessly) perfumed, and also waiting for a suitably impressive courier. He finally hit on Pietro Niccolini, the ambassador's brother and the grand duke's suc-cessful candidate for archbishop of Florence.[134] Eight copies went with Filippo Magalotti, perhaps not until July, among them one for Campanella.[135] Maga-lotti was probably a relative of Francesco Barberini's mother and her brother, former secretary of state Cardinal Lorenzo Magalotti, then in deep disgrace.[136] Galileo thought Scheiner might have a copy by 17 May, and on the same day Castelli wrote of two copies in Rome, including one for Francesco Barberini, which he had read and was rereading "with a few friends."[137] Scheiner, who may or may not have had his own *Dialogue*, was profoundly upset by the book.[138] Ciampoli requested an unbound copy, apparently to speed its passage through the plague quarantine, and Castelli begged Galileo to comply, while asking for two copies for himself.[139] Why Ciampoli wanted this copy is un-clear, since he already had one of his own.[140]

Is the Pope Catholic? Borja's Protest

Barely two weeks after the *Dialogue* issued from the press came Borja's infa-mous protest. The Thirty Years' War had entered its most dangerous phase as the Swedish Lutheran king Gustavus Adolphus defeated anything the German Catholics could throw at him. It looked as if he would drag the whole empire into the Protestant camp. Almost as bad, Rome had been reluctant to grant the Spanish Crown the right to collect a large contribution from its clergy to the war effort. In retaliation, the Spanish threatened a second Reformation.[141]

The temper and bad manners usually manifested on both sides between Cardinal Borja and Urban VIII thus far fade almost to insignificance at the most notorious moment of their strained relations. This is Borja's "protest" of 8 March 1632. There is no missing its diplomatic significance. It marked the end of a Spanish attempt to secure an alliance with the papacy against France and its replacement by Urban's protracted campaign to assemble a coalition against Spain to be headed by the grand duke. The pivotal moment came about a month earlier when Borja temporarily took over as Spanish ambassador to the pope.[142] According to the most authoritative study, Borja first officially appeared as ambassador in a coram of the Holy Office, dramatically flaunting his new authority.[143] Perhaps drawing on his deep wells of obtuseness, perhaps deliberately manifesting his contempt for Urban and proper modes of doing business, Borja raised an objection about a matter that had nothing to do with the Inquisition, attacking Urban's claim to tax the Spanish clergy. As usual, the decree registers take no notice of Borja's action. The following Monday Borja took his offensive into consistory, appearing in a body with the other nine Spanish cardinals, demanding a new subsidy for the emperor. Baldassare Moscoso y Sandoval rather than Borja took the lead, urging Urban to set an example to Christendom, but the pope told Moscoso he had already spoken to the Spanish cardinals about the matter and to be quiet.[144] Next, the papal master of ceremonies rebuffed an effort to secure a collective extraordinary audience, which Borja chose to interpret as Urban's refusal of any kind of audience.[145] This became the pretext for his actions in the consistory of 8 March.

The protest took the form of a Latin oration Borja delivered complaining about how slowly Urban had helped the emperor.[146] Urban listened until Borja either called him "cunctator" (delayer) or accused him of delaying ("cunctatur," as the best text of the protest reads).[147] At that point, when Borja had come near the end of his text, Urban ordered him to stop speaking, according to at least one account shouting his command. Borja tried to continue, but Urban again shouted at him to be silent. Antonio Barberini, Sr., "a little angry," approached Borja and asked him to cease. He probably also either took Borja's hand or grabbed his sleeve, a breach of protocol that bulked large in Spanish reactions. Moscoso intervened and told Antonio not to speak to another cardinal like that, and may have added that it was "indecent" for a Capuchin (Antonio's order) to take the pope's part in a matter of such importance to religion. Urban asked Borja in what capacity he spoke, whether as ambassador or cardinal. Borja replied "as ambassador," and Urban told him he could not act as such in consistory. Instead, Borja should request an audience like any other ambassador. Borja retorted that he had been refused a meeting, which Urban called a lie. Then Cardinal Colonna tried to defuse the situation by ringing the bell signaling the consistory's end. Neither Borja nor Urban paid any attention. Only when Borja got Urban's agreement to take a written copy of the protest did he agree to leave. One account has him leave three copies for the heads of religious orders before marching out in company with Scaglia.[148]

More important than the event is the sequel. Borja took his protest into that week's coram of the Inquisition, which it appears Urban had tried to prevent him from attending.[149] At any rate, Borja shouted at Commissary Lanci accusing him of failing to send that day's agenda.[150] Interestingly enough, Borja allegedly tried after the meeting to apologize for his behavior, and Urban apparently tried to mollify him.[151] By contrast, on at least one other occasion, the pope refused to give Borja the usual audience after a coram.[152] Both Borja and the pope set their propaganda machines to work, Borja quickly sending out copies of his protest, Urban a little more slowly through Cardinal Francesco convening his loyalists (Laudivio Zacchia, Gessi, Giulio Sacchetti, Camillo Pamphili, Fabrizio Verospi, Giovanni-Francesco Guidi di Bagno, Francesco Barberini, and Antonio Barberini, Jr.) to draw up their version of what had happened. It went at least to the nuncio in Madrid.[153] In this rendition, Urban's action was justified on the grounds that the pope did not have to follow councils, much less cardinals, and if anyone objected that the cardinals could weigh in on matters affecting the *respublica christiana*, the nuncio was to reply that the pope's power "is absolutely monarchical."[154]

Over the next month or six weeks, Urban exacted harsh revenge on most of the Italian cardinals in Borja's party, especially Ludovisi and Roberto Ubaldini, whom he accused of being the chief conspirators.[155] He forced them out of Rome along with the Florentine Cardinal Luigi Capponi.[156] More important, Urban tried to act in exactly the same a-legal fashion he had in the cases of Morandi and Fra Innocenzo. He tried to get the fiscal general of Rome, Febei, to raid Ubaldini's palace and seize his writings, as well as imprisoning him in Castel Sant'Angelo. Febei refused to do so without evidence and demanded a breve authorizing him to act. The pope flatly ordered him to obey, and only Cardinal Francesco's intervention saved Febei from the pope's anger. Nevertheless, it was thought that he had lost his chance to move up to governor and might lose office altogether.[157] No papal legal officer could have missed the moral of the story, but by the same token a conscientious official, inclined to obey the law, might have taken heart from the fiscal's resistance. Either way, the legal consequences of Borja's protest cast a long shadow over Galileo's case. Next, Urban tried to manipulate the record. He wanted Ludovisi out as vice-chancellor of the church, a highly lucrative office, and tried to intrude his favorite Marzio Ginetti, an Inquisitor. Only fear of the viceroy in Naples led him to back down. Still, Ginetti alone had the pope's writing on the matter, which might well not be entered into the consistorial acts because Urban wanted no trace of Borja's protest there.[158] Ambassador Niccolini also thought himself "embarassed" with Francesco Barberini because he had visited Borja's palace on the same day as the protest.[159]

Urban Cleans House

Beginning in the immediate wake of Borja's protest in April and May 1632, a dramatic turnover took place in the administration of the city of Rome and also in the papal secretariat of breves. Just for good measure, the first signs appeared of an even more important changing of the guard in the Roman Inquisition (see the next chapter). This last development directly affected Galileo's trial. While the precise nexus between it and a good deal of the rest of this change is often more difficult to demonstrate than I would like, the first two episodes led to the fall of men involved in the publication of Galileo's *Dialogue*, Antonio Ricciulli and Ciampoli. Ricciulli, the man who had licensed the dialogue on behalf of Rome's urban administration, may have lost his post by coincidence, and Ciampoli may have as well, but there is no doubt that Galileo suffered in the second case from the loss of his long-time sycophant. All these changes probably formed part of Urban's attempt to have his revenge on Borja and the Spanish in general, and had nothing special to do with Galileo. Nevertheless, as a client of their staunch ally the grand duke, none of this worked to Galileo's advantage. It was his bad luck that the second phase of his trial fell into an especially difficult geopolitical conjunction.[160] Late spring and summer 1632 makes an exceptionally complicated moment, in part and unusually for the history of Galileo's trial because of too much often conflicting information. I offer here one plausible scenario of what happened.

The first sign of the changes in personnel came on 11 May 1632, when Cesare Raccagna or Racagni became governor of Rome, perhaps having shouldered Febei aside. Roman gossip said Urban chose him as a person "totally dependent on him [the pope] who must obey any of his holiness's nods without any reservation whatsoever" and "serve him [Urban] in his [probably the pope's] manner in angry matters (*materie rabbiose*)."[161] Raccagna's career bears out these judgments. From Brisighella, which may make him a client or perhaps a relative of Inquisitor Galamini, he had first come to prominence in 1621, when Gregory XV made him governor of Avignon in one of his first appointments.[162] That Raccagna later attracted and kept Urban's favor is a little odd, since later that pope did his best to clear away Gregory's men (see the next chapter for Commissary Lanci, for example). On his return to Rome in 1627, he became "auditor [judge] of his most holiness the pope," or general commissary of the Camera apostolica, a post he held until 1630.[163] He moved thence to the more remunerative position of *commendatore* of the Ospedale dello Santo Spirito, replacing Urban's long-time client-administrator Giuseppe Anselmi, a consultor of the Inquisition.[164] While still *commendatore* (to 1632), Raccagna served as one of four members of a congregation particularly dear to Urban, that for the government of his new territory of Urbino.[165] In order to give him more weight as governor of Rome, Urban made him bishop of Città Castello in July 1632.[166]

Raccagna never had anything directly to do with Galileo, except through his nominal control of Morandi's *processo*. Ricciulli (1582–1642) did. As vicegerent of Rome, deputy governor under the cardinal vicar, he had given one of the licenses for the *Dialogue*. Originally a Ludovisi client (he dedicated his first book to Cardinal Ludovico), he successfully moved to Francesco Barberini's clientage.[167] Barberini had just used him in early May to visit his abbey of Farfa. This combined with the fact that, within a week of Galileo's sentence, Ricciulli became "inquisitor" of Naples suggests that his move to the bishopric of Umbriatico now probably has little or nothing to do with Galileo. Then again, he was on record as thinking that "errors about natural things," including "astronomical theses" did not constitute heresy.[168]

Much more important to Galileo than either of these changes, the post of assessor of the Roman Inquisition also changed hands, in exceedingly irregular fashion. Alessandro Vittrici was suddenly dismissed in mid-July 1632. Vittrici was the son of one of Filippo Neri's leading penitents, wardrober of Gregory XIII, and more important the husband of the niece of Maffeo Barberini's poetry teacher Aurelio Orsi.[169] By September 1624 he was a consultor of the Inquisition when Urban VIII allowed him to attend corams, and two months later the pope ordered him to sit in on the examination of suspects.[170] In a huge jump, on 29 March 1627 he became assessor.[171] Most of what is known of him during his tenure has to do with his role or rumored role in other congregations and posts, for example, the bruit that he would replace Prospero Fagnani as penitentiary or again that he would become secretary of the powerful congregation of immunities that jealously guarded papal jurisdiction.[172] We do know that the Inquisitors allegedly thought highly of him.[173] It may be that his major attraction to Urban VIII had little to do with his legal skills or experience. Vittrici's copious dedication of his edition of Orsi's "Caprarola Aurelii Ursi Epigrammatis illustrata" to Urban, as well as his father's assiduous collecting of Caravaggio, may have meant much more.[174]

Then, without warning, an *avviso* of 17 July 1632 excitedly reported that Vittrici "had been deprived of his post with most rigorous words." He had worsened his situation by refusing to accept the bishopric of Ripatransona offered by Francesco Barberini, because its income was too small.[175] That rejection annoyed the cardinal nephew, and Vittrici seemed on the way out of court. The *avviso* writer claimed that Vittrici's ejection had stunned everyone, since he had been in such high favor with the pope and the rest of the Barberini that two months earlier he had been mentioned as a possible secretary of the congregation for bishops and regulars or maybe even cardinal. Various conjectures circulated about the cause of Vittrici's fall from favor. Some said he had been aligned with Borja's party and had spent six hours with him the night before the protest.[176] Others thought him addicted to astrology and had let slip that Urban would die this year. He was also implicated in the case of Giovanni Battista Pari Dalla Torre, executed in 1630.[177] Many of his letters were found among Pari's papers. The engine of Vittrici's disgrace was supposed to have been Cardinal Ludovisi's former secretary who had entered Francesco Barberini's service.[178] This is plausible, since the timing of the secretary's switch of allegiance coincides with Urban's general offensive against the Ludovisi clientage.[179] After hanging on for most of the summer, in late August and early September Vittrici became bishop of Alatri and in November received a fat pension in order to maintain his style.[180] He did not in the end become governor of Campagna, but he did make a comeback as governor of Rome in 1647 (until his death in 1650) after bribing Innocent X, bitter enemy of the Barberini, with his collection of Caravaggios.[181]

Whatever the reasons for Vittrici's removal, it was so precipitous that no successor had been arranged. As late as 7 July, the man who would replace him, Alessandro Boccabella, was still subordinate to Vittrici but named in such a way in the attendance list that he may already have been acting for Vittrici.[182] A week later he was given the unusual title "vice-assessor" before, on 28 July, being assigned the superior position without any notice of installation in office.[183] An *avviso* of 17 July called him assessor "pro interim" in Vittrici's place.[184] The fact that in between he was nominated an auditor of the Rota at Francesco Barberini's instance suggests that he was never meant to be assessor.[185] An *avviso* claimed that his principal qualification to replace Fagnani, one of the most distinguished canonists of the seventeenth century, was "his spirit conformed to [Francesco] Barberini and [the fact that] he breathed devotion," while grudgingly admitting that he was "a good theologian."[186] Francesco Barberini pushed hard for Boccabella, while Urban backed Francesco's own general auditor, Antonio Cerri, a competition that says a lot about relations between uncle and nephew just as the second phase of Galileo's trial was about to begin. When Boccabella reappears in office in 1636 after his removal in January 1633, his title varies from assessor to vice-assessor to pro-assessor.[187] This was the man on whom (and on whose insecure position) Ambassador Niccolini would lean heavily later in the year (see the next chapter).

Boccabella was as qualified as his predecessor. A theologian, he became a qualifier (not consultor) on 27 November 1624. In 1627 he was appointed deputy fiscal and managed on several occasions to shoulder his way past the real fiscal, Carlo Sincero, in the attendance lists.[188] As Vittrici had been, a year later he was admitted to the secret part of corams.[189] Whatever his academic credentials, an *avviso* announcing Boccabella's appointment as assessor gave his best qualification as the same as Vittrici's, "utter devotion" to Francesco Barberini.[190] Francesco Beretta's speculation that Boccabella drafted the particular congregation's report on the publication of Galileo's *Dialogue* together with his characterization of that document as strongly slanted against Galileo suggest another reason for Boccabella's appointment: he came in to spearhead Galileo's prosecution (see the next chapter). As Boccabella's actions will instead demonstrate, he came to help. Doing so would cost him his job, despite efforts to adhere to the new approach to the trial unfolding in early 1633.

Ciampolata

Among those incriminated in Borja's protest was Ciampoli, secretary of papal letters to princes and for a long time one of Urban's most favored protégés, certain to become a cardinal. Urban thought so highly of him that he ordered Ciampoli to write his official biography despite the fact that another man had already finished one for Cardinal Francesco.[191] Ciampoli's job gave him the coveted daily access to the pope that only one or two other officials could boast.[192] He used his position to leak Urban's "most minute private things" to both the Spanish lobby in Rome in general and also the Ludovisi faction in particular.[193] Ciampoli, after beginning as Urban's client when the pope was still a cardinal, had moved into Ludovisi's uncle's service. When the uncle became Pope Gregory XV, he trained Ciampoli to exercise the office he kept under Urban.[194] Urban intensely disliked the enormously wealthy and therefore dangerous Cardinal Ludovisi from the time he tried to block Urban's election.[195] Urban's attack on his faction partly explains Ciampoli's fall. He allegedly visited Borja secretly at night beforehand.[196] This may be no more than a nasty rumor, but it crops up repeatedly in the stories of his fall. Ciampoli was also close to another of the Borja offenders, Cardinal Ubaldini.[197] By keeping up his ties to his former patrons, Ciampoli also made himself guilty of the worst offense in the eyes of all the Barberini: insufficient loyalty.

Ciampoli's status had gone to his head, and he indulged a bad habit of rewriting the pope's letters, including the crucial one in reply to Borja's protest, not only wounding the poet Urban's overweening pride in his literary talents but also putting his papacy in acute political danger.[198] Urban knew Ciampoli's habit well enough to give it a name, "ciampolata," which covered what Urban saw as Ciampoli's deceit in getting the license for Galileo's book.[199] For his part, Ciampoli supposedly said that Urban had only middling intelligence and no more education than a man in the street.[200] He put the same point in general terms in his description of the papal court: "No patron can bear that a servant be good for anything, nor more intelligent than he, and when the patron seems to honor his client he is really damning him."[201] In a work written in exile, he noted that "the proud [also called the great, like Urban] cannot stand to find something in a book that is not in their own head."[202] Inquisitor Guido Bentivoglio, with whom Ciampoli continued to correspond after his disgrace, understandably wondered whether he suffered from too much vanity or too little judgment.[203]

As he usually did, Urban calmed down fairly rapidly except that he utterly rejected Ciampoli's restoration, refusing to talk to him and banning him from the papal antechamber, a sure sign that he would be fired "in an angry and sharp manner," as a newsletter put it.[204] Ciampoli's big mouth left him without friends, naked before Urban's anger. His chief in the secretariat of state, Cardinal Francesco, led the charge against him, trying to get him away from Urban because Ciampoli spoke too freely to the pope and more seriously because of the increasingly worrisome perception that his uncle spent all his time writing poetry and hobnobbing with poets.[205] Ciampoli tried to negotiate his exit from Rome, but Urban turned down his request to go to Naples.[206] Then Ciampoli dug in his heels and said he would have to be chased out of the Vatican palace with a stick.[207] He wound up with the next best thing to a beating, a posting to the ungracious doghole of Montalto in the Marches, which gloried in being Sixtus V's birthplace and not much else. Ciampoli left Rome for the last time on 23 November 1632.[208] Perhaps in spite, he took all the breves he had written with him.[209] Urban continued to denigrate him after his departure.[210] He spent the rest of his life in exile as governor of similar places, putting his time to use writing strongly Galilean tracts containing such blunt pronouncements as "Aristotle is the destroyer of all religion."[211]

Urban's official biographer Andrea Nicoletti gave what he called "the true and solid cause" of Ciampoli's fall as his intervention on behalf of Galileo.[212] Ciampoli's nineteenth-century biographer Domenico Ciampoli thought it was "most clear" that the imprimatur for the *Dialogue* had brought his ancestor down.[213] However motivated, his departure dealt Galileo a severe blow.

The *Dialogue*'s Publication Is Suspended

Galileo probably knew nothing of these disquieting developments. Then, out of the blue at the end of July, Riccardi ordered Egidi to collect all copies of the *Dialogue* and at the same time also used unofficial channels to try to recover those in Rome.[214] After discussing the book with Galileo's agent Magalotti over the course of two weeks, Riccardi asked him for all the copies he had brought, promising to return them within ten days.[215] He would not have had much difficulty locating his own copy and not much more those given to Cardinal Nephew Francesco and to Ludovico Serristori, a consultor of the Inquisition who will play a possibly important role in Galileo's trial (see the next chapter). The others had gone to Niccolini, Ciampoli, Campanella, Magalotti himself (who lent it to Taddeo Barberini's *maestro da camera*), and Leone Santi, S.J. It is easy enough to see how most of these qualified as presentees, but not Santi (1585–1651/2). Mainly known as a dramatist, Santi may have been targeted by Galileo because he taught mathematics for a time in the Collegio Germanico.[216] It may indicate how much Galileo's standing with the Society of Jesus had slipped that Santi was its most authoritative member Galileo could find. Riccardi's actions, both official and unofficial, might appear to mark the first irregularity in the events leading to the second phase of Galileo's trial. Ordinarily, the master of the sacred palace (Riccardi's office) engaged only in prepublication censorship. It fell to the Index and the Inquisition to exercise censorship after a book had appeared. In fact, as Magalotti intuited, Riccardi was acting on behalf of the Holy Office, a point Magalotti repeated later in his letter.[217]

Among the reasons Riccardi alleged for the book's recall was one that Magalotti regarded as silly, the device of three dolphins on the title page that was read as a satire on Urban's nepotism. It was really the printer Landini's mark. Riccardi's other objection carried more weight, "that the book was not printed there [Florence] in conformity to the original, and that, among others, it lacked at the end two or three arguments invented personally by the holiness of our lord, with which he pretends to have convinced Lord Galileo and declared false Copernicus's position."[218] Magalotti thought this too a "cover," and that the real problem arose from the Jesuits, whom Riccardi openly said were "persecuting him [Galileo] most sharply." If all was in order with the version as printed, Magalotti advised the grand duke to complain about Riccardi and approach Francesco Barberini. Whatever action the Florentines took, Magalotti begged that his name be kept out of it, emphasizing that Castelli was also acting "very cautiously."

By coincidence, on 7 August Riccardi wrote Egidi again, ordering a precise accounting of how many copies of the *Dialogue* had been printed in order that all of them could be tracked down (while also telling the inquisitor to "console" Galileo), and Galileo wrote Fulgenzio Micanzio, Sarpi's long-time collaborator and another source of steady consolation, that a ban of the *Dialogue* lay in the offing.[219] Galileo's news may have been no more than an inference. Nevertheless, the machinery to suppress the book had been set in motion.

CHAPTER 6

The Second Phase of Galileo's Trial Begins

In mid-August 1632, in the fraught context of Urban's moves against the Spanish in Rome, including the disgrace of Galileo's idolater Giovanni Ciampoli, and in the deteriorating military situation in the empire as Gustav Adolf's threat loomed ever larger, a particular congregation assembled to consider how Galileo's *Dialogue on the Two Chief World Systems* had come to be licensed for publication.[1] It deserves emphasis that the congregation's charge seems to have had little to do with examining the book for heresy, except insofar as such evidence would support a conclusion about its publication. Florentine ambassador Francesco Niccolini first noted its existence on 15 August, when he reported that Cardinal Nephew Francesco Barberini headed it and that all its members were hostile to Galileo.[2] Six days later Galileo's defender and Urban's astrologer Tommaso Campanella confirmed Niccolini's judgment that its theologians knew nothing of mathematics and "hidden things." He suggested to Galileo that the grand duke ask that he and Benedetto Castelli join the congregation to counterbalance "Dominicans, Jesuits and Theatines." He also advised Galileo to "demand an advocate and a proctor in this case," that is, to treat the proceedings as a formal trial, "and if we do not win, take me for a beast." Campanella was sure Urban did not know what was going on and "when he is informed, etc.," that last word a sign of the caution Campanella had learned after years of fighting the Roman Inquisition.[3] He was wrong on both points: a trial was the last thing Galileo should have wanted, and Urban certainly did know what was afoot. Galileo would have been much better off to take the Inquisition's invitation to negotiate, giving him a chance to make an impact on the terms of its judgment or at the least spinning out proceedings, always a good tactic in Inquisition cases. The pope was also in poor health, a factor previously overlooked as reinforcing his naturally choleric temperament, being forced to skip the Feast of the Assumption of the Virgin at Santa Maria Maggiore because of gout.[4]

Campanella probably erred further by putting in the plural the members of the three orders he named. On Niccolò Riccardi's testimony, the congregation numbered three men, whose identities it took Niccolini almost a month to ferret out.[5] Two of them served as consultors of the Inquisition. They were Riccardi himself, master of the sacred palace, and consultor ex officio and the pope's personal theologian and almoner Agostino Oreggi. The last was an unnamed Jesuit Oreggi had suggested, probably Melchior Inchofer, who had no official status; he became a consultor of the Index only in 1640 and never held that post in the Inquisition.[6] Although educated by the Jesuits and a protégé of Roberto Bellarmino, Oreggi did not become a member of the Society, instead serving as a secular priest after taking degrees in both theology and law. He became a consultor not later than 1624 and a cardinal in 1634.[7] A Hungarian Lutheran who had converted to Catholicism, Inchofer had several times been in trouble with the Inquisition, only to escape possibly in part because he was too valuable an example of successful efforts to bring the empire back into the Catholic fold. Born ca. 1585, Inchofer received a papal dispensation to take priest's orders in 1605 and entered the Jesuits two years later.[8] He taught at their college at Messina from at least 1616 to 1629, the year he first encountered the Roman Inquisition. This time he quickly extricated himself, perhaps already with Francesco Barberini's aid.[9] Inchofer, called a "sly and crafty fellow" by Francesco Barberini's librarian Gabriel Naudé, may about now also have offered a second opinion on Galileo's *Assayer*, supporting the conclusion of the notorious "G3," discovered by Pietro Redondi, that Galileo's atomism threatened the doctrine of transubstantiation.[10] If the usual date of this opinion is correct, it indicates that the congregation cast its net beyond the *Dialogue*.[11] The fact that it decided not to include the *Assayer* may support the conclusion offered below that the particular congregation did its best to go easy on Galileo.[12] Then again, since Inchofer's opinion is undated, it seems more likely to come from his tenure as consultor to the Index, which began in 1640, and to have nothing to do with the particular congregation.

This particular congregation raises a number of questions, beyond the presently unanswerable one of its legal and constitutional status. Above all, did the Inquisition assemble it? Urban gave ambiguous answers, originally discussing the congregation in the context of Inquisition matters before insisting that its point was to see whether Galileo could be spared the Inquisition, and later in effect endorsing Niccolini's insistence that the congregation had nothing to do with the Inquisition, when he said that the congregation concluded that such a course could not be avoided.[13] Contrariwise, Filippo Magalotti assured Galileo that the Inquisition had created the congregation, and Riccardi spoke of the two bodies in parallel, at least.[14] Two pieces of evidence may clinch the case for the particular congregation's independence. First, its report said it had been drawn up on the pope's orders alone, and second, one of its three members was not an Inquisition consultor (see below for both points), and I have found no other instance of an Inquisition particular congregation using an outsider. That last point may not prove entirely compelling, since nothing is known of how the Inquisition assigned consultors to vet books. That Francesco Barberini headed the congregation probably signifies little, since he was both increasingly Urban's right-hand man and an Inquisitor. In any case, none of its three members had strong ties to him, so he might almost have served as a figurehead for a committee appointed by someone else, perhaps Urban himself, as the pope appeared to claim at one point.[15]

The grand duke reacted strongly to Niccolini's news of 15 August. Nine days later Andrea Cioli, Florentine secretary of state, summarized "long discussions" with his master. First, he was surprised that a book properly reviewed and licensed by the Roman authorities could be suspended two years later. Second, the book argued no case, instead presenting "observations and experiments [*esperienze*]" for the Ptolemaic and Copernican sides "solely for the Church's benefit," including by demonstrating how "the truth. . .agreed with holy scripture." Further, the grand duke was sure the "movement" arose from animus against Galileo, not his book, and therefore demanded that Galileo be allowed to mount a defense. To that end, the charges should be put in writing and sent to Florence, a point Cioli made twice. The duke endorsed Galileo's own view (as he transparently did throughout) that the trouble came from "enviers and evil persecutors."[16]

Niccolini's efforts to get to the bottom of the particular congregation were doubtless not helped by a major precedence dispute between him and one of Urban's household officials, either his *maestro da camera* or his cup-bearer.[17] The same day he had no more to report than that Francesco Barberini had referred him to Riccardi.[18] Magalotti did better after another discussion with Riccardi, although he thought the master's optimism might have been pretended. He told Magalotti that had he been a member of the Index in 1616 Copernicus's book would never have been suspended. He added that Galileo had done a good job in the scriptural arguments of the "Letter to Christina" and asked Magalotti if he had a copy. Magalotti, properly put on guard by this request, replied that he had one when he left Rome in 1625 and would have a search made for it. He proposed to consult Castelli before turning it over to Riccardi, and the master agreed. After reading it, Riccardi pronounced it superior to the *Dialogue* and asked why it had not been printed. Magalotti replied that Galileo had written it only in his defense and then the Index's decree had supervened. He had just sent Riccardi a carefully corrected copy. Riccardi made a big show of being a simple agent, which probably helped Magalotti downplay the importance of Riccardi's revelation of himself as supporting Tycho. Magalotti advised patience, while admitting that he still did not know the particular congregation's composition.[19]

Immediately after finishing his letter, Magalotti received Galileo's missing one of 23 August and quickly replied. He assured Galileo that he did not think that, even if the majority of the congregation thought "the Copernican opinion" false, the Holy Office, which had appointed the congregation ("d'ordine della quale si è instituita questa per questo particolare"), would still not condemn it. According to Riccardi, the outcome would likely be "a most pleasing moderation of the *Dialogues* [sic]."[20]

The next day Niccolini had much worse news.[21] The ambassador opened his letter with the gloomy expectation that "the world will fall." Discussing the Holy Office's matters, Urban "burst out in great anger" that Galileo too had entered where he should not have, "and in the gravest and most dangerous matters that in these times could be raised." To Niccolini's reply that the book had been properly licensed and that he personally had sent the preface and conclusion, Urban continued in the same "heat" that "he" (apparently meaning Galileo) and Ciampoli had tricked him and that Ciampoli had assured him that Galileo would do all that the pope ordered. The pope also complained about Riccardi, but said that Ciampoli had also tricked him into issuing the imprimatur, which had been improperly used in Florence since the book took no account of the orders sent to its inquisitor. Niccolini brought up the particular congregation and asked that Galileo be allowed to defend himself. Urban retorted that the Holy Office—implicitly admitting that the congregation arose from it—proceeded in only two steps: censure and recantation. When Niccolini asked whether Galileo should not know the charges, Urban shot back "violently" and correctly that the Inquisition did not do that, catching Niccolini in basic ignorance of how the Holy Office conducted its business. Urban insisted that he knew what the problems were and therefore so did Niccolini from their earlier conversations. Then Niccolini pointed out the book's dedication to the grand duke, to which the pope replied that he had banned books dedicated to himself and, given how heinous Galileo's offenses were, the grand duke should join in prohibiting the book. Urban added that the grand duke should not weigh in as he had in Mariano Alidosi's case, since he could not come out with honor.[22] Niccolini persisted in saying that the book could not be condemned without Galileo being heard. Urban agreed that was the least he could do, and claimed disingenuously that he was trying to keep the matter away from the Holy Office by setting up the particular congregation of theologians and other experts who were going over the *Dialogue* "word for word." It contained "the most perverse material that one could ever have in one's hands," a point he repeated after adding further complaints about Ciampoli. Urban instructed Niccolini to write the grand duke to stay out of the matter and imposed secrecy on the ambassador, while allowing him to give the duke a full report, emphasizing how gently Galileo was being handled since the case had not been turned over to the Inquisition but instead to the "newly created" particular congregation. Niccolini nevertheless judged that Urban's attitude could not be worse.

An interview with Riccardi had gone better, the master assuring Niccolini that all would be well and that the book would not be prohibited provided some points were "emended and corrected." Riccardi regretted that he could not tell Niccolini more. He once more objected to the slippage between the book as printed and the orders to the Florentine inquisitor about it, especially that the preface was set in a different typeface and that the end and the beginning did not correspond.

Niccolini closed with his own advice. In a nutshell, it was to stay away from Urban and deal with his ministers instead, especially Francesco Barberini. As far as the pope was concerned, the matter was already "expedited" ("spedita"); he would only dig in his heels further if threatened. It was best to come back again and again "without shouting" ("senza strepito") and work only through the ministers. He added that it would have been better to win over the nuncio in Alidosi's case, a broad hint about how to handle Galileo's. Niccolini concluded that "the thing goes with extreme secrecy."

The Precept Comes to Light

Niccolini's next weekly dispatch began with Riccardi's strong advice not to push hard on Galileo's behalf.[23] Violence would not move the pope, since he was sure the matter concerned not mathematics but "holy scripture, religion, and the faith," the ominous first appearance of the heresy interpretation of Galileo's trial. Not only had the book not been printed according to order, but the pope's views had often been declared "insupportable." Riccardi thought that, had the book been printed in Rome and gone over "sheet by sheet," the problems would have been averted; Niccolini agreed that it had been a serious mistake to print in Florence. The only safe approach was to go "sweetly and without shouting," Riccardi suspiciously echoing Niccolini's words. Meantime, he would go over the book and try to find ways to "adjust" it before taking it to the pope. Only then might it work to raise a few mild objections on behalf of the grand duke. Even should the Holy Office allow such (it did), demanding Campanella or Castelli as "advocates and procurators" was impossible since the first had both written a book "almost the same as was prohibited" and was also a convict and the second was objectionable for various unnamed reasons in addition to being *diffidente* (untrustworthy?).[24] As for the particular congregation, Riccardi had to defend Galileo's book, not least because he had licensed it, Oreggi "had a good will," and the Jesuit member "walks with a right intention." Above all, Riccardi confided in strict secrecy that it had been discovered in "the Holy Office's books that about twelve years ago it being heard that Lord Galileo had this [Copernican] opinion and was spreading it in Florence, and for this reason made to come to Rome, he was prohibited in the name of the pope and of the Holy Office by Lord Cardinal Bellarmino to be able to hold this opinion and that this alone is enough to ruin him." (It is worth noting here the first appearance of the false claim that Galileo had been summoned to Rome in 1616.)

Riccardi's revelation marks the pivotal moment of Galileo's trial: the discovery of the precept of 1616 and the first appearance of the interpretation of his trial based on it in competition with the heresy interpretation that Urban had just floated. Not that the precept itself would have been particularly hard to find, since Galileo's dossier contained the best text and was, unlike the decree registers, easy both to locate and also to use.[25] The precept became the red thread linking the two halves of the proceedings against Galileo. A remarkably flexible tool, its use changed from an alembic to a relatively lenient outcome to an express route to condemnation. Galileo gave his judges an opening by failing to take the opportunity offered by the precept's first use; indeed, he made matters worse by dismissing it as utterly insignificant.

The Case Goes to the Inquisition

On 18 September Niccolini passed on the bad news that Urban had sent one of his secretaries, Pietro Benessa or Benessi, three days earlier with word that Galileo's case had to go to the Inquisition.[26] Niccolini made his usual objection about the book's prior approval, but Benessa said he knew little on that head other than what he had gathered from Urban's conversation when given the order, that is, that Galileo's was not the first such case. He added that the Holy Office did not customarily hear an "individual defense." This claim was false but provides another indication of Urban's strong disinclination to follow the rules. Niccolini then went to see the pope the morning of his letter. The ambassador objected that Urban could have allowed Galileo to defend himself, since the case had been heard only in a *giunta particolare* "which has nothing to do with the Holy Office," and its proceedings could not therefore offend against the Inquisition's "constitutions" that allowed for no more than "censure, prohibition and forced recantation," taking Urban at his word about Inquisition procedure. Urban replied that it was all the same and the "giunta" had been set up solely out of respect for the grand duke and Galileo and to see whether the Inquisition could be avoided. After another attempt to emphasize the grand duke's honor, Niccolini asked whether anyone on the Congregation of the Holy Office knew about mathematics. Yes, said Urban, Guido Bentivoglio and Fabrizio Verospi did. The pope further warned the grand duke that Galileo's teaching not be allowed to cover the dissemination of error in his states. Through clenched teeth, Urban also granted that some members of the particular congregation might be invited to attend congregations. Urban closed the interview by letting Niccolini report to Florence, but only under the Inquisition's strict secrecy, which meant that he had to write the letters himself.

The same day Riccardi ordered Inquisitor Egidi to produce the original manuscript of the *Dialogue* together with Giacinto Stefani's approval and send them immediately either to the Holy Office or to him.[27]

The Particular Congregation's Report

According to Francesco Barberini, the particular congregation met five times before it reported, probably about the time Urban announced to Niccolini the transfer (if such it was) of Galileo's case to the Holy Office and certainly before the cardinals met on 23 September and decided to summon Galileo.[28] In his later *censura* on the *Dialogue*, Oreggi apparently claimed that he and Riccardi wrote the document, referring to "the observations in writing" that they had made about the *Dialogue* "at the pope's command."[29] Francesco Beretta thinks Alessandro Boccabella was also deeply involved, not only presenting the finished report to the Congregation on 23 September (as he probably did), but also writing its text "in a form entirely unfavorable to Galileo, in orienting all attention to the infraction of the prescription [*sic*] of 1616."[30] In addition to weak palaeographical evidence, Beretta cites Inchofer's reference in his funeral oration for Riccardi to their mutual friendship with Boccabella as further, equally weak evidence of the assessor's involvement.[31] If Beretta were right, that would cast Boccabella's apparent efforts to help Galileo in a much different light. Whoever wrote it, the report, too, made clear that it had been drawn up at papal command. Its subject was "the whole series of facts that occurred about the printing of Galileo's book." It is in two parts, the first an executive summary of the second, perhaps redacted by a single member of the congregation or an Inquisition functionary (almost certainly not Boccabella).[32] Headed "in fact," it offers a detailed history of the *Dialogue*'s publication (nos. 1–5 in *DV*) followed by a list of points "that are to be considered as the body of the crime (*corpo di delitto*)." Galileo had done the following: misused the Roman imprimatur; printed the preface in such a way as to separate it from the rest of the book and put "the medicine of the end in a fool's mouth"; failed to argue hypothetically; treated the issue as undecided (thereby ignoring the Index decree of 5 March 1616); abused authors on the other side and "those of which Holy Church made most use"; claimed that human and divine intellect comprehended geometry in the same way; asserted that Ptolemaians sometimes became Copernicans but never the opposite; and used the earth's motion to explain the tides. Then the report offered a conclusion that has often been overlooked or downplayed: "All which things could be emended if there should be judged some utility in the book for which he [Galileo] should be done this grace." It was the particular congregation's judgment that the book could be fixed. This sounds like an offer to negotiate, which the Inquisition liked to make.[33] But then the framer or framers added another paragraph with no obvious connection to what had gone before: "The author had a precept of 1616 from the Holy Office," which was then quoted in the strong form found in Galileo's dossier. This passage is marked off by a vertical pen stroke in the margin.[34]

The executive summary reduced the detail of the publication history as well as the potential charges. The original eight had become three. First, Galileo had violated "the orders [from the pope about how to write the *Dialogue*] by going away from hypothesis by asserting absolutely the earth's mobility and the sun's stability"; second, he had used the earth's nonexistent motion to explain the tides, these two being "the principal charges" ("capi"); and, finally and of greatest significance to the trial's course, he "had *fraudulently* kept silent about a precept given him by the Holy Office in the year 1616." What had been no more than an interesting piece of information in the first report had become the foundation of the third charge in the second. It ends with the words "one must now consider the manner of proceeding both against the person and also about the now printed book."[35]

The addition of the adverb "fraudulently" represents the most significant difference between the two documents and reduces much of the possibly positive impact of the shortened list of charges in the summary. It also elided the orginal report's recommendation that the book could be fixed, apparently closing the door to negotiation. This moment presents major difficulties of interpretation. It looks as if an original effort to frame the charge as narrowly as possible and, therefore, give Galileo the best chance to strike a deal would appear to have been overtaken by another plan requiring greater severity. It is as hard to avoid the conclusion that the precept's appearance out of place at the end of the first report did the damage in the transition to the second as it is that the congregation suffered from divided counsels. Were the report in Boccabella's hand, and were Beretta right that Boccabella was brought in to lead the prosecution of Galileo, the summary would support both points, and we would have a nice, tidy reading of this moment. Unfortunately, the document is almost certainly not in Boccabella's hand. That fact, together with his subsequent actions, nearly all of which appear to have been intended to help Galileo, wrecks that interpetation, as it supports that of divided counsels. The party that appeared to have sealed its win with the summary had not yet swept the field. The option of negotiation, as reflected in at least some of Boccabella's later moves, remained open. Whichever party "won" at this moment, the only element of the congregation's report with a future ahead of it was the precept, including its fraudulent use. All the other charges failed to reappear in Galileo's sentence.

One reason the report is so confusing is that it encapsulates the two competing but not mutually exclusive theories of Galileo's trial. The author/s jumbled together two different issues: the licensing and publication of the *Dialogue* and Galileo's violation of Urban's instructions about how to handle

Copernican ideas. The first is an essentially disciplinary issue of control of the press, with which the Inquisition dealt regularly. A trial would merely have to establish whether Galileo had received a precept in 1616 and whether he told Riccardi about it. This is the precept interpretation of his trial. The second violation might also seem a matter of discipline, but it inches close to a vastly more serious charge, heresy. This would demand a much more complicated trial over much more dangerous questions, above all of intention. The tension between these two interpretations, precept and heresy, continued to shape Galileo's trial even after it ended.

Citation to Rome

Negotiation did not seem in the offing in the immediate sequel to the particular congregation's report. In a coram of 23 September, the Congregation of the Holy Office—missing only Francesco Barberini—took up the document.[36] On its basis, Urban ordered Galileo to Rome by the end of October. He added instructions about how Inquisitor Clemente Egidi in Florence was to execute his command: "and [the inquisitor is to] receive from him [Galileo] the promise to obey this precept which should be made to him in the presence of a notary and witnesses [damage; reconstructed reading], who, in case he should not wish to admit it [that he had promised] and pretend that he had not, they might testify to the fact, if need be."[37] Urban had become fond of precepts, and we should not therefore be surprised to see him using one here (see Chapter 4). We might be a little more surprised that this order gave rise to the spectacular mess Francesco Barberini and Benessa made two days later. This moment of citation, according to some the most critical step in a trial, deserves extra attention in Galileo's case since what happened in September 1632 has frequently been misleadingly used to elucidate the precept of 1616, especially by Giorgio de Santillana.[38]

It is puzzling that both the cardinal and Benessa, the same man Urban had just used to notify Niccolini that the Inquisition would get Galileo's case, had legal training, Benessa at Bologna, and the secretariat of state was familiar with precepts (see Chapter 4), yet Barberini and Benessa still seemed to have little idea what such a thing might be. Benessa (1580 or 1586–1 May 1642), from Dubrovnik, had studied at the Collegio Romano, including with Christoph Clavius. Shortly after Urban's accession Cardinal Lorenzo Magalotti, Urban's original right-hand man, summoned him to Rome where he began a career

in the secretariat of state that lasted until his death. In 1626–27, he also served
as Francesco Barberini's private secretary, a post he took over permanently in
September 1630. That same year he was licensed "to involve himself in criminal cases," making his weak grasp of precepts that much harder to explain.
In November 1632, he became de facto secretary of state for two years.[39] An
avviso then made the inaccurate claim that he had little experience in writing
and handled oral negotiations badly.[40] In fact, he had been and would be again
a human writing machine.[41] Benessa's struggles over the precept of citation
would, therefore, seem further to demonstrate how much the Barberini valued
loyalty over competence.[42]

Cardinal Secretary Antonio Barberini transmitted the Inquisition's order
to Egidi on 25 September, spelling out exactly the inquisitor's responsibilites.[43]
According to the secretary, the order to come to Rome was *not* a precept,
which Galileo was to receive only if he refused to obey. The same day Francesco Barberini and Benessa had to try twice to get their version right, a second letter seemingly being drafted almost immediately after the sending of
the first, but not enciphered for three days. According to them, the citation
was a precept, even if Galileo readily accepted it.[44] To judge from nearly all
the rest of the Inquisition's records before January 1633, Cardinal Francesco
and Benessa were wrong about whether the citation to Rome was a precept.
Beginning with Galileo's *fede* of 1 October accepting it, calling it a *comman-
damento* as he did again in his first interrogation, right through to December
1632, no document refers to the order of 23 September as a precept.[45] Only on
10 January 1633 does the term appear in Antonio Barberini's letter transmitting
a new order to Florence to have Galileo dragged to Rome in chains if necessary, saying that "by this Congregation [of the Inquisition]. . .it is very badly
understood [taken very badly] that Galileo Galilei has not promptly obeyed
the precept given to him to come to Rome."[46] Perhaps the disciplinarian cardinal secretary meant to deepen Galileo's difficulties by threatening him with
contravention of a second precept.

The same day as Galileo's citation to Rome, after acknowledging Riccardi's order of a week earlier to send "the original already printed book of Sig.
Galileo" ("il libro originale, stampato già"), Egidi sent it instead to Cardinal
Antonio as "safer."[47] Riccardi had asked for the manuscript, together with Stefani's censure of it. Galileo's biographer Vincenzio Viviani claimed that "P. Rosati" either "shredded" or "took home" the original manuscript.[48] That Egidi
was never called to task for failing to find it or send the censure must mean
that Riccardi and Antonio Barberini were not communicating well. A note on

Egidi's letter by an Inquisition functionary deepens the mystery. "I do not see this book," he wrote on 2 October, guessing that it might be at the "Castello," that is, in the papal archives at Castel Sant'Angelo, or "in the post." It cannot be that the official was too impatient in expecting the book to arrive in Rome and make it through processing only a week after it was dispatched, since he did have Egidi's covering letter, which *had* come from Castel Sant'Angelo. A printed copy of the *Dialogue* would be used in Galileo's first interrogation. For now Egidi's copy had gone missing. Riccardi kept after the book, ordering Egidi on 7 October to find out how many copies had been printed in order to gather them all in.[49]

Into this already confused situation the egregious Campanella lobbed another of his grenades. Still, on 25 September, he wrote Galileo both that he had failed to be "admitted" with defenses of him and also that he had informed a cardinal leading "the contradictors." Campanella did not say where he been denied entrance. It has usually been assumed that he meant the Holy Office. His opaque reference to the cardinal and his posse of "contradictors" thus seems to mean that the Inquisition, like its particular congregation about the *Dialogue*, was of two minds. There are other scraps of evidence that seem to point to the same conclusion, especially the fact that only seven of the ten Inquisitors signed Galileo's sentence. That point at least is probably insignificant (see below). Nevertheless, the Inquisition unquestionably had factions, and one of them might have been more favorable to Galileo than another.[50] Still, it must be emphasized that the evidence is thin.

Castelli and Lanci

A week after receiving the order to cite Galileo, Egidi administered it on 1 October and Galileo produced the *fede* with witnesses as specified; the chancellor of the Florentine Holy Office also signed.[51] Just as formal proceedings gathered momentum, Castelli, recently returned to Rome, urged Galileo to accept them. Assuring Galileo that from the first he had declared that if "this excellent and holy tribunal [the Inquisition]" did not follow its "due manner" it would wreck "the reputation and reverence owed to it," he did not even care if the condemnation of Galileo's book resulted, as long as "it [the Inquisition] proceeded in a way that after the fact they could say what it was that they had prohibited."[52] Castelli had made the same point to Riccardi and his "companions" (*compagni*). Further, using a jousting metaphor, he warned them that "if there were courses run at one who had written as modestly as possible," etc., then others would really blast away. They might have the authority to prohibit books, but not to change the way the universe worked nor to prohibit "God and nature" from revealing their secrets.

Then Castelli got to the meat. He had a long talk with the Inquisition's commissary offering to explain those parts of the *Dialogue* that treated the earth's motion. Because the commissary was "di molto garbo" (roughly "an adroit operator") and especially close to Castelli ("mio particolar amorevole"), he made two arguments about why it was licit to believe that the earth moved. He gave Galileo the exact speech, which contained three points. The first argument had two parts. First, the case from patristics: "I find written in St. Augustine expressly that this question, whether the earth moves or no, has been well considered by sacred writers, but not decided and taught, not signifying anything to the salvation of souls." Second, an argument from authority: Copernicus had been "stimulated" to write by Cardinal Nikolaus Schönberg, dedicated *De revolutionibus* to Paul III, and the church had used the book in reforming the calendar. Castelli concluded, "I freely confess that I have no scruple about holding that the earth moves with those movements assigned to it by Copernicus, persuaded by most effective reasons and so, so many proofs of experience [or experiments] and observations." Like his master Galileo, Castelli drew a distinction between the church and nature, which was what counted. Perhaps realizing what he had just said and thinking of his audience, Castelli hurried on to note that he had had many discussions with theologians, none of whom had contradicted him. Therefore, he concluded, he saw no reason to prohibit the *Dialogue*. There is nothing all that significant in Castelli's presentation. There is in the commissary's response. As far as he was concerned, "he was of the same opinion, that this question ought not to be determined by sacred scripture. And he said further that he wanted to write on the subject, and that he would have shown the piece" to Castelli.[53] Castelli closed by telling Galileo that he was honored that the grand duke had chosen him as "proctor in this case," even if he could not enter congregations of the Holy Office. The grand duke seems to have ignored Niccolini's advice not to proceed thus.

The commissary's answer to Castelli sounds like dynamite stuff. Unfortunately, from Favaro until recently, historians have thought this hero was Vincenzo Maculano.[54] In fact, it was his predecessor, the seasoned and experienced Ippolito Lanci. That Maculano would shoulder Lanci out of office by the end of the year spelled the worst possible news for Galileo. At any rate, such a conversation with any commissary would have pleased Galileo.

On 6 October, a non-coram of the Congregation heard Egidi's letter of 25 September.[55] Its action left no trace in the decree register, a common occurrence. This congregation also transacted an unusual amount of secret business.[56] The reason was that, from 30 September until 30 October, the pope was at Castel Gandolfo.[57] His absence should have affected Galileo's case, since both his brother Secretary Antonio and nephew Francesco Barberini went with him.[58] Among several possible consequences of this triune disappearance from Rome may be the fact that the Congregation did not read Michelangelo Buonarroti's letter of 12 October to his old literary companion Urban until 25 November.[59]

Galileo's First Response to the Citation

In another of the numerous synchronicities between events in Rome and in Florence, also on 6 October Galileo wrote Cioli.[60] It seems his memory must have been acting up, since he opened by dating his citation by Egidi "three days ago," not five as his autograph *fede* cited above correctly had it. Galileo announced his intention to leave the following Sunday [10 October] for Siena to consult with the grand duke about "these mad ideas and provisions" ("quei partiti e provisioni") "through which I can show myself at the same time, as I am, most obedient to and zealous for the Church, and also desirous of protecting myself, as much as possible, against the persecutions of unjust suggestions," hitting two of his most constant themes. In the event Galileo, although expected momentarily in Siena on the 9 October and again on the 12th when Cioli thought he would be on the way to Rome, was still in Florence on the 16th.[61]

Despite Galileo's failure to consult any of the grand duke's advisers, and possibly anyone else, he decided to write directly to Francesco Barberini on 13 October.[62] He protested that "the purity of my conscience" would make it easy to show his innocence and he hoped to be given "a field" to that end. Not only would he come to Rome out of obedience but also to "the top of the world." Citation before the Inquisition had "afflicted" him gravely, so much so that he intended to burn all the work he had in hand. The "affliction" together with various bodily ailments meant he could not arrive in Rome alive. He begged for Cardinal Francesco's intervention, not to escape giving an account of his actions but only to bring the Inquisitors to see how they could help him accomplish that end.

Two possibles modes occurred to Galileo. One, he could write a complete account of all his works from the very beginning that would demonstrate "the sincerity of my intention (*mente*)" as well as his "affection" to the church, for which he had done everything. Then Galileo threw in a tantalizing remark:

> Finally, my ultimate confirmation in this proposal [to write] impressed itself on me in hearing a very brief but most holy and admirable pronouncement, that, almost as an echo of the Holy Spirit, issued unexpectedly from the mouth of a person most eminent (*eminentissima*) in learning and to be venerated for holiness of life; such a pronouncement that contained in itself in fewer than ten words accompanied with such brilliant stylishness (*leggiadria*) as much as is collected from long discourses spread in the sacred doctors' books.

Galileo forebore to name the person, since the affair concerned only himself. This trick of a nudge and a wink was a favorite of Galileo's, who tried to use it again in his first interrogation by telling the commissary that he had to tell the pope a secret. In neither case did he follow through and either name or make public. It seems this time that Galileo may have meant to refer by the word *eminentissima* obliquely to a cardinal, since that came close to the new title of *eminenza* that Urban had forced on them in 1628 (decree not published until June 1630).[63] Niccolini called this mystery man first "un eminentissimo," a cardinal, and then "a great subject," which may well mean the same thing.[64] Whomever Galileo meant, if his first plan were not endorsed, then Galileo suggested a trial in Florence, which had "inquisitor, nuncio, archbishop and other ministers of Holy Church" whom he thought had dealt with serious cases and to whom Galileo graciously conceded "the freest authority to remove, add or change at their judgment (*arbitrio*)" anything in his book.

Galileo's attempt to negotiate came to nothing in another complicated tale. On 16 October, calling Galileo "the most afflicted man in the world," Cioli forwarded a copy of the letter to Niccolini, but not the original, which Galileo had not sent.[65] Cioli ordered Niccolini to find out whether Francesco Barberini had it. Then he wrote Galileo (the court was in Siena).[66] He told him the grand duke had seen the copy of his letter, which Cioli hoped was not too long. Since he did not have the original, he could not send it with the order to Niccolini. A week later Niccolini wrote Galileo.[67] After telling him that the Holy Office's business was so "strict" that talking about it could not help, the ambassador said he could not deliver the letter since Cardinal Francesco was away until the end of the month and Castelli, with whom he wanted to consult, was also at Castel Gandolfo. In his opinion, the letter might do more harm than good. The urge to condemn him might increase in direct proportion to Galileo's protests about his innocence. While there was no chance of having the case heard in Florence, it might be possible to get a short delay. Niccolini advised Galileo to defer to the Congregation on the points to which it objected and instead "withdraw in the manner that its cardinals wish to do," in other words, beat a tactical retreat. "Otherwise there will be great difficulty in the expedition of your case as has happened to many others. Nor, speaking Christianly, can one claim other than what they want, as the supreme tribunal which cannot err." Niccolini emphasized that following his advice might aid in the "expedition of your case" which could not be pursued without making formal process, and as a result some kind of confinement for Galileo. Finally, Galileo's introduction of "an *eminentissimo* from whom you heard a pronouncement as an echo of the Holy Spirit" was a bad idea because Barberini would have to present the letter to the Congregation and they would want to know who he was. Therefore, Niccolini held the letter back until he could discuss it with Castelli. Wishing he could offer his own blood in Galileo's defense, Niccolini closed by observing that the Inquisition was not like other papal congregations and, because of the censures threatened (for breaches of its secrecy), no one ever responded to information or recommendations.

Galileo pursued his own strategy, sending Castelli at Castel Gandolfo a letter addressed to one of Francesco Barberini's secretaries, using him as a conduit to the cardinal, since Castelli apologized that an answer would have to wait until Barberini returned to the papal court.[68] Castelli was a team player and wanted to consult with Niccolini just as much as Niccolini wanted to see him. He expected to be in Rome in two days. (Castelli added the melancholy news that Giovanni Ciampoli had been made governor of Montalto.)

Worse than the missing letter to the secretary, Galileo went ahead and sent Niccolini his original to Francesco Barberini.[69] Niccolini quickly wrote Cioli that there was no possibility of presenting Galileo's letter to the cardinal. Cardinal Francesco would immediately turn it over to the Congregation "where it will be scrutinized and pondered," and the Inquisitors would especially want to know who the unnamed "great subject" was and would go after Galileo by any means to find out. That would mean a "restriction of habitation" for Galileo, as Niccolini delicately put it, and force him either to deny the statement "or to write against that one who published it," an especially gnomic statement at this crucial juncture. Either way, there was no hope that Galileo's reasons would carry the day and they might not even be heard. The best the Florentines could hope for was a delay, since Urban had already rejected all the other proposals in conversations with Niccolini. Niccolini promised to demand a delay from Francesco Barberini as soon as he returned to Rome. The ambassador still wanted to see Castelli, whom he thought might have negotiated something about Galileo's letter to Cardinal Francesco. Cioli replied five days later—meaning this correspondence went by express courier—that he thought a delay likely, had no advice about whether to present the letter, and that it would be easy to unmask "that great personage."[70] Castelli did meet Niccolini almost the moment he returned from Castel Gandolfo, and despite the ambassador's earlier insistence that the letter could not possibly reach its addressee he accepted Castelli's advice to hand it in, although he had not been able to do so that day.[71]

No surprise that Niccolini could not present Galileo's letter, since the court only came back to Rome on the day he met Castelli, 30 October. An *avviso* reported that Urban was in optimal health after a change of regimen halfway through his vacation, perhaps triggered by Francesco Barberini's concern over his visible decline.[72] Urban must indeed have been in fine fettle, since the day after Cardinal Gaspar Borja, the pope's principal Spanish nemesis, sang mass at the Quirinal.[73]

On 2 November Castelli had a brief chat with Riccardi, who complained that he, too, was in difficulties over the *Dialogue*.[74] Nevertheless, he thought a delay likely. About the same time the master finally received the "*processo*, I mean Galileo's book" from the Inquisition; receipt of it had been delayed by Antonio Barberini's absence at Castel Gandolfo.[75] The delay arising from the secretary's absence suggests that he had the volume forwarded to him there, since the Congregation continued to conduct a great deal of business in his absence. There is unfortunately no confirmation of the tantalizing possibility that he was involving himself so directly in Galileo's trial. Riccardi's reference to a *processo* suggests that he meant the manuscript of the *Dialogue*, which he had demanded on 25 September and which could not be found a week later (see above).

It took Niccolini a week to give Galileo's letter to Cardinal Francesco. The audience in which he did so must have been a little tense, since Niccolini began by speaking to the cardinal about Mariano Alidosi's case.[76] The order in which Niccolini discussed his topics is significant: a feudatory of the grand duke first and only then his first mathematician and philosopher.[77] Their cases would be inextricably bound together right through the end of Galileo's. It is likely that this linkage helped neither, especially since they had both put up impressive displays of recalcitrance. As always, Cardinal Francesco refused to descend to particulars, while expressing himself "most kind" toward Galileo and gave Niccolini the impression that a delay would be possible.

It appears that Niccolini drew the wrong inference from Francesco Barberini's behavior about the possibility of a delay and that Riccardi was mistaken on the same score. In a coram on 11 November Urban ordered no concessions; Galileo was written to obey, and Egidi to compel him to come to Rome.[78] Curiously, Urban claimed Niccolini had sought the delay by means of his secretary on the sole grounds of Galileo's great age. There is no sign of this approach in the ambassador's correspondence. If Urban's statement is true, then the Florentine camp seems to have been in almost complete disarray as Niccolini actively resisted Galileo's, but more important, the grand duke's wishes. The mystery of this moment deepens when we try to take account of a note on the original of Galileo's letter to Francesco Barberini in Urban's own hand that "this business was dealt with in the last congregation of the Holy Office [probably 11 November]; it is enough to find out from the assessor whether the order given in that congregation has been executed."[79] Since Urban knew this letter, as he told Ambassador Niccolini two days after the coram (see below), and must have had it from Francesco Barberini, the Congregation should have as well. There is no sign in the *decretum* that it did. Is this an oversight, another instance of the Inquisition's lackadaisical handling of documents, or did someone think it wise deliberately to keep the letter away from the Inquisitors, perhaps because whoever did so feared they might be inclined to accept its proposals? No evidence supports either conjecture. However all this may be, on the following Saturday, 13 November, the usual day for the secretary to see to the Inquisition's correspondence, Antonio Barberini executed the order, managing to intensify the "nothing" ("nihil") of Urban's order by substituting "anything at all" ("cosa alcuna").[80]

Niccolini Approaches Cardinal Ginetti and Boccabella

Castelli and Niccolini saw eye to eye about the next step, an approach to Marzio Ginetti, Urban's long-time favorite, his "fourth nephew," but the most junior Inquisitor.[81] Castelli's interview did not produce much substance other than "rather good words in general" and the impression that a delay "will be conceded."[82] Niccolini got Ginetti, Urban's "beloved creature [cardinal promoted by the pope]" to put Galileo's case to the Holy Office, as Niccolini was sure he had.[83] Ginetti must have done so in the coram of 11 November. If so, his representations had no effect. Another strategy, possibly more productive, had occurred to Niccolini, that is, to speak to the Inquisition's assessor, Boccabella, as well as that morning to the pope. The most the ambassador could get out of the pope was that Francesco Barberini, prefect of the new congregation of health, would shorten the plague quarantine for Galileo. Making the rounds, Niccolini then went to Cardinal Francesco who excused himself by saying that "he could not have opinions contrary to his holiness" but would do what he could about the quarantine. It is worth emphasizing the cardinal's explicit statement that he could not contradict his uncle, since many interpretations of the second phase of Galileo's trial turn on a supposed opposition between the two.[84] Frustrated by Francesco Barberini, Niccolini had gone back to Boccabella about the delay and had promised to push the plea hard, despite the fact that the order had just been "strictly" written "this evening" that Galileo had to come to Rome.

In a letter to Cioli, Niccolini sounded less optimistic.[85] He had seen Ginetti and Boccabella and given them Galileo's excuse about his age and poor health. (The ambassador continued to stay away from Galileo's more high-powered objections.) Since neither had replied, he had seen the pope, who he expected had read Galileo's letter to the cardinal nephew. He had indeed. His only response was that Galileo had to come to Rome. Slow stages in a litter should lessen the journey's rigors. Urban added that God should pardon Galileo for having gotten into such an intrigue, from which, he, as cardinal, had freed him, apparently a reference to the Index decree against Copernicus that did not mention Galileo. When Niccolini brought up the imprimatur, Urban interrupted that Ciampoli and Riccardi "had carried themselves badly, and that those servants who did not do what their patrons wished are evil familiars." As Urban's actions for some years had demonstrated, this statement expressed his views exactly; it will be worth remembering through the rest of Galileo's trial. Ciampoli in particular had always assured Urban that all was well, although the pope had "sniffed out" trouble. When Niccolini then saw Francesco Barberini, all he got was the question what Urban had said and a promise to lighten the quarantine. Having gained little from either pope or cardinal nephew, that morning Niccolini sent his secretary to see Boccabella. The assessor promised to bring the matter of a delay up "in his first audience" and to push it "with all efficacy."[86]

A week after the order to force Galileo to Rome went out, Egidi executed it, somewhat curiously without mentioning an order to do so.[87] He had first listened to Galileo's excuse of age and infirmity, before giving him a month to appear before the Holy Office, a notary and witnesses recording the event.[88]

The Boccabella card still appearing to be his best play, Niccolini tried to find him on 20 November but had to wait until the following day.[89] The assessor had disappointing news.[90] He had failed to induce Urban to grant a delay, since he regarded Galileo's coming as a sign of obedience. Boccabella suggested going around the pope through Egidi. Galileo should negotiate a delay using his usual excuses, and Egidi could then pass them on to Rome. In any case, there was no chance of the case being heard in Florence. Although it does not seem that Niccolini had gotten much out of Boccabella after all, the assessor's suggestion does raise the possibility that Egidi favored Galileo. Castelli sent Galileo an almost inconsequential letter in the same packet, except for his opinion that the Holy Office's latest decisions "will never be prejudicial" to Galileo.[91]

No progress, Niccolini disappointedly wrote Galileo on 5 December, not even in winkling out of Boccabella where Galileo would stay.[92] The assessor would say only that it depended on "your [Galileo's] examination and your responses." It would be a "vanity" for Niccolini to assure Galileo that he could stay at the embassy in Palazzo Firenze. On Friday Niccolini had seen Francesco Barberini, who had recently become vice-chancellor of the church, a lucrative financial office.[93] This was a big break for Urban, since the opening arose by the death of his archenemy Cardinal Ludovisi.[94] Borja and the other Spanish cardinals had attended the consistory in which Francesco took office, while utterly refusing to add to the hosannas for the new occupant.[95] Niccolini could get nothing out of Cardinal Francesco about "this blessed delay" except that Galileo should come as soon as possible.

Cardinal Francesco may have already known that Urban was about to threaten Galileo with being brought to Rome by force, as he did in the coram of 9 December.[96] Antonio Barberini dutifully executed the order two days later.[97] That same day Niccolini wrote Cioli that his last hopes of a delay had vanished and that Galileo had better head for a place near Siena where he could begin twenty days of quarantine.[98] Nor had he had any better luck learning where Galileo would stay, such was the Inquisition's secrecy. Boccabella, "as a friend," suggested orally that the hardships of the trip might count as part of Galileo's punishment. The assessor also wanted his name kept out of it. The next day Niccolini wrote Galileo a rather different letter, beginning with the news that Urban had not been at all pleased by the month Egidi had given Galileo to leave for Rome, an echo of the last coram.[99] The pope's main sticking point was that he thought Galileo had tricked him ("si sia preteso d'aggirarla"). Niccolini even feared that Galileo would be imprisoned, albeit with "all possible comforts." He closed by urging Galileo to set out for Aquapendente where he would undergo quarantine.

The Death of Gustav Adolf

No wonder that Niccolini could get no information on 11 December. That day in the German national church, Santa Maria dell'Anima, Urban sang a *Te deum* for the death of Gustav Adolf. What should have been one of the high points of his papacy the Spanish cardinals chose to interpret as a major gaffe. They violated protocol by wearing improper vestments for Advent, while Urban wore the green garb of the season and celebrated only low mass, omitting ceremonies for great occasions.[100] As a result, at the end of December Borja refused to complete a deal intended as an apology for his protest.[101]

Gustav Adolf's death had more direct significance for Galileo.[102] The political motives that had already inspired Urban to move against the *Dialogue* now became even stronger thanks to the papacy's and the German Catholics' much improved position. Not only had the *Dialogue* failed to provide Urban with propaganda in the empire, robbing its publication of purpose in the pope's eyes, but severe action against its author now had the additional merit of averting another action like Borja's protest as it continued to demonstrate Urban's new hard line as defender of the faith.[103]

Meanwhile, Castelli had come up with another tactic, perhaps drawing on Riccardi's actions earlier in the summer. He began to show Galileo's "Letter to Christina" to various people, especially to "a gentleman of Mons. Raimondi."[104] The tactic was doubly new in that the target's master, probably Francesco Raimondi, was a clerk of the Apostolic Chamber, a papal financial official of middle rank. He had bought his office in late 1629 after failing to secure his uncle Giovanni Battista's post at his death a year earlier.[105] For what it is worth, he was also close to Assessor Alessandro Vittrici, whose fall in July 1632 might have hurt him, too.[106] He helped Vittrici financially thereafter.[107] Since one of the best explanations of Vittrici's end turns on faction, it may be that Castelli meant to use it to help Galileo.[108]

In the next week only one significant event occurred. Things moved so slowly that Castelli wrote Galileo on 18 December that he had nothing to say.[109]

On that very day Egidi dispatched to Rome a *fede* testifying to Galileo's poor health, signed by three physicians.[110] They found him to suffer from "frequent dizzy spells, 'hypochondriacal melancholy,' stomach weakness, wakefulness and pains wandering around his body" ("veritigini frequenti, di melancolia hipochondriana, debolezza del stomaco, vigilie, [and] dolori vaganti per il corpo"). They also noted Galileo's most serious ailment, an erupted hernia.

A Dangerous Change of Personnel: Vincenzo Maculano Becomes Commissary

Four days later one of the most decisive events in Galileo's trial took place when Maculano was sworn in as commissary of the Roman Inquisition, the man who conducted most of the trial.[111] Instead of Castelli's friend Lanci, Galileo got Maculano. Lanci's fall had begun already in late 1629 after the death of his patron, Secretary Gian Garzia Millini.[112] New Secretary Antonio Barberini, Sr., in highly irregular fashion, seized on an accident to Lanci to replace him with his *socio* Maculano on Urban's orders. The notary had no idea how to handle this event and inserted Cardinal Antonio's letter into the decree register, and noted that the order had been carried out in the presence of witnesses. Lanci clawed his way back in a few months, getting rid of Maculano in the process and regaining Urban's confidence by mid-1630. At just the time of Urban's changing of the guard two years later, Lanci allegedly fell ill, opening the way to his permanent replacement by Maculano. Explanations of his fall include his close relationship with Vittrici, revenge on him by Antonio Barberini, Jr., faction (Urban's final settling of scores with the Ludovisiani in the wake of Borja's protest), as well as a clearing of the decks to make way for Galileo's prosecution, the least likely possibility.

Maculano's arrival provided the clearest possible sign of a new and dangerous direction in Galileo's trial. Galileo's in-law Giovanfrancesco Buonamici, probably reflecting Galileo's own views, blamed him for Galileo's fall, as did even more strongly Francesco Barberini's client and later librarian Lucas Holstein. "In addition [to Jesuit machinations]," wrote Buonamici, "there was the hatred and 'friarly' persecution of Father Firenzuola [Maculano], commissary of the Holy Office, much loved by His Most Holiness for knowing more about drawing [that is, engineering] and savings than preaching or theology, against the Father Monster [Riccardi], master of the sacred palace, approver of the book [the *Dialogue*]. The pope did not know how to deny Firenzuola the formation of complaints [that is, a trial] against Galileo in order to ruin the Father Monster and Ciampoli, Galileo's friend and favorer. It was allowed to cite him [and] make him come to Rome." Holstein was even blunter. "[A]ll this storm," he wrote, "is believed to have risen from the particular hatred of one monk. . . . He is now commissary of the Holy Office."[113] Historians have been reluctant to put much trust in Buonamici's story.[114] We should remain cautious about both tales, especially about the motive Buonamici alleged. Much of the rest of Holstein's report to Galileo's French supporter Nicholas Fabri de Pieresc is patently false, especially the claim that the Holy Office had clapped Galileo in chains.[115] He further asserted that he had warned the "deputatos" considering Galileo's book, "men who openly dealt with ecclesiastical authority," that the "first authors," apparently meaning Pythagoras and Copernicus, were mathematicians especially good at ferreting out the truth. Did Holstein mean that he had contacted the particular congregation or the parent body, neither very likely, the second virtually impossible? These two key but almost certainly false claims throw some doubt on Holstein's concluding sally about Maculano, however close it may come to making a true point almost by accident. Nevertheless, it raises eyebrows that Maculano wound up eventually in Riccardi's job as master of the sacred palace and used it as a springboard to a cardinalate and several mentions as a possible pope, while Riccardi found himself silenced, his career almost at an end.[116] For the last century at least, those who thought Galileo was railroaded have made Maculano the hero.[117] They miscast him badly in that role. It was his job to secure Galileo's conviction, and he got it. In tandem, Urban and his brother Antonio used their nephew Francesco and Maculano to by-pass the Inquisition until Urban could not avoid hiding behind it (as popes always did) when it came time to sentence Galileo.

Someone, the pope or Secretary Barberini or both in tandem, was in a great hurry to get Maculano into office, since he took his oath at a prison visitation during which ordinarily the Congregation did no business. He had been rumored to be in line to replace Lanci already on 13 November when a newsletter writer noted that he had been intruded as vicar of the Dominican order in a coup against its general, Niccolò Ridolfi.[118] This had first happened two years earlier at Urban's behest.[119] On 4 December the same informant wondered what would happen to Maculano, since he could not act as vicar while Ridolfi was in Rome.[120] Nevertheless, he kept the post when he ascended to commissary, leading Lanci allegedly to marvel out loud that a man who was "most ignorant" of Inquisition matters had gotten the office and Ridolfi to have his complaint to Francesco Barberini about the vicariate rejected on the grounds that the pope wanted Maculano to keep it.[121] The same *avviso* also linked Riccardi to Lanci and Ridoldi and, therefore thought him likely to suffer a similar fate.

Whether or not Maculano (1578–1666) had it in for Riccardi, he probably owed his original appointment as the commissary's *socio* in 1623 to Lanci; at least, it is likely that the commissary had the privilege of naming his own substitute.[122] In late 1629, after the first attempt to supplant Lanci, Maculano became the Dominican proctor-general, an office that sometimes qualified its holder to sit as an Inquisition consultor. Maculano had begun doing so in February 1629. By now if not earlier, Maculano was also a Barberini client. His first assignment was to help bring down his Order's general. The right patrons had a lot to do with his advancement. He had certainly not earned his brevet promotion to commissary by hard work. He had an indifferent record both as *socio* and as inquisitor, first in Pavia and then in Genoa. Although the *socio* usually attended less than half the Congregation's meetings, Maculano managed to appear for only about a third. Then, while serving as inquisitor in Pavia, he was frequently lent to the Genoese to work on their fortifications. He was gone so much that he failed to notice that the inquisition's building in Pavia was falling down. Making him inquisitor of Genoa in 1627 neatly solved the problem of his commute. Even after his short stint there and return to Rome, he continued to work for the Genoese and appears to have spent much of the year before he became commissary in Genoa. The volume of his correspondence as provincial inquisitor is significantly lower than that of two of his predecessors as commissaries when they held similar posts, Michelangelo Seghizzi and Desiderio Scaglia, both of whom wrote much more frequently than Maculano, or than his immediate predecessor in Genoa, Eliseo Masini, who, to judge from his widely circulated manual for inquisitors, *Sacro arsenale*, worked at his job. No, something else besides dedication to work distinguished Maculano from the other possible candidates. It was almost certainly his ties to Cardinal Antonio, Sr., that put him over the top.

A New Strategy for Galileo

It may not be a coincidence that Maculano's appointment nearly coincides with a new strategy by Galileo's Florentine supporters, apparently suggested by Galileo before he left for Rome.[123] After spinning their wheels ineffectually for quite some time, it involved Cardinal Carlo de' Medici's writing a letter to the general of the Capuchin order (so identified in all three letters reporting the scheme), including a passage drafted by Galileo. Geri Bocchineri, a grand ducal secretary and Cioli's client whose sister married Galileo's son Vincenzio, sent the signed but unsealed letter to de' Medici's servant Pietro Lagi so that Galileo could be sure it was as he wished.[124] In his last letter about the scheme, dated 29 January, Bocchineri mentioned two letters, one to the general, the other to his *compagno*, both unsealed.[125] Later he assured Galileo that "Antonino, our Capuchin brother," was praying for him.[126]

Such a strategy suggested that someone had realized the importance of Secretary Barberini, a member of the Capuchin order, and wished the general to intervene with him. Favaro identified the man in question as Giovanni Antonio (or Camillo) Montecuccoli da Modena, but he was not elected general until either 13 or 15 May 1633.[127] Instead, at this moment, the order had no general, Montecuccoli's predecessor, Francesco Denegri (Francesco da Genova) (1580–1650), serving as the order's proctor and vicar general by Urban's (illegal) appointment of 28 September 1632. Because Antonio Barberini, Sr., thought him too valuable as a preacher in Rome, he was taken out of the running for general in 1633 when he was continued in office as proctor and vicar at Urban's request.[128] Unfortunately, not much more is known of him outside a few other signposts of his career in the order and his publication of two sermons.[129]

On 26 December Niccolini reported to Cioli that Ridolfi and others had confirmed the rumor that Riccardi was under threat.[130] Niccolini had approached Boccabella again, who was "embarassed" to address the pope, since he was "most badly inclined." As Niccolini had told Galileo the day before, the assessor wanted to wait for the medical *fede* as a pretext before trying again. Boccabella's hesitation led the ambassador to pronounce himself out of ideas about how to proceed.[131] Also the day before, Niccolini had told Galileo that Boccabella "has always shown himself to sympathize with you, as it appears to me certain that he is ready to help and serve you in all that the duty of his office permits." Both Niccolini and Castelli again urged Galileo to set out for Sienese territory as a token of obedience.[132] Castelli also thought it wise for Galileo to write "a good letter" to the pope and another to Francesco Barberini.

On 30 December in a coram at the Vatican attended by Borja, Scaglia, Antonio Barberini, Sr., Laudivio Zacchia, Berlinghiero Gessi, and Ginetti, the Congregation reacted to the medical *fede* that had arrived two days earlier.[133]

(Francesco Barberini began a month-long absence after attending the Wednesday meeting the day before.) Urban gruffly dismissed it, saying that he and the Congregation "by no means can or ought to tolerate these kinds of stratagems (*subterfugia*)." They therefore ordered a commissary and physicians sent from Rome to examine Galileo. If he proved fit to travel, he was to be sent back there "imprisoned and bound with chains." To compound Galileo's pain, he was to pay the envoys' expenses. The decree ended with an order to give Galileo a precept "at an opportune time" if he refused to come and obey. On 1 January Antonio Barberini passed on the instruction enclosed in a brief letter allowing Egidi to read it to Galileo.[134] As usual, the secretary intensified the Congregation's decree, converting "stratagems" into "fictions" and adding "nor dissimulate about his coming here," as well as the phrase "if he does not obey immediately" before getting to the instruction about the commisssary, which he concluded with an extra flourish of "he [Galileo] has abused this Congregation's kindness." He did not, however, say anything about a precept, concluding "you [Egidi] will execute what is imposed on you and report here," completely changing the sense. The same day Francesco Barberini did what he did best and soothed Cioli, who had written on 13 December, telling him that the pope remained as well inclined to Florence as ever, saying nothing specific about Galileo.[135] Nuncio Bolognetti duly executed the cardinal nephew's instructions, but not until 5 February after the court returned from Pisa.[136] Egidi responded on 8 January 1633, saying he had read Galileo Antonio Barberini's letter and "exhorted and persuaded him to come," which is not quite what the pope had demanded.[137] When Egidi's letter was read in a congregation on 20 January—after a report about Mariano Alidosi—no action was taken, nor did anyone complain about his fudging of his instructions.[138]

Still, Niccolini could get nothing out of Boccabella about whether the medical *fede* had arrived and, therefore, could not say whether "these lords, or to say better, his holiness" had determined to go easier on Galileo. Niccolini, anyway, was sure Urban had charge.[139] The ambassador was reduced to assuring Galileo vaguely that, if Boccabella had a say, a delay would be granted, but it was also possible that other orders had gone to Egidi. When Boccabella announced that the *fede* had arrived, he also said it had not been taken seriously, as written only for Galileo's "service."[140] The assessor could only advise Galileo to come to Rome.

Finally, the grand duke blinked and ordered Galileo to Rome on 11 January.[141] Cioli tried to soften the blow by saying that Galileo would travel in a grand ducal litter and could stay with Niccolini. Galileo dragged his feet, writing Elio Diodati in Paris on 15 January that he was about to leave and Cardinal de' Medici that he would do so on 20 January.[142] In his first letter, he blamed the Jesuits for his troubles. On 15 January Bolognetti passed to Francesco Barberini the news from the vicar of the Florentine inquisition that Galileo would leave on the 19th. He also noted heavy pressure on Alidosi's behalf.[143] Galileo delayed his departure two days, until the 21st.[144] For a short time thereafter, Niccolini was out of action in Livorno, mourning his mother's death.[145]

Boccabella and Bellafaccia, or the Inquisition Finds a New Assessor

On 26 January 1633, the Inquisition made a further personnel move that was nearly as ominous for Galileo as Maculano's appointment. The helpful Boccabella gave way to Pietro Paolo Febei, a man with zero experience in any kind of inquisition, certainly none of the usual on-the-job training in the central tribunal. Like Boccabella and Maculano, his principal qualification was unswerving fidelity to the Barberini. Although he had recently bucked Urban over the pope's order to raid Cardinal Roberto Ubaldini's premises, refusing to do so without written authorization, he had learned his lesson and from then on did exactly as he was told.[146] Boccabella's removal and replacement by another soldier dependent on Francesco Barberini strongly suggests the beginning of a new, less flexible, approach to Galileo's trial, as it does that Cardinal Francesco was not in Galileo's corner. The two-edged precept no longer served as a negotiating tool but as the best means to hurry a condemnation.

Unlike Boccabella, we know a lot about Febei (12 October 1585–4 August 1649) before he became assessor, and none of it is reassuring.[147] He may have been a highly qualified lawyer, but he knew absolutely nothing about how the Holy Office worked. Febei was woefully unprepared because, instead of coming up through its ranks, he had been for close to twenty years a criminal judge, getting most of his training from his uncle Giulivio Cartari in various tribunals in the papal states.[148] In 1624 he brought his wife and six or seven children to Rome when he became criminal judge on the Campidoglio.[149] Then he went back out to the provinces to Ferrara before taking up his most important post as auditor of the Torrone in Bologna (for about eighteen months—one biography says only six—between 1627 and 1629), responsible for the whole territory of that major papal legation.[150] One of the cases he apparently heard in Ferrara involved contravention of a precept.[151] Among the major cases he handled in Bologna was a dispute over straw.[152] This appointment also represented the fruition of his uncle's strategy of introducing him to the Barberini, beginning with Urban's uncle Francesco.[153] He owed the job especially to Urban's brother and Francesco Barberini's father Carlo, general of the Church.[154]

Meantime, Febei's wife had conveniently died, allowing him to enter the clergy—as he insisted he always wanted to do—and become eligible for higher office.[155] In early 1629, he returned to Rome and replaced his uncle as fiscal general, chief prosecutor in the city courts, the closest he ever came to filling the assessor's job description.[156] Even here Febei does not compare well to a recent former fiscal, one of the most famous defense attorneys of the day, Prospero Farinacci, author of a treatise on the Inquisition Cardinal Bellarmino had endorsed for publication.[157] Despite these weak credentials, all of a sudden, Febei found himself assessor of the Holy Office. He probably earned the post on the strength of his role in the prosecution of Orazio Morandi, the astrologer abbot (see the last chapter).

Febei did have one other qualification: he cut a good figure. In his hometown of Orvieto, they called him "Bellafaccia," "Pretty Face," and the portrait bust on his cenotaph in Santa Anastasia al Palatino, erected by his son Francesco Maria, makes him look handsome. Unlike some epitaphs that go on for pages, his is brief and singles out his status as "ex-assessor of the Holy Office" and bishop of Bagnoregio, the summit of his career after he lost the post of assessor in July 1635 to be replaced by Boccabella as substitute for one of the most distinguished assessors, Francesco Albizzi.[158]

It would be nice to say that the assessor's job came open because Boccabella had drawn a richly deserved promotion, but in fact he had been demoted, following the reverse of the normal career, going down to become an auditor of the Rota.[159] Usually even the top-ranking auditor, the dean Giovanni Battista Coccino for example, proudly served as a consultor of the Inquisition.[160] Boccabella's career had gone fast in reverse. Or so it appears. A tiny entry in the Inquisition register in early fall 1633, shortly after Galileo's trial ended, hints at major behind-the-scenes developments. On 20 September, Boccabella was listed among the Inquisitors.[161] Yet another slip by the notary, whom we can almost see nodding off as he wrote up yet another in the interminable parade of attendance lists? Or had he heard an interesting bit of gossip? Although just about anybody could be rumored to be cardinal material, in Boccabella's case, there may be more substance than usual to the diarist Giacinto Gigli's entry recording his death, saying that he would have become a cardinal at the next promotion.[162] And instead of slinking off to the Rota with his tail between his legs, Boccabella continued regularly to attend Inquisition meetings, rising steadily in precedence, coming first among the consultors more than once.[163] It might, therefore, be that his removal as assessor is part of another Barberini illusion, masking yet another trick at Galileo's expense.

However that may be, with either Boccabella's or Febei's appointment as assessor, the Inquisition had become almost completely beholden to the pope, from the top of the professional staff to the Congregation. Six of ten Inquisitors (Antonio and Francesco Barberini, Gessi, Ginetti, Verospi, and Zacchia) were Urban's creatures, and, except for Borja, the other three (Bentivoglio, Felice Centini, and Scaglia) might as well have been.[164]

Galileo Arrives in Rome

After putting it off as long as he could, Galileo reached Rome on the evening of 13 February after a trip of twenty-five days, including a quarantine that Niccolini managed to shorten by two days.[165] The next day Boccabella communicated with Galileo via Niccolini (whether in person or by messenger is unclear, probably the first), "not as a minister of the Holy Office, since it has been sixteen days since he left his post as assessor, but as to a friend." Under pretext of thanking Galileo for "such a good disposition," Boccabella "advised him [Galileo] how he must govern himself, as he had begun to do giving him some notes (*qualche ricordo*)." Niccolini had immediately addressed himself to the new assessor, whom he did not name, and Boccabella apparently tried to see Maculano without success.[166] Maculano's friend Girolamo Matti had already intervened for Galileo with the commissary and offered to continue to do so for the grand duke's sake.[167] Niccolini had, therefore, thought it worthwhile to speak to Matti but had not been able to accomplish anything yet. He also meant to see Francesco Barberini the following morning, seeking permission for Galileo to stay in the embassy.

Niccolini never said any more about Matti, but he did succeed with Cardinal Francesco, via Maculano, provided Galileo remained in close confinement.[168] Maculano also promised to tell the Holy Office about Galileo's willingness to obey. As always stressing that it was almost impossible to learn what the Inquisition was doing, Niccolini still thought there would not be "a great evil," the first of many optimistic prognostications. Francesco Barberini, who did not usually attend congregations on Wednesday (non-corams),

had gone that day, which meant the Congregation had discussed how to proceed.[169] He might, however, have gone because a marriage dispensation for the
duke of Mantua was on the agenda. Niccolini could not confirm that from
Padre Paolo Bombino, the duke's agent, with whom he regularly conferred.[170]

Galileo, too, sounded upbeat in a letter to Cioli of 19 February, slightly
misquoting *Orlando Furioso* to support his point.[171] He was behaving himself
by staying indoors, making this sound as if it were his idea: "one of the lords
of the Congregation [of the Holy Office]" had been to visit him twice, giving
Galileo a chance to insist on his "most sincere and obsequious intention,"
which he thought had gone over well. Niccolini identified him as Ludovico
Serristori (ca. 1600–1656), a Florentine and a consultor. Serristori, whom Galileo had known since at least 1624 and who had been sent a *Dialogue* via
Filippo Magalotti and whom he called in a later letter "my friend and patron
of many years," had almost as odd a preparation for service in the Inquisition
as had Maculano.[172] A lawyer (degree from Pisa), he had made his mark as
vice-legate of Romagna and commissary of its papal army.[173] He held both
posts until named inquisitor of Malta in May 1630, an office he kept until
appearing (irregularly) as a consultor on 10 March 1632, perhaps as part of the
general rearrangement of papal personnel beginning about then.[174] Galileo
interpreted Serristori's visits as authorized (Niccolini agreed) and therefore a
sign of gentle treatment to come "and completely different from the threatened torture, chains, prisons, etc." Niccolini and he had decided to pursue
the same strategy Galileo had already employed by approaching the Capuchin
general, getting letters of recommendation from the grand duke to powerful
men, now Inquisitors Scaglia and Bentivoglio. The grand duke's letters were
both dispatched, unsealed, to Galileo by 24 February.[175] Galileo thought that
to Scaglia had produced the best results one could wish.[176] The Florentines
pushed this approach hard, despite its fatal flaw: it was illegal.[177] This seems to
be another instance where lack of knowledge of how the Inquisition worked
hamstrung a defense.

This blunder might not have counted for much. Galileo made a much
bigger one in his persistent treatment of the precept as insignificant. He did
that for the first time in a letter to Bocchineri of 25 February 1633.[178] The only
thing either he or Castelli knew, wrote Galileo, was that "so many and so
serious charges have been reduced to a single point." Galileo vaunted that he
would have no trouble dealing with it and had already begun a whispering
campaign "with some of these supreme ministers" who could not help but
listen and respond. He expected that once Scaglia and Bentivoglio had their

recommendations from the grand duke, it would be easy to persuade the other Inquisitors. Since he was under house arrest, in effect, Galileo had not been able to deliver the letters to the Capuchin general (but see above) and his *compagno*. His in-law Buonamici had done so in his stead, especially with the second who had been his close friend in the empire. The "general" had also kept a copy of the "Letter to Christina." Ten days later Galileo forwarded the vicar general's reply to Cardinal de' Medici, but the man knew nothing, nor had Buonamici been able to see the general.[179]

Two Lawyers with Access to the Inquisition

Buonamici's (1592–1669) appearance is important, not only for his connections but also for his expertise.[180] A lawyer, Buonamici had pursued a diplomatic career, beginning as secretary of the Florentine legation to Paul V, his tenure perhaps overlapping Niccolini's. After service with the nuncio in Vienna (when he met the Capuchin general's *compagno*), from the mid-1620s he acted as the duke of Neuburg's agent. Buonamici was in Rome now on the duke's behalf.[181] Neuburg wanted an annulment, about which Urban proved even more stubborn than he had with the duke of Mantua, a case that also went to the Inquisition because Neuburg wanted to marry a heretic (that is, a Protestant, which he himself had once been).[182] Buonamici as both a lawyer and a person in direct touch with the Inquisition could have been a useful adviser to Galileo, but he received little more attention than Galileo gave anyone else.

Another Tuscan lawyer could have been even more useful. Niccolò Gherardini (4 March 1607–4 May 1678) was Urban's "nipote cugino" and first cousin of the bishop of Fiesole, Lorenzo Della Robbia, with whom he had apparently come to Rome sometime during the second phase of Galileo's trial.[183] Probably at this time he acted as Della Robbia's vicar general and at an unknown time as auditor of the Tuscan nunciature.[184] After his time in Rome, he tried to retire to the family benefice of S. Margherita a Montici in order to be near Galileo at Arcetri, but was forced to take up legal duties again.[185] According to the "Vita" of Galileo he finished probably in 1654, Gherardini claimed to have been ideally placed to aid Galileo:

> In 1633 I began to deal with Sig. Galileo Galilei since I was staying at that time in the city of Rome, where he was equally found in

order to justify himself against certain accusations . . . and having
some familiarity with one of the principal ministers of the Holy
Office, I offered my effort to help him [Galileo], which truly
could not consist in other than advising him of some particular
suggestions for his governance. I was moved to do this by the
same prelate, who was inclined to withdraw him [Galileo] from an
imminent and too severe mortification, not only by the effective
recommendations made to him by those who protected Sig.
Galileo's case and person, but also to make a counterweight in part
to the evil intention of another personage who had great authority
in that tribunal. Sig. Galileo showed himself to enjoy my offer and
my service; but, either because he thought the subject [the minister]
too weak, or because he suspected some trick, or indeed because he
trusted too much in his innocence, as he said, he showed himself
little amenable to believe some of that prelate's advice, whom I
could not name in order not to break the seal [of secrecy]. Perhaps
Sig. Galileo's hardness in listening to the otherwise helpful advice
came from that silence.[186]

For what it is worth, Gherardini put Galileo's light sentence down to Niccolini.

Gherardini's failure to name his informant has given rise to a good deal of
speculation about his identity, all of it misguided. Since Gherardini described
his acquaintance as a "minister," literally a servant, he could not have been
one of the Inquisitors as Favaro, De Santillana, D'Addio, Fantoli, and others
have thought.[187] Except that Gherardini's man must have been a member of
the professional staff, there is nothing more by which to identify him. I might
speculate that he was a Florentine (Serristori, Corbuzio) or that Gherardini
meant Boccabella, but I do so with all due diffidence.

Galileo apparently never told Niccolini about either of these possible
openings, and the ambassador instead continued to push the recommendation strategy with anyone who would listen "in the manner which the quality
of the tribunal of the Holy Office permits" ("nella maniera che permette la
qualità del Tribunal del S. Offizio").[188] He spelled out what Galileo had tried
to gloss over, that the precept of 1616 posed "the greatest difficulty," giving its
content as an order "not to dispute nor discuss this [Copernicus's] opinion."
Galileo objected to that version, alleging that it said "not to hold or defend,"
which is indeed much closer to its language. It is worth emphasis that he did
not object to the precept itself. It would be easy to defend himself, since his

Dialogue had done neither. Nevertheless, Niccolini thought it would be hard for Galileo to escape being "retained" by the Holy Office.

In a second dispatch of the same day, Niccolini reported an audience with Urban.[189] The first topic, although given short shrift in the published text, held much greater importance than Galileo's case and provides a vital context for it. This was an alliance the pope wanted with the grand duke, nominally against the Turks but really intended to drive the Spanish out of Italy.[190] The plot explains why Francesco Barberini worked so hard to convince the grand duke of Urban's benevolence. He displayed less of that to Galileo. Urban replied to Niccolini's assurance of Galileo's "most devoted, reverent observance" that he had treated Galileo exceptionally well by allowing him to stay with Niccolini, while a cadet of the house of Gonzaga, for example, had been imprisoned in Castel Sant'Angelo.[191] Acknowledging this great favor, Niccolini asked for "expedition" of Galileo's case, as did the grand duke in March.[192] The ambassador's use of the term here and elsewhere is ambiguous enough to leave it unclear whether he meant the pivotal moment of an Inquisition proceeding when a case went to sentence.[193] The pope replied that the Inquisition usually took its time, and a quick expedition was probably unlikely since process was only just being formed. Galileo had been most unwise to publish his opinions, Urban calling that a "ciampolata," which had also contravened an "order" given to him in 1616 by Cardinal Roberto Bellarmino in the name of the Index, a mistake for the Inquisition. (Urban's memory was not entirely reliable.) Besides, the Inquisition could not let Galileo off too easily since it had publicly called him to Rome. Niccolini had as usual next seen Francesco Barberini, again recommending Galileo, since Urban had seem calmer than usual. The cardinal replied that the matter was "delicate," especially since Galileo had spread his ideas in Florence, "where I knew that intellects were rather subtle and curious," that is, given to intellectual novelties.

CHAPTER 7

The End

Divine Omnipotence

In a Sunday audience with the pope on 13 March, Niccolini began with an-other request for "expedition" (*speditione*) of Galileo's case.[1] Urban responded that "calling" (*chiamar*) Galileo to the Holy Office could not be avoided, which must mean that he at least did not take "expedition" in the technical sense. Niccolini and Urban went back and forth several times on this point, Urban refusing to budge. The pope then returned to his usual line about the nature of the case, saying Galileo would have done much better "to go with the common [interpretation of the earth's movement]," before again blaming Ciampoli. Galileo had been the pope's friend, but the matter concerned "faith and religion." Then Urban introduced a new argument, of which a great deal has been made recently[2]: "God is omnipotent and can do everything; if He is omnipotent, why do we want to force him (*necessitarlo*)?"[3] Niccolini admitted that he found himself out of his depth faced with this basic nominalist argu-ment, but tried anyway. If God were omnipotent, then he could also have made the world as it was. This annoyed Urban, who, "heating up," retorted that "necessity ought not to be imposed on blessed God." Seeing the pope's fury (*escandenza*) mounting, Niccolini backed down and reassured Urban that Galileo was in Rome only "to obey, annul, or retract all that could be shown to be of service to religion." Niccolini tried again to have Galileo "habilitated" from confinement, a technical term used by the Inquisition. Galileo heard only part of this report, not including his likely summons before the Holy Office. At the end of his dispatch, Niccolini returned to Galileo's "expedition," repeating what both the pope and Maculano had said, disagreeing among themselves about when that might happen, Urban saying he had no idea,

Maculano "as soon as possible." On the strength of this letter, Andrea Cioli largely capitulated and ordered Niccolini to try to get permission for Galileo to return to Palazzo Firenze for the night while undergoing interrogation.[4]

Niccolini's dispatch had gone by express courier. The reason had nothing to do with Galileo. The grand duke had two more urgent concerns, the fief of Castel del Rio (and Mariano Alidosi) and the troubles of the house of Lorraine, which naturally interested Grand Duchess Mother Christina. Alessandro Paoli correctly inferred that the grand duke once again had other, more important things than Galileo on his mind.[5]

Sheltered from the worst by Niccolini and being fed rosy reports by his Candide, Castelli, Galileo plowed ahead with the strategy of recommendations from the grand duke to the rest of the Inquisitors. Niccolini sent their names.[6] Geri Bocchineri sent them all unsealed to Galileo on 26 March.[7] Though Castelli did not say so, he had reason to be optimistic, as Mario Guiducci explained to Galileo.[8] His evidence was hearsay and recycled from Florence, but it still looked promising. Giovanni Rinuccini, returned from Rome, told Guiducci that "the most eminent lord [a cardinal] that he [Rinuccini] does not name" had been reading the *Dialogue* with Castelli and had begun substantially to change his opinion of it. That change should help "the cause and the truth." It turned out that Rinuccini had after all told Guiducci the man's name, which Guiducci did not repeat. It leaked in Florence, anyway: Desiderio Scaglia.[9] The news that Cardinal Luigi Capponi, in exile from Rome in Florence, was also trying to read the *Dialogue* and thought Copernicus's ideas "not erroneous" caused less excitement.

Galileo may have seized on Capponi nonetheless. If so, Guiducci thought Galileo's suggestion for "that lord" to write "his colleagues" about the *Dialogue* was a bad idea, as did his war council (which included the Florentine reviewer of the *Dialogue* Giacinto Stefani and probably his teacher and eminent Dominican Michele Arrighi). The principal reason Capponi's writing would not help was that he had no standing with the Barberini, nor was it wise to put any more in writing than absolutely necessary. Instead, his *confidentissimo* Francesco Nerli could approach other cardinals in person in Rome.[10] Guiducci understated Capponi's problem. Urban had personally told Capponi to go to his diocese in late 1630 as part of his drive to clean the Spanish out of Rome; he had then left for Naples in company with Cardinal Ludovico Ludovisi and another Spanish cardinal.[11] Capponi remained in close touch with Ludovisi after both were forced out of Rome.[12] In February 1633, the Venetian ambassador called Capponi "the greatest enemy" (*inimicissimo*) of the Barberini over a failed marriage negotiation.[13] Galileo's reach of Roman politics exceeded his grasp.

As March wore into April and the Inquisition did nothing, Galileo's hopes rose. He wrote Guiducci a missing letter in which among other causes for optimism he again cited Scaglia's expected role.[14] Unfortunately, Castelli had to leave Rome at this moment. His departure was Galileo's fault. He sent his disciple back home to Brescia to check on a small pension owing to him.[15] Bocchineri acknowledged another positive letter from Galileo a week later.[16] He also referred to a mysterious writing that Niccolini had given Francesco Barberini. A week later Galileo credited it with having opened his trial.[17]

Niccolini probably presented that writing to Francesco Barberini in an audience to which the cardinal summoned the ambassador on 7 April.[18] Barberini informed him that the Congregation had decided "to the end of expediting Sig. Galileo" (*a fine di spedir il S.or Galileo*) to call him (*chiamar*) to the Holy Office. Since Barberini did not know "whether he could be expedited quickly (lit. "in two hours"; *in due hore lo potessero spedire*), Galileo might have to be retained. Respect for the grand duke demanded that Barberini warn Niccolini. Niccolini went back to his usual refrain about Galileo's health and antiquity and requested that Galileo be allowed to return to Palazzo Firenze in the evening. This seemed unlikely to Barberini, who offered special lodging instead. In an unusual Friday audience with Urban, the pope played his usual tune about the danger Galileo's ideas posed to religion but said nothing else. Galileo was "extremely afflicted" by the news, and Niccolini feared for his life. Finally, Niccolini claimed to have delivered all the recommendations from the grand duke.

Galileo's First Interrogation

Even though it may be no more than a coincidence and nothing to do with Galileo's communication to Francesco Barberini, the second phase of his trial opened on 12 April 1633. Galileo managed to sound upbeat about it, writing Bocchineri that he was lodged in three rooms of the fiscal's suite in Palazzo del Sant'Uffizio and was in good health. It seems that he had not grasped the full implications of undergoing interrogation.[19]

Galileo was summoned to the commissary's rooms, not the hall of examinations as usual, perhaps another sign of favor. Maculano handled the questioning in the presence of Fiscal Carlo Sincero and a notary. After establishing when Galileo arrived in Rome and that he had been cited by the Holy Office, Maculano asked the usual possibly self-incriminating question whether Galileo knew or "imagined" why he had been ordered to Rome. Galileo chose the second option and said the cause "was to give an account of my book recently printed." Then Galileo made his first mistake, misunderstanding Maculano's question whether he would "recognize" his book and giving a sarcastic reply that he hoped he would. Maculano's question was legally required to establish a firm link between author and work, as indicated by his subsequent question whether Galileo recognized all its content as his work. The Congregation had ordered the same questions put to Campanella, for example.[20]

It did not take Maculano long to get to his principal concern. After an almost throw-away question about how long it had taken to write the book, the commissary asked Galileo whether he had been in Rome on other occasions, specifically in 1616. Now Galileo made a serious mistake, unveiling a strategy he followed throughout the interrogation. He lied. This claim may sound harsh or overly critical of Galileo, but I fail to see how to avoid it. His answer: "hearing doubts raised about Nicholas Copernicus's opinion about the earth's movement and the sun's stability and the order of the heavenly spheres, in order to make myself more certain to hold none but holy and Catholic opinions, I came to hear what it was proper to hold about this matter." Galileo in fact went to Rome—against advice—to lobby all and sundry on behalf of Copernicus's ideas.[21] Maculano pressed on. Had Galileo come of his own volition or been summoned? By my choice, replied Galileo, adding "In Rome I dealt with this matter with some lord cardinals of those who were above the Holy Office at that time, in particular with Lord Cardinals Bellarmino, [Agostino] Galamini, [Giovanni Battista] Bonsi, [Ferdinando] Taverna, and [Felice] Centini." Why did you deal with them?" Maculano demanded. Because, averred Galileo, "they wanted to be informed about Copernicus's teaching" and "In particular they wanted to understand the disposition of the heavenly spheres according to Copernicus's hypothesis."

Seizing on the motive Galileo claimed for his visit, Maculano asked what had been decided about Copernicus's book. Galileo once more skated around the truth, making the Index say what Bellarmino had a year earlier in a letter to Paolo Antonio Foscarini.[22] In that letter Bellarmino advised Foscarini (and Galileo) to deal with Copernicus's ideas hypothetically. The Index decree of 5 March 1616 instead suspended the book implicitly as contrary to holy scripture and "Catholic truth." To jumble things further, Galileo continued that Bellarmino had informed him of the Index's decree. The commissary then wanted to know what Bellarmino had said and under what circumstances. Galileo again trotted out the cardinal's letter to Foscarini:

> Lord Cardinal Bellarmino indicated to me that the said opinion
> of Copernicus can be held hypothetically, as that Copernicus had
> held it, and his eminence knew that I held it hypothetically, that
> is, in the manner that Copernicus held it, as is seen from a reply
> by the same lord cardinal made to a letter of Father Master Paolo
> Antonio Foscarini, Carmelite Provincial, of which I have a copy,
> and in which are these words: "I say that it seems to me that your
> paternity and Lord Galileo do prudently to content yourselves to
> speak hypothetically and not absolutely." This letter of the said lord
> cardinal is dated 12 April 1615. Otherwise, that is, taken absolutely,
> it must not be either held, or defended.

This answer did not satisfy Maculano who ordered Galileo to "say what was resolved, and notified to you then, that is, in the month of February 1616." Galileo had not referred to this event, making Maculano's command dangerously close to a violation of the Inquisition's prohibition of leading questions[23]:

> In the month of February 1616 Lord Cardinal Bellarmino told me
> that because Copernicus's opinion taken absolutely was contrary
> to holy scripture, it could not be held nor defended, but it could
> be taken hypothetically, and made use of. In conformity to this,
> I have an affidavit (*fede*) of the same Lord Cardinal Bellarmino
> made in the month of May, on the 26th, 1616, in which he says that
> Copernicus's opinion cannot be held nor defended because it was
> against holy scripture, of which affidavit I present a copy.

Galileo added that he also had the original in Rome with him. Maculano pressed Galileo on the situation in which Bellarmino had notified him, asking who else was present. Galileo remembered some Dominicans, but not their names.

Now Maculano got to the point, with another question perilously close to leading. "In the presence of the said fathers by them or anyone else was any precept given you about the same matter, and [if so,] what?" Galileo's reply and Maculano's follow-up questions deserve to be quoted in full, especially since key elements of them have usually been overlooked or denied.[24]

Galileo: I remember that the business passed in this manner. One morning Lord Cardinal Bellarmino sent to summon me and told me a certain[25] detail that I would like to speak in His Holiness's ear before others, but the conclusion then was that he told me that Copernicus's opinion could not be held nor defended as contrary to holy scripture. I do not remember whether those fathers of St. Dominic were there before or came after, nor do I remember whether they were present when the lord cardinal told me that the said opinion could not be held. It could be that some precept was given to me that I not hold nor defend the said opinion, but I do not remember because this is a matter of some years ago.

Maculano: If what was then said to you and told you with a precept were read to you, will you remember them?

Galileo: I do not remember that anything else was said to me nor can I know whether I would remember what was then said to me, and also when it is read to me, and I say freely what I remember, because I do not claim not to have broken that precept in any way, that is, not to have held nor defended in any way the said opinion of the earth's motion and the sun's stability.

Maculano: Having been told that in the said precept given to you then in the presence of witnesses is contained that you could not in any fashion hold, defend, or teach the said opinion, say only whether you remember "in any fashion," and by whom this was told you.

Galileo: I do not remember that this precept was told to me by others than orally by Lord Cardinal Bellarmino, and I remember that the precept was that I could not hold nor defend, and it could be that there was also nor teach. I also do not remember that there was that detail, in any fashion, but it could be that it was there, since I have not reflected [on the event] or formed another memory, because a few months later I had that affidavit of the said Lord Cardinal Bellarmino

under date of 26 May 1616 presented by me, in which was
indicated the order to me not to hold nor defend the said
opinion. I have not kept a memory of the other two details
now notified to me, that is, nor teach, and in any fashion, I
think because they were not explained in the said affidavit, to
which I referred myself, and held as my memory.

The most important point in this exchange is that Galileo gradually admitted
the precept, finally conceding that he might have received it in the full form
of "nor hold, teach nor defend the same otherwise in any manner in word or
writing," using the term precept three times in the course of his damning answer.[26] Blaming his poor memory and claiming to have relied instead on Bellarmino's *fede* as an explanation of why he had forgotten the precise wording
reduce only a little the impact of his statement that he had received a precept
from Bellarmino. The only important point that Galileo never admitted and
about which Maculano never asked directly was whether Commissary Michelangelo Seghizzi had played a role. Maculano's silence is hard to explain, since
it appears that he had in front of him the full form of the precept, contained
in Galileo's dossier. It spelled out precisely Bellarmino's and Seghizzi's actions.
The other significant point is Galileo's opening wish to whisper something to
the pope. This both betrays a deep lack of comprehension of how the Inquisition worked—heightening the necessity of Galileo's seeking advice about
it—and also reflects Galileo's habit of claiming secret information that can
only have hurt him.

    Having established the precept's reality and content, Maculano turned
to its connection to the imprimatur for the *Dialogue*. Galileo claimed not to
have mentioned the precept because far from defending Copernicus, his book
refuted him. In response to Maculano's question about whether Galileo had
obtained an imprimatur, Galileo gave a reasonably straightforward account of
how he had done so, including the change of printing venue, ascribing that to
the plague without mentioning Federico Cesi's death. He closed with another
stubborn insistence that he had not told Riccardi about the precept because
his book did not defend Copernicus.

    His first interrogation manifests the strategy Galileo followed through
all three of his confrontations with Maculano. He told untruths. Whatever
we think of the rights and wrongs of this struggle, the fact remains that most
of Galileo's versions of the precept until the very last and his explanation of
why he did not tell Riccardi about it do not agree with other sources or with

the manifest content of the *Dialogue*. Almost as serious given how important intention was to establishing degree of heresy, Galileo misrepresented his purpose in coming to Rome in 1615–16. Trying to pull Bellarmino's long shadow over himself was probably the strongest move Galileo made. Unfortunately for him, his citation of Bellarmino's letter to Foscarini has no relevance to what the Index (or his precept) said, and Bellarmino's *fede*, despite its centrality to Galileo's defense, is equally irrelevant to establishing what happened in 1616. On the other side, Maculano's questioning does not offer a model of proper procedure as he often came to the brink—if he did not fall over it—of leading Galileo along. Maculano's approach also reveals the advantage the questioner had over a suspect when it came to catching him in answers that varied from one question to the next. Curiously, Maculano did not take advantage of Galileo's tergiversation. The commissary's actions show a man vaguely aware of how to do his job, which is what we might expect given his lack of solid preparation or at least failure to take advantage of his training.

Niccolini put Galileo's first interrogation in context four days later in his regular weekly dispatch.[27] He at least did not regard it as an urgent matter. The reason may have been that he thought it had gone remarkably well. Maculano had "received him [Galileo] with loving demonstrations" and given him good rooms; Barberini told the ambassador that the commissary "has helped also with the pope in mitigating His Blessedness's animus in an extraordinary way." The rest of Niccolini's letter largely repeated that of 9 April, adding that Guido Bentivoglio had also assured him "that it [the case] will be expedited quickly," as Urban and Francesco Barberini had already told him. Now Niccolini admitted that the grand duke's recommendations might not have worked as well as had been thought, since some of the addressees not only had not responded but "also were doubtful about receiving them, out of fear of falling under the censures." Although Francesco Barberini had accepted his letter, he had refused to tell Niccolini's secretary what was going on, "not even whether he [Barberini] can or cannot speak."

The Consultors Weigh In

Urban spent 16 April to 3 May at Castel Gandolfo.[28] While there he spent most of his time purging and, therefore, did little business.[29] In his absence, Agostino Oreggi, Melchior Inchofer, and Zaccaria Pasqualigo handed in censures on the *Dialogue*.[30] It is not immediately clear in what capacity they did so, especially since Inchofer was not an Inquisition consultor. Even if he were, the threesome could not have acted as consultors at the moment of *expeditio*, since they did not offer a judgment on the evidence assembled in the *summarium*. It is most likely that they constituted a particular congregation that has left no other signs of its existence, unless, as Oreggi's censure suggests, it was somehow a continuation of that of summer 1632 with Pasqualigo taking Riccardi's place. Maculano called it "the congregation about the book" (see below). All three opinions were probably discussed at a congregation of some kind held on 21 April. Oreggi's is the only dated one, 17 April 1633.[31] He rested his brief censure on "the work's whole text [or structure or context; *contextu*] and especially" on the particular congregation's report of summer 1632 which he said he wrote with Riccardi. He concluded that in the *Dialogue* "is held and defended the opinion that teaches the world moves and the sun remains quiet." Nothing was said of teaching.

Only Pasqualigo's opinion spells out the issue he was to consider. It opens by saying he had been asked "whether Sig. Galileo Galilei had violated the precept in publication of his *Dialogues* [sic] in which he treats the Copernican system, by which he was prohibited by the Holy Office to hold, teach, or defend in any way whatsoever in word or writing this opinion of the earth's motion and the sun's stability in the center of the world." The Theatine Pasqualigo was Inquisitor Marzio Ginetti's theologian, which may explain Niccolini's earlier approach to the cardinal (see the last chapter). Trained in both theology and law, he had a distinguished career in his order and published numerous books, some of which got him in trouble with the Index.[32] Like Inchofer, Pasqualigo submitted a censure in two parts, one short, one more detailed. Both answered the question about the precept in the affirmative. The long form established that Galileo had contravened the precept by teaching, defending, and holding Copernicus's ideas.

Inchofer's is by far the most extensive censure. He keyed its second section to the printed *Dialogue*. His conclusion fell between Oreggi's and Pasqualigo's in length and complexity but made the same point: "I judge that Galileo not only taught and defended the sun's stability or quiet as the center of the universe, around which, both the planets and the earth turn with their own motions, but also by his firm adherence to this opinion makes himself vehemently suspect also of holding it." Although he did not mention the precept, Inchofer drew his three points directly from it. As Francesco Berretta in particular has insisted, none of these three censors found Galileo guilty of any explicit heresy.[33] The closest anyone comes is Inchofer's use of the adverb "vehemently." Heliocentrism had not to this point been adjudged a heresy except implicitly in the Index decree of 5 March 1616, which had no juridical or theological force. Nevertheless, as far as the consultors were concerned, both interpretations of the trial, precept and heresy, were solidly in play.

"The Case Is Deformed Forcefully": Maculano Takes a Hand

According to Maculano, on Thursday, 21 April, "the congregation about the book [the *Dialogue*]" ("la Congreg.ne sopra il libro") had met and "it was resolved that in it [the book] the opinion reproved and condemned by the Church is defended and taught and that therefore the author makes himself suspect also of holding it."[34] The commissary for one did not care in the least what the opinion was, nor whether the church had condemned it, as none of the consultors had claimed. He either did not see the consultors' opinions or did not read them carefully, since he said nothing about the precept. Since Urban was in Castel Gandolfo, this meeting could not have been a coram, nor does it appear that the Congregation met on this date. The next entry in the decree register after the coram of 14 April is damaged, but the date seems to be 20 April, the normal Wednesday non-coram. Maculano must, therefore, have meant a meeting of the three consultors alone. Given their judgment, he thought the "the case can more quickly be reduced to a state of expedition," awaiting only Francesco Barberini's orders. (It is worth pointing out that Maculano's letter began with Mariano Alidosi.)

Armed with the consultors' judgment, Maculano said he had visited Galileo twice, most recently the morning of his letter, finding him in great pain on both occasions. Galileo said that Sincero had also been in attendance.[35] Maculano's assurance that "his case will be sped up as soon as possible" ("quanto prima si sbrigherà la sua causa") had seemed the "best medicine" for Galileo. The commissary and fiscal had expressed "the firm intention to expedite me (*spedirmi*) immediately [after] I got out of bed" and told Galileo to cheer up.[36] He did. He probably did not understand what the Inquisition officials meant, since he said "expedite me" instead of "expedite my case." Galileo thought his troubles would shortly have a good outcome; they meant his case was going to the phase of *expeditio* when he would be sentenced.

This moment brings the commissary's strategy into crystal-clear focus. In response to Galileo's evasions and straightforward lies, Maculano gladly replied in kind. He had to have Galileo's confession and could get it by deceit if needed.[37] The nearest thing to an official manual for inquisitors, Nicolau Eymeric's *Directorium Inquisitorum*, written in the fourteenth century and printed nine times between the end of the fifteenth and beginning of the seventeenth centuries, made clear that inquisitors could bamboozle the accused in the interests of justice.[38] Besides, heretics worked overtime on their tricks, so turnabout made fair play. Eymeric discussed ten kinds of heretical skullduggergy followed by a corresponding list of ten "cautions" against them. Countersubterfuge number 5 could serve as a transcript of Maculano's conversation with Galileo.[39] Eymeric suggested that the inquisitor display compassion for the recalcitrant heretic, telling him, "I will expedite you and your case and you will not remain thus a captive since you are in delicate health and can easily become ill." That is exactly what Maculano told Galileo, without revealing that he had already been found guilty.

Even as Maculano tried to outwit Galileo, the Inquisition continued to make extraordinary concessions to him, including allowing letters to Niccolini every day. Most of these have been lost. Even had they not been, they would require careful handling, since Maculano would almost certainly have read them before dispatch.[40] Galileo apparently did not report his visit from Maculano to Niccolini who the next day still knew no more of Galileo's proceedings than his first interrogation.[41] Optimism became the order of the day, Niccolini opining that "this party will land on someone else's head." Once the pope returned from Castel Gandolfo before Ascension (5 May), Galileo would be freed. Niccolini's new attitude arose in part because he was badly informed about what had happened, perhaps by Galileo himself, who still did not realize what he had given away in his first interrogation. As far as the ambassador knew, nothing was asked about the book, and the only point pursued concerned Riccardi's role in issuing the imprimatur. Neither statement is true. No matter how ill informed, Niccolini continued to pursue the strategy of recommendations to powerful cardinals, approaching Antonio Barberini, Jr., the night before the pope left for Castel Gandolfo, probably 15 April.[42] This had been an especially good move, thought Niccolini, because the young cardinal "likes to be esteemed" and "he really acts when he is approached." Niccolini put Maculano's promises down to Antonio Barberini, Jr.'s intervention. Were he right, that would mean the Barberini, beginning with Urban, had formed a united front and left the Inquisition in the shade.

A Negative Heretic

True to his word, on Wednesday, 27 April, Maculano, casting aside Cardinal Francesco's smokescreen and explicitly acting on Urban's orders, referred (reported on) Galileo's case before the Congregation.[43] It approved what he had done thus far and then considered "various difficulties" in the way of expedition, "especially Galileo's denial in his [first] interrogation what manifestly appears in the book composed by him, from which standing in the negative would follow the necessity of greater rigor in justice and less regard to the respects that there are in this business" ("massime havendo il Galileo negato nel suo constituto quello che manifestamente apparisce nel libro da lui composto, onde dallo stare così negativo ne seguirebbe la necessità di maggior rigore nella giustitia e di riguardo minore a gli rispetti che si hanno in questo negotio"). Galileo had made himself a "negative heretic," one who had refused to confess in the face of damning evidence, the penalty for whom after conviction was death, at least according to the *Directorium Inquisitorum* and its commentator and long-time Inquisition consultor Francisco Peña. Such a judgment arose

> when delated for heretical pravity, the merits of the *processo* having been diligently discussed with the good counsel of legal experts, [the defendant] is found to be caught in heresy on the evidence of the fact or the legitimate production of witnesses, not by his own confession . . . although he is thus convicted and caught, he persists firmly in the negative and constantly confesses the holy Catholic faith.[44]

Eymeric gave as illustrations of the *facti evidentia* publicly preaching heresy or the testimony of (unanimous) witnesses, leading himself into a contradiction since preaching provided solid proof.[45] Either made the suspect an impenitent heretic. The treatment was "hard prison" in chains. If despite numerous adjurations to confess he refused, he was to be turned over to the secular arm. Witnesses might be reexamined or sent to reason with the prisoner. If they refused to recant and he to confess, death became inevitable. A change of heart "frequently and very frequently" resulted in mercy. Peña called this practice "most absolute" and Eymeric's opinion "true and common;" his first citation was a Rota decision. He emphasized that conviction of a negative heretic followed not only from his words but from any heretical act.[46] The Rota had applied five conditions, all of which were required *ex principio*. First, the heresy had to be "true and formal." Second, the words used had to be "certain and clear," plainly manifesting a dichotomy between them and Catholic belief. Third, the witnesses had to be beyond exception (above reproach). Fourth, the fact or speech had to be recent. Finally, the suspect had to have asserted the contrary, apparently meaning continued belief in Catholic doctrine.[47] On the other hand, long-time assessor Albizzi claimed that he had never seen a negative heretic convicted, despite Rota decision 875.[48]

Admitting that politics had thus far played a large role in Galileo's trial, Maculano faced the necessity of following the Inquisition's procedure and the trouble that would mean for Galileo. He therefore proposed as a way of avoiding "the greater rigor of justice" that the Congregation grant him authority (*facoltà*) to deal with Galileo extrajudicially "to the end of making him aware of his error and reduce him to the point when he recognizes it of confessing it" ("a fine di renderlo capace dell'error suo e redurlo a termine, quando lo conosca, di confessarlo"). The plan to convince Galileo with "reasons" met resistance until Maculano told the Congregation "the foundation" that had brought him to make his proposal. If by "foundation" he meant the danger to a "negative heretic," then his extrajudicial move appeared to pervert the course of justice. That very evening after dinner, the commissary had started in with Galileo and "after many, many arguments and replies," he made Galileo "touch his error with his hand" and recognize that he had made a mistake. Galileo acted as if he were "most consoled" and "was disposed to confess it [his error] judicially." He asked time "to make his confession honest" ("honestare la confessione"), which Maculano thought would go in "the manner as below" ("maniera soddetta") which he did not give.

Maculano had immediately reported to Francesco Barberini without telling anyone else so that the cardinal and the pope would be "satisfied" by the plan to bring the case to expedition "without difficulty": "The tribunal [of the Inquisition] will keep its reputation, kindness can be used with the suspect/ convict (*reo*), and in whatever manner expedited, he [Galileo] will know the grace that will have been done to him" ("Il Tribunale sarà nella sua reputatione, co'l reo si potrà usare benignità, e in ogni modo che si spedisca, conoscerà la gratia che li sarà fatta"). Maculano meant to examine Galileo that day about his intention and "give him his defenses."[49] "That done, he can be habilitated to his house as prison." Maculano's dismissal of a defense as formulaic violated the Inquisition's rules, if not its practice.[50] The commissary said nothing of a sentence, which may mean he intended his plan to spare Galileo abjuration.[51] Such a lenient outcome does not square well with Maculano's handling of

Galileo as a negative heretic nor with one possible consequence of an extrajudicial confession, as we shall see.

The move Maculano proposed was extrajudicial in all senses of the word, including leaving no trace in the decree register. The Inquisition often resorted to this tactic, including in a proceeding not unlike Galileo's, that of his fellow Florentine Girolamo Vecchietti.[52] In Galileo's case, the tactic was more than usually extrajudicial, since Maculano by not mentioning the precept ignored the entire course of the trial to that point. His failure to spell out the "foundation" behind his suggestion left the door open to speculation that he meant Urban's desire to avoid torturing Galileo while keeping him locked up.[53] If so, Urban changed his mind quickly since it was he who would decree a final interrogation under threat of torture.

The same day as Maculano broached his plan, an unexpected event transpired that could have worked against Galileo. Felice Centini, an Inquisitor since 1611 but in exile in Macerata for most of the time since 1618 except for a year in 1625–1626 and another interval in 1628, arrived in Rome and immediately went to Castel Gandolfo to see the pope. He came about the case of his nephew Giacinto Centini, in trouble for trying to kill Urban by black magic.[54] (Urban's handling of that case sheds a great deal of light on how he dealt with Galileo, especially in his complete disregard of the Inquisition's rules and procedures.)[55] More important, Centini was the only Inquisitor who could have impeached Galileo's testimony about what had happened in 1615–16. He attended most congregations through 16 March 1634, although not that of 16 June when Galileo's sentence was proposed. His absence does not mean that he could not have spoken to his fellow Inquisitors or members of the Inquisition's staff at other times.[56] He did attend Galileo's formal sentencing and abjuration on 22 March.[57]

Galileo's Second Interrogation

On 30 April 1633, Galileo appeared for interrogation as envisioned in Maculano's plan.[58] Maculano opened by acceding to Galileo's wish to be heard. Now Galileo finally realized the precept's importance, even though Maculano seemingly did not. He began by saying he had reflected "for many days" about his first interrogation "in particular about whether I was given a prohibition sixteen years ago by order of the Holy Office not to hold, defend or teach in any way whatsoever the opinion—indeed then condemned—of the earth's mobility and sun's stability." It occurred him to reread the *Dialogue* "in order diligently to observe whether, against my most pure intention through my inadvertence there came out of my pen a thing through which the reader or superiors could argue in me not only some stain of disobedience, but also other details through which one could form an idea of me breaking the Holy Church's orders." The book seemed written by somebody else, said Galileo. Nonetheless, he was prepared to make his confession:

> *I[59] freely confess that it* [the book] *presented itself to me in many*
> *places drawn out in such form that a reader not conscious of my*
> *innermost thoughts would have had cause to form an idea that the*
> *arguments brought for the false part* and that I intended to refute
> were pronounced in such appearance that, for their effectiveness,
> they were rather powerful to constrain [that is, they worked as
> proof] than easy to be dissolved, and two in particular, one about
> sunspots, and the other about the flux and reflux of the sea truly
> come to the reader's ears with strong attributes and powerfully
> reinforced more than might appear proper to one who holds
> them for inconclusive and who wished to refute them, as I indeed
> internally and truly thought and think them inconclusive and to be
> refuted.

Several points emerge forcefully from this passage. First is Galileo's concern with his intention. Not new to his broader defense, it suggests here that Galileo had learned of its significance in a heresy proceeding. Second, the two points on which Galileo thought he had particularly offended raise several problems. That he was prepared to give them up must mean that the seriousness of his situation had dawned on him. It would have pained him greatly to abandon what he regarded as his best proofs of the earth's motion. Would he have hit on his failures by himself? If not, where did he get them? The argument about the tides is easier to track down. Urban had objected to it when the *Dialogue* manuscript was undergoing vetting in Rome, and the particular congregation had twice made it one of the charges against Galileo.[60] Galileo could have remembered Urban's reservations, or Maculano could have leaked part of the congregation's report. Sunspots, on the other hand, despite being the origin of the Inquisition's interest in Galileo, did not appear there. Did Maculano make good use of Galileo's dossier and dig out the censures of February 1616? But Galileo did not give as much ground as might at first appear. After all this, he doggedly stuck to his insistence that he had not meant his book to defend Copernican ideas.

Galileo blamed his mistake on love of glory, quoting Cicero. (Even in so serious a situation, he could not resist a rhetorical move.) "It is therefore my error, and I confess it, of vain ambition and pure ignorance and inadvertence." And that was that; the interrogation ended. Or almost. After a bit, Galileo came back—too late—with an offer he must have invented himself. Given the chance, he would take the opportunity built into the *Dialogue* and add a day or two in order to revisit "the arguments already brought up in favor of the false and condemned opinion and refute them in a more effective manner." His initial confession seems to have been forgotten.

Maculano still thought he had what he needed. As soon as the interrogation ended, he allegedly talked to Urban ("facto prius verbo cum Sanctissimo").[61] This may be a formula and does not mean that Maculano literally got on his horse and galloped the sixteen miles to Castel Gandolfo.[62] Still, a courier must have made an express round trip. Alleging his motive as Galileo's poor health and great age, with the pope's agreement Maculano ordered Galileo "habilitated" to the Florentine embassy "in place of prison," not to communicate with anyone beyond the "familiars and domestics of that palazzo," and "to present himself in the Holy Office whenever it was required under penalty at the will (*arbitrio*) of the Holy Congregation." Three witnesses, all officials of the Inquisition, appended their signatures in order to testify to Galileo's promise to obey what at the end was identified as a precept. Its text was standard form.[63]

Niccolini told a different story the next day in his usual Sunday dispatch to Florence.[64] Galileo had appeared unexpectedly the previous day, his "exam" not being finished. Maculano had approached Francesco Barberini, who released him on his own authority without the Congregation. "The same father commissary intends to intervene so that this case is put to an examination and silence is imposed."[65] Niccolini's claim about Cardinal Francesco directly contradicts Maculano's official record of this moment. The ambassador's source seems likely to have been Galileo, perhaps drawing on information from Maculano who wished to mask the pope's role. Or Francesco may himself have intervened in a missing document in order to burnish his reputation. Niccolini repeated the same information in another letter to Cioli of 3 May, adding more praise of Maculano "continuing in this business to do all the pleasing things possible and to show himself most well inclined to this most serene [grand ducal] house" ("continuando verso questo negozio di farci tutti i piaceri possibili et di mostrarsi benissimo inclinato verso cotesta Ser.ma Casa").[66]

Urban may not have been in a good mood when he considered Maculano's request. He had not had a good purge because of the weather and instead celebrated mass every day at a nearby church, probably San Tommaso de Villanova.[67] Still, he may have been better inclined to Galileo than he had been recently, since it was rumored that he was about to come to terms with the Florentines, even without an agreement about artillery in Urbino.[68]

Maculano's solution to Galileo's stubbornness produced two unexpected results. First, the grand duke planned to cut off Galileo's support within a month.[69] Second, Clemente Egidi, inquisitor of Florence, tried to quit, alleging that he had to return home "for domestic matters." The Congregation denied his request on 19 May.[70] As an extra complication, Francesco Barberini as prefect of the congregation of health ordered a new quarantine of Florence.[71]

Galileo's Defense

Following his plan and still acting without the Congregation's knowledge or approval, on 10 May Maculano summoned Galileo and assigned him eight days to prepare his defense.[72] Instead of taking advantage of that fairly standard interval, Galileo immediately handed Maculano the original of Bellarmino's *fede* as his sole defense "to show the sincerity and purity of my intention [and] not indeed to excuse my having exceeded in some part."[73] Despite there being no note of it in the act, Galileo also handed in a memorandum in his defense.[74] It mainly responded to the last question in his first interrogation (Galileo mistakenly called it an "interrogatory," the word for the list of questions to be put to witnesses in the *repetitio* of an Inquisition trial), whether he had told Riccardi about the "command" of 1616 when seeking the imprimatur for the *Dialogue*. Galileo blamed Maculano for not having further interrogated him about why he had not. "Now it seems necessary to me to say it in order to demonstrate my most pure mind [or intention], always opposed to using dissimulation or fraud in any of my actions," in the last clause rejecting the particular congregation's allegation that would reappear in his sentence. Galileo's rebuttal rested on Bellarmino's *fede*, amplifying a claim he had made in his first interrogation, that it said only "that one could not hold nor defend the teaching attributed to Copernicus of the earth's mobility and the sun's stability, etc.," which was a "general pronouncement concerning everybody." Galileo meant to refer to the Index's decree suspending Copernicus's book. Since Galileo kept the *fede*, he claimed he had forgotten the other two points in the precept that it did not include, "'in any way whatsoever teach,' [evidently separating "in any way whatsoever" and "teach"] which I hear are contained in the command given to me and registered, have come to me as most new and unheard." Galileo hammered on his point:

> I do not believe that I ought not to be trusted that in the course
> of fourteen or sixteen years I had lost all memory, especially since
> I had no need to reflect upon it in any way, having thus the valid
> reminder in writing. Now, when the said two details are removed,
> and only the two noted in the present affidavit are retained, there
> is no point in doubting that the command given in it is the same
> precept given in the Sacred Congregation of the Index's decree.

Galileo then repeated his claim in his second interrogation that he had not intended to violate any order and had acted solely out of "vain ambition," which failing, "I will promptly repay and emend with all possible effort whenever I am either commanded or allowed by these most eminent lords." After pleading health and age, Galileo closed with one last reference to Bellarmino in defense of his "honor and reputation."

The content of this memorandum is virtually identical to that of Galileo's second interrogation in which he was supposed to confess according to Maculano's plan. In neither did he admit to any error in the *Dialogue*. Instead, as he gradually had over the course of his first interrogation, Galileo concentrated on the precept and its relation to the imprimatur, thereby failing to comply with Maculano's scheme. The extrajudicial phase of Galileo's trial had not saved him. Galileo's lack of effort to mount a serious defense is a large part of the reason. The common assertion that he prepared his defense carefully is one of the most misleading claims about his trial.[75] The document Antonio Favaro titled accurately "Per la licenza di stampa del *Dialogo dei Massimi Sistemi*" and suppositiously dated 1633 probably has nothing to do with the trial, as Favaro supposed.[76] The latest text cited in it is probably Riccardi's letter of 24 May 1631, which makes it more likely to be a summary of the negotiations over the imprimatur designed to force the master's hand.

The Final Expedition

Five days after Galileo's defense, Niccolini wrote that his "case for now has not received expedition" ("la sua causa non riceve per ancora speditione").[77] Part of the reason may have been that Urban had spent the previous week purging.[78] Galileo remained optimistic about a "quick and happy expedition," as Mario Guiducci concluded from a missing letter a week later.[79] He was almost right about the quick part. The next day Niccolini, writing hurriedly, said he had lost no time since his audience with Urban the previous day.[80] Both Urban and Francesco Barberini had assured him that Galileo's case "will be terminated" in the Inquisition's second coram in eight days, apparently meaning on 26 May.[81] The only solid date to emerge for this event is 9 June, again coming from Urban, on which day the Congregation failed to decree expedition.[82] Niccolini feared that the *Dialogue* would be prohibited unless Galileo were allowed to write an *apologia* for it, as Galileo had proposed in his second interrogation and defense. He would also have to suffer some "salutary penance" for having violated "the orders of 1616 given him by Cardinal Bellarmino." Niccolini was breaking the news to Galileo slowly.

In fact things did not move as quickly as the pope and Cardinal Francesco had promised. The next action the Congregation took—leaving no trace in the decree register—was to agree to Niccolini's request to Maculano to allow a "habilitation" of Galileo to Villa Medici for exercise.[83] The Congregation last met on the 24th, another meeting in a string from 12 May to 14 July not attended by Francesco Barberini, to whom Maculano had made the same request "particularly," as he informed Niccolini. The interval between the meeting and Niccolini's dispatch may mean that the Congregation was not involved at all, despite Maculano's claim. However that may be, the news of its putative action went to Florence by *staffetta*.[84]

The *Summarium*

Sometime before 16 June, someone, probably Assessor Pietro Paolo Febei, drew up the *summarium* of Galileo's case, the document on which the Congregation rested its judgment.[85] Beretta claims the Inquisition's notary "in all probability" drew up the sentence, following Maculano's direction, he in turn following orders from his Barberini superiors.[86] The object was to "manipulate" the whole *processo* in order to exculpate Riccardi.[87] Beretta's interpretation does not agree with at least one anonymous inquisitorial manual in BAV, Barb. lat. 1502, which said it was the assessor's job to draft the sentence at the commissary's instruction.[88] It is often said that whoever wrote this "indictment" slanted it strongly against Galileo.[89] This claim both lacks much support in the text except for one distorted statement near the beginning and a passage substantially rewritten from its original shortly thereafter and also overlooks a number of places where the bias tilts in Galileo's favor. Working from the front of Galileo's dossier, the *summarium* begins with Niccolò Lorini's letter of February 1616, covering a copy of Galileo's "Letter to Castelli." The summary is accurate enough except for the conclusion of Lorini's letter.[90] Where he had written "the occasion of this writing was one or two public readings made in our church of Santa Maria Novella by Father Master Tommaso Caccini," the *summarium* has instead "such writing was made *deliberately to contradict* certain lectures given in the church of Santa Maria Novella by Father Master Caccini."[91]

There follows the only original section of the *summarium* and the other place where it departs from its sources. Instead of the three propositions censured in the consultor's report of 1616 on the "Letter to Castelli," all to do with scripture, none of them serious, come five propositions, only two of them in the censure. The first is a near-quotation from the "Letter" ("there are many propositions found in holy scripture that are false as to the plain sense of the words," where the letter read "in the scripture there are many false propositions as far as the plain sense of the words"), followed by two more complaints about Galileo's handling of scripture, both also nearly exact quotations: "That in natural disputes it should be reserved to the last place" and "That scripture in order to adjust itself to the people's incapacity did not refrain from perverting some of its principal dogmas." The fourth point makes the blanket claim that "In a certain way he wants philosophical to prevail over sacred argument in natural things," which is not found in precisely that form in the "Letter," before this passage concludes with the fifth assertion, Galileo's contention that Joshua addressed his command to stop to the Primum Mobile, not the sun. The oddity here is not so much the substance of the propositions as it is the origin of those not in the consultor's report of 1616. All five are underlined in the copy of the "Letter" in Galileo's dossier, but there is no way to say when that might have happened.

Next came a brief resumé of Tommaso Caccini's deposition, reducing its substance to two points: "That God is an accident," etc., and "miracles that are said to be done by saints are not real miracles." The testimony of witnesses

Caccini had named led to the deduction "that the said propositions were not [made] assertively by Galileo or his disciples but only disputatively."[92] This is a point where it could well be said that the *summarium* slanted in Galileo's favor, since not only did it properly neutralize part of Caccini's testimony, but he had also given other damaging evidence it omitted.

Next came the heart of the *summarium. Sunspot Letters* and the consultor's opinion [of 24 February 1616] accurately quoted that "The sun is the center of the world and completely immobile by local motion" and "The earth is not the center of the world, and completely moves according to itself, even with daily motion." Both statements were philosophically absurd, while the first was "formally heretical" and the second "at least mistaken in faith." The *summarium* linked the censure to Paul V's order of 25 February and its execution the next day, both given in summary except for a truncated quotation of the precept: "Its tenor is that 'he abandon the said opinion, nor hold it in any way whatsoever, nor teach or defend [it], otherwise he would be proceeded against in the Holy Office'." The precept minute read that "he completely give up [or abandon] the abovesaid opinion . . . nor hold, teach or defend the same otherwise in any manner in word or writing; otherwise he will be proceeded against in the Holy Office."[93] Leaving out "the same otherwise in any manner in word or writing" could only have worked to Galileo's benefit.

The narrative then jumps to 1630 and Galileo's effort to secure the imprimatur from Riccardi. The account is again compressed, but does no violence to the documents it summarizes except to say that Riccardi "considered the book and found that Galileo had violated the orders and the precept given him by moving away from hypothesis," when Riccardi never said anything about the precept beyond noting its discovery as the *summarium* shortly admits.[94] This passage also does Galileo the enormous favor of omitting the claim that he acted fraudulently when concealing the precept from Ricccardi. Without mentioning the particular congregation's report, the *summarium* noted Urban's order of 23 September citing Galileo under precept to Rome.

A precis of Galileo's first interrogation follows, accurately enough interpolating into Galileo's standard defense of weak memory the statement "He confesses the precept, but rel[ies] on that affidavit [Bellarmino's], in which the words 'in any way teach' are not registered."[95] A brief capsule of how the *Dialogue* came to be printed in Florence is succeeded by an accurate version of Galileo's statement that "In asking the said license, he kept the said precept quiet from the master of the sacred palace, thinking it was not necessary to tell him about it, not having with his said book held or defended the opinion of the sun's stability and the earth's mobility, indeed in it he showed the contrary, and that Copernicus's reasons were invalid."[96] Marked "30 April," the *summarium* quotes almost all of Galileo's interrogation of that date when he was supposed to confess according to Maculano's plan. Galileo's defense is summarized in three paragraphs beginning with his presentation of the original of Bellarmino's *fede*, his weak memory and his age and poor health.

All in all, a succinct and mainly level-headed account of some of the evidence against Galileo, which if anything works to his advantage. The material mainly comes from the "Letter to Castelli," the censures on *Sunspot Letters*, and Galileo's own testimony. The most damaging hostile deposition, Caccini's, receives cursory treatment and other testimony discredits what little evidence from it made it into the *summarium*. Only two statements do not adhere closely to their originals among the documents in Galileo's dossier: the rewritten conclusion of Lorini's letter and the five propositions drawn from the "Letter to Castelli." The first point might have damaged Galileo by assigning him a hostile intent, which, even so, could not have materially exacerbated his offense. The five propositions altered from those in the consultor's report mark the only significant irregularity and might have harmed Galileo more seriously. Otherwise, the few other even marginally significant changes are the truncation of the precept and the assignment to Riccardi of responsibility for deciding that Galileo had violated it. The first of these helps Galileo, the second Riccardi. The precept holds the *summarium* together, agreeing perfectly with most of the course of Galileo's trial.

The Trial Moves to Sentence

After referring properly to the reporting of Galileo's case (including implicitly the *summarium*), together with the required consultors' opinions on it, in the coram of 16 June 1633 attended by six of the ten Inquisitors (Bentivoglio, Scaglia, A. Barberini, Gessi, Verospi, and Ginetti), Urban proposed Galileo's sentence.[97] He did this at an unusual moment, as the last act of the congregation's secret session, before the consultors entered.[98] Ordinarily, sentences were handed down at the end of the entire meeting. Before passing judgment, Urban ordered one more interrogation under threat of torture. If Galileo sustained it ("si sustinuerit"), meaning continued to refuse to confess, he was to abjure vehement suspicion of heresy, "be condemned to prison at the Sacred Congregation's discretion," and "enjoined" not to deal "in any way" with the earth's movement under pain of treatment as a relapsed heretic, that is, sentenced to death.[99] The *Dialogue* was to be prohibited and in a major departure from procedure copies of the sentence were to be sent to all nuncios and inquisitors "who will publicly read the sentence in a full congregation assembled of many professors of the mathematical art." Urban did not order the copies of the sentence returned (nor did Antonio Barberini, Sr., when transmitting the papal will), and most remained where they had been sent.[100]

Now that the trial was moving again, it went fast. Niccolini had another Sunday audience with Urban in which he again sought expedition.[101] The pope replied that it was done and that Galileo would be summoned one morning next week to hear sentence. Niccolini begged for mercy in the grand duke's name, to which Urban responded that there was no need, since he already had already given Galileo "every habilitation" (*habilità*) and could do no less than to prohibit "that opinion" as contrary to scripture. As for Galileo, he would, as ordinarily happened, remain imprisoned in Rome for some time for having "contravened the orders that he had since 1616." Urban thus combined both interpretations of the trial, just as the sentence would. Once it was published, they could negotiate about how to mitigate it, but some "personal demonstration" was required. To Niccolini's old song about Galileo's condition, the pope could say only that he had to be confined in "some convent," Santa Croce in Florence, for example (which happened to be the headquarters of the Florentine inquisition). For now, Urban alleged, a tiny bit disingenuously, that he could not say what the Congregation might do, "which all united, no one disagreeing, walked in these senses of [treating] Galileo as a penitent" ("la qual tutta unitamente et nemine discrepante caminava in questi sensi del penitenziario"). Niccolini had told Galileo only of the expedition and prohibition of the *Dialogue*, in part because Urban had ordered him not to disturb Galileo further. This declaration, too, rings a little false in light of Urban's recent wish to threaten Galileo with torture.

On the evening of Monday, 20 June, Galileo was summoned to appear before the Holy Office the next morning.[102] There he gave his final deposition.[103] It followed almost exactly the formula in Eliseo Masini's *Sacro Arsenale* for an examination under torture "sopra il fatto" (on the fact) combined with that "sopra l'intenzione solamente" ("solely on intention").[104] Maculano began by asking whether Galileo had anything to say "spontaneously." Galileo replied "I have nothing whatever to say." Maculano then asked whether he had ever held heliocentric views. Basing himself on the Index's decree and the precept, Galileo said he had abandoned his undecided position and adopted

"Ptolemy's most true and undoubted opinion." Accused on the strength of his book of holding the opposite, Galileo insisted that he meant his book to lay out "the natural and astronomical reasons that can be produced for one side and the other," and did not therefore think he "held the condemned opinion after the superiors' determination." Taxed again with holding Copernican ideas and threatened with "the remedies of the law, and suitable things of fact" ("devenietur contra ipsum ad remedia Iuris, et facti opportuna," which is almost the exact phrase in Masini), Galileo bluntly claimed, "I do not hold nor have I held this opinion of Copernicus's after I was told with a precept that I should abandon it." Then explicitly threatened with torture, Galileo gave the same answer. Maculano gave up. If Urban had really hoped to get evidence about Galileo's intention, he failed miserably.

Torture

Despite Emil Wohlwill's best efforts, not many historians ever thought Galileo was tortured, rather than threatened with torture, and almost none do now.[105] This consensus is not terribly well grounded, since, except for Wohlwill's book and Léon Garzend's largely ignored discussion, the question has received little attention, and the examination *sopra intenzione* has been misunderstood. As Jules Speller establishes on the basis of the manuals, that examination did not seek the suspect's reasons for his actions but rather to establish "beliefs that are wrong or impious insofar as they are contrary to the faith of the Church and are voluntarily and obstinately held."[106] As we have seen, intention is the critical variable in establishing degree of heresy, even though in Galileo's case Urban already knew what it was before ordering the final examination. Speller also critiques Garzend's argument that Galileo could not have been tortured, largely on the grounds of age and ill health.[107] Commentary on both points is more ambiguous than Speller makes it appear. One of his favorite sources, Francesco Bordoni, whose book appeared after Galileo's trial and may not have had much status, said "old and weak sixty-year olds *at the judgment of the inquisitor* cannot be tortured, [but] they can be terrified as the doctors say."[108] Speller overlooks the italicized qualification, nor does he note that the only source Bordoni adduced, the more authoritative Antonino Diana, consultor of the Sicilian inquisition, said old people were not to be tortured but added that age was not measured chronologically, leaving the judgment based on numerous other factors up to the inquisitor; nor did he cite any sources, leaving

Bordoni's "doctors" unidentified.[109] Peña noted that the numerous exceptions to torture in other crimes, including age, did not apply in heresy cases, offering an analogy to torture in treason trials, before concluding that most exceptions, including age, did, after all, still apply.[110]

While Urban's decree had made clear that he meant torture, the sentence by contrast speaks of a "rigorous examination" (which Galileo had passed with flying colors.) One of the first to claim that a "rigorous examination" did not mean torture was Philip Gilbert in 1877 working from Eymeric, Peña, Bordoni, Cesare Carena, and Diana.[111] Most recently, Speller makes the same point.[112] Neither Gilbert nor Speller consider Masini's explicit statement that "it is necessary in order to have the truth to come against him [a negative heretic] to a rigorous examination, torture being precisely invented in order to supply the defects of the witnesses, when they [inquisitors] cannot bring complete proof against the the suspect."[113] Masini justified torture by the necessity of securing a confession in order to save the heretic's soul. When discussing the examination *sopra intenzione* Masini adhered to the same line, spelling out that he meant torture, not the threat thereof, was to be applied to the suspect about his "mala Credulità" (bad belief).[114] His description of the scene also omits any threat of torture, as the suspect is taken from the usual site of interrogation directly to the torture chamber.[115] The "Avvertimenti per formare le sentenze nel Tribunale del S. Offizio" flatly defined "esamine rigoroso" as torture.[116] So did Scaglia.[117] Diana agreed that a suspect who was either convicted of or confessed to heretical acts or words was to be tortured.[118]

Masini's prescription exactly fits Galileo's case. Other commentators gave other reasons why he would have qualified for torture. One of the most interesting takes us back to Maculano's extrajudicial move, which it casts in a yet harsher light. This is the claim that an extrajudicial confession opened a suspect to torture. Diana was especially clear beginning from his opening list of the conditions allowing torture, which included such a confession.[119] He spelled out that "an extrajudicial confession suffices for inquisitors to be able to torture a suspect, because it is not to be believed that anyone would falsely impose a crime on himself." Whittling down Pietro Follerio's fourteen requisites, Diana thought such a confession had four: it had to be "verisimilar," "done seriously, not jokingly or out of anger," "specific not general as to place and time," and "proved by the testimony of two witnesses."[120] Like Masini, Diana explained the necessity of a forced confession in circumstances like Galileo's: "When the crime is vehemently evidenced and the accused denies [it], the inquisitors cannot punish him by some extraordinary punishment, but they must torture him and elicit the truth," a principle supported by Roman law. This was "especially [the case] in the Inquisition's tribunal, in which not so much punishment of the *reo* as his improvement is intended, which is obtained once the truth is confessed."[121] Bordoni, Carena, and Peña all agreed with Diana.[122]

The *Repertorium inquisitorum* added an important qualification. Any decision to torture should involve an advocate, a point Peña also made forcefully.[123] Diana added that the defendant must get a copy of the evidence and time to mount a defense before torture, following Spanish practice.[124] Scaglia's "Prattica" demanded the *repetitio* before torture.[125] Galileo did not have an attorney and may not have received the written information against him.

Thus torture (or threat thereof) in Galileo's trial was handled irregularly for either of two reasons. As the commentary makes clear, he should have been tortured, not merely threatened with it, and, if he were, at least two safeguards should have been in place. Orio Giacchi came closest to being right about the lack of torture as the only serious irregularity in Galileo's trial, that is, except for the missing *repetitio*.[126] Urban may after all have gone easier on Galileo than the law demanded.

Sentence

In any case, the result of Galileo's final deposition hardly mattered, since Urban had already proposed his sentence. In its meeting the next day, the Congregation duly approved it, finding Galileo "vehemently suspected of heresy."[127] Even though sentences apparently varied widely in form, Galileo's conforms well to the sketch offered in "Avvertimenti per formare le sentenze nel Tribunale del S. Offizio."[128] It began with a narrative of the case based on Galileo's *processo* designed to spell out his crimes. This should have followed the *summarium*, but instead it adds a great deal of detail not to be found in it, for example, two points drawn directly from Caccini's deposition about Galileo's "disciples" and his correspondence with Germany. Next came the two propositions from *Sunspot Letters* followed by the precept and its administration, giving its text in the strongest form: "you must completely leave the said false opinion, and that in the future you could not hold, nor defend, nor teach it in any way whatsoever, not orally nor in writing." The Index's decree against Copernicus was also mentioned.

Skipping over the *summarium*'s treatment of the imprimatur for the *Dialogue*, the sentence said "in it [the book] was found expressly the violation of the said precept that was given to you" by defending "the said, already condemned, opinion [of the earth's motion and the sun's "stability"]" which was "a most serious error, since an opinion declared and defined as contrary to divine scripture can in no way be probable."

The next section summarized Galileo's interrogations, which the "Avvertimenti" did not consider necessary. It also again did not follow the order of the *summarium*, skipping from his opening "recognition" of the *Dialogue* to his concealment of the precept from Riccardi and, for good measure, adding to the time of writing "after you were given the precept." His admission to ambition and vainglory deserved mention before the most accurate part of the sentence, the precis of Galileo's defense, which is also its longest section. Its most significant move is to take Bellarmino's affidavit as confirmation of Galileo's guilt, linking it to "the license [the imprimatur] you fraudulently and hotly extorted." The narrative ended with Galileo's inconclusive "rigorous examination," with a careful note that he had answered "without prejudice to any of the things you [Galileo] confessed." As Diana explained, this *clausula* was required when torturing a suspect over intention since, if he continued as a *negativus*, that "purges all proofs." With the *clausula* added, he would be subject to "ordinary punishment" whatever he said or did not.[129]

The narrative and list of crimes omitted three points considered essential by the "Avvertimenti." (1) It lacked any claim of Galileo's *mala fama*.[130] (2) Nor did it describe his imprisonment, perhaps because technically speaking he had not been imprisoned. (3) More important, it did not say that the decision to threaten Galileo with torture had been done on the strength of consultors' opinions. A fourth point might be added, the necessity of providing circumstantial detail about the crime. Nowhere in Galileo's dossier apart from Pasqualigo's and Inchofer's censure on the book are any passages from the *Dialogue* quoted as evidence.

The sentence itself made Galileo guilty "of being vehemently suspected of heresy, that is, of holding and believing doctrine false and contrary to the sacred and divine scriptures, that the sun is the center of the earth [or in most texts, "world"] and that it does not move from east to west, and that the earth moves and is not the center of the world and that an opinion can be held and defended as probable after it has been declared and defined as contrary to holy scripture." His punishment was suppression of the *Dialogue*, imprisonment, and recital of the seven penitential Psalms once a week. As usual, the sentence ended with the reservation to the Congregation of the right to modify it in any way at any time.[131]

Interpreting the Sentence

While we can safely leave on one side the dispute about its theological significance and relation to the papal magisterium, Galileo's sentence still poses difficulties of interpretation, including its textual status.[132] Beretta has brought out a number of these, from the question of authorship (see above) to the document's unusual use, its widespread diffusion to inquisitors and nuncios (see below).[133] Much of the the commentary on the sentence, including Beretta's, descends ultimately from Garzend. He originally floated the theory that Galileo's condemnation rested on disciplinary grounds.[134] While allowing that the sentence had doctrinal aspects, Garzend insisted it did not concern the faith.[135] More recently, Mario D'Addio has argued vociferously for the sentence as "exquisitely" disciplinary, seconded by Bruno Neveu and Pierre-Noël Mayaud, while Speller has been about the stoutest critic of that thesis.[136]

The single biggest problem in making sense of his sentence is that Galileo was convicted of suspicion of a heresy that did not exist, nor do we know officially what Urban thought the heresy was, except by implication from the "injunction" included in the proposed sentence.[137] The closest heliocentrism had previously come to condemnation was in the consultors' opinions on *Sunspot Letters*, but those opinions had never been formally endorsed by the Congregation, much less the pope. The only possible way to make them into a properly condemned heresy might go through the precept, but there is no precedent so far as I know for using them, even in full judicial form, to such an end. Beretta argues plausibly that the sentence depended for its doctrinal content on the Index's decree against Copernicus.[138] It is also odd that, after all the stress on Galileo's violation of the precept right through the narrative in the sentence, it did not enter into his conviction, even though contravention of it could easily have been treated as a crime in itself (see Chapter 4). Niccolini certainly thought that Galileo was sentenced solely for violating it.[139]

One more oddity to my knowledge has never been observed. The argument about divine omnipotence Urban used implicitly to condemn Galileo when talking to Niccolini was perfectly acceptable theology. Why did he, or his acolyte Oreggi, not use it explicitly in Galileo's sentence? If with all due caution we use Oreggi's representation of Urban's position in his 1629 *De deo uno*, it will become clear how easy it would have been to deploy the pope's position against Galileo.[140] The argument began from God's foreknowledge and its impact on free will, a hot topic since at least the twelfth century, the second an issue that had spawned many heresies from early in the history of

Christianity. Urban moved on to the necessity that the earth's motion pass the test of agreement with scripture before raising the possibility that God in his "infinite power" could have made the universe in another fashion. Since Galileo thought his mathematics revealed the universe's "true [and only possible] constitution," it would have been easy to demonstrate that Galileo not only thought he could force God's hand but had done so through his numerous statements that experiments and experiences should take first place over scripture in questions of natural phenomena. Similar claims appeared in the *Dialogue*, if not as strident as earlier ones found in *Sunspot Letters* or the "Letters" to Castelli and Christina, the first of them known to the Inquisition, and probably the second as well since at least Riccardi had read it in summer 1632. It looks as if the heresy interpretation ran such a distant second to the disciplinary interpretation (it occupies a much smaller part of the sentence) that their victory at the moment of sentence almost surprised its backers.

Much has been made of the absence of three of the Inquisitors' signatures on the sentence ever since Sante Pieralisi observed but did not interpret that fact in 1875.[141] Favaro constructed from it a factional interpretation that has often surfaced since then.[142] The three nonsigners were Francesco Barberini, Borja, and Zacchia. Beretta is correct, although on doubtful grounds, that the first did not oppose the sentence.[143] While the rest of the Congregation met on the morning of 22 June at Santa Maria sopra Minerva, Barberini and Borja were busy elsewhere, in an audience with Urban—at the usual time—about a more important subject, an anti-Spanish libel published in Bologna.[144] Cardinal Francesco also presided over a meeting of the congregation of health that issued eleven decrees on that day, a record number.[145] The only slightly mysterious missing signature is Zacchia's. He certainly attended the coram that finalized the sentence the next day.[146] For what this is worth, the number of Inquisitors who attended congregations that passed sentences varied as widely as it did at any other congregation.[147]

Vehement suspicion

The crime of which Galileo was convicted also needs explication, whatever its intellectual basis. Conviction of vehement suspicion of heresy was one of thirteen modes of terminating a trial listed by Eymeric followed by Masini and Carena.[148] Of these the most serious for a person neither contumacious nor relapsed were the three degrees of suspicion requiring abjuration, *de levi, de vehementi*, and *de violenta*, the last of which had collapsed into the second by Galileo's day.[149] As Eymeric had already acknowledged, in cases of contumacy, vehement suspicion led directly to "violent," the "superlative comparative" degree.[150] Eymeric defined the three in reverse order as "levis, vehemens, maxima" ("light, vehement, the highest").[151] Carena explained that *de levi* meant suspicion of the second grade.[152] Eymeric discussed *de vehementi* in qq. 55 and 56 of book 2. Vehement meant "strong" (*fortis*). In general, Eymeric defined those "vehemently suspected" as "those who did such vehement and strong things, that from them arises vehement and great suspicion against them of some heresy or error. And thus where anyone is found vehemently suspected of heresy, by no means is he a heretic, nor can he be condemned as a heretic" ("illi, qui talia vehementia & fortia peragunt, quod ex eis oritur vehemens & magna suspicio contra eos de aliqua haeresi vel errore. Et ubi quis sic invenitur de haeresi vehementer suspectus, nullatenus est haereticus, nec potest ut hereticus condemnari").[153] Ten kinds of persons were guilty of vehement suspicion: anyone who (1) is contumacious; (2) "knowingly impedes the Holy Office of the Inquisition"; (3) aids such impeders; (4) advises a suspect to lie; (5) is excommunicated for any reason; (6) defends or promotes heretics; (7) associates with heretics; (8) receives heretics; (9) is convicted of perjury or lying in a heresy case; and (10) "often says or does anything against the faith."[154] Of all these, only the catch-all no. 10 seems to apply easily to Galileo, and tells almost nothing about the crime of which he was convicted. Just in case a reader missed the point, Peña stressed that there were no limits to what might count as vehement suspicion.[155] Given Galileo's behavior throughout the last phase of his trial, it would be tempting to bring in nos. 4 and 9, except that it seems doubtful a suspect could be convicted of advising him- or herself to do anything, and there is no question of Galileo being convicted of perjury.

Abjuration

Eymeric's claim that punishment for vehement suspicion demanded a general and specific abjuration looks more helpful.[156] As the first act of the non-secret part of the same session that passed sentence, Galileo knelt before the Congregation to make just that act.[157] His enemy Christoph Scheiner claimed there were twenty witnesses, which nearly agrees with the eighteen listed in the decree register.[158] It was a special grace to allow Galileo to abjure before such a small body and essentially in private, probably in the Dominican general's apartments in Santa Maria sopra Minerva where, after 1628, the Congregation usually met.[159] Other abjurations of well-known figures also took place there, for example, Marcantonio De Dominis.[160] Although the sentence proper had glossed over the precept, the abjuration began with it: "But because by this Holy Office for having, after being juridically informed with a precept of the same [the Holy Office] that I [Galileo] must completely (*omniamente*) leave the false opinion" of the earth's mobility and the sun's stability, he made himself guilty of vehement suspicion of heresy as in his sentence.[161] The rest of the abjuration contained standard language about permanently swearing off such belief, reporting other heretics, and promising to submit to punishment if he failed to do either. As he apparently told his future son-in-law Buonamici who then put the claim into his brief biographical sketch, the first such, Galileo refused only to admit that he had committed fraud in concealing the precept from Riccardi.[162] As Beretta has several times brought out, the abjuration contains the same "ambiguity" as the sentence, since it simultaneously condemned Copernicus's ideas as a heresy and found Galileo "vehemently suspected" of holding them.[163]

The day after Galileo abjured, in a coram attended by all the Inquisitors save Borja and Francesco Barberini, Urban "rehabilitated" Galileo to Villa Medici at Trinità dei Monti as his prison.[164] Niccolini had already begun negotiating the terms of imprisonment, since neither the pope nor Cardinal Francesco would allow a pardon, trying to commute the sentence to confinement in Siena, perhaps in Archbishop Ascanio Piccolomini's house or a convent there before a move to Florence. The ambassador had not been able to see Francesco Barberini because of a public consistory for the extraordinary French ambassador, who among other topics complained about the suspension of the anti-Spanish book to which Borja had objected.[165] Six days later Niccolini, at Francesco Barberini's encouragement, appeared before the Congregation to ask leniency; his appeal left no trace in the decree register's entry for that non-coram.[166] Nor was Niccolini's supplication mentioned the following day when Urban approved the plan it contained, although the note of it in Galileo's dossier says it was "read" then and that the pope "did the ambassador the grace of [allowing Galileo] to go to Siena."[167] According to Niccolini, the Congregation also decided that Urban would negotiate with him on the following Saturday.[168]

Urban took a more important action on the 30th. Before granting Galileo's petition, he ordered a copy of the sentence and abjuration sent to the inquisitor of Florence—to be read to professors of philosophy and mathematics—as well as to nuncios and inquisitors, especially of Bologna and Padua; the Holy Office's diocesan vicars were to spread the news to all such professors.[169] Urban's decree is unusual, but not unprecedented. Paul V had ordered Fulgenzio Manfredi's sentence published in 1610, as Urban had De Dominis's in 1624.[170] The meaning of Urban's action has engendered debate. Michele Cioni probably correctly called it "more juridical than doctrinal or scientific."[171] Beretta, by contrast, makes it an important part of his argument that one of the central issues in Galileo's trial was the hierarchy of the disciplines.[172] He also argues that a desire to preserve the supremacy of scripture motivated Urban.[173] Neveu and Mayaud, in common with their attempt to empty the sentence of theological content, argue that its publication has nothing to do with its dogmatic status and was intended as an "act of administrative vigilance" to get rid of the imprimatur.[174] Their point might be recast as an attempt to broadcast Galileo's precept and stretch it to cover all his peers.

That seems to have been Antonio Barberini's intention. His order covering the sentence's dissemination, together with the reactions of nuncios and inquisitors, may shed a little light on the object of the exercise. Writing to the inquisitor of Florence, Secretary Barberini opened with Galileo's violation of the precept and concealment of it when seeking the imprimatur before concluding pithily that his "punishment will be an example to others such that they abstain from such excesses nor dare to adhere to opinions against holy scripture and condemned, as is this, by the holy apostolic see."[175] This formulation almost perfectly encapsulates confusion about the sentence's nature while putting Galileo's punishment front and center. For some reason, Florence did not get the standard letter the secretary drew up, even though the copies of both versions went out on the same day.[176] The second text was much clearer both about the sentence and about the reason for its publication. Those hearing it read would know how Galileo had been treated and would comprehend "the seriousness of the error committed by him, in order to avoid it together with the punishment which they would receive if they fell into it." There was nothing about condemnations by the Holy See, apart from an opening reference to the Index's decree of 1616.

One group of responses to Antonio Barberini's circular parrotted back, sometimes virtually word for word, his stress on Galileo's punishment.[177] Another group zeroed in on the Inquisition's prohibition to Galileo, and hence even more clearly on the precept theory.[178] The inquisitor of Perugia somehow got things exactly right, writing that Galileo "for having contravened the precept . . . has been judged vehemently suspected of having held that [opinion, that is, the earth moved and the sun did not]," even though the secretary's usual letter did not use the language in the inquisitor's opening phrase.[179] Perhaps he got a version like that to Florence, which, of course, takes us back to the mystery of why there should be two versions of the letter.

Florence's letter seems not to have been its only oddity. Mario Guiducci gave Galileo a detailed report on what the vicar of the Florentine Holy Office read out to the assembled philosophers and mathematicians. According to his second-hand report, Galileo was condemned because, despite having had "a particular and special precept given to him in Rome by the commisssary in Cardinal Bellarmino's presence not to hold nor teach such [Copernican] doctrine, . . . he had fraudulently extorted the license to print it [the *Dialogue*] for not having confessed that he had that precept."[180] The Florentine version put the heaviest stress of all on the precept theory.

Rehabilitation

The following Saturday, 2 July, saw the execution of Urban's rehabilitation of Galileo.[181] First, the pope talked to Niccolini about it, saying it was too early to reduce Galileo's punishment but that he would still negotiate, even though the cardinals opposed it. Urban gave Niccolini nearly all he wanted. Then Niccolini wrote Maculano asking him to come to his palazzo as soon as possible to issue the necessary orders. The commissary told Niccolini that Riccardi and Egidi were also in trouble, while making plain that Galileo's punishment arose from his having "contravened the orders of the Congregation, since sixteen years ago this [Copernicus's] opinion was condemned" as Bellarmino's *fede* testified along with the printed Index decree. Galileo should have told Riccardi about the precept and Riccardi should have known "the edicts, orders and prohibitions;" further, the *Dialogue* did not speak hypothetically as ordered so the Holy Office had to proceed rigorously and make him abjure "the opinion of the earth's mobility." Maculano made the precept properly central to his summary, finally toeing the line about the nature of Galileo's offense. In addition to doing what Niccolini asked, Maculano also brought a notary to attest to his notification to Galileo of Urban's decree of 30 June.[182] That same Saturday, Antonio Barberini, Sr., sent Urban's order about publication of Galileo's sentence to various inquisitors and nuncios, as well as to Archbishop Piccolomini.[183] Egidi duly read the sentence to a group of Florentine mathematicians, including Guiducci, on 12 July.[184] The inquisitor failed to report having done so until August, apparently after Nuncio Giorgio Bolognetti, acting on the Congregation's orders, had checked to see whether he had.[185] Echoing the particular congregation's report of summer 1632, Guiducci summarized the sentence as turning on the precept and the "fraud" Galileo had committed in not telling Riccardi about it.

Nuncios and inquisitors were not the only men to get copies of Galileo's sentence and abjuration. Galileo did, too, through Buonamici's agency, shortly before returning to Florence in mid-September.[186] Buonamici's success further supports the supposition that he was one of the persons best placed to serve as Galileo's intermediary with the Holy Office.

From then until 23 March 1634, Galileo and Niccolini tried repeatedly to get permission for Galileo to return to Florence from his villa at Arcetri, until Urban finally ordered Galileo not to make further appeals.[187] Thus, Galileo's trial ended first in the banning of his book and then in permanent house arrest.

Conclusion

In order to understand Galileo's trial as a legal event, it will help to compare it to the course of a proceeding before the Roman Inquisition, the whole of which I have called a trial from the opening of a dossier, in keeping with the Inquisition's usage.[1] A "typical" one ran through eleven phases, although any particular one might have more or less. Any phase that might harm the defense could never be left out. A denunciation opened a trial, while two witnesses were required to proceed further. The inquisitor took over at the second step, the investigative phase during which he determined whether there was enough evidence to support the denunciations. Witnesses and the accused were examined, the second under an oath that might produce self-incrimination. In step three, one of the most essential, the accused was cited to stand trial. Further interrogations (step 4) followed and then charges were laid that the suspect answered (step 5). In the next stage, step 6, the *repetitio*, all witnesses previously heard were reexamined along with any the defendant named. With an attorney's help, he could draw up a list of questions to be put to them. The Roman Inquisition had a *procurator reorum*, in effect a public defender, if an accused could not afford his own counsel. Usually the defendant was allowed only one attorney of his nomination, although a few cases are known when two or more appeared for the defense. Conducted with or without expert input, the *repetitio* was of the trial's "substance."

After the questioning, the accused was offered a defense (step 7) within an assigned term. The suspect and his or her attorney received a copy of all testimony—minus any identifying details—to which they replied in writing. A number of "exceptions" could be raised against both witnesses and their evidence. The best defense was a solid alibi, or failing that a good excuse, including drunkenness or great age, any claim that would reduce responsibility.

Recommendations from patrons, however, were strictly forbidden. At the defense's conclusion, the trial entered in equal parts the liminal and pivotal moment of "expedition" (step 8). It had three steps: compilation of the *summarium* of evidence, normally the only document the cardinals saw when deliberating; the consultors' opinions on it; and the Congregation's decree, including proposed sentence. Of these three, the consultors' judgment of the nature and degree of heresy in the alleged acts was most important. On the basis of their views and the cardinals' discussion, the pope then proposed sentence (step 9), although apparently he could ignore both. Like the *expeditio*, the sentence was also triune. First came a sufficiently detailed narrative of the crime to support the charge. There followed a note that the consultors had been heard and the Congregation had discussed their opinions. The document concluded with the sentence proper, including punishment and abjuration, as well as a final clause allowing the Congregation to alter any part of the sentence at any time. Once sentence was accepted, the abjuration (step 10) took place, usually in public, but probably fairly often in private. Last of all, the sentence was made public (step 11); often this step came before the abjuration. Publication did not necessarily mean revelation of the sentence's content; in fact the details of the case were usually suppressed in order not to give observers ideas. Rather, it became part of the "public" record of the trial. Torture might be applied at just about any moment, including during the accused's first interrogation if he or she refused to answer or gave conflicting replies, through to almost the end of the trial in the examination over intention. The accused's advocate was supposed to be involved in any decision to torture.

Galileo's trial followed this pattern perfectly through step 1, denunciation. Two members of the Florentine Dominican conspiracy, Niccolò Lorini and Tommaso Caccini, collaborated to bring Galileo to the Inquisition's attention, the first in a letter covering a copy of Galileo's "Letter to Castelli," which Lorini unconvincingly said he did *not* wish to be taken as a legal document, the second through a deposition to the Inquisition in Rome. Galileo's attackers also included information about his reputation (*publica fama*, as Caccini explicitly called it), the element that had originally launched an *inquisitio*. An investigation began (step 2), largely on the strength of Caccini's deposition, but Galileo was not examined, even though he was then in Rome and rumors ran around that he had been deposed (and condemned). The preliminary investigation continued into early 1616, when, instead of a citation to appear before the Inquisition, Galileo got his precept, which most commentators thought did not function in lieu of citation to begin a trial. Instead, Galileo had to wait until 22 September 1632 to be cited to Rome (step 3). What seems to be another investigative phase (step 2) conducted by the particular congregation of Niccolò Riccardi, Agostino Oreggi, and, probably, Melchior Inchofer may have had nothing to do with the Inquisition. The congregation skipped step 4, or at least modified it to consist solely of written evidence, before producing the charges in what should have been step 5. Except what followed was not step 6, the *repetitio*, but rather step 3, Galileo's citation. Then came his first interrogation of 12 April 1633, the only moment of step 4; no other witnesses were examined. Nor did Galileo ever formally respond to the charges (step 5), although he did rebut them in the course of this and his subsequent two interrogations. His trial never had a *repetitio* (step 6), even though two of the four witnesses examined in 1615 were still alive, including Caccini. Nor is there any sign that Galileo ever got written copies of the evidence against him, though such might easily have been destroyed by Galileo's acolytes when they cleaned house of his papers after his conviction.

Galileo's trial went most seriously off the usual rails with Commissary Vincenzo Maculano's extrajudicial move, apparently designed to secure Galileo's admission of guilt without imposition of a formal sentence; the extrajudicial confession Maculano wanted also could and did lead to at least the threat of torture against Galileo. Galileo offered his defense at more or less the right place (step 7), even if its content did not correspond well to what was needed. By then his trial had already gone into the *expeditio* (step 8), which included the required three elements, the *summarium*, the consultors' opinions, and the cardinals' proposed sentence, followed by the pope's sentence (step 9). The consultors' intervention marked an anomaly, since one of their number, Inchofer, did not serve the Inquisition in that capacity. The *summarium* was if anything slanted in Galileo's favor. Still, it can be difficult to map it onto the sentence and the abjuration, since the first and the third turn on the precept, as does the narrative of the sentence, before the sentence proper ignored it. The abjuration (step 10) followed the normal course, before probably the strangest and as we have seen the hardest to interpret moment of Galileo's trial, the literal publication throughout Catholic Europe of his sentence (step 11).

In sum, Galileo's trial contained nearly all the required phases, albeit not in the expected sequence; the most serious omission was the *repetitio* (6). The trial began in 1615 with denunciations and an investigation (phases 1–2) before being suspended by the precept, restarted in 1632 with another investigation (phase 2) resulting in a list of charges (5) including violation of the precept and "fraudulently" concealing it when seeking permission to publish the *Dialogue*, followed by citation (3) and interrogation (4) of Galileo alone. Galileo never mounted much of a defense (7), with or without a lawyer's assistance. The next most serious irregularity after the missing *repetitio* involved the *expeditio*, which was jumbled up both with an attempt to end formal proceedings without the necessary outcome as well as with Galileo's defense. The last part of the trial came close to the normal sequence of steps, including threatened torture in the examination over intention, until the bloody-mindedly literal publication of his sentence (step 11).

Legal Improprieties

It, thus, seems that those who have argued that Galileo fell victim to a "legal impropriety" are partly right, even though they did not know why.[2] His trial contains a number of elements that might be so qualified. Two of the three "substantial" parts of the defense, broadly speaking, were either handled oddly or skipped altogether, the *repetitio* and the defense itself. (Assuming that his dossier is complete, as Francesco Beretta has demonstrated most recently.) To be fair, the decree registers almost never explicitly mention the *repetitio*—only twice—which may be hidden under the formula "datis defensionibus" ("having been given defenses").[3] Perhaps significantly, of the six cases that pose exceptions to the general silence, including the two in the registers, four of their suspects had legal representation.[4] There are also questions about Maculano's plan for an extrajudicial confession, which led to threats of torture. Galileo's attempt to rely on recommendations as one of the two principal planks of his defense proved a crucial blunder, since they were in no case to be allowed. These peculiarities could not but harm Galileo's ability to argue his case successfully. The responsibility for these damaging deviations from the Inquisition's usual trial course must be shared among nearly all the participating parties: Pope Urban; Secretary Antonio Barberini, Sr.; Commissary Maculano; probably Assessor Pietro Paolo Febei, who learned his lesson about displaying unswerving loyalty to his Barberini masters; as well as the Congregation, most of whose members were heavily dependent on those same masters. Urban's penchant for increasingly autocratic behavior, including his housecleaning of the papal administration beginning in mid-1632, and blithe disregard for the law, in which his brother Antonio almost matched him, manifested in the cases of Orazio Morandi, Fra Innocenzo, Tommaso Campanella, and Giacinto Centini, should not be downplayed, any more than his acute sense of the international situation and especially his attempts to restore his position in Rome and the empire in the wake of Cardinal Borja's protest, which also cost Galileo some important backers, certainly Giovanni Ciampoli, perhaps Ippolito Lanci, and others. It was Galileo who decided to ground the heart of his defense in lies and thereby gave Maculano the opening to secure conviction. He also played directly into Maculano's scheme to secure an extrajudicial confession, another blunder he might have avoided had he retained counsel.

Galileo need never have come to that desperate pass. He bears much of the responsibility for finding himself in a formal trial at all. He might have avoided nearly all his difficulties had he told Riccardi—or, better, Urban—about the precept not later than the protracted negotiations over an imprimatur for the *Dialogue*. Once he missed that opportunity, much of the rest of the problem probably stems from Galileo's failure to understand the necessity of effective counsel.[5] At least two lawyers with contacts in the Inquisition offered their services, Giovanfrancesco Buonamici and Niccolò Gherardini, and he might also perhaps have shared Mariano Alidosi's effective advocate, Francesco Baffadi.[6] Nor should we forget that the Inquisition's semi-assessor, Alessandro Boccabella, at least gave the strong impression of trying to help Galileo, whatever deeper game he might also have been playing. The Tuscan ambassador, although a lawyer who had practiced before other papal courts, did not understand much about the Inquisition nor prove helpful as a legal advisor. Above all, Galileo should have done everything possible to take the Inquisition's offer to negotiate in late summer 1632, *before* Urban had a chance to redirect the trial's second phase in March 1633. Instead, Galileo at least implicitly followed the advice of two incompetent advisers, one of whom at least had lots of experience with the Inquisition, Campanella, and Galileo's devoted disciple Benedetto Castelli, neither of whom knew much about law. Galileo intuited that he needed help; his mistake lay in choosing the wrong kind. It is unfortunately an open question how much Galileo or any similarly literate suspect could or might have known about Inquisition procedure. Manuals were available, especially *Sacro arsenale*, but we know next to nothing about whether laymen could and did get access to them.

Then again, it might be claimed that the deck was stacked against Galileo beginning with the slippery precept. On the one hand, taken as a disciplinary device originally intended to silence him, it might yet on the other hand in 1632 have given him a way out of his troubles or at least a means seriously to lessen them by avoiding a charge of doctrinal heresy, as some members of the particular congregation apparently intended. Then again, martinet Antonio Barberini, Sr., could on the precept's basis easily make Galileo's case a simple instance of disobedience. He had the Inquisition's own jurisprudence on his side much more than those who tried to use the precept to help Galileo. When combined with the overhaul of the Inquisition's personnel in 1632, Maculano's deliberate trickery, Urban's quick anger, a threatening international situation, the loss of most of Galileo's Roman backers, and so on, it does look as if by late 1632 or early 1633 Galileo had little chance of escaping condemnation.

Two Alternative Theories of the Trial

Throughout the second phase of Galileo's trial, the Roman authorities continued to work with the competing theories of it that had arisen during its first phase. The first, the heresy interpretation, arose first and also failed first. It came from forces inside the Inquisition, probably spearheaded by Cardinal Roberto Bellarmino, perhaps even including Paul V. Urban VIII resurrected it late in the trial's second phase, albeit with different arguments than those put forward originally. It made Galileo's crime heresy. The second, the precept theory, although grounded in judgments that Galileo had espoused at least antiscriptural ideas in *Sunspot Letters*, one of them "formally" heretical, naturally turned on the precept minute of 26 February 1616, which says nothing about heresy other than to note "the above-mentioned opinion." Even the slightly more forthcoming act ordering the precept dated the day before merely mentions the "censures of the father theologians" without saying what they were. It simply ordered Galileo to "abstain from teaching or defending or dealing with this doctrine and opinion [Copernicus's]," which the minute embellished with the phrase "in any way at all."[7] In an interesting conundrum, it seems also to have come from Bellarmino and more clearly from Paul V. Galileo's enemies had tried to have him condemned for heresy and failed. They did, however, manage to silence him. From this point forward, if Galileo so much as mentioned Copernicus he would violate the precept and become subject to conviction therefor. Not even that would make him a heretic. The two theories were distinct but compatible, even if their combination would have weakened one of them. The second theory would have strengthened the first, but not vice versa, since the first would largely have overwhelmed the second's much more limited disciplinary force. In the trial's second phase, Niccolò Riccardi, the master of the sacred palace, emphasized the precept theory, which made the issue a disciplinary one, perhaps in an attempt to get himself out of trouble for having issued the imprimatur.

These two theories remained in tension right through Galileo's abjuration and indeed after. At only one point do they nearly uncouple: the report of the particular congregation in summer 1632 at the launch of the trial's second phase. The two parts of the report read almost as if drafted by different hands. The second part of the document probably came first, preceded now by a sort of executive summary. The *corpus delicti* in the first text include charges of defending Copernicus's ideas, but do not identify either it or any of the other errors in the *Dialogue* as heresy. Its last point mentions the precept, without explaining its significance. It concluded that all the problems identified could easily be fixed. The later text reduced the charges to two, still not calling either heretical, but mentions the precept twice, the second time accusing Galileo of "fraudulently" suppressing it when seeking the imprimatur. At this moment, the precept seemed to be winning out. While the particular congregation was meeting, Riccardi announced the precept's discovery, saying it alone would ruin Galileo. Urban's decree of 23 September summoning Galileo to Rome, issued immediately after the particular congregation's report, put the precept second after the imprimatur. Neither was said to involve heresy.

Between then and 27 February, we hear nothing about the nature of the charges. On that date Niccolini identified the precept as "the greatest difficulty," and Urban, too, spoke of Galileo's having "contravened the order given him in 1616 by Lord Cardinal Bellarmino at the order of the Congregation of the Index [*sic*]" before the pope first hinted at the heresy interpretation by referring to Galileo's "evil doctrine" ("dottrina . . . cattiva") without elaboration. The full-blown heresy interpretation came out on 13 March, when Urban explained what he had meant a few days earlier. He prefaced his revelation by saying, "We are dealing with new doctrines and the holy scripture. . .[and] the interests of the faith and of religion." Then he floated—forcefully—his argument about divine omnipotence. Niccolini quickly gave up defending Galileo in order not "to speak some heresy," but Urban did not yet call Galileo's ideas themselves heretical. On the day, 9 April, that Niccolini learned Galileo would be interrogated, the pope repeated that the matter was "most serious and of great consequence for religion." The precept seemed to be losing ground.

Yet when the last phase of Galileo's trial began, the precept came right back. Its discovery and implications formed most of the substance of his first and longest interrogation on 12 April when Maculano as much as led him into admitting that he had received it in the strongest form. Similarly, there it is as *the* issue in Zaccaria Pasqualigo's censure of ca. 17 April. As Francesco Beretta quite correctly says, neither Pasqualigo's nor the other two consultors put forward the heresy interpretation by name, although all do implicitly.

During the brief extrajudicial move of roughly 20–22 April, the precept disappears, to be replaced by a mysterious alternative. The only plausible one is the heresy interpretation. It seems likely that Maculano had shifted to that line, especially in light of my reading of the extrajudicial move and its sequela as designed to damage Galileo as much possible.

Then again, perhaps Maculano did slip the precept in; at any rate Galileo himself brought it up in his second interrogation on 30 April, defending himself against having violated it by claiming that the *Dialogue* did not defend Copernicus. In his final deposition on 10 May, Galileo alleged that the precept applied to everybody. During the *expeditio* and sentencing, the *summarium* first truncated the precept into an order "to abandon the said opinion, nor hold it in any way whatsoever, nor teach or defend [it]" before Urban abandoned his earlier line and told Niccolini on 19 June, three days before sentence, that Galileo had been imprisoned for having "contravened the orders that he had since 1616." The tension between the two interpretations runs clearly through most of Galileo's sentence, the prototypical committee-built camel. The danger to the second of being attached to the first comes out equally clearly in the penalty clause, which contains only a conviction for heresy. The precept bounces right back as the cause of his offense in the abjuration.

And there the precept stays for the next several months, Niccolini reporting to Florence on 26 June 1633 that Galileo had been sentenced for violating it, Maculano at Galileo's 2 July 1633 rehabilitation saying he had "contravened the orders of the Congregation" sixteen years ago," while making the precept central to his sum of the sentence, before Mario Guiducci on 27 August— reporting the sentence's reading in Florence—remembered it as turning on "a particular and special precept." It is anybody's guess whence arose the further charge that Galileo had "with fraud extorted the license to print it [the *Dialogue*], because he had not confessed to having that precept" ("un particolare e speciale precetto . . . [and] con fraude estorto facultà di stamparlo, per non avere confessato di avere tal precetto"). The accusation of fraud had disappeared as soon as the particular congregation had put it foward. The heresy in Galileo's sentence is hard to find before that point.

A Political or Factional Interpretation?

Two theories do not necessarily mean two factions. In the present state of knowledge it is impossible to make a convincing argument on those grounds, and it seem unlikely that we are ever going to have signficantly more information about most of the principal actors. Still, Galileo's trial manifests the Inquisition's political nature in straightforward fashion.

The principal argument for the role of faction in the first phase of Galileo's trial involves the guerrilla warfare between Dominicans and Jesuits.[8] That does not make it easy to find signs of their dispute in Galileo's trial. On the contrary, on at least two important occasions we find members of the two groups cooperating. The first comes during the Florentine conspiracy, when Jesuit Emanuele Ximenes talked another Jesuit out of attacking Dominican Tommaso Caccini. While important, the second moment is much more so: the seamless cooperation between the Jesuit Bellarmino and Dominican Michelangelo Seghizzi in the administration of the precept.

Probably all papal courts have factions. Usually one of the most powerful was that formed by the adherents of a previous pope, often headed by his surviving cardinal nephew. Urban VIII had the misfortune to face two such factions, Paul V's led by Scipione Borghese and Gregory XV's whose leader was Ludovico Ludovisi. (There were also Clement VIII's partisans who had become many fewer in number.) Borghese had at least pretended to favor Galileo in 1615, so Urban's rejection of his request to become an Inquisitor might have worked against Galileo.[9] There is little other indication that Borghese involved himself or directed his partisans during the trial. Neither did Ludovisi, who died in December 1632 just before its second phase opened. Earlier that year his faction suffered a sweeping defeat that certainly did effect Galileo's trial. Urban's mid-year housecleaning swept out Assessor Alessandro Vittrici, replacing him with Alessandro Boccabella, and later in the year he jettisoned Commissary Ippolito Lanci and introduced Maculano; Antonio Ricciulli was also forced out as vicegerent of Rome. All three were or could have been favorable to Galileo or, in Boccabella's case, at least pretended to be. Ludovisi and his dependents met their fate in part because of grand political faction, allegiance to the Spanish party in Rome, whose temporary defeat further worked to Galileo's disadvantage by costing him Giovanni Ciampoli.

This kind of faction has been used effectively to elucidate Galileo's trial.[10] More has been made of faction inside the Inquisition.[11] The blame falls to

Tommaso Campanella, seconded by Niccolò Gherardini, who might have been in a better position to know. Campanella wrote Galileo in September 1632 just after the particular congregation's report had led Urban to order Galileo to Rome that "indeed I informed a cardinal, who sustains the force of the contradictors," apparently of his failure to gain admission to the Inquisition's discussion ("e pur informai un Eminentissimo, che sostenne l'impeto di contradicenti").[12] "Contradictors" has been taken to refer to a party among the Inquisitors opposed to prosecuting Galileo. Gherardini used similar language in his sketch biography of Galileo. He claimed that because he knew "one of the principal ministers of the Holy Office, I offered my effort to help him [Galileo]. . . . I was moved to do this by the same prelate, who was inclined to withdraw him [Galileo] from an imminent and too severe mortification, not only by the effective recommendations made to him by those who protected Sig. Galileo's case and person, but also to make a counterweight in part to the evil intention of another personage who had great authority in that tribunal."[13] Following Campanella's and Gherardini's lead, most historians have tried to ferret out only a pro-Galileo faction, assuming that Urban headed the antis. Their candidate for leader of Galileo's defenders has always been Francesco Barberini, faithfully assisted by his creature Maculano. These a priori assumptions have distorted the record in remarkable ways, not least by creating a virtually bicephalic leader. That assumption lays this analysis open to a simple, fatal objection: Maculano had charge of executing both theories of the trial. He was already pushing the relatively lenient precept theory when forced (?) to switch extrajudicially to the harsher heresy theory.

Jules Speller is the most recent of a long line of Francesco Barberini's champions. He almost manages to outdo Annibale Fantoli. Speller brings Francesco on stage as head of the particular congregation of summer 1632, with typical hyperbole endorsing Stillman Drake's judgment that the cardinal "was Galileo's ablest and most highly placed protector at Rome," adding that he "fully deserv[es]" that title as "revealed by an endless series of facts."[14] Most of these "facts" consist of various observers *claiming* the cardinal's goodwill to Galileo, including Galileo himself, rather than *demonstrations* of his attitude. The only solid actions Speller can cite are trivial: allowing better conditions of confinement or the obvious suggestion after his sentence that Galileo ask for some measure of relief, as he had already begun to do through Niccolini.

Cardinal Francesco has usually been thought to have helped Galileo most through the extrajudicial move. As Speller says, there was "some kind of complicity between the Commissary and the Cardinal," accidentally using just the right word.[15] Reinterpreting this moment as damaging to Galileo, as I have done, automatically wrecks the rosy view of both cardinal and commissary.

My rereading also squares well with another interpretation of Francesco's role, not as Galileo's defender but as Urban's spokesman. So does one other moment that seems to show Francesco Barberini specially favoring Galileo: Galileo's premature release from the Holy Office before his "exam" had ended. According to Niccolini, Maculano had asked and received permission to let Galileo go from Cardinal Barberini alone, the Congregation having no involvement. Along with Maculano's letter of 28 April, Barberini's alleged action provides one of the central moments behind the interpretation of him as Galileo's principal protector. There is an immediate problem. Maculano himself said the authority came from Urban.[16] The slippage between Maculano's and Niccolini's texts produces the likelihood that Francesco Barberini's role was magnified, to say the least. Instead of proving his priority, this moment demonstrates the degree to which Francesco acted for the pope. Whatever the smooth and close-mouthed Francesco did, he could only have done with Urban's backing. Early in his career as cardinal nephew he had suffered two major failures as a diplomat and either had not yet realized how important the Inquisition could be as a base of power or was staying out of his two uncles' way. As a junior colleague of the other Inquisitors (the second newest appointee), he found himself in a difficult position. His power came from his status in the Roman hierarchy as cardinal nephew and, beginning in November 1632, as vice-chancellor of the Church. Even if he had favored Galileo, he lacked the political skills, and possibly the will, to battle both uncles and a majority of the Inquisitors. Francesco's role was to keep proceedings as obscure as possible and the grand duke as happy as possible while acting as messenger-boy for his papal uncle. It is also a sign of the degree to which the papal diplomatic apparatus had come to supersede the Inquisition.[17]

If Francesco Barberini did not stand up for Galileo, did anyone else? Was there a "pro-Galileo" faction? Niccolini suggested such a thing when he reported on 19 March 1633 that "And for now it is understood that Lord Cardinals [Desiderio] Scaglia and [Guido] Bentivoglio walk rather united in protecting and favoring him [Galileo]" ("et per hora s'intende che il S.r Card.l [sic] Scaglia e Bentivogli camminano assai uniti in protegerlo e favorirlo").[18] Niccolini had an interest in his assertion, since winning them over via recommendations from the grand duke was a major plank in the Florentine defensive strategy. Their support would have shown that the ambassador did his job well. In these two cases, the evidence that either one favored Galileo during the second phase of his trial is even thinner than for Francesco Barberini's attitude. There is no documentation for Bentivoglio except for his statement years later that when Galileo had appeared before the Holy office "where then I exercised the place of a supreme inquisitor general . . . I tried to help his case as much as I could" ("dove allora io esercitava un luogo di supremo Inquisitore generale, e dove procurai d'aiutare la sua causa quanto mi fu possibile").[19] Scaglia's assistance might seem more tangible, since he enlisted Castelli to walk him through the *Dialogue*. An Inquisitor with a lot of experience vetting books, he might have done so as easily in order to look for heresy as because he wished to help its author. There is no evidence either way.

These three—Francesco Barberini, Bentivoglio, and Scaglia—exhaust the possible members of a putative pro-Galileo alignment. All the rest of the Inquisitors were Urban's creatures, from whom he demanded unswerving loyalty, and therefore would have formed a solid bloc prepared to follow the papal line on Galileo.[20] Urban has usually been treated as their leader, but, as pope and sole head of the Inquisition, he had no need to direct a faction. Its obvious head has been completely ignored, the pope's brother Antonio Barberini, Sr., the Inquisition's secretary. In addition to the best institutional post from which to lead a faction, evidence of his hostility to Galileo is pronounced. We need only look at how he intensified the already harsh language in the decrees when communicating them via letter. Nor should his patronage of Maculano—and possible hostility to Commissary Lanci—be forgotten. As a notorious zealot and martinet, Barberini, Sr., was perfectly suited to ram through a verdict resting largely on disciplinary grounds.

Perhaps Urban should be allowed the last word about faction in Galileo's case. Speaking to Niccolini on 19 June 1633, three days before Galileo's sentence, he told the ambassador, "the whole Congregation, all united and no one dissenting," had agreed to punish Galileo ("la qual [la Congregatione] tutta unitamente *et nemine discrepante* caminava in questi sensi del penitenziario").[21]

Frequency of Precepts (1597–1633)

This table categorizes precepts by type of offense (only if explicitly included in the precept), by action ordered (for example, appearance before the Inquisition), by outcome, and by punishment or threatened punishment. It records precepts only, without regard to whether an individual might have had more than one or a single precept covering more than one offense.

Action Taken

Dismissal	56
Appearance	49
Relegation	41
Galleys[1]	27
Exile	16
Secrecy	11
Renewal	10
Fine	9

Offense

Blasphemy	46
Gaming	28
Sorcery	25
Medicine	20
Magic	19
Press	13
Talking	10
Superstition[2]	8
Contravention of earlier precept	7

Polygamy	7
Preaching	6
Interference with Inquisition	6
Exorcism	4
Prohibited books	4
Mass	3
Pretensed sanctity	3
Alleged witches	2
Theology	2
Astrology	1
Rebaptism	1
Seclusion	1
Obscenity	1
Magnetic baptism	1
Invocation of demons	1

[1]Both as threat and as punishment.
[2]Overlaps with magic, etc.

ABBREVIATIONS

ACDF   Archivum Congregationis Doctrinae Fidei
ACDFSO   Archivum Congregationis Doctrinae Fidei Sanctum
              Officium
ACDFSO:DSO   Decreta Sancti Officii
    *NB In multiple citations to this source in the same note, only the year of
    subsequent volumes is given after the initial reference.*
St. st.   Stanza storica
AdS   Archivio di Stato
ARSI   Archivum Romanum Societatis Iesu
ASF:AMdP   Archivio di Stato, Florence, Archivio Mediceo del
              Principato
ASMod   Archivio di Stato, Modena
ASMod:AE   ASMod, Cancelleria Ducale, Avvisi dall'Estero
    *NB All volumes are divided into fascicles by month; these are not indicated
    unless an* avviso *is misfiled; all are also unfoliated.*
ASR   Archivio di Stato, Rome
ASV   Archivio Segreto Vaticano
Seg. Stato, Nunz. Segretaria di Stato, Nunziatura
ASVe   Archivio di Stato, Venice
ASVe:SDR   Archivio di Stato, Venice, Senato Dispacci Roma
BAV   Biblioteca Apostolica Vaticana
    Barb. lat. MSS Barberiniani latini
    Urb. lat.   MSS Urbinates latini
BC   Biblioteca Casanatense, Rome
BEM:RC   Biblioteca Estense Universitaria, Modena, Raccolta
              Campori
Beretta, *Galilée* Francesco Beretta, *Galilée devant le Tribunal de l'Inquisi-
              tion*, ThD thesis, Universitè de Fribourg, 1997, privately
              published

Cadène, "Collectio"	Félix Cadène, "Collectio decretorum responsorumque S. Officii," *Analecta ecclesiastica. Revue romaine* 2, 3, 4 [1894, 1895, 1896]: 318–21, 360–62, 407–12, 493–95 and 32–33, 79–82, 115–22, 167–69, 262–63, 297–302, 352–54, 457–65, 494–98 and 76–83, 123–28, 179–92, 273–77, 361–66, 421, 462–65
Cioni, Documenti	Michele Cioni, *I documenti galileiani del S. Uffizio di Firenze* (Florence: Giampiero Pagnini, 1996; reprint of Florence, 1908 ed.)
DBI	A. M. Ghisalberti, ed., *Dizionario biografico degli italiani* (Rome: Istituto dell'Enciclopedia italiana, 1960–; www.trecani.it)
DSI	Adriano Prosperi with John Tedeschi and Vincenzo Lavenia, *Dizionario storico dell'Inquisizione*, 5 vols. (Pisa: Edizioni della Nazionale, 2010)
DV	Sergio M. Pagano, ed., *I documenti vaticani del processo di Galileo Galilei (1611–1741). Nuova edizione accresciuta, rivista e annotata* (Città del Vaticano: Archivio Vaticano, 2009; Collectanea Archivi Vaticani 69)
Edit16	http://edit16.iccu.sbn.it
EN	Antonio Favaro, ed., *Le Opere di Galileo Galilei*, 20 vols. (Florence: G. Barberà, 1933; reprint of 1890–1909 ed.)
Finocchiaro	Maurice A. Finocchiaro, ed., *The Galileo Affair: A Documentary History* (Berkeley: University of California Press, 1989)
HC	Patrice Gauchat, ed., *Hierarchia catholica medii et recentioris aevi*, 4 (Münster: Regensburger Bibliothek, 1935)
IT/ICCU	Istituto Centrale per il Catalogo Unico, Ministero per i Beni Culturali e Ambientale at http://www.internetculturale.it/opencms/opencms/it/main/strumenti/; numbers are to catalogue entries
MOPH	Socii Instituti Historici Fratrum Praedicatorum, ed., *Monumenta Ordinis Praedicatorum Historica*, 30 vols. (Rome: Institutum historicum Ordinis fratrum praedicatorum, 1896–)
QE	Jacques Quétif and Jacques Échard, *Scriptores ordinis praedicatorum recensiti, notisque historicis et criticis illustrati*, 2 vols. (Paris: Ballard and Simart, 1721)

"Requiem"	The database of cardinals established by Wolfgang Reinhard. The url is usually http://www2.hu-berlin.de/requiem/db/suche.php?function=b_ausgabe&grabmalID=768&PHPSESSID=bebf5bc2ee3fbbe0c54414b3fb5609fc. Searches often do not produce stable URLs. They have been given when they can be verified.
RI	Thomas F. Mayer, *The Roman Inquisition in the Age of Galileo* (Philadelphia: University of Pennsylvania Press, 2013)
SI	Thomas F. Mayer, *The Roman Inquisition on the Stage of Italy, ca. 1590–1640* (Philadelphia: University of Pennsylvania Press, 2014)
SRRD	*Sacrae Rotae Romanae Decisionum recentiorum a Prospero Farinaccio j.c. Romano selectarum, pars prima [-partis decimae nonae tomus secundus]* (Venice: Paolo Balleoni, 1716; 19 vols. in 25)
TCD	Trinity College, Dublin
TG	Thomas F. Mayer, ed., *The Trial of Galileo, 1612–1633* (Toronto: University of Toronto Press, 2013)

NB References to printed books are assumed to be to pages unless folio/s is given. References to MS sources specify page or folio.

NOTES

INTRODUCTION

NB: After an initial reference in a note to ACDFSO:DSO, subsequent citations give only the year of the decree register.

1. Dava Sobel, *Galileo's Daughter* (New York: Walker, 1999), 232.

2. Adriano Prosperi, "L'Inquisizione fiorentina al tempo di Galileo," in *Novità celesti e crisi del sapere*, ed. Paolo Galluzzi (Florence: Giunti Barbèra, 1984), 97–124, 315; reprinted in Prosperi, *L'Inquisizione romana, letture e ricerche* (Rome: Edizioni di Storia e Letteratura, 2003), 183–98, 184.

3. Rather than offer detailed criticism of even the most important of these earlier studies, I refer readers to occasional discussion in the notes below and especially to Maurice A. Finocchiaro, *Retrying Galileo, 1633–1992* (Berkeley: University of California Press, 2005).

4. While both have received study recently, much of the basic work on the Roman "constitution" remains to be done, without which no social-historical study of panoply and power, for example, can make full sense. See, e.g., Paolo Prodi, *Il sovrano pontefice: Un corpo e due anime: la monarchia papale nella prima età moderna* (Bologna: Il Mulino, 1982); Irene Polverini Fosi, *All'ombra dei Barberini: fedeltà e servizio nella Roma barocca* (Rome: Bulzoni, 1997) and *La giustizia del papa: Sudditi e tribunali nello Stato Pontificio in età moderna* (Rome-Bari: Laterza, 2007), together with the expanded and revised English translation by Thomas V. Cohen, *Papal Justice: Subjects and Courts in the Papal State, 1500–1750* (Washington, D.C.: Catholic University of America Press, 2011), and the work of Wolfgang Reinhardt and students.

5. See Conclusion for further discussion.

6. This interpretation resembles that put forward by Jules Speller in *Galileo's Inquisition Trial Revisited* (Bern: Peter Lang, 2008).

7. Orio Giacchi, "Considerazioni giuridiche sui due processi contro Galileo," in *Nel terzo centenario della morte di Galileo Galilei*, ed. Università Cattolica del Sacro Cuore (Milan: Vita e Pensiero, 1942), 383–406.

8. Pio Fedele, "Dei precetti ecclesiastici," in *Scritti giuridici in onore di Santi Romano*, 4 vols. (Padua: CEDAM, 1940), 4: 267–310.

9. Giacchi, "Considerazioni," 392–93.

10. *RI*, 11.

11. See *RI*, 22–26.

CHAPTER 1. THE FLORENTINE OPPOSITION

1. Antonino Poppi, *Cremonini, Galilei e gli Inquisitori del Santo a Padova* (Padua: Centro Studi Antoniani, 1993), 54. Poppi cites Silvestro Pagnoni's denunciation in Padua of 21 April 1604, which reads "sua [Galileo's] madre mi ha anco detto che in Fiorenzza glie fu mandato un cartelo a casa dal S. Officio." This "cartelo" is unlikely to have been an admonition as Poppi thinks; see Chapter 3 below. As he implicitly admits later in the note, it was probably a citation to appear delivered *ad domum*, that is, if the document ever existed. See *RI*, 178. John Heilbron follows Poppi in calling this episode an "admonition." J. L. Heilbron, *Galileo* (Oxford: Oxford University Press, 2010), 2, 105.

2. Poppi, *Cremonini*, 62–63.

3. 17 May 1611. ACDFSO:DSO 1611, p. 202 and 1610–1611, fo. 313v; *EN* 19: 275.

4. Thomas F. Mayer, "The Censoring of Galileo's *Sunspot Letters* and the First Phase of his Trial," *Studies in the History and Philosophy of Science, Part A* 42, 1 (2011): 1–10.

5. Luigi Guerrini, *Galileo e la polemica anticopernicana a Firenze* (Florence: Polistampa, 2009), 68.

6. Ibid., 41, 42. On 67, Guerrini speaks of "the multi-layered anti-Galilean 'party' of Florence."

7. E.g., Annibale Fantoli, *Galileo for Copernicanism and for the Church*, 3rd English ed., trans. George V. Coyne (Vatican City: Vatican Observatory Publications, 2003), 98.

8. Guerrini, *Polemica*, 36n and 37.

9. *Descrizione di ciò che intervenne nel traslatare il corpo di santo Antonino arcivescovo di Firenze* (Florence: Giorgio Marescotti, 1589; IT\ICCU\CFIE\034010); *La trionfatrice Cecilia vergine, e martire romana: Di F. Bastiano Castelletti . . . Con gli argomenti del P. F. Raffaello delle Colombe* (Florence: Filippo Giunti, 1594; IT\ICCU\BVEE\016782); *Vita ammirabile di santa Agnesa Poliziana* (Florence: Giunti, 1604; IT\ICCU\PALE\000498). See Guerrini, *Polemica*, 42, for Delle Colombe's role in the promotion of new saints.

10. Ibid., 38–39.

11. Guerrini, *Polemica*, 40, and Stefano Orlandi, *La biblioteca di S. Maria Novella in Firenze dal sec. XIV al sec. XIX* (Florence: Il Rosario, 1952), 78 and 80n.

12. Guerrini, *Polemica*, 53.

13. Lorenzo Cantini, *Saggi istorici d'antichità Toscane*, 5 (Florence: Albizzini, 1796), 217–18; and Giacinto Stefani, *Delle pompe, o vero degli abusi del vestire* [no pub. data; no title page, nor colophon, title from p. 1], sigg. a4r and a4v.

14. Marzi Medici apparently used Seripando (13 April 1567–3 November 1622) as his regular consultor. See his opinion and the archbishop's linked approval for various parts of Vincenzo Puccini, *Vita della Veneranda Madre Suor M. Maddalena de' Pazzi Fiorentina* (Florence: Guinti, 1611), 364, and unpaginated. He ceased to act as consultor shortly after

this moment. Niccolò Lorini, *Elogii delle più principali sante donne del sagro calendario* (Florence: Zanobio Pignoni, 1617) has an authorization to give an opinion dated 31 October 1613 from Marzi Medici to Pierlorenzo Zaffini, Th.D.

15. Deposition of Rodrigo Alidosi, 30 April 1609 (BEM:RC, MS ʾY.O.4.26, fos. 37v–8r) and *fede* of Baccio Bandinelli, Carmelite of Florence, 21 May 1609 (BEM:RC, MS ʾY.O.4.23, fo. 79r–v). The Alidosi were lords of Castel del Rio (between Imola and Firenzuola), a fief under the Medici grand dukes, who for thirty years protected them against papal threats delivered via the Inquisition until Urban VIII finally wrested the territory away from both the Alidosi and the grand duke. This case quite often had priority over Galileo's. For Alidosi's trial, see *SI*, chapters 5 and 6.

16. Guerrini, *Polemica*, 53, infers that the interval between permissions and publication means that these volumes underwent "amplification." Such a delay appears to have been normal in Florence (see Niccolò Lorini's publication history below), and there is no evidence that authors used the time to add material. Doing so would appear to violate the purpose of the permissions.

17. Guerrini, *Polemica*, 64–65.

18. "Gli huomini del mondo son tanto lontani da questa umiltà, che non è cosa che più si studino di nasconder che l'ignoranza, né di manifestare che la scienza; e pure la scienza humana se non è temperata con l'acqua della sapienza divina, non è altro che una briachezza. . . . la superbia ha perturbata la vista . . . . [develops parallel to drunkenness] Così se chi bee il vino della scienza del mondo, se non vi mette dell'acqua di cui è scritto, *Aqua sapientiae salutaris potabit illum*, darà nel delirio e farà di pazzie. E qual maggio pazzia che negar Dio come Protagora, o la divina provvidenza, come Averroé, e simili cose? Qual maggior stultizia che far l'anima mortale, come Galeno? . . . Qual cosa più sensata che il veder che *Deus firmavit orbem terrae qui non commovebitur*, e con tutto ciò che i Copernici [*sic*] dicono che la terra si muove e il cielo sta fermo, perché il sole è il centro della terra, per la qual cosa si può dir di questi che habbian le vertigini, *Dominus miscuit in medio eius spiritum vertiginis et errare fecerunt sicut errat ebrius et vomens*." *Delle prediche sopra tutto gli Evangeli dell'anno* (Florence: B. Sermartelli e fratelli, 1613), quotation from 2nd ed. 1619, 56, 62, 61; partly quoted in Guerrini, *Polemica*, 55–56.

19. Guerrini, *Polemica*, 57 and 61, where he makes Delle Colombe's "aversion" to Galileo "complete."

20. Ibid., 59–60, makes the following passage in a sermon dated 6 December 1615 another attack on Galileo, but this seems unlikely: "Intendete ogni cosa passare e mutarsi non quanto alla sostanza, ma quanto a gli accidenti, perché insino gl'istessi cieli non si moveran più, dicon gli Scolastici. Ma vuoi vedere la malignità del peccato, che appesta insino i cieli e fa nero il Sole e oscura le Stelle?" (Do you understand that everything passes and changes not so much as to the substance but as to the accidents, until the same heavens no longer move, as the Scholastics say? But do you want to see sin's malignity that stinks to the heavens and makes the sun black and obscures the stars?).

21. None of Delle Colombe's sermons are dated by year. This one bears the day "feria seconda della prima domenica di Queresima" (the second weekday [i.e., Tuesday] after the

first Sunday of Lent). Guerrini, *Polemica*, 65, thinks the year date must be 1614 because (1) the day of delivery in 1613 would have come shortly before the publication of the *Istoria*; and (2) 1615 is "very improbable" because Delle Colombe had given two more sermons against Galileo by then. The first point is not as telling as Guerrini claims, given the Inquisition's prepublication censorship. Given how much Galileo was told, it seems not impossible that the revisors' allies would also have known what the Inquisition censors were doing. The second point has no weight at all.

22. "Mentre dura il Mondo dura anco la nostra ignoranza, poco conosciamo gli altri, e niente noi stessi, verrà tempo, che si spiegherà la tela, che si svolgerà il viluppo di questo cuore, s'aprirà il nascondiglio di questo seno: e come disse San Pietro Damiano, *Cunctaque cunctorum cunctis arcana patebunt*. Quell'ingegnoso nostro Mattematico Fiorentino si fà beffe di tutti gli antichi, che facevano il Sole nitidissimo, e netto da qual si sia minima macchia, onde ne formarono il proverbio, *Querere maculam in Sole*, però egli con lo stromento detto da lui Telescopio fa vedere, che ha le sue macchie regolari, come per osservation di giorni, e mesi ha dimostrato; ma questo farà piu veramente Iddio, perche *Coeli non sunt mundi in conspectu eius*, se si troveranno le macchie ne' Soli de' giusti, pensate voi, se si troveranno nelle Lune de gli instabili peccatori," *Prediche della Quaresima* (Florence: B. Sermartelli e fratelli, 1622; first ed. 1615), also quoted in Guerrini, *Polemica*, 57–58; and *Cosmologie in lotta: Le origini del processo di Galileo* (Florence: Polistampa [Mauro Pagliai], 2010), 142. Translation from *TG*, doc. 5a.

23. I have not been able to identify this quotation in St. Peter Damian's works. Other sources ascribe it to pseudo-Bernard of Clairvaux. Its ultimate source may be Bede. This and all other quotations are in Latin in the original.

24. Delle Colombe also used this proverb in the next sermon.

25. Job 12.33.

26. A paraphrase of Matthew 5.45.

27. "Fu pensiero di Seneca, che lo specchio fusse ritrovato per poter contemplare il Sole. Non pareva convenevol cosa, che l'huomo non potesse considerar la bellezza della maggio luce, che comparisca nel teatro del mondo. Ma, perche l'occhio mortale per la debolezza della sua vista non può fissare lo sguardo per lo troppo suo gran lume; almeno il rimiri in un chiaro Cristallo dentro cui la sua bella immagine il sole vi rappresenti. Quindi un ingegnoso Accademico tolse per impresa uno specchio nel cospetto del sole col motto, *Receptum exhibet*. Voleva dire, che haveva scolpito nell'animo non so che amato sole. Ma come va meglio questo a Maria? Chi potrebbe l'infinita luce del divin sole fissamente risguardare, se non fusse questo Verginale specchio, che in se il concepisse, e al mondo lo rende? *Nobis natus, nobis datus ex intacta Virgine*? Questa di che *Receptum exhibet*. D'uno che cerchi difetto, dove non è non dicevano gli antichi, *Querit maculam in sole*? Il sole è senza macchia, e la madre del sole senza macchia. *De qua natus est Iesus*." *Dupplicato avvento di prediche* (Florence: Sermartelli, 1627), 355–56, also quoted in Guerrini, *Polemica*, 60, and *Cosmologie*, 145–46. Translation from *TG*, doc. 5b.

28. This was the device of Niccolò di Tommè Gori. It is illustrated and interpreted as a love token in Scipione Bargagli, *Delle imprese* (Venice: Francesco Franceschi, 1594), 394.

Gori may have been a relative of another Florentine Dominican of Santa Maria Novella, Domenico Gori. "Academic" means a member of one of the numerous academies in early modern Italy that devoted themselves mainly to literature and the arts and sometimes to science, as in the case of the Lincean Academy, for instance.

29. From a hymn by Thomas Aquinas.

30. Matt. 1.16.

31. Guerrini, *Polemica*, 47 and 50.

32. Guerrini, *Cosmologie*, 89–104. For more on Dominican science, see, e.g., J. L. Heilbron, *The Sun in the Church: Cathedrals as Solar Observatories* (Cambridge, Mass.: Harvard University Press, 1999).

33. Tolosani's work was "De coelo supremo immobili et terra infima et stabili," finished in 1544 according to a note on the MS, Florence, Biblioteca nazionale centrale, MS Conv. Soppr. J.I.25, from San Marco. Salvatore I. Camporeale, "Giovanmaria dei Tolosani O.P.: 1530–1546. Umanesimo, riforma e teologia controversista," *Memorie Domenicane* n.s. 17 (1986): 145–252, 186. See also Robert S. Westman, "The Copernicans and the Churches," in *God and Nature*, ed. David C. Lindberg and Ronald L. Numbers (Berkeley: University of California Press, 1986), 76–113, 99 (summary of Tolosani on 87–88); Irving A. Kelter, "The Refusal to Accommodate: Jesuit Exegetes and the Copernican System," *Sixteenth Century Journal* 26 (1995): 273–83, 283; M. A. Granada, "Giovanni Maria Tolosani e la prima reazione romana di fronte al *De revolutionibus*: la critica di Copernico nell'opuscolo *De coelo et elementis*," in, eds., *La Diffusione del copernicanesimo in Italia, 1543–1610*, ed. Massimo Bucciantini and Maurizio Torrini, Biblioteca di Nuncius. Studi e testi 21 (Florence: L. S. Olschki, 1997), 11–35; and Michel-Pierre Lerner, "Aux origines de la polémique anticopernicienne I. L'*Opusculum quartum* (1547–1548) de Giovanmaria Tolosani," *Revue des Sciences Philosophiques et Théologiques* 86 (2002): 681–721.

34. Guerrini, *Cosmologie*, 101. See also 125–26, etc. For Guerrini's undue stress on Tolosani's importance, see, e.g., the unsubstantiated claim that Domenico Gori "undoubtedly" read Tolosani. Ibid., 118.

35. Ibid., chapter 1.

36. Lorini's birthdate is an inference from the date of his profession on 2 April 1561. Elettra Giaconi and Maria Camilla Pagnini, *Il monastero domenicano di S. Caterina da Siena a Pistoia dalla fondazione alla soppressione (1477–1783): Cronaca e documenti*, Memorie domenicane 36–37 (Florence: Nerbini, 2007), 193n. That he was still alive in 1617 seems to be confirmed by his reference to himself as seventy-three in the preface to his *Elogii*. Giaconi and Pagnini, *S. Caterina da Siena*, cite two legacies to San Marco in "Annalia conventus S. Marci" (Biblioteca Medicea-Laurenziana, MS 370, fos. 39r and 121r). These must have dates, but I have not been able to consult the source.

37. If not from Mugello, the family at least had property there, and in 1613 Lorini discovered the relics of S. Cresci there and delivered "Ragionamento nella Invenzione delle Reliquie e de' santi corpi di s. Cresci martire e de' compagni," in *Elogii*, 358–73, n.d. http://www.radiomugello.it/blog.asp?C=mugello, accessed 10 November 2010; and Marco Antonio de' Mozzi, *Storia di S. Cresci* (Florence: Anton Maria Albizzini, 1710), 103. For his

profession, see Giaconi and Pagnini, *S. Caterina da Siena*, 193n citing "Annalia conventus S. Marci" (Biblioteca Medicea-Laurenziana, Florence, MS 370, fo. 38v. The source of the mistake is probably *QE*, 2:1, 406b. He was again a brother of S. Marco when he denounced Galileo (see below). For preaching in Genoa, see Lorenzo Gorini–Olivieri Gorini [in Florence], Genoa, 29 March 1577; ASF:AMdP 695, fo. 61rf at http://documents.medici.org/ (Accessed 9 November 2011).

38. He was later a general preacher by the patronage of Cosimo II. *QE*, 2:1, 406b. He also took a first degree in theology before 14 June 1580 when he became prior of S. Domenico, Fiesole, before moving to S. Gimignano in 1582. http://moro.imss.fi.it/lettura/ (Accessed 12 July 2010).

39. *Oratio r.p.f. Nicolai Lorini Florentini sac. Ord. praedicatorum in Romana provincia lectoris, ac praedicatoris generalis. Habita in cappella summi pont. Sixti papae quinti. In prima dominica Adventus Domini 1585* (Rome: Heirs of Antonio Blado, cameral printers, 1586; IT\ICCU\UBOE\019582); and *Oratio admodum r.p.f. Nicolai Lorini Florent. sac. Ord. praedic. in Romana provincia doctoris theol. ac praedicatoris generalis, habita in cappella summi pont. Sixti papae quinti. In prima dominica Advent. Dom. 1585* ([Camaldoli]: Press of the Hermitage of Camaldoli, 1589; IT\ICCU\CFIE\030581).

40. *Sermone del reverendo p.f. Niccolo Lorini, lettore, et predicatore generale dell'Ordine dei predicatori. Fatto nella Metropolitana fiorentina, il giorno della commemoratione di tutti i morti, l'anno 1584* (Firenze: Francesco Tosi & Co., 1584; CNCE 34935 in Editi6; no entry in IT/ICCU).

41. Giuliano de' Ricci, *Cronaca (1532–1606)*, ed. Giuliana Sapori, Documenti di filologia 17 (Milan: Ricciardi, 1972), 382.

42. Ibid., 478.

43. Ibid., 477, 478, and 498–99.

44. *MOPH*, 10: 343.

45. See Chapter 4 below.

46. 18 May 1602, Claudio Acquaviva–Agabito Gervasio, Rome. ARSI, Roma 15 I, fo. 156r.

47. 22 May 1602, Claudio Acquaviva–Girolamo Costa, Rome. ARSI, Roma 15 I, fo. 156v. De' Medici's vicar has not been identified. The last known such, Sebastiano de' Medici, died in 1595, http://www.treccani.it/enciclopedia/sebastiano-medici_%28Dizionario-Biografico%29/, accessed 14 March 2013. The next known, Pietro Niccolini, was said to have been in office "for twenty-five years" as of June 1632. *HC* 4: 188.

48. "Quod in futurum quilibet ipsorum non audeat, nec aliquo modo praesumat tam in concionibus, quam in lectionibus, nec alias, discutere, vel alio modo tractare articulum pluries ab ipsis, diebus elapsis in controversiam concionando, deductum, An, scilicet, Confessio sacramentalis per scripturam, vel per nuncium fieri possit, sub poena excommunicationis latae sententiae." ASV, Seg. Stato, Nunz. Firenze, 14A, fo. 325r-v.

49. Massimo Bucciantini, "Reazioni alla condanna di Copernico: Nuovi documenti e nuove ipotesi di ricerca," *Galileiana* 1 (2004): 3–19, 7 and 17 identify de' Medici as the ringleader of the Florentine opposition to Galileo.

50. Ascanio Jacovacci–Pietro Aldobrandini, 19 May 1602, Florence. ASV, Seg. Stato, Nunz. Firenze, 14A, fo. 322r–v. For the nuncio's identity, see Klaus Jaitner, "Der Hof Clemens VIII. (1592–1605): Eine Prosopographie," *Quellen und Forschungen aus Italienischen Archiven and Bibliotheken* 84 (2004): 137–331, 153; http://www.treccani.it/enciclopedia/ascanio-jacovacci_%28Dizionario_Biografico%29/, accessed 14 March 2013.

51. Ascanio Jacovacci–Pietro Aldobrandini, 11 August 1602, Florence. ASV, Seg. Stato, Nunz. Firenze, 14A, fos. 255r–6r.

52. ACDFSO:DSO 1602, pp. 427–28.

53. Ibid., p. 430.

54. Ibid., pp. 509–10. The nuncio's letter of 15 September is in neither ASV, Seg. Stato, Nunz. Firenze, 14 (June–December 1602) nor 14A, nor in the closest cipher of 16 September (ASV, Seg. Stato, Nunz. Firenze, 14, fo. 292r, decipher in ASV, Seg. Stato, Nunz. Firenze, 14A, fo. 335r, wrapper including date of decipher on fo. 336r). 14A has only a handful of letters from the right time in 1602 and none of 15 September (fos. 330r–45r).

55. Giaconi and Pagnini, *S. Caterina da Siena*, 279.

56. *Preparazione e frutto del Ss.mo Natale di Cristo divisa in venti Prediche i Vangeli, e le Pistole, Sponenti delle Domeniche dell'Avvento, ove la Sostanza del Senso Letteral dichiarata, tutto'l resto ne Santi Sentimenti Morali si stende . . . predicata in Roma nella Chiesa di San Giovanni dell'Illustrissima Nazion Fiorentina l'Anno 1605 e 1606. All'Illustrissimo & Reverendissimo Sig. il Sig. Cardinal Capponi Legato di Bologna* (Florence: Giunti, 1615). Despite the title, the sermons actually cover the whole Christmas season through the second Sunday after Epiphany.

57. Ibid., 5.

58. Lorini accepted astrologers' explanation of how the Pleiades caused April rain. *Elogii*, 72.

59. The reference to Copernicus is on 17. Lorini had meant to publish earlier. The book bears an imprimatur from Niccolò Sermartelli, master of the Dominicans' Roman province, and Vincenzo Cambio, "lector et socius," given at Santa Maria sopra Minerva 12 August 1614, "dummodo serventur ea quae servanda sunt." On 31 October 1613, Archbishop Alessandro Marzi Medici assigned the book to the parish priest Pierlorenzo Zaffini (later identifed as holding a doctorate in theology) to review, his opinion coming on 3 June 1614, leading Marzi Medici to license publication of "these sermons" on 13 June 1614, if the inquisitor of Florence agreed. That did not happen until "Ludovicus Iacobonius Vice Inquis. Florentiae" gave approval on 20 April 1616. Yet another year went past before the grand ducal censor, Niccolò dell'Antella, added "Stampisi questo di 29. di Maggio 1617." There was often a substantial delay between permissions and publication, as we have seen in the case of Delle Colombe's sermons, but almost four years raises questions about what kind of trouble the book had encountered.

60. Ibid., sig. A2r.

61. Ibid., 29.

62. Ibid., 30.

63. "molta proporzione si ritrova fra le virtù, e i gioelli, imperochè i gioelli non

son'altro, che vapore, e una esalazione secca della terra congelato, ò pietrificate dal freddo, per virtù del Cielo, e operazion del Sole, e ridotti da loro a somma digestione, da quali Cielo, e Sole riceve la diversità de' colori, e bellezze, e varie proprietadi e virtù; perche trovandosi in terra ci sono però generat [sic] per bontà, e virtù del Cielo, come le virtù sono nella terra dell'anime sante, per dono di Dio." Ibid., 32–33.

64. Ibid., 33.

65. Ibid., 299.

66. http://moro.imss.fi.it/lettura/LetturaWEB.DLL?AZIONE=UNITA&TESTO=Eb3 &PARAM= 826–437586–39720&VOL=20&RADIO=B, accessed 12 July 2010. Guerrini uses Lorini's dual position to point out the lack of study of the "interconnections" between the study of theology in monasteries and at the university. *Cosmologie*, 103n.

67. Matteo Caccini–Alessandro Caccini, 4 May 1612, Rome. Antonio Ricci-Riccardi, *Galileo Galilei e fra Tommaso Caccini: il processo del Galilei nel 1616 e l'abiura segreta rivelata dalle carte caccini* (Florence: Le Monnier, 1902), 42.

68. Lorini–Galileo, 5 November 1612, Florence. *EN* 11: no. 793.

69. See *EN* 11: note 1109 and Domenico Zanrè, "Ritual and Parody in Mid-Cinquecento Florence: Cosimo de' Medici and the Accademia del Piano," in Konrad Eisenbichler, ed., *The Cultural Politics of Duke Cosimo I de' Medici* (Aldershot: Ashgate, 2001), 189–204. Nothing is known of the Ghignoni. The two "companies" may also be a pun on the name of Savonarola's followers, the Piagnoni.

CHAPTER 2. FORMAL PROCEEDINGS BEGIN
(LATE 1614–MID-FEBRUARY 1616)

1. Antonio Ricci-Riccardi, *Galileo Galilei e fra Tommaso Caccini: il processo del Galilei nel 1616 e l'abiura segreta rivelata dalle carte caccini* (Florence: Le Monnier, 1902), 15, quoting his brother Alessandro's memoirs. The entry in *DBI* 16: 35–37 is largely based on this book and is riddled with errors.

2. Ricci-Riccardi, *Galileo*, 28; Luigi Guerrini, *Galileo e la polemica anticopernicana a Firenze* (Florence: Polistampa, 2009), 26–28; Alfredo Damanti, *Libertas philosophandi: Teologia e filosofia nella Lettera alla Granduchessa Cristina di Lorena di Galileo Galilei*, Temi e Testi 71 (Rome: Edizioni di Storia e Letteratura, 2010), 63, states as fact that Ludovico delle Colombe planned Caccini's lecture.

3. Guerrini, *Polemica*, 65, 67.

4. The sermon is known only at second hand from Luigi Maraffi, O.P.–Galileo, Rome, 10 January 1615. *EN* 12: no. 1070. In the context of Caccini's December reading, he reported that Cardinal Giustiniani, while legate of Bologna, had forced Caccini to retract by force of the police "a similar escapade" committed while preaching in San Domenico ("lo [Caccini] fece ricantare a forza di sbirri per una simile scappata fatta in pergamo"). Ricci-Riccardi, *Galileo*, 28, citing no documentation, made this into an attack on Galileo, but there is no certainty Maraffi meant that, nor did he date the event precisely. It must have been before

Giustiniani ceased to be legate in mid-summer 1611. Nicole Reinhardt, *Macht und Ohnmacht der Verflechtung: Rom und Bologna unter Paul V. Studien zur Frühneuzeitlichen Mikropolitik im Kirchenstaat* (Tübingen: Bibliotheca Academica, 2000), 105n245. Matteo Caccini at the same time as Maraffi also reported Giustiniani's actions "to calm him [Caccini]" but located them "in these days" and said nothing about Bologna. Matteo Caccini–Alessandro Caccini, 9 January 1615, Rome. *EN* 18: no. 1069bis.

5. The reading's content is known from Caccini's deposition of 20 March 1615. *DV*, no. 8. Most observers overlook liturgical niceties and incorrectly call his performance a sermon. It was not the main sermon for the day, the pericope for which came from the book of Luke. According to the Tridentine *Breviarium romanum*, the Advent texts are from Isaiah and St. Paul's Epistles, while Joshua is for Lent, ruling out any possibility that Caccini delivered a sermon. Nor was Caccini then a preacher. Instead, as he said himself, he held the office of reader in the Bible. His lecture was a *lezione* of the type produced by his fellow Dominican Domenico Gori. Guerrini, *Polemica*, 49, and *Cosmologie in lotta: Le origini del processo di Galileo* (Florence: Polistampa [Mauro Pagliai], 2010), 116–17. Despite his awareness of the two genres, Guerrini identifies Caccini's performance as a sermon. See also the distinction "tam in concionibus, quam in lectionibus," a precept to Niccolò Lorini, and "tam in concionando, quam in legendo," a precept to the rector of the Jesuit house in Florence, both n.d., but enclosed in a letter from the nuncio of 19 May 1602. ASV, Seg. Stato, Nunz. Firenze, 14A, fo. 325r–v. For medieval practice through 1200 including cross-contacts with preaching, see Duncan Robertson, *Lectio Divina: The Medieval Experience of Reading* (Collegeville, Minn.: Liturgical Press, 2011) and Eliana Corbari, *Vernacular Theology: Dominican Sermons and Audience in Late Medieval Italy* (Berlin: De Gruyter, 2013).

6. Giuseppe Galli, "Il cardinale Vincenzo Maculano al processo di Galilei," *Memorie domenicane* (1965) fasc. I–III: 24–42, 65–101, 146–75, 82n; and Ricci-Riccardi, *Galileo*, 206.

7. This sally may be mythical. It is not documented before the late eighteenth century. Maurice A. Finocchiaro, *Retrying Galileo, 1633–1992* (Berkeley: University of California Press, 2005), 115. Damanti, *Libertas*, 61, takes it as fact.

8. The MS bears a note that "publicae lectioni exposuit Fr. Thomas Caccinus . . . 1635." Massimo Bucciantini, *Contro Galileo: Alle origini dell'Affaire* (Florence: Olschki, 1995), 37n.

9. He arrived on 19 February. Ricci-Riccardi, *Galileo*, 115–16.

10. Despite Matteo Caccini's assurance on 7 February 1615 that he had the patent for the office, a week later he wrote that there was "little hope" for it, a view he contradicted two days later, and so it went. *EN* 18: no. 1078bis (Ricci-Riccardi, *Galileo*, 91) and Bucciantini, *Origini*, 38–39n (Ricci-Riccardi, *Galileo*, 99–100) and 39n. It was certainly still in play in November 1615 and possibly as late as June 1616 before going to another man. Matteo Caccini–Alessandro Caccini, 13 November 1615, Rome (Ricci-Riccardi, *Galileo*, 135) and do–do, 25 June 1616 (Guerrini, *Cosmologie*, 221), but the second text refers only to Tommaso's *negozio* without naming the office. The *negozio* might have been a permanent appointment as regent of studies, which he had received temporarily in late 1615. The problem was that the convent had elected that man and only then had the Dominican general tried to intrude Caccini. Bucciantini, *Origini*, 37n.

11. Ricci-Riccardi, *Galileo*, 91, and snippet in *EN* 18: no. 1078bis.

12. See, e.g., Matteo Caccini–Alessandro Caccini, 9 January 1615, and Matteo Caccini–Tommaso Caccini, 14 February 1615, both Rome. *EN* 18: nos. 1069bis and 1080bis.

13. *DV*, 13. Bucciantini, *Origini*, 32, overstates the case in saying that Lorini wrote in the name of the convent of San Marco.

14. Bucciantini, *Origini*, 33.

15. Francesco Beretta claims that Lorini and Caccini tried to mobilize the Inquisition since they knew its majority shared their view, trying to use an organ of "intellectual regulation" for their factional end. "Melchior Inchofer et l'hérésie de Galilée: Censure doctrinale et hiérarchie intellectuelle," *Journal of Modern European History* 3 (2005): 23–49, 27. There is no evidence for this assertion.

16. *HC* 4: 12 and *avviso* of 14 September 1611. BAV, Urb. lat. 1079, fo. 631v. Galamini swore the oath on 16 November. ACDFSO:DSO 1610–1611, fo. 435r. For a more complete biography, see *RI*, 64–66.

17. *Avvisi* of 5 November (?) and ca. 14 December1611. BAV, Urb. lat. 1079, fos. 763v and 846v.

18. Bucciantini, *Origini*, 39, although he may go beyond the evidence when saying that Caccini's "conversations . . . with Cardinal Arrigoni, but above all with Aracoeli [Galamini] must have been frequent."

19. For Sfondrato, see *RI*, 62–63.

20. For Sfondrato and Seghizzi, see *RI*, 112.

21. *RI*, 63.

22. X.-M. Bachelet and S. Tromp, eds., "Epistolae S. Roberti Bellarmini ab initio cardinalatus S. R. E." (typescript, PGUR), 1541, cited in Peter Godman, *The Saint as Censor: Robert Bellarmine Between Inquisition and Index* (Leiden: Brill, 2000), 174.

23. *DV*, 14. The fact that Lorini thought a letter might count as a deposition—it could not, as Bucciantini points out (*Origini*, 36)—by contrast with Caccini's legally impeccable deposition may provide further evidence that someone (Galamini?) helped Caccini prepare carefully.

24. See Chapter 4 below.

25. The translation is from *TG*, 49–55.

26. Ibid., 50–51. Here and throughout, italics represent passages underlined in the text found in Galileo's dossier.

27. For Galileo's ideas both of experiment and "necessary demonstrations," see Peter Machamer, "Galileo's Machines, His Mathematics, and His Experiments," in *The Cambridge Companion to Galileo*, ed. Peter Machamer (Cambridge: Cambridge University Press, 1998), 53–79, 67–70.

28. Galileo–Piero Dini, 16 February 1615, Florence. *EN* 5: 291–95.

29. Mauro Pesce, "Le redazioni originali della Lettera Copernicana di G. Galilei a B. Castelli," *Filologia e Critica* 17 (1982): 394–417.

30. Ludwig von Pastor, *The History of the Popes from the Close of the Middle Ages*, 25, trans. and ed. Ernest Graf (London: Kegan Paul, Trench, Trübner, 1937), 32.

31. *EN* 12: no. 1071.

32. Richard S. Westfall, *Essays on the Trial of Galileo* (Vatican City: Vatican Observatory Publications, 1989), 13. Bucciantini, *Origini*, 42.

33. Roberto Bellarmino, *De Ascensione mentis in Deum* (Rome: Giacomo Mascardi, 1615).

34. *EN* 12: no. 1090.

35. *EN* 5: 297–305.

36. *EN* 12: no. 1099.

37. ACDFSO:DSO 1615, p. 98. The building is the present Collegio Bellarmino, via del Seminario 120, even though the Jesuits now know nothing of this connection and the name appears to be pure happenstance.

38. *DV*, no. 8, and ACDFSO:DSO 1615, p. 166; EN, 20, 568, and 513.

39. *EN* 12: no. 1115, Dini–Galileo, Rome, 2 May 1615. Dini had offered a series of excuses over the previous month as to why he had not shown Bellarmino the letter.

40. Bucciantini, *Origini*, 42n.

41. Domenico Moreni, *Bibliografia storico-ragionata della Toscana*, 1 (Florence: Domenico Ciardetti, 1805), 126. He was appointed consultor of the Index 10 May 1616. Pierre-Noël Mayaud, *La condamnation des livres coperniciens et sa révocation à la lumière de documents inédits des Congrégations de l'Index et de l'Inquisition* (Rome: Editrice Pontificia Università Gregoriana, 1997; Miscellanea historiae pontificiae, 64), 60–61.

42. *EN* 12: no. 1070, Luigi Maraffi–Galileo, Santa Maria sopra Minerva, Rome, 10 January 1615. Cesi described the "great affection" Maraffi had to Galileo when reporting his death. Cesi–Galileo, Rome, 8 October 1616. *EN* 12: no. 1228.

43. *EN* 18: nos 1067bis and ter; and Bucciantini, *Origini*, 37–38n from the MS.

44. *EN* 18: nos 1069bis.

45. Ricci-Riccardi, *Galileo*, 24.

46. *SI*, Chapter 4.

47. 17 May 1611. ACDFSO:DSO 1611, p. 202, and 1610–1611, fo. 313v; *EN* 19: 275.

48. Christian Wieland, *Fürsten, Freunde, Diplomaten. Die römisch-florentinischen Beziehungen unter Paul V. (1605–1621)* Norm und Struktur 20 (Cologne: Böhlau, 2004), 211–17, VSR either 1609 (Christoph Weber, *Die Päpstlichen Referendare 1566–1809. Chronologie und Prosopographie*, 3 vols. [Stuttgart: Anton Hiersemann, 2003], 2:586–87) or 1607 (Bruno Katterbach, *Referendarii utriusque Signaturae a Martino V ad Clementem IX et Praelati Signaturae Supplicationum a Martino V ad Leonem XIII*, Studi e Testi 55 [Città del Vaticano, 1931], 243).

49. Bucciantini, *Origini*, 143.

50. *DBI*, 40: 158–59.

51. Thomas F. Mayer, "A Tale of Two Vigne: Galileo, the Telescope and Roman Elites, 1611," forthcoming.

52. E.g., *EN* 12: no. 1049, Galileo–Michelangelo Buonarroti the younger, 13 October 1614, asking him to have the inquisitor of Florence appoint a particular reviewer of his *Risposta alle opposizioni del S. Lodovico delle Colombe*, etc.

53. *EN* 12: no. 1084.

54. Cosimo II–Francesco Maria Del Monte, 27 February 1611, Florence. *EN* 11: no. 485.

55. *DBI* 16: 35–37.

56. *Requiem* (*sic.* *)

57. For Maffeo Barberini, see *RI*, 100–109.

58. *EN* 12: no. 1085.

59. Dini–Galileo, Rome, 14 March 1615. *EN* 12: no. 1095.

60. Ciampoli–Galileo, Rome, 28 February 1615. *EN* 12: no. 1085.

61. Ibid.

62. The fact that Sfondrato was an Inquisitor makes it unlikely that he acted as head of the Index when passing Lorini's letter to the Holy Office. Bucciantini, *Origini*, 32.

63. ACDFSO:DSO 1615, p. 98.

64. Lelio Marzari–Millini, Pisa, 7 March 1615. *DV*, no. 7. For Marzari's career, see *SI*, Chapter 5.

65. Castelli–Galileo, 12 March 1615, Pisa. *EN* 12: no. 1094.

66. Castelli–Galileo, 18 March 1615, Pisa. *EN* 12: no. 1097. Guerrini says that Gori criticized Caccini's *toni* and took a "less peremptory" approach (*Cosmologie*, 114 and 122), but these readings dilute Castelli's words. Castelli's letter also does not support Guerrini's claim (ibid., 112) that Bonciani asked Gori as his confessor for an opinion on Caccini's sermon.

67. Castelli–Galileo, 25 March 1615, Pisa. *EN* 12: no. 1101.

68. Stefano Orlandi, *La biblioteca di S. Maria Novella in Firenze dal sec. XIV al sec. XIX* (Florence: Il Rosario, 1952), 77–78.

69. Guerrini, *Cosmologie*, 105.

70. Orlandi, *Biblioteca*, 77.

71. *QE* 2: 415, and Guerrini, *Cosmologie*, 105.

72. Ibid., 106–7, 116–17, and *Polemica*, 49n.

73. Guerrini, *Cosmologie*, 115 and 127.

74. Castelli–Galileo, 25 March 1615, Pisa. *EN* 12: no. 1101.

75. Emanuele Boaga, "Annotazioni e documenti sulla vita e sulle opere di Paolo Antonio Foscarini, teologo 'copernicano'," *Carmelus* 37 (1990): 173–216, 178.

76. Boaga, "Foscarini," 187–88; cf. Cesi–Galileo, 7 March 1615, Rome (*EN* 12: no. 1089), and for Foscarini's readiness to debate, Dini–Galileo, 27 March 1615, Rome (*EN* 12: no. 1102).

77. Stefano Caroti, "Un sostenitore napoletano della mobilità della terra: Il padre Paolo Antonio Foscarini," in E. Lomonaco and M. Torrini, eds., *Galileo e Napoli* (Naples: Guida, 1987), 81–121.

78. Ibid., 87n and *EN* 12: p. 165.

79. *EN* 12: no. 1110.

80. Boaga, "Foscarini," 191–92.

81. *DV*, 2. The document is undated, but must postdate the receipt in Rome of the copy Lorini sent that bears an order dated 26 February 1615 (*DV*, 13).

82. The document may be misplaced in Galileo's dossier, since it is now only half the original bifolium. *DV*, 12.

83. Guerrini, *Origini*, 43–44n53.

84. *DV*, 6.

85. For a more detailed biography, see *RI*, 64–66.

86. *RI*, Table 3, 219–21.

87. BAV, Barb. lat. 4676, fos. 19v–20r.

88. Bucciantini, *Origini*, 23.

89. Ricci-Riccardi, *Galileo*, 98–100.

90. Ibid., 104, 106 and 122.

91. *DV*, 23. English translations in *TG*, no. 10, and Finocchiaro, *Retrying*, 136–41.

92. *RI*, 166–68.

93. *DV*, 24.

94. 1555–1609, Serrarius was born in Alsace but crossed the Rhine to make his career in the Empire. Augustin de Backer, Aloys de Backer, and Auguste Carayon, *Bibliothèque de la Compagnie de Jésus*, ed. Carlos Sommervogel, 12 vols. (Brussels: O. Schepens, Paris: A. Picard, 1890–1932), 7: c. 1134–45, c. 1143. Caccini drew on his *Commentaria in librum Josue*, 2 vols. (Mainz: Johannes Albinus, 1610).

95. *DV*, 25.

96. I have found two strong suspects for this never identified preacher: Patrizio Colombini and Giacomo Fuligatti. Both appear as "concionator" (preacher) in the 1615 "Catalogus primus" in ARSI, Roma 55, fo. 30r. Colombini is further described as only moderately skilled, while Fuligatti was praised as a natural preacher (fo. 67r). Fuligatti is particularly interesting since he also taught mathematics and would write the first life of Bellarmino. Cesi told Galileo on 20 June 1615 that he was happy that preaching in Florence had been effective, but nothing is known of this campaign. *EN* 12: no. 1127. A third possibility is Claudio Seripando. Giulio Cordara, *Historiae Societatis Jesu pars sexta . . . sub Mutio Vitellescho*(Rome: n.p., 1750), 1: 352. Josephus Fejér, ed., *Defuncti primi saeculi Societatis Iesu, 1540–1640*, 2 vols. (Rome: Curia Generalitia S.J. , 1982), 1: 233 says Seripando preached all over Italy but gives no details. A native of Naples, he died there 3 November 1622 (ibid.). He was in Florence as recently as 31 August 1613, when he signed an approval for Raffaello Delle Colombe, *Prediche della Quaresima* (Florence: Sermartelli, 1615). See also Chapter 1 above.

97. Emanuele Ximenes (25 May 1543–bef. 6 February 1616; 1611 catalogue in ARSI, Roma 54, fo. 284r, and Roma II, fo. 334r) was admitted as a Jesuit on 4 September 1565 and took his fourth vow on 20 December 1590. 1611 catalogue in ARSI, Roma 54, fo. 284r. He had both an I.U.D. and a Th.D. and taught philosophy, but his real talent was for cases of conscience. ARSI, Roma 54, fo. 213r, and 1611 catalogue in Roma 54, fo. 315r. As consultor to the Florentine inquisition, he witnessed Inquisitor Cornelio Priatoni's oath 19 January 1612 (Michele Cioni, *I documenti galileiani del S. Uffizio di Firenze* [Florence: Giampiero Pagnini, 1996; reprint of Florence, 1908 ed.], 2, 3) and probably in the same capacity gave the imprimatur "per ordine del S. Offizio" for Raffaelel Delle Colombe's *Prediche della*

Queresima, dated "del nostro Collegio della Compagnia di Giesù," 2 September 1613. He was supposedly the son of Odoardo Ximenes and Isabella di Rodrigo Rodriguez, http://moro. imss.fi.it/lettura/LetturaWEB.DLL?AZIONE=UNITA&TESTO=Eb3&PARAM=1596 -575189-51307&VOL=20&RADIO=B. Ferdinando Ximenes, regent of Santa Maria Novella and deponent against Galileo, was probably his cousin. See below, REF.

98. *DV*, 25.

99. Bardi (1570–1622), bishop 19 December 1603–† August 1622 (certainly bef. 19 December). *HC* 4: 166. VSR 1600, papal governor 1593–ca. 1602, his brother Cosimo was archbishop of Florence, 1630–31. Weber, *Referendare* 2: 438. He was also a leading member of the Accademia della Crusca.

100. *DV*, 26.

101. *DV*, 27.

102. See *SI*, Chapter 3. Caccini's was not the only effort to link Galileo and Sarpi. Potentially more damaging, two Tuscan ambassadors to Venice did the same thing before Galileo came to Florence. Bucciantini, *Origini*, 46.

103. ACDFSO:DSO 1612, p. 112.

104. *RI*, 181.

105. ACDFSO:DSO 1615, p. 166; *EN* 20: 568 and 513. *DV*, no. 10. The decree register confirms Bucciantini's speculation (*Origini*, 56) that Bellarmino knew of Caccini's deposition when he wrote to Foscarini on 12 April (see above).

106. Dini–Galileo, 18 April 1615l; Rome and do-do, 2 May 1615; Rome. *EN* 12: nos. 1112 and 1115.

107. Dini–Galileo, 16 May 1615; Rome. *EN* 12: no. 1122.

108. Dini–Galileo, 20 April 1615; Rome. *EN* 12: no. 1114.

109. *EN* 5: 367–70. English translation in Richard J. Blackwell, *Galileo, Bellarmine, and the Bible* (Notre Dame, Ind.: University of Notre Dame Press, 1991), Appendix IX.

110. Dini–Galileo, 2 May 1615, Rome. *EN* 12: no. 1115. As a lawyer, Dini should not have meant "under the protection" to have the ominous technical legal meaning that an accused could not be molested by other courts until the proceedings already under way in a superior court had been completed. As the context of his letter indicates, Dini used it to mean that Foscarini had become Millini's client.

111. This sketch is extracted from the more detailed biography in *RI*, 43–50.

112. Despite his longer than average tenure as an auditor, Millini did not have much of an impact on Rota jurisprudence until long after his death. The editor of the most comprehensive printed collection of the Rota's recent decisions, Prospero Farinacci, did not think much of him and included only a handful of his cases. His manuscript decisions are usually exceptionally short, as even his nephew was forced to admit in his gushing biography, rarely concern high-profile cases, and are not very numerous, especially in proportion to how long he served. A volume of them appeared in print only in 1649, whereas other auditors had their decisions printed during their lifetimes, often more than once. It seems not to have mattered what kind of lawyer he was. His skills lay elsewhere.

113. This sketch is extracted from *RI*, 96–100.

114. Massimo Firpo and Dario Marcatto, eds., *Il processo inquisitoriale del Cardinal Giovanni Morone*, 6 vols. (Rome: Istituto Storico Italiano per l'Età Moderna e Contemporanea, 1981–95).

115. Tracy L. Ehrlich, *Landscape and Identity in Early Modern Rome: Villa Culture at Frascati in the Borghese Era* (New York: Cambridge University Press, 2002).

116. Jack Wasserman, "The Quirinal Palace in Rome," *Art Bulletin* 45 (1963): 205–44, 232–38.

117. Pietro Guicciardini–Cosimo II, 4 March 1616, Rome. *EN* 12: no. 1185.

118. Steven F. Ostrow, *Art and Spirituality in Counter-Reformation Rome: The Sistine and Pauline Chapels in S. Maria Maggiore* (New York: Cambridge University Press, 1996).

119. Steven F. Ostrow, "Cigoli's Immacolata and Galileo's Moon: Astronomy and the Virgin in Early Seicento Rome," *Art Bulletin* 78 (1996): 218–35; and Sara Elizabeth Booth and Albert Van Helden, "The Virgin and the Telescope: The Moons of Cigoli and Galileo," in *Galileo in Context*, ed. Jürgen Renn (Cambridge: Cambridge University Press, 2001), 193–216.

120. Magno Perneo, "De gloria Pauli V," BAV, Barb. lat. 3282–3288.

121. Abraham Bzowski, *Paulus quintus Burghesius* (Rome: Stefano Paolini, 1624).

122. *Avviso* of 25 June 1611. BAV, Urb. lat. 1079, fo. 458r.

123. *DV*, 11.

124. *DV*, 12.

125. *DV*, 13.

126. For his career, see *SI*, Chapter 5.

127. For his career, see *SI*, Chapter 5.

128. Bucciantini points out that the Florentine inquisition took no independent initiative against Galileo. *Origini*, 70.

129. As Alfredo Damanti has shown in great detail, the "Letter to Christina" reworks nearly all the material in Galileo's 1613 "Letter to Castelli" and can therefore be said to have been begun then. *Libertas*, Chapter VIII. Despite the "Letter to Christina" being his book's centerpiece (he prints an edition in an appendix), he makes no effort to date it. Blackwell (*Galileo*, 75) and Fantoli flatly say the letter was probably completed by June 1615. Annibale Fantoli, *Galileo for Copernicanism and for the Church*, 3rd English ed., trans. George V. Coyne (Vatican City: Vatican Observatory Publications, 2003), *For Copernicanism*, 434.

130. Nick Wilding, "Manuscripts in Motion: The Diffusion of Galilean Copernicanism," *Italian Studies* 66 (2011): 221–33, 231.

131. *DV*, nos. 14 and 12.

132. Tommaso Ximenes (Jiménez de Aragón) (1571–1633), son of Rodrigo Jiménez de Aragón (1534–1581), VSR 1608, reader in law at Pisa, canon of Florence 1596–1608 (Weber, *Referendare* 2: 986–87), "Cler. Antwerpien.," former canon, provided bishop of Fiesole 16 November 1620 on grand duke's nomination, consecrated by Millini 22 November 1620, † bef. 6 August 1634 (*HC* 4: 187). Their uncle and head of the family's Florentine branch, Sebastián de Tomás Jiménez de Aragón, had also been born in Portugal and still headed the family's Lisbon branch bank. http://documents.medici.org/people_details.

cfm?personid=2340&returnstr=orderby=Name@is_search=1@result_id=0, accessed 1 June 2011.

133. BAV, Urb. lat. 1099 I, fo. 337r.

134. *DV*, no. 16. English translation in *TG*, no. 15, and Finocchiaro, *Retrying*, 141–43.

135. No fewer than five Ridolfis were knights of Santo Stefano in 1615. http://moro .imss.fi.it/lettura/LetturaWEB.DLL?AZIONE=UNITA&TESTO=Eb3&PARAM=1271 -516584-46334&VOL=20&RADIO=B, accessed 12 July 2009.

136. This chronology appears impossible unless we assume that Caccini lectured on Joshua for quite some time in 1614, not just during the Advent season.

137. *DV*, no. 17.

138. Ca. 1580/82–1657. He had just become parish priest of S. Ippolito in Castel-fiorentino. http://moro.imss.fi.it/lettura/LetturaWEB.DLL?AZIONE=UNITA&TESTO =Eb3&PARAM=122–300486-27665&VOL=20&RADIO=B, accessed 21 June 2008.

139. *RI*, 182 and 183.

140. *RI*, Chapter 4 passim.

141. Marzari's covering letter is dated 15 November, and its receipt was noted on the 21 November and acknowledged six days later. *DV*, nos. 17, 15; *EN* 20: 569, no. 1141bis (Cioni, *Documenti*, no. XI). The congregation took place on 25 November. *DV*, no. 17; *EN* 19: 278; *DV*, no. 122 (ACDFSO:DSO 1615, pp. 542 and 544).

142. ACDFSO:DSO 1615, pp. 542 and 544. The recommendation from the grand duke is dated 2 December. *EN* 12, no. 1147.

143. Antonio Banfi, *Galileo Galilei* (1961), 143, quoted in Bucciantini, *Origini*, 42.

144. Bucciantini, *Origini*, 31, thinks there may have been a leak in the Inquisition, but it seems much more likely that Galileo would have had the news from a Florentine source.

145. *EN* 12: no. 1150.

146. *EN* 12: no. 1149.

147. *EN* 18: nos. 1149bis and 1153bis.

148. Matteo Caccini–Tommaso Caccini, 25 December 1615, Naples. *EN* 18: no. 1154bis; Ricci-Riccardi, *Galileo*, 138.

149. Galileo–Curzio Picchena, 12 December 1615, Rome. *EN* 12: no. 1152. Bucciantini, *Origini*, 74, alleges that Galileo said little at this point because he was bound by the Inquisition's secrecy, but Galileo had never been administered the oath.

150. Galileo–Picchena, 16 January 1616, Rome, and Picchena–Galileo, 19 January 1616, Florence. *EN* 12: nos. 1168 and 1169.

151. Galileo–Picchena, 8 January 1616, Rome. *EN* 12: no. 1164.

152. Antonio Querenghi–[Alessandro d'Este], 1 January 1616, Rome. *EN* 12: no. 1161. Giovanni Sagredo–Galileo, 11 March 1616, Venice; ibid., no. 1188. In between the Venetian ambassador reported on 27 February that Galileo had been summoned to Rome by the Inquisition, as did Matteo Caccini from Naples on 19 February. *EN* 20: 570; 18: no. 1181bis.

153. Galileo–Picchena, 8 January 1616, Rome. *EN* 12: no. 1164.

154. The best treatment of Ingoli is Bucciantini, *Origini*, 85–97. See also J. L. Heil-bron, *Galileo* (Oxford: Oxford University Press, 2010), 219, 261–63.

155. *EN* 5: 403, and see Bucciantini, *Origini*, 88–97. Ingoli's side of the discussion became "De situ e quiete terrae contra Copernici systema disputatio." Galileo did not write up his side until 1624.

156. Bucciantini well observes that Galileo's attitude "certainly did not serve to calm" his opponents. He also speaks of Galileo's "irresponsible . . . behavior" as partly responsible for the decree of 5 March. *Origini*, 77, 78.

157. Picchena–Galileo, 19 January 1616, Florence. *EN* 12: no. 1169. Galileo's letter is missing.

158. Querenghi–Alessandro d'Este, 20 January 1616, Rome. *EN* 12: no. 1170.

159. Querenghi–Alessandro d'Este, 27 January 1616, Rome. Ibid., no. 1172.

160. Galileo–Picchena, 23 January 1616, Rome. Ibid., 12: no. 1171.

161. *Avviso* of 13 January 1616. BAV, Urb. lat. 1084, fos. 25r and 41v. Orsini was created 2 December 1615. *HC* 4: 13.

162. http://www2.hu-berlin.de/requiem/db/suche.php?function=p_ausgabe&kaID=283, accessed 19 July 2008. For Orisini and the status of his house and role in Florentine-papal relations, see Wieland, *Fürsten*, 409–24.

163. Ibid., 424–28.

164. Ibid., 429, 432–33.

165. Ibid., 430 and 432.

166. *Avviso* of 15 May 1610 in BAV, Barb. lat. 6344, fo. 83v and Wieland, *Fürsten*, 432–33.

167. *Avvisi* of 2 September 1615; 13, 16 January; 30 March; 6 April; 14 May 1616. BAV, Urb. lat. 1083, fo. 444r, and Urb. lat. 1084, fos. 24v, 26r, 123r, 135r, 186r.

168. *EN*, 5: 373 and 377; the work is on 377–95.

169. Galileo–Picchena, 30 January 1616, Rome. *EN* 12: no. 1173.

170. Galileo–Picchena, 6 February 1616, Rome. Ibid.: no. 1174.

171. Ibid. Guerrini, *Cosmologie*, 213, makes this meeting the end of his period since he thinks it marked a complete defeat for Caccini. There is reason to doubt that sweeping interpretation. See further *Cosmologie*, 224–37, for a careful if sometimes tendentious reading of the episode.

172 http://moro.imss.fi.it/lettura/LetturaWEB.DLL?AZIONE=UNITA &TESTO=Eb3&PARAM=248-327171-30097&VOL=20&RADIO=B; http://moro.imss.fi.it /lettura/LetturaWEB.DLL?AZIONE =UNITA&TESTO=Eb3&PARAM=1547-565979-50511& VOL=20&RADIO=B, both accessed 24 September 2007. Venturi succeeded Pietro Niccolini as archdeacon of Florence in 1632, the year Niccolini became archbishop, not 1639 as Favaro said. *HC* 4: 188.

173. See the biography in *RI*, 51.

174. *EN* 12: no. 1174.

175. PS to Galileo–Picchena, 13 February 1616, Rome, and Scipione Borghese–Cosimo II, 13 February 1616, Rome. Ibid., nos. 1177 and 1179

176. Ibid., no. 1177.

177. Picchena–Galileo, 13 February 1616, Florence. Ibid., no. 1178.

178. Galileo–Picchena, 13 February 1616, Rome. Ibid., no. 1177 (*sic.* *)

179. The best date for Tommaso Campanella's *Apologia pro Galilaeo* is February 1616. See Tommaso Campanella, *Apologia per Galileo*, ed. Salvatore Femiano (Milan: Marzorati, 1973), 22–27, and for Caetani's commission, Campanella's dedication, 40.

180. For Campanella's trials, see *SI*, Chapter 2.

181. See Paolo Ponzio, Introduction to Campanella, *Apologia per Galileo* (Milan: Bompiani, 2001).

182. He was assigned the review 7 May 1615. ACDFSO:DSO 1615, p. 280.

183. Leen Spruit, "Cremonini nelle carte del Sant'Uffizio Romano," in *Cesare Cremonini: Aspetti del pensiero e scritti*, ed. Ezio Riondato and Antonino Poppi, 2 vols. (Padua: Academia Galileiana, 2000), 1: 193–204, 200.

184. Galileo–Picchena, 20 February 1616, Rome. *EN* 12: no. 1182.

185. Ibid., no. 1183.

186. *DV*, no. 18.

187. Ibid., pp. 6–7; *EN* 19: 403.

188. *DV*, 45; *EN* 19: 321.

189. *EN* 11: no. 555, from "Bibl. Naz. Fir. Mss. Gal., P. III, T. VII, 1, car. 51–55," a contemporary copy. In vol. 18 in an addition to no. 555, Favaro printed a few lines from another copy that belonged to Gilberto Govi, which then eventually passed to Stillman Drake and is now in the Fisher Rare Book Library at the University of Toronto (Drake Italian MSS collection, Box 28, folder 3). This passage on fo. 12v in Drake's copy is identical to Favaro's text except for a couple of orthographical variations.

190. The form of points condemned by the Inquisition—direct quotations or propositions abstracted from them—may be insignificant. My former student John Frymire of the University of Missouri, who has worked extensively in the Index's records, tells me that the Inquisition's sister congregation might censor either propositions or quotations and says in conclusion that "what you describe re: the propositions in his [Galileo's] *Sunspot letters* does not seem to me to be completely uncharacteristic of the place by any means." E-mail of 27 May 2010. Almost none of the Inquisition's *censurae* survives, making it impossible to describe its usual practice directly.

191. See, e.g., *EN* 11: no. 555, p. 7n. Guerrini, *Cosmologie*, 175, insists they come from Caccini's testimony through the agency of Commissary Seghizzi. There is no evidence for the second claim, and the first is less than certain.

192. Piero Guicciardini–[Cosimo II], 4 March 1616, Rome. *EN* 12: no. 1185.

193. Jerome J. Langford, *Galileo, Science and the Church*, 3rd ed. (Ann Arbor: University of Michigan Press, 1992), 87.

194. *DV*, no. 19.

195. There is something odd about the order of the signatures. Ordinarily the regular consultors gave their oral opinions in reverse order of seniority, although they were put into the attendance lists in rough order of their status in the hierarchy. Neither principle appears to hold here. For all those not otherwise cited, see *RI*, 150–52.

196. http://www.oxforddnb.com/view/article/16953, accessed 7 June 2008.

197. See *SI*, Chapter 1.

198. S. L. Forte, "I Domenicani nel carteggio del card. Scipione Borghese, protettore dell'Ordine (1606–1633)," *Archivum fratrum praedicatorum* 30 (1960): 351–416, 370 and 354; ACDFSO, Decreta S.O. 1613, p. 528; and *HC* 4: 181–82.

199. See *RI*, 112–18.

200. ACDFSO:DSO 1615, pp. 150 and 249; *HC* 4: 334.

201. Hugo Hurter, *Nomenclator literarius recentioris theologiae catholicae*, 3 vols. (Innsbruck: Wagner, 1903–11), 1: 268–70.

202. De Backer, ed., Sommervogel, *Bibliothèque*, 3: cc. 1489–91.

203. Antonio Francesco Vezzosi, *I scrittori de' cherici regolari*, 2 vols. (Rome: Sacra Congregazione di Propaganda Fide, 1780), 2: 207–8.

204. ACDFSO:DSO 1617, p. 160, and 1620, p. 289.

205. Christopher F. Black, "The Trials and Tribulations of a Local Roman Inquisitor: Giacomo Tinti in Modena, 1626–1647," www.giornaledistoria.net, accessed 15 December 2012.

206. Against Giorgio Stabile, "Linguaggio della natura e linguaggio della Scrittura in Galilei. Dalla 'Istoria' sulle macchie solari alle lettere copernicane," *Nuncius* 9 (1994): 37–64, 46; Maurice A. Finocchiaro, "Galileo as a 'Bad Theologian': A Formative Myth About Galileo's Trial," *Studies in History and Philosophy of Science, Part A* 33, 4 (December 2002): 753–91; and Ernan McMullin, "Galileo's Theologial Venture," in *The Church and Galileo*, ed. Ernan McMullin (Notre Dame, Ind.: University of Notre Dame Press, 2005), 88–116, 111–12.

CHAPTER 3. THE PRECEPT OF 26 FEBRUARY 1616

1. This chapter is a rewritten and expanded version of my "The Roman Inquisition's Precept to Galileo (1616)," *British Journal for the History of Science* 43, 3 (2010): 327–51. For the historiography of the controversy, see my "The Status of the Inquisition's Precept to Galileo (1616) in Historical Perspective," *Nuncius* 24, 1 (2009): 61–95; and Sergio Pagano, "Il precetto del Cardinale Bellarmino a Galileo: Un falso? con una parentesi sul radio, Madame Curie e i documenti Galileiani," *Galileiana* 7 (2010): 143–203. To these discussions should be added the treatment in Luigi Guerrini, *Cosmologie in lotta: Le origini del processo di Galileo* (Florence: Polistampa [Mauro Pagliai], 2010), 207ff. He argues that the first phase of Galileo's trial marked a major defeat for his Florentine opponents. To do that, Guerrini made two critical mistakes, speaking only of an "admonition" and incredibly enough asserting that Galileo "emerged personally unblemished from the *processo*."

2. *RI*, passim, especially Chapter 1.

3. http://www.law.cornell.edu/wex/index.php/Injunction, accessed 19 December 2012, and see the next chapter.

4. *DV*, no. 20.

5. *DV*, nos. 21 and 123.

6. *DV*, no. 124.

7. *DV*, no. 25.

8. *DV*, no. 1, 7.

9. *DV*, no. 114.

10. Only a few scholars have raised doubts about the evidential value of Bellarmino's certificate. The first was Thomas Henri Martin in *Galilée: Les droits de la science et la méthode des sciences physiques* (Paris: Didier, 1868), 76–80, who thought Bellarmino manufactured it in order not to reveal the precept and thus breach the Inquisition's secrecy. Martin's account is so oddly argued throughout and so sloppily documented, despite its impressive almost thirty-page "Notice bibliographique," as to render any part of it suspect. See Emil Wohlwill, *Der inquisitionsprocess des Galileo Galilei: Eine prüfung seiner rechtlichen grundlage nach den acten der römischen inquisition* (Berlin: Robert Oppenheim, 1870), 19–21. Bruno Neveu and Pierre-Noël Mayaud, "L'Affaire Galilée et la tentation inflationiste: À propos des notions d'hérésie et de magistère impliquées dans l'affaire," *Gregorianum* 83 (2002): 287–311, 295, make the same claim as Martin.

11. *RI*, 16–17, 27–28.

12. See, e.g., Giovanni D'Andrea, *In primum [-quintum] decretalium librum novella commentaria*, 5 vols. in 4 (Venice: Francesco Francesco, 1581), 2, fos. 121A–122r. See also the next chapter.

13. The four texts read respectively: (1) "omnino abstineat huiusmodi doctrinam et opinionem docere aut defendere, seu de ea tractare" (*DV*, no. 20); (2) "omnino relinquat, nec eam de caetero, quovis modo teneat, doceat aut defendat, verbis aut scriptis" (no. 21); (3) almost quotes the last except it substitutes "verbo" for "verbis" (nos. 25, 53.); (4) "omnino desereret dictam opinionem, nec etiam de caetero illam quovis modo teneret, doceret et defenderet," with all verbs put into the imperfect).

14. "In qua propositae fuerunt infrascriptae causae, quas in notam sumpsit idem Dominus Assessor et mihi Notario tradidit, videlicet: . . . Facta relatione per illustrissimum Dominum cardinalem Bellarminum, quod Galileus Galilei mathematicus, monitus de ordine Sacrae Congregationis ad deserendam opinionem quam hactenus tenuit. . .acquievit." *DV*, no. 124. The opening clause through "videlicet" was standard boilerplate. See, e.g., *EN* 19: no. 275.

15. Those arguing that Galileo received no more than a "charitable admonition" fail to note the slim bit of evidence for their case in that adverb "benignly."

16. Based on my experience reading the registers (granted, more difficult than it would have been then since many of them are badly damaged now), it might have taken in the vicinity of three months to go through the previous sixteen years worth of them.

17. The contemporary indices added to the front of most of the decree registers suggest that such searches must have been fairly common. I have noted two orders for them, 3 January 1604 for a case from 1559 (!) (ACDFSO:DSO 1604, fo. 2r); and 23 August 1608 for letters from 1550 (1608–1609, fo. 176v and 1608, p. 364).

18. *RI*, 20–22.

19. As evidenced by the existence of various collections of such precedents, e.g.,

Assessor Girolamo Casanate's volumes, among them BC, MS 2631, as well as the decree registers themselves and possibly correspondence registers like that in BAV, Barb. lat. 6334. Cf. Pierroberto Scaramella, *Le lettere della Congregazione del Sant'Ufficio ai tribunali di fede di Napoli 1563–1625* (Trieste: Edizione Università di Trieste, 2001), xlii.

20. *RI*, 26–37.

21. See, e.g., ACDFSO:DSO 1615, pp. 327 and 490.

22. First entry for the meeting without the pope of 12 December 1628: "Ill.mus D. Card.is Millinus retulit mihi assessore (?), S.mus mandasse, ut literae commendationes quarumque personarum inquisitarum in S. Off.o, quae commendationes vigore decreti S.mus mense Januarii praeteriti emanaret (?) non sint recipiandae, legand. [*sic*] quando proponend. (?) causae et processus praedictorum reorum." ACDFSO:DSO 1628, fo. 206v.

23. "Dichiaratione di Concistori," etc. in BAV, Chigi N. III 84, fo. 63r. The text probably dates from ca. 1604. The exclusion of the notary from the secret session may have given rise to Pagano's misapprehension that decisions made then were not entered into the decree registers.

24. Beretta, *Galilée*, 34–35, alleges that the Inquisition's de facto head, Millini, kept close tabs on the assessor's accuracy, citing *Vita dell'eminentissimo Signor Cardinale Gio. Garzia Mellino Romano: Scritta dal Sig. Decio Memmoli suo Segretario* (Rome: Gio. Paolo Rocchetti, 1644), 35. Memmoli said that Millini "Stava in oltre attentissimo alle risolutioni, che si pigliavano accioche se l'Assessore, il quale ha la cura di stendere i decreti, non havesse preso bene il senso della Congregatione potesse farvelo avvertito. Ne le bastava la sustanza del decreto, se non si sodisfaceva anco del modo di spiegarlo." But see *RI*, 46–47, and for the assessor's handling of the agenda, 14 and 27–28.

25. Pierre-Noël Mayaud, *La condamnation des livres coperniciens et sa révocation à la lumière de documents inédits des Congrégations de l'Index et de l'Inquisition*, Miscellanea Historiae Pontificiae 64 (Rome: Editrice Pontificia Università Gregoriana, 1997), 47–48; and Neveu and Mayaud, "L'Affaire Galilée," 294.

26. Pagano, "Il precetto," 192.

27. See my "Status of the Inquisition's Precept," passim.

28. The phrase is omitted from the translation in *The Galileo Affair: A Documentary History*, ed. Maurice A. Finocchiaro (Berkeley: University of California Press, 1989), 147, nor does any commentator take cognizance of it. As he often did, Guido Morpurgo-Tagliabue, *I processi di Galileo e l'epistemologia* (Rome: Armando Armando, 1981, rev. ed.; 1st ed. Milan: Edizioni di Comunità, 1963); originally published in *Rivista di Storia della Filosofia* (1947), nn. 2, 3; (1948), n. 1, 20, accidentally used exactly the right legal language to describe Galileo as "costituto quasi l'avvocato del sistema copernicano," but with reference to No. 1, not No. 2.

29. Sigismondo Scaccia, *Tractatus de iudiciis causarum civilium, criminalium et haereticalium, Liber primus* (Venice: Giovanni Battista and Giovanni Bernardo Sessa, 1616), fo. 154r.

30. X.3.5.19 and 33, X.3.8.11 and 12, etc.

31. See, e.g., Giason del Maino's commentary on C.6.43.2. "Omne verbum significans

testatoris legitimum sensum legare vel fideicomittere volentis utile atque validum est, sive directis verbis, quale est "iubeo" forte, sive precariis utetur testator, quale est "rogo," "volo," "mando," "fideicommitto" sive iuramentum posuerit, cum et hoc nobis audientibus ventilatum est, testatore quidem dicente partibus autem huiusmodi verbum huc atque illuc lacerantibus.

32. Two marginal notes to Francisco Peña, *Scholia* to q. 4 in *Directorium Inquistorum* (1578: In aedibus Populi Romani, 1578), LXXIIII, 196, and LXVI, 197.

33. Beretta, *Galilée*, 183–84.

34. For orders, see, e.g., X.3.3.6 and X.3.11.3; it appears together with the meaning in the last note in, e.g., X.3.32.15; the second phrase is in X.3.5.14.

35. See my "Status," 65–68.

36. Francesco Beretta, "Le procès de Galilée et les Archives du Saint-Office: Aspects judiciaires et théologiques d'une condamnation célèbre," *Revue des Sciences Philosophiques et Théologiques* 83 (1999): 441–90, 479. Annibale Fantoli agrees, "The Disputed Injunction and Its Role in Galileo's Trial," in *The Church and Galileo*, ed. Ernan McMullin, Miscellanea Historiae Pontificiae 64 (Notre Dame, Ind.: University of Notre Dame Press, 2005), 117–49, 121–22, 138.

Beretta's work, both thesis and a number of later articles, deserves another word, not least because it put the study of Galileo's trial on an almost entirely new footing, without thus far saying much about the trial itself. As I do, he emphasizes the precept that he—almost alone these days—thinks was forged, before concluding that it had little to do with the trial's outcome. Furthermore, he studies the Roman Inquisition's procedure (often building on the work of John Tedeschi) and, to a degree, its personnel. He has also turned up a few new sources, though here, as on the score of several arguments he claims as original, some of the most important of both were put forward in the nineteenth century, especially by Domenico Berti, Sante Pieralisi, and Franz Reusch. Beretta's most serious limitation is that he is a theologian, and no matter how much he insists that his work goes beyond the apologetic nature of older studies, it is equally so in an antipapal way and as a result makes some crucial blunders or at least serious overstatements, including probably that Galileo's trial represented a moment in Urban VIII's effort to maintain the hierarchy of the disciplines with theology on top. Francesco Beretta, "Orthodoxie philosophique et Inquisition romaine au 16e–17e siècles: Un essai d'interprétation," *Historia Philosophica* 3 (2005): 67–96; "Melchior Inchofer et l'hérésie de Galilée: Censure doctrinale et hiérarchie intellectuelle," *Journal of Modern European History* 3 (2005): 23–49, 26; "La Condamnation de Galilée (1633)," 48; and "Galileo, Urban VIII and the Prosecution of Natural Philosophers," in McMullin, ed., *The Church and Galileo*, 234–61.

37. Beretta, "Le procès," 477.

38. Ibid., 476.

39. Ibid., 457, 459, and the appendices.

40. Ibid., 447–48, and "Galilée," 170.

41. Beretta, "Le Procès," 460.

42. Fantoli, "Injunction," 145n16. He bases his judgment on the photograph in Sergio

M. Pagano and Antonio G. Luciani, eds., *I documenti del processo di Galileo Galilei*, Collectanea Archivi Vaticani 21 (Città del Vaticano: Archivio Vaticano, 1984), pl. 1 (Fantoli says it is on 256, but all the plates follow that page).

43. Most of the Inquisition's *processi* have been lost.

44. For the special handling of such suspects, see, e.g., Nicolau Eymeric, ed., Francisco Peña, *Directorium inquisitorum* (Rome: Giorgio Ferrari, 1587), 409ff, or Francesco Albizzi, *De inconstantia in iure admittenda* (Amsterdam: Jean Antoine Huguetan, 1683), 68–81.

45. Beretta, "Procès," 475.

46. To Beretta's brief discussion, Stefania Pastore adds an article about *correctio fraterna*, which despite its promising title is almost entirely irrelevant. "A proposito di Matteo XVIII,15: Correctio fraterna e Inquisizione nella Spagna del Cinquecento," *Rivista Storica Italiana* 63 (2001): 323–68.

47. For Scaccia, see the next chapter. For the other two, *RI*, 159–60 and 152–53.

48. *RI*, 159 and Daniele Bartoli, *Della vita di Roberto cardinal Bellarmino* (Rome: Niccolò Angelo Tinassi, 1678), 219–20.

49. Prospero Farinacci, *Tractatus de haeresi* (Rome: Andrea Fei, 1616), 667–68; and *RI*, 170.

50. Beretta, *Galilée*, 152–58. Cf. Henri de Bohic, *In quinque Decretalium libros commentaria* (Venice: Girolamo Scoti, 1575 [1576]), 2, fo. 183r.

51. Francesco Beretta, "Le Siège apostolique et l'affaire Galilée: Relectures romaines d'une condamnation célèbre," *Roma Moderna e Contemporanea* 7 (1999): 421–61; 455n36 refers to Dorn's work without expressing an opinion about it.

52. Matthias Dorn, *Das Problem der Autonomie der Naturwissenschaften bei Galilei*, *Sudhoffs Archiv*, Beiheft 43 (Stuttgart: Franz Steiner, 2000), 167–77.

53. Ibid., 175.

54. Henri L'Épinois, *Les pièces du procès de Galilée précédées d'un avant-propos* (Rome: Palme, 1877), plate facing 40. For one effect of the manuscript's deterioration, see *DV*, 14n48. The original is now in the *Reserva* of the ASV and allegedly inaccessible for consultation, although Frajese was allowed to see it after I made my request. The photocopy made available to me is useless for most questions of palaeography and obviously all those of codicology.

55. Pagano, "Il precetto," 172–91, offers other criticisms, backed up by photographs he was ideally placed to procure.

56. Fantoli, "Injunction," 146n24.

57. For the first post, see Giovanni Mocenigo–doge, Ferrara, 26 June 1598 (ASVe:SDR, f. 41, fo. 313r), and X.-M. Le Bachelet, *Bellarmin avant son Cardinalat 1542–1598: Correspondence et documents* (Paris: Beauchesne, 1911), 385n; and for the second Giacomo Fuligatti, *Vita del Cardinale Roberto Bellarmino della Compagnia di Giesù* (Rome: Heirs of Bartolomeo Zannetti, 1624), 150, and X.-M. Le Bachelet, *Auctarium Bellarminianum: Supplément aus oeuvres du Cardinal Bellarmin* (Paris: Beauchesne, 1913), 458.

58. Fuligatti, *Bellarmino*, 150; 1626 edition, sig. HHr–v; and 1631 edition, 247. His

place of origin was probably Badia S. Quirico delle Rose, also called "a Nasciano," a former Camaldolese monastery, near Pozzo in Val di Chiana, attested from the eleventh to the thirteenth century and still a villa ca. 1833, now Foiano della Chiana (province of Arezzo). Emanuele Repetti, *Dizionario geografico fisico storico della Toscana*, 1 (Florence: A. Tofani, 1833), 156; and Fabio Gabbirelli, *Romanico Aretino: Architettura protoromanica e romanica religiosa nella diocesi medievale di Arezzo* (Florence: Salimbeni, 1990), 188. I am grateful to Erik Gustafson for helping locate this place.

59. Fantoli, "Injunction," 145n15. He extends a point made by Beretta in "L'Archivio della congregazione del Sant'Ufficio: Bilancio provvisorio della storia e natura dei fondi d'antico regime" in *L'inquisizione romana: Metodologia delle fonti e storia istituzionale*, ed. Andrea Del Col and Giovanna Paolin (Trieste: Edizioni Università di Trieste, 2000), 119 –44, 126.

60. "[I] registri degli atti emessi in forma pubblica dal notaio," ibid., 124. He cites as examples ACDFSO, L-3-a and Q-1-a through s.

61. Fantoli, "Injunction," 121–22 citing Morpurgo-Tagliabue, *I processi*, 18–20, *recte* 21.

62. Frajese published his work in at least three forms, first as "A proposito del processo a Galileo: Il problema del precetto Seghizzi," *Annali della Scuola Normale Superiore di Pisa, Classe di Lettere e Filosofia* ser. 5, 1/2 (2009): 507–34, and then both as an on-line article, "A proposito di falsi: Ritornando sul processo a Galileo," in *Dimensioni e problemi della ricerca storica* 1 (2010): 123–47, at http://dev.dsmc.uniroma1.it/dprs/sites/default/files/frajese.pdf, accessed 23 July 2010., and as a short book *Il processo a Galileo Galilei: Il falso e la sua prova* (Brescia: Morcelliana, 2010), neither adding to the original article's argument. See my review of the last in *Renaissance Quarterly* 66 (2013): 637–38.

63. Frajese, *Annali*, 507. He also calls Bellarmino's action a "verbal admonition" (508) and a "fraternal admonition" (510), as well as being "in fraternal and extrajudicial form" (511).

64. For the signatures' significance see, e.g., ibid., 514.

65. Ibid., 512–13, 523.

66. Ibid., 524.

67. Ibid., 526.

68. Frajese appends to his book (*Il processo*, 103–6) a report by an expert in medieval palaeography demonstrating the same point.

69. Frajese, *Annali*, 530–31.

70. Ibid., 518–19 and 516n, arguing against Fantoli in *Il caso Galileo: Dalla condanna alla "riabilitazione:" una questione chiusa?* (Milan: BUR, 2003), 114.

71. Frajese, *Annali*, 520.

72. Ibid., 521.

73. Ibid., 533.

74. Pagano also speaks of a "secret admonition" and a "formal admonition," as well as of a verbal warning followed by a written precept. "Il precetto," 145–46.

75. Ibid., 177–78.

76. Ibid., 185–86.

77. Ibid., 179–81. Pagano draws the further more debatable inference that the time delay between orders and notes of action taken was short.

78. Ibid., 188–90.

79. Ibid., 191.

80. Ibid., 187.

81. Ibid., 183; *RI*, 12, 19, 20–21.

82. E.g., *EN* 12: no. 1187 and see below.

83. *EN* 12: nos. 1187 and 1189.

84. These rumors came from especially worrisome sources, Castelli and Sagredo. *EN* 12: nos. 1195 and 1198.

85. Massimo Bucciantini, *Contro Galileo: Alle origini dell'Affaire* (Florence: Olschki, 1995), 28, thinks Galileo wanted the affidavit to show to the grand duke.

86. "Noi Roberto cardinale Bellarmino, havendo inteso che il sig. Galileo Galilei sia calunniato o imputato di havere abiurato in mano nostra [*la dottrina del Copernico circa la mobilità della terra, et immobilità del sole* cancelled], et anco di essere stato per ciò penitentiato di penitentie salutari, et essendo ricercati della verità, diciamo che il suddetto sig. Galileo non ha abiurato in mano nostra né di altri *qua in Roma, né in altro luogo che noi sappiamo, alcuna sua opinione, o dottrina [phrase added in margin], né manco [*meno* in the draft] ha ricevuto penitentie salutari né d'altra sorte, ma solo [added above *si bene, che* cancelled] gli è stata denuntiata la dichiaratione fatta da Nostro Signore et publicata dalla Sacra Congregatione dell'Indice, nella quale si contiene che la dottrina attribuita al Copernico, che la terra si muova intorno al sole, et che il sole stia nel centro del mondo senza muoversi da oriente ad occidente, sia contraria alle Sacre Scrit[tu]re, et però non si possa difendere né tenere. Et in fe[de] di ciò habbiamo scritta et sottoscritta la presente di nostra propria mano, questo dì 26 di maggio 1616." *DV*, no. 43. The draft is in ARSI, Opera nostrorum, 243 I, fo. 243r, printed in Ugo Baldini and George V. Coyne, eds. and trans., *The Louvain Lectures (Lectiones Lovanienses) of Bellarmine and the Autograph Copy of His 1616 Declaration to Galileo* (Vatican City: Specola Vatican, 1984), 25–26, with facsimile reproduction. I am grateful to T. M. McCoog, S.J., for sending me a copy of the manuscript.

87. Neveu and Mayaud, "L'Affaire Galilée," 296, although they are kinder to Galileo than I am. I am grateful to Massimo Firpo for discussion of the translation of *ma si bene*.

88. Pagano, "Il precetto," 193, observes that there was no reason for Bellarmino's *fede* to say anything about the event of 26 February since that was not its purpose.

89. Ibid., 197. He attenuates the force of his observation by endorsing Galileo's own defense that he had relied on Bellarmino's *fede* and therefore forgotten what had happened in the cardinal's palace.

90. *DV*, no. 69.

91. *EN* 12: no. 1110.

92. Franz Reusch, *Der Process Galilei's und die Jesuiten* (Bonn: Eduard Weber, 1879), 144.

93. *DV*, no. 70.

94. *DV*, no. 9.

95. *DV*, no. 42, italics in original.

96. Pagano, "Il precetto," 198.

97. *DV*, no. 48.

98. "Ma perché da questo S. Off.io, per aver io, dopo d'essermi stato con precetto dall'istesso giuridicamente intimato che omninamente dovessi lasciar la falsa opinione che il sole sia centro del mondo e che non si muova e che la terra non sia il centro del mondo e che si muova, e che non potessi tenere, difendere né insegnare in qualsivoglia modo, né in voce né in scritto, la detta falsa dottrina, e dopo d'essermi notificato che detta dottrina è contraria alla Sacra Scrittura, scritto e dato alle stampe un libro nel quale tratto l'istessa dottrina già dannata e apporto ragioni con molta efficacia a favor di essa, senza apportar alcuna soluzione, sono stato giudicato veementemente sospetto d'eresia, cioè d'aver tenuto e creduto che il sole sia centro del mondo e imobile e che la terra non sia centro e che si muova." *EN* 19: no. 406. English translation from *TG*, no. 82.

99. Wohlwill, *Der inquisitionsprocess*, 4–5, 7, 57.

100. Karl von Gebler, *Galileo Galilei und die römische Kurie nach den authentischen Quellen* ([n.p.]: Emil Vollmer, [n.d.]; reprint of Phaidon edition itself reprint of Stuttgart: J.G. Cotta, 1876), 54.

101. Fantoli, "Injunction," 120.

102. Quintiliano Mandosio and Pietro Vendramino, eds., *Repertorium inquisitorum pravitatis haereticae* (Venice: Damiano Zenaro, 1575), 431.

103. First published 1621. I quote from the expanded edition of Genoa: Giuseppe Pavoni, 1625; the 1639 edition contains the same text. For Gilbert, see my "Status," 73–77.

104. The only glimmer of hope in the entry in *Grande dizionario della lingua italiana*, ed. Salvatore Battaglia and Giorgio Bàrberi Squarotti, 21 vols. (Turin: UTET, 1961–2002), 7: 355, is the application of the term to the legal succession of an heir that may or may not in reality follow "immediately," with no interval of time whatsoever, on the death of the testator. See further below. I am grateful to Stefania Tutino for advice on this point.

105. Beretta, *Galilée*, 192.

106. Francisco Peña, "Introductio, sive Praxis Inquisitorum." BAV, Barb. lat. 1367, fo. 118v/1544, p. 46.

107. ACDFSO:DSO 1608, pp. 43 and 52; 1612, p. 600.

108. Luigi Amabile, *Frà Tommaso Campanella e la sua congiura, i suoi processi e la sua pazzia. Narrazione con molti documenti inediti politici e giudiziari, con l'intero processo di eresia e 67 poesie di 'Frà Tommaso' fin'oggi ignorate*, 3 vols. (Naples: Morano, 1882), 3, nos. 310, 314, 335, 260, 265, 298.

109. BEM:RC, MS 'Y.O.4.22, fos. 20v, 38v, 116r, 118r, 119r, 123r.

110. "Successive examinatus" (AdS Roma, Governatore, Processi, sec XVII, b. 251, fo. 523r); Successive cariter pro recognitione supradicti cadaveris (fo. 525v); "successive et incontinenti idem D. Jo. Bapta. Gentiultius ad effectum exequendi de mandatum ordinem et mentem (?)" of governor (fo. 860v); "etiam incontinenti" (fo. 553r).

111. Charles du Fresne du Cange, *Glossarium mediae et infimae Latinitatis*, 5 vols. (Graz: Akademische Druck- und Verlagsanstalt, 1954; reprint of 1883–89 ed.), s.v. 3: 331.

112. I have used a copy of the *Thesaurus* formerly in the Augustana College Library. It is missing the title page and I have not been able to provide bibliographical details. It does not appear in Worldcat, for example. The dedication is dated Leipzig 1717. This is probably one of the many updatings of Robert Estienne's dictionary of 1531 and later. Spartianus's text is part of the *Historia Augusta*.

113. It went through at least two editions, the first known that of Eustace Vignon, 1573. The work is relatively rare with only seven holders in Worldcat.

114. *Novus Linguae et Eruditionis Romanae Thesaurus* (Leipzig: Widow of Caspar Fritsch and Bernhard Christoph Breitkopf, 1749), 4: 625.

115. E. g., in Lactantius, *De falsa sapientia philosophorum* (J.-P. Migne, ed., *Patrologiae cursus completus . . . Series latina*, 217 vols. [Paris: Garnier, 1844–65], 6, col. 425B); Gregory the Great, *Moralia* (76, col. 500A); William of Malmesbury, *De antiquitate glastoniensis ecclesiae* (179, col. 1684A); Alan de Lille, *De fide catholica contra haereticos sui temporis* (210, col. 316B); or a number of occurrences in Innocent III's correspondence, 214, 215. http://pld.chadwyck.com.

116. Melchior Adam, *Vitae Germanorum iureconsultorum et politicorum . . . et Germanorum Theologorum* ([Frankfurt am Main]: Heirs of Johann Rosa; Heidelberg: Johannes Georg Geyder, 1620), 6, 758, and 770, as well as two occurrences in a file of Inquisition cases.TCD, MS 1232, fos. 432v and 450r, probably both from 1636.

117. The sixteenth-century humanist jurist Andrea Alciati put it among *inusitata vocabula* in Roman law. Karl Andreas Duker, ed., *Opuscula varia de latinitate iurisconsultorum veterum* (Leipzig: Fridi. Gotth. Iacobaeerum, 1773), 356 [389].

118. *Alberici de Rosate bergomensis iurisconsulti celeberrimi Dictionarium iuris tam civilis, quam canonici*, ed. Gianfrancesco Deciani (Venice: n.p., 1581), no foliation or pagination. I am grateful to Whitney S. Bagnall, former librarian of Special Collections in Law at Columbia, and Ryan Greenway for their help with this text.

119. *Commentariorum iuris utriusque summi practici Domini Alberici de Rosate Bergomensis pars prima super codice*, 2 vols. [(Lyon: George Regnault, 1545), fo. 87v.

120. E.g., Pardulph Du Prat, *Lexicon iuris civilis et canonici, sive potius thesaurus, de verborum, quae ad ius pertinent, significatione* (Lyon: Guillaume Rovilli, 1567), fo. 104r.

121. Felino Sandeo, *Commentariorum . . . ad quinque libros Decretalium pars prima [-tertia]*, 3 vols. (Venice: [Sub signo aquilae renovantis; Società dell'Aquila che si rinnova,], 1600–1601), 3, fo. 140v. See also one of his *Consilia* in a separately foliated appendix to the same volume, fo. 89r.

122. Menochio twice said the length of time was entirely up to the judge. *De arbitrariis judicum quaestionibus et causis libri duo* (Venice: Heirs of Girolamo Scoti, 1613), Bk II, c. 10, 159.

123. Ibid., 159–60.

124. *Repertorium Inquisitorum*, 431, cited in Philippe Gilbert, "La Condamnation de Galilée et les publications recentes," *Revue des Questions Scientifiques* (April 1877): 353–98; (July 1877): 130–94, 142, not entirely accurately.

125. "[V]ariam secundum rem propositam interpretationem recipit. Incontinenti,

cum aliquo moderato spatio interpretamur." *B. Brissonii in suprema parisiensi curia advocati, De verb. quae ad ius pertinent, significatione, libri XIX* (Frankfurt-am-Main: Johannes Fabricius, 1578; also later editions), col. 278. For other similar entries, see Antonius Nebrissensis [Antonio de Lebrija (died 1522)], *Vocabularium utriusque iuris* (Venice: Giovanni de Albertis, 1599), sigg. 154v and 131v; and Christoph Besold, *Thesaurus Practicus* (Nürnberg: Wolfgang Endter, 1643), 356, 654.

126. Simon Schard, *Lexicon iuridicum*, preface dated 16 March 1616, signed by Johannes Gymnicus (Cologne: Ioannem Gymnicum sub Monocerote, 1616), unpaginated and unfoliated. Johann Kahl in his popular *Lexicon iuridicum iuris caesarei* (Geneva: Matthieu Berjon for the Societas Caldoriana, 1612), p. 1338 [*recte* 1308] followed Schard almost word for word. The work went through at least fifteen editions after it first appeared in 1600. http://www.richardwolf.de/latein/kahl.htm.

127. Thomas Kurig, "Ein gravierender Fehler in der Übersetzung und Interpretation der Akten des Galileischen Inquisitionsprozesses," *Berichte zur Wissenschaftsgeschichte* 10, 1 (1987): 15–16, 16. "Im lateinischen Original sind die beiden Maßnahmen durch die drei Wörter 'successive, [*sic*] ac incontinenti' getrennt. Man muß sie etwa folgendermaßen übersetzen: 'darauf folgend [entsprechend dem päpstlichen Willen] und, da Galilei unwillig war. . . .' Das Partizip *incontinenti* bezieht sich eindeutig im Dativ auf den später folgenden Galilei und muß kausal übersetzt werden. Man kann es auch mit 'sich nicht mäßigend,' 'frech' wiedergeben." The English abstract confuses the issue by having Kurig say that Galileo really did refuse, which would make the precept legitimate, which Kurig doubts, apparently thinking it a forgery. Only Dorn, *Problem*, 172, has taken note of Kurig's point, and only to reject it. His criticism is founded in an incorrect characterization of the wide separation between *incontinenti* and *praedicto Galileo* as "high classical" style and on an originally eighteenth-century dictionary of classical Latin that took no account of later developments.

128. By Joseph Clark in 1964 at the Galileo conference at Notre Dame, cited in Jerome J. Langford, *Galileo, Science and the Church*, 3rd ed. (Ann Arbor: University of Michigan Press, 1992), 96. For some reason his paper was not included in *Galileo: Man of Science*, ed. Ernan McMullin (New York: Basic Books, 1967). Giorgio De Santillana predictably savaged Clark's suggestion, calling it a sign of the poor state of modern Latin instruction! "Nuove ipotesi sul processo di Galileo," in *Pubblicazioni del Comitato nazionale per le manifestazioni celebrative del IV centenario della nascita di Galileo Galilei*, 3:2, ed. Carlo Maccagni, *Saggi su Galileo Galilei* (Florence: G. Barbèra, 1972), 474–86, 482–83. I am grateful to my colleague Emil Kramer for further advice on this point.

129. Emil Wohlwill, *Ist Galilei gefoltert worden? Eine kritische Studie* (Leipzig: Duncker and Humblot, 1877), 138n. For his translations see *Inquisitionsprocess*, 4–5 ("und darauf folgend und sofort"); 7 ("ohne ihm [Galileo] zur Antwort Zeit zu lassen" or "ohne Pause"); and 57 ("unmittelbar darauf").

130. Masini's text postdates it by five years, the two instances Beretta cites from TCD, MS 1232 by twenty. T. K. Abbott, *Catalogue of the Manuscripts in the Library of Trinity College, Dublin* (Dublin: Hodges & Figgis, 1900), 257.

131. For these famous volumes, see John Tedeschi, *The Prosecution of Heresy: Collected Studies on the Inquisition in Early Modern Italy* (Binghamton, N.Y.: MRTS, 1991), 25–26.

132. "Successive ac incontinenti facta per custode de mandato perquistione super persona eiusdem Innocentii inventae fuerunt aliquae scripturae et alia fragmenta tracta de reperientis thesauris, et similibus, quae omnia ab(?) ipso subscripta fuerunt hic inserta, et signata." TCD, MS 1232, fo. 217v/181v (the volume has two foliations, neither of which is exactly right). There is also one case of the older "in continenti [*sic*]" used by itself (fo. 243r/246). Beretta, *Galilée*, 192.

133. TCD, MS 1232, fo. 453r/416r.

134. *Deinde*: TCD, MS 1232, fos. 83r/74r, 86/77v, 87/79/78, 178/147r, 456v/419v (in the midst of torture); *tunc*: fos. 257v and 296/273r.

135. The laurea is reproduced in pl. 5 part 2 in Candida Carella, *L'insegnamento della filosofia alla "Sapienza" di Roma nel Seicento: Le Cattedre e i Maestri* (Florence: Olschki, 2007), and the second is in ASV, S. R. Rota, Processus in admissione auditorum, b. 1, no. 67 (Alessandro Boccabella).

136. For a fuller treatment, see *RI*, 112–18.

137. ACDFSO:DSO 1601, fo. 213r.

138. ACDFSO:DSO 1603, fo. 188v and 1608–1609, fo. 397v.

139. *RI*, 117.

140. See the typical run of his correspondence from Milan in late 1613 with letters of 22 and 31 October; 5, 6 (either two separate letters or two problems in the same letter) and 13 November (ACDFSO:DSO 1613, pp. 543, 557, 563, 567, and 586) and 4 December (1614, p. 3). If anything, he wrote even more frequently from Cremona.

141. He swore the oath of secrecy on 25 February 1615. ACDFSO:DSO 1614, pp. 98 and 99.

142. BAV, Urb. lat. 1084, fos. 197r and 204r.

143. ACDFSO:DSO 1616, p. 208, and ASV, Archivio concistoriale, Acta miscellanea, 97, fo. 893r.

144. ACDFSO:DSO 1616, p. 369.

145. Ibid., 1616, p. 329, and 1619, p. 419. In 1626 he was transferred to Modena. BAV, Barb. lat. 6334, fos. 22v–3r. For Tinti, see Christopher F. Black, *The Trials and Tribulations of a Local Roman Inquisitor: Giacomo Tinti in Modena, 1626–1647* at www.giornaledistoria.net, accessed 15 December 2012.

146. For impressionistic evidence suggesting that commissaries named their own *socii*, see *RI*, 303n77.

147. *DV*, no. 20; English translation in *TG*, doc. 23.

148. The Latin text makes a grammatical mistake here.

149. The usual translation of *recusaverit*, but it also has the weaker sense "to be reluctant."

150. *DV*, no. 21; Reader, doc. 24.

151. The Index met on 1 March. Mayaud, *Condamnation*, 37–38. Bellarmino reported

its action to the Inquisition on the 3 March. ACDFSO:DSO 1616, p. 99, middle of page; *EN* 19: no. 278; *DV*, no. 124.

152. *DV*, no. 22.

153. Mayaud, *Condamnation*, 42–43.

154. See part of Giovanfrancesco Buonamici's "diary," dated 2 May 1633, in *EN* 15: no. 2492, and Michele Camerota, *Galileo Galilei e la cultura scientifica nell'età della Controriforma* (Rome: Salerno Editrice, 2004), 320–21. Among other sources for the story about Cardinal Barberini and Copernicus, see "Memorie intorno la Vita di PP. Urbano cavate dall'originale di Mon. [apparently Francesco] Herrera al quale S. Ma. le dettava," in BAV, Barb. lat. 4734, fo. 245v. Castelli told Galileo the story at third hand fifteen years later. *EN* 14: no. 1993.

155. Ingoli served as Caetani's auditor when the cardinal was legate of Romagna. Josef Metzler, "Francesco Ingoli, der erste Sekretär der Kongregation (1578–1649)," in *Sacrae Congregationis de Propaganda Fide Memoria Rerum 1622–1972*, 3 vols. (Rome: Herder, 1971–76), 1: 197–243, 200. Mayaud, *Condamnation*, 60–61, calls Ingoli Caetani's secretary for whom he undertook the revision of Copernicus. See also Bucciantini, *Origini*, 88.

156. Mayaud, *Condamnation*, 56–57.

157. ACDFSO:DSO 1616, p. 99 in middle of page; *EN* 19: no. 278; *DV*, no. 124.

158. *EN* 12: no. 1185.

159. See *SI*, chapters 5 and 6.

160. *DV*, no. 22, a printed copy of the decree included in Galileo's *processo*.

161. Decio Carafa–Millini, 2 June 1616, Naples, and decree in response of 9 June 1616 ordering the archbishop to pursue the printer. *DV*, nos. 23 and 24; *EN* 19: no. 279.

162. Querenghi reported that the Inquisition handed down the decree (*EN* 12: no. 1186), the Venetian ambassador agreed (while adding that Galileo had been "ammunito rigorosamente") (*EN* 20: no. 570), and so did an anonymous reporter to Giovanni de' Medici on 26 March, misdating the decree to 7 March (Massimo Bucciantini, "Reazioni alla condanna di Copernico: Nuovi documenti e nuove ipotesi di ricerca," *Galileiana* 1 [2004]: 3–19 and 18–19 [text]), as did Matteo Caccini writing to his brother Alessandro on 11 June 1616, Rome, misdating the event in the same way (*EN* 12: no. 1208).

163. *EN* 12: 1186.

164. Bucciantini, "Reazioni," 6–7 and 18–19.

165. The first letter just cited referred to "Dr. Bellabarba delli Amadori" and other Galileisti as not at all bothered. Amadori was probably the Florentine physician Giovanni Battista, a close friend of Ludovico Cigoli, Benedetto Castelli, and Luigi Maraffi. For Cigoli, see *EN* 10: no. 273, and 11, nos. 468, 791, 840, 870; for Castelli, *EN* 11: nos. 842 and 951; and for Maraffi, *EN* 18: no. 842bis, a letter to an unknown correspondent to which Amadori appended a list of prohibited books he wished permission to read.

166. *EN* 12: no. 1187.

167. Picchena–Galileo, 20 March 1616, Livorno. *EN* 12: no. 1191.

168. Francesco Maria Del Monte–Cosimo II, 4 June 1616, Rome, and Alessandro Orsini–Galileo, 26 June 1616, Rome. *EN* 12: nos. 1207 and 1210.

169. Galileo–Picchena, 12 March 1616, Rome. *EN* 12: no. 1189.

170. Galileo–[Picchena], 26 March 1616, Rome. *EN* 12: no. 1192.

171. Sfondrato–inquisitor of Modena, 2 April 1616, with orders to print the letter as soon as possible, and a general circular of 9 April. *EN* 12: no. 1193; and Ugo Baldini and Leen Spruit, "Nuovi documenti galileiani degli archivi del Sant'Ufficio e dell'Indice," *Rivista di Storia della Filosofia* 56 (2001): 661–99, 675–76.

172. Avviso of 9 April 1616 in BAV, Urb. lat. 1083, fo. 136v.

173. Bucciantini, *Origini*, 53, emphasizes that Caccini did not suffer disgrace by the affair. His brother Matteo may even have gone over to the enemy, possibly writing the anonymous report to Florence cited above that included the news about Lorini's reaction to Galileo's condemnation. At any rate, Matteo made the same mistake about the date of the Index decree as the writer of that letter, assigning it to the Feast of St Thomas Aquinas, March 7. See also Guerrini, *Cosmologie*, 210, who notes the likelihood of a common source, "undoubtedly Roman," and speculates wildly that Seghizzi might have sent the news to Florence.

174. Ricci-Riccardi, *Galileo*, 182.

175. Ibid.

176. Matteo Caccini–Alessandro Caccini, 18 January 1619, Rome. *EN* 18: no. 1370bis.

177. Ricci-Riccardi, *Galileo*, 191.

178. "Mi dispiace poi che il P. Caccini pregiudichi tanto a' Principi e al S.to Officio stesso, se però è vero che vadia dicendo che, se non fusse lo scudo di diversi Principi, V. S. sarebbe stata messa all'Inquisizione, quasi che i Principi impedischino il S.to Officio e protegghino persone di mal affare, e insieme il S.to Officio porti rispetti a' Principi nel procedere contro l'impietà; e mi pare che il Padre Caccini meriti d'esser messo all'Inquisizione, perchè non fa il debito suo per rispetti de' Principi." Castelli–Galileo, 6 December 1623, Pisa. *EN* 13: no. 1604.

179. *Storia del primo concilio niceno (History of the First Nicene Council)* (Lucca: Pellegrino Bidelli, 1637), Caccini–Francesco Barberini, 3 July 1638. BAV, Barb. lat. 6540, fo. 34r. Ricci-Riccardi, *Galileo*, 219, cited a letter from Tommaso of 24 May 1640 saying the cardinal had Caccini's works read at table.

CHAPTER 4. THE LEGAL MEANING OF 1616:
THE JURISPRUDENCE AND USE OF ADMONITIONS AND PRECEPTS

1. A condensed version of this chapter was presented at the UCLA School of Law in October 2013. I am grateful for much helpful feedback.

2. Prospero Farinacci's *Tractatus de haeresi* (Rome: Andrea Fei, 1616) could perhaps have provided a link between jurisprudence and Inquisition practice, but it treats precepts only in the context of apostasy of persons under religious obedience, which he decided was (surprise!) heresy.

3. E.g., Francesco Zabarella in his commentary on X.2.1.13, Innocent III's *Novit* (*Super*

primo [–quinto] Decretalium subtilissima commentaria (Venice: Luca Antonio Giunti, 1603), 3, fos. 17r and 47r) or Filippo Decio on X.1.29.24, *Consuluit (In decretalium volumen perspicua commentaria* [Venice: Giunta, 1593], fo. 127 no. 76).

4. *In primum [-sextum] decretalium librum commentaria*, 7 vols. (Venice: Giunta, 1581), 2, fo. 84r–v nos. 3–4.

5. E.g., Innocent IV (Sinibaldo de' Fieschi), *In quinque decretalium libros, necnon in decretales per eundem Innocentium editas . . . commentaria doctissima* (Venice: Bernardino Maiorini, 1570), fos. 288r (X.5.1.2) and 289v (X.5.1.16). He also left the waters in need of clarification by speaking of "evangelicae denunciationis correctionis sive monitionis" (fo. 154r); Enrico Da Susa used similarly confusing language. *Commentaria*, 5, fo. 4v. Henri de Bohic was among the first to try to clean up the terminology. *In quinque Decretalium libros commentaria*, 5 vols. (Venice: Heirs of Girolamo Scoti), 5, fo. 111r.

6. De Bohic, *Commentaria*, 5, fo. 83r. Domenico Da San Gimignano, *Super Decretorum volumine commentaria* (Venice: Giunta, 1578), fo. 164r, gave twice in the case of evangelical denunciation, three times for judicial.

7. Antonio Da Budrio, *Super prima [-secunda] primi [-secundi] Decretalium commentarii . . . Tomus primus [-septimus]*, 7 vols. (Venetiis: apud Iuntas, 1578), 1, fo. 23r.

8. For the usual position about the equivalence of admonition and evangelical denunciation, see, e.g., Da Susa, *Commentaria*, 5, fo. 4v. De Bohic unusually distinguished *monitio* and *denunciatio* but did not define the second. De Bohic, *Commentaria*, 5, fo. 111r. See also San Gimignano for *canonica admonitio* as equivalent to *citatio*. San Gimignano, *Commentaria*, fo. 232r no. 1.

9. See Innocent IV, *Commentaria*, fo. 118v.

10. The fourfold scheme represented the addition of one ("regular") to Enrico Da Susa's original three, which Francisco Peña still cited. BAV, Barb. lat. 1367, fo. 28r–v; 1544, p. 29.

11. San Gimignano, *Commentaria*, fo. 164r. Zabarella offered a very similar discussion. Zabarella, *Commentaria*, 2, fo. 5v.

12. San Gimignano, *Commentaria*, fo. 164r.

13. Da Budrio, *Commentarii*, 3, fos. 17v–21r. For D'Andrea, see San Gimignano, *Commentaria*, fo. 164r. Zabarella, Da Budrio's contemporary, said the four types were "commonly" given. Zabarella, *Commentaria*, 2, fo. 5v.

14. Cf. De Bohic, *Commentaria*, 2, fo. 183r.

15. Da Budrio, *Commentarii*, 4, fo. 5v on X.2.28.5.

16. Paolo Da Castro, *Consiliorum . . . volumen primum [-tertium]*, 3 vols. (Venice: [Società dell'Aquila che si rinnova], 1580–1581), fos. 17v–18r.

17. Breve of 16 [*sic*] June 1618 in ASV, Sec. Brevi 561, fos. 31r–34v.

18. Although fathered on Giovanni Calderini, *Repertorium Inquisitorum* was probably written considerably later by a notary of the inquisition in Spain and edited by Miguel Albert before its first publication in Valencia in 1494. Andrea Errera, *Processus in Causa Fidei: L'evoluzione dei manuali inquisitoriali nei secoli XVI–XVIII e il manuale inedito di un inquisitore perugino* (Bologna: Monduzzi, 2000), 93–94.

19. Pseudo-Giovanni Calderini, *Tractatus novus aureus et solemnis de haereticis* (Venetiis: ad candentis Salamandrae insigne [Damiano Zenaro acc. Biblioteca Angelica catalogue information], 1571), 544–56.

20. For Caccini and Lorini, see Chapter 2.

21. *De iudiciis*, 144–45.

22. Da Budrio, *Commentarii*, 4, fos. 22v–23r.

23. For *constitutus* and its significance, see Chapter 3 and *RI*, 177.

24. Eliseo Masini, *Sacro arsenale, ovvero prattica dell'officio della S. Inquisizione ampliata* (Genoa: Giuseppe Pavoni, 1625), 41. But see the draft citation discussed below, which included the charges.

25. Sigismondo Scaccia, *Tractatus de iudiciis causarum civilium, criminalium et haereticalium* (Frankfurt: Officina Paltheniana, 1618), 149–54.

26. *Repertorium locupletissimum in omnes Bartoli a Saxo Ferrato Lecturas* (Turin: Heirs of Niccolò Bevilacqua, 1577), unfoliated, e.g., fos. 9 no. 48, 4 no. 53, 8 no. 42, 5 no. 130, and 8 no. 77.

27. Cino was commenting on D.3.3.73 and D.5.1.21. Pietro D'Ancarano, on *Dudum et infra, De rebus ecclesiasticis non alienandis* [VI.3.9.1] in *Super sexto Decretalium acutissima commentaria* (Bologna: Societas Typographiae Bononiensis, 1583), 310 no. 4.

28. Bartolo, *Gemma legalis seu compendium aureum . . .* (Venice: Giunti, 1596), v. 11 of *Opera omnia*, 8 part II, fos. 49r (both), "Praeceptum omne iudicis facientes ad causam dicitur sententia interlocutoria," in l. quoties. nu. 6. C. de digni. lib. X (1577) 12. (1596) with reference to next (9 no. 46); 9 no. 46v, "Praeceptum faciens ad causam est interlocutorie [sic] sententia" in § ad excludendas no. 10 in Auth. de litig.; cf. also 9 no. 48.

29. "Praeceptum iudicis debet exequi, licet antequam exequatur iudex removeatur de officio . . . videtur quod ista iussio, seu praeceptum extinguatur morte eius causa cui facta est, vel eius officio finito, nam mandatum morte mandatarii extinguitur." Ibid., fos. 53v no. 56 (Bartolo Da Sassoferrato, *Repertorium*, unfoliated), and 46v, "Praeceptum faciens ad causam est interlocutorie [sic] sententia in § ad excludendas no. 10 in Auth. de litig."

30. Bartolo, *Gemma*, fo. 2* no. 139v, "Praeceptum absque Ordine iudiciario factum potest etiam absque causae cognitione, & citatione revocari. Alex. [unidentified] in add. l. minor. ff. de evict. in ver. Gl. ver. Et per istam col. 4." For these two crucial moments of legal process, see *RI*, 187 and 177–80.

31. Bartolo, *Gemma*, 8/76v no. 3, "Quod praeceptum habet vim cuiusdam citationis, sed est nullum, etiam si fit praeceptum iudicis in l. 1. nu. 3. C. de execu. rei. iud." In case of an order to pay before sentence, the letter has the force of citation "& praeceptum, quando continetur est nullum. Et istam formam citandi tangit gl. in l. de pupillo, § meminisse, ff. de no. ope. nun & ibi dixi."

32. Lanfranco da Oriano, *Repetitio on Quoniam contra* [2], in *Repetitionum in universas fere Iuris canonici partes, materiasque sane frequentiores*, 6 vols. (Venice: Luca Antonio Giunti, 1587), 3, fos. 227v [sic]–28r.

33. "Praeceptum iudicis non est sententia diffinitiva, sed interlocutoria," commenting on *De re iudicata*, l. 3, C.7.52.3. Paolo Da Castro, *In Pandectarum, Iustinianeique Codicis,*

titulos commentaria, 8 vols. (Venice: Giunta, 1593–1594 [Venice: Giunta, 1592–1593]), 8, fo. 133v. See also 1, fo. 125v to D.5.1.21, "Si debitori meo."

34. Comment on D.I.3. Da Castro, *In pandectarum . . . commentaria*, fo. 10r.

35. Quoted in Decio, *In decretalium . . . commentaria*, fo. 59r.

36. Da Castro, *Consiliorum*, 48 in 2, fo. 23v. See also *consilium* 20 in 3, fos. 17r–18r.

37. Del Maino, *Commentaria*, 2, fo. 158r–v.

38. For citations of Paolo, see, e.g., Giacomo Menochio, *De arbitrariis iudicum quaestionibus et causis libri duo* (Venice: Heirs of Girolamo Scoti, 1613), I, Quaestio LXIX, p. 84 (quoting somewhat beside the point Paolo's consilium 48, misnumbered 438), or Filippo Decio, *Super decretalibus [libri]* (Lyon: Mathieu Bernard and Etienne Servani, 1564), fos. 17r–18r, referring to D.I.3 on the force of precept relative to counsel.

39. The Collateral of Naples cited him in the course of a long-running contest of secular jurisdiction on 26 January 1630. J. P. Wickersham Crawford, "The Life and Works of Christóbal Suárez de Figueroa: A Dissertation Presented to the Faculty of the Department of Philosophy of the University of Pennsylvania" (Philadelphia, 1907), 107–21.

40. San Gimignano, *Commentaria*, fo. 156r–v, citing "Ugo.," probably Huguccio, author of an influential late twelfth-century *Summa* on the *Decretum*.

41. *Repetitio on Canonum statuta, De constitutionibus* [X.1.2.1]. D'Ancarano, *In quinque Decretalium . . . commentaria*, 2, fo. 56v.

42. C.14.q.1.c.3 §. 2. "Quod precipitur inperatur; quod inperatur necesse est fieri; si non fiat, penam habet." § 3. "Ubi consilium datur, offerentis arbitrium est; ubi preceptum, necessitas servientis."

43. C.33.q.2.c.3. "Preceptum est ab inperatore lege lata, ut primo permitteretur ei libere rem familiarem diutius ordinare; tunc deinde responderet obiectis. Hoc omnes leges tam ecclesiasticae quam uulgares publicaeque recipiunt."

44. See also D. 4. c. LXXXIII, D. 4, *De consecratione*, and c. V, *De consecratione*.

45. See, e.g., D. 55. c. 12, D. 19. c. 2 and 5.

46. "Mandatum consistit inter consilium & preceptum. Est enim ultra consilium & citra preceptum. Mandatum enim cogit sicut & preceptum & peccatur si non adimpletur. & in hoc differt a consilio & accedit ad preceptum sed pena non infligitur antequam preceptionis verbum recipiat & condemnatur. & in hoc differt a precepto & consonat consilio," citing *Relatum*. Comment on C.14.q.1.c.3 § 2. Guido Da Baysio, *Rosarium super decreto* ([Venice], 1494), fo. [235r].

47. If "alius superior committat inferiori & dicat precipimus iubemus ut iussus & preceptum necesssitatem imponat. Si autem dicat mandamus vel volumus non. . . . Si autem dicat mando expirat tunc morte mandantis & non imponit necessitatem, . . but qui delegat precipit. . . . hoc non est verum. qui dicit quod omne verbum necessitatem imponit." After a discussion of judges delegate and mandates, Guido concluded "preceptum non obligat semper & ad semper & simpliciter." *Rosarium*, fo. [235r].

48. "Precepta sunt quae aut quid faciendum sit aut non faciendum docent, precipere est imperare seu occupare iubere, & componitur preceptum a pre & capio, iussio, enim facta est secundum papi. vel dic planius preceptum dicitur a precipio, pis [*sic*] quid est pre

aliis capere, quia precepta pre aliis capienda sunt a faciendum eo quod homo tenetur illa perficere; unde componitur ut predixi, vel preceptum dicitur precedentis sive precellentis ceptum.id est captum quod a solo precedente sive precellente capitur a subdito . . . & non quia preceptum obligat semper & ad semper." Comment to D.i.c.5, De consecratione, c. precepta). Guido Da Baysio, *Super decreto [liber]* (Lyon: Ugo da Porte, 1549), fo. 379v, no.1.

49. The revised code of 1983 gave rise to similar amounts of commentary on precepts, of no use for present purposes.

50. Raymond de Peñafort assumed this sense, the only one he discussed, in *Summa de Poenitentia* (Rome: Giovanni Tallini, 1603), 381.

51. Willy Onclin, *De territoriali vel personali legis indole*, Dissertationes ad gradum magistri in Facultate Theologica vel in Facultate Iuris Canonici consequendum conscriptae, Universitas Catholica Lovaniensis, ser. 2, vol. 31 (Gembloux: J. Duculot, 1938), 131.

52. G. Paolo Montini, "I rimedi penali e la penitenze: un'alternative alla pene," in Zbigniew Suchecki, ed., *Il Processo Penale Canonico* (Rome: Lateran University Press, 2003), 75–101.

53. *Repertorium in omnes commentarios Ioannis a Turre Cremata super Decretum* (Venice: Heirs of Girolamo Scotti, 1578), 138. Among those citing Da Baysio were Decio (*Super decretalibus*, fos. 17r–18r; X.I.2.4, *Nam concupiscentiam*) and Da Budrio (*Commentarii*, 1, fos. 12v–13r). Durand said much the same as cited by Menochio, *De arbitrariis*, Quaestio 498 n. 41 (p. 869). See also Antonio Burgos's popular *repetitiones* on *Canonum statuta, De constitutionibus* [X.1.2.1] and *Quae in ecclesiarum, De constitutionibus* [X.1.2.7] in *Repetitionum in universas fere Iuris canonici partes, materiasque sane frequentiores*, 6 vols. (Venice: Luca Antonio Giunti, 1587), 2, fos. 78r and 151v. Felino Sandeo, who was otherwise among the most hard-nosed canonists about precepts, cited this particular notion only in a *consilium*, so far as I can see. *Consilia Felini Sandei . . . His subiectis est index in omnia eiusdem Felini opera* (Venice: [Sub signo aquilae renovantis], 1601), fo. 118v.

54. See, e.g., *Dominorum de Rota decisiones novae, antiquae et antiquiores* (Cologne: Gymnich, 1581), p. 364 (10/3 antiq de consue.).

55. "Praeceptum generale datum pro tota communitate et ad eius bonum commune non est lex, et in nullo alio differt a lege, nisi in perpetuitate." Francisco Suarez, *De legibus*, vol. 5, L. I. c. 10, no. 6, cited by Onclin, *Indole*, 236 giving a long list of other early modern commentators who agreed with Suarez.

56. A precept "non attingunt statum et perpetuitatem legum. . .ideo ab homine vocantur." Suarez, *De legibus*, XXIII, *De censuris*, disp. III, sect VIII, n. 4; see also disp. III, sect I, n. 2. and further bibliography cited by Onclin, *Indole*, 239.

57. "Qui enim potest per praeceptum perpetuum legem condere, potest etiam praecipere communitati, non condendo legem, sed ad tempus. Solum vero praeceptum quod ponit legislator perpetuo duraturum vocatur lex; illud contra quod tantum ad tempus, simpliciter praeceptum nuncupatur." Suarez, *De legibus*, V, L. I. c. I, n. 11–12, quoted in Onclin, *Indole*, 237.

58. "Inde fit ut lex ratione suae perpetuitatis aequiparetur consuetudini et censeatur nota omnibus et omnibus proposita ut ab eis servetur; praeceptum vero non ita aequiparatur

consuetudini nec illam introducit, cum facile mutetur, nec ita solet esse notum et ideo praeceptum de se solum obligat incolas terrae et subditos." Suarez, *De Legibus*, V, L. III, c. XXXIII n. 12, quoted in Onclin, *Indole*, 240.

59. Pio Fedele, "Dei precetti ecclesiastici," in *Scritti giuridici in onore di Santi Romano*, 4 vols. (Padua: CEDAM, 1940), 4: 267–310, 273 and 294–95.

60. Giuido's principle drew wide acceptance. As Zabarella put it, "mandatum & praeceptum differentiam inter haec, mandatum enim non importat necessitatem, praeceptum sic." X.1.3.7, *Eam te, De rescriptis. Commentaria*, 1, fo. 33r.

61. Fedele, "Precetti," 299. This is a slight misquotation, Decio putting *semper* between *se* and *habet*. *In decretalium . . . commentaria*, fo. 59r.

62. Fedele, "Precetti," 301.

63. According to Fedele, the *Glossa* here assimilated a precept to an interdict in Roman law. Ibid., 305.

64. X.5.39.21. Da Budrio, *Commentarii*, 7, fos. 120r–121v.

65. "Dic quod statuta, quae ut edicta dependentiam non habent perpendiculariter super potentia statuentis, et sic ipsam non assumit pro causa permanendi, sed producendi, et eo quod prodita a se vires sumunt, durant, et extinguuntur extinctione iurisdictionis. . .[i.o.] Sententia vero quae perpendiculariter habuit suum effectum et vim promovendi a pronunciante, et ab eius potestate perpendiculariter dependet, prout sententia est in fieri, quia nondum ex contraventione laqueum iniecit, extinguitur." Filippo Decio, *Super librum primum-quintum Decretalium commentarii*, 8 vols. in 5 (Venice: Giunti, 1578), fo. 121r–v, no. 11; *Commentaria in decretalium* (1593), fo. 118r, no. 46 on X.1.29.19, both cited in Fedele, "Precetti," 305n.

66. Fedele, "Precetti," 305n. Fedele noted but did not pursue Decio's claim that Goffredo Da Trani also thought precepts expired with the death of the issuer.

67. "Secus autem est in precepto, quod sit alias habenti potestatem quia tunc solum antiqua potestas excitatur; in tali casu preceptum per mortem non extinguitur." Decio, *Super decretalibus*, fo. 126v.

68. Decio reported Goffredo's views as reported by Zabarella that "natura precepti communiter est, quod fiat ei, qui alias habet potestatem: ideo statim quod emanavit, suum habet complementum & per mortem non extinguitur." Ibid.; *In decretalium*, fos. 117v–18r. I have not been able to verify Zabarella's quotation, which almost certainly comes from the *Summa*, by far Goffredo's most widely diffused work. http://www.treccani.it/enciclopedia/goffredo-da-trani_%28Dizionario-Biografico%29/, accessed 23 November 2012.

69. Decio, *Super decretalibus*, fos. 125v–6v; *In decretalium*, fos. 117v–118r.

70. Fedele, "Precetti," 306n, emphasis added.

71. "[S]ed licet tunc mandatum expiret: non tamen preceptum factum a quocumque iudice mortuo vel translato." Guillaume Durand, *Speculi pars prima [-tertia et quarta]* (Lyon: n.p., 1543), fo. 13r.

72. Niccolò De' Tudeschi, *Prima [-ultima] p[ar]s Abb. Panor. sup[er] primo [-quarto [et] q[ui]nto] Decre[talium]* ([Lyon?]: Jean Petit, 1521–1522), 1, fos. 79v–80r. See also De' Tudeschi, *Omnia quae extant commentaria, primae [-tertiae] partis, in primum [-quintum] Decretalium librum*, 9 vols. (Venice: Giunta, 1588), 1, fos. 47r–8r.

73. Zabarella, *Commentaria*, fos. 249v–52r. See also fos. 33r–35r and 244r–45r.

74. "Secus dicit [Durand] in praecepto: quia commissio pendet ex voluntate mandantis, quae finitur morte: praeceptum non habet dependentiam ex voluntate, sed ex necessitate, quo quod est mandatum.in Spe.de dele.§.restar.ver. [*recte* Restat videre] item mortuo." Antonio Da Budrio, comment on X.1.29.19, *Relatum, De officio et potestate iudicis delegati* in *Commentarii*, 2, fo. 32r–v, citing "Spe.de dele.§.restar.ver.[*recte* restat videre] item mortuo;" the closest Durand comes to Da Budrio's quotation is on fo. 13r: "sed licet tunc mandatum expiret: non tamen preceptum factum a quocumque iudice mortuo vel translato."

75. De' Tudeschi, *Prima pars Decretalium*, 1, fos. 47r–8r on X.1.3.7, *Eam te, De rescriptis*.

76. Comment on X.1.2.4. *Compendium aureum totius lecturae d. Abbatis Panormitani super decretalibus* (Venice: Michele Tramezino, 1564), fo. 20r–v.

77. X.1.3.5. Ibid., fo. 46r–v.

78. X.1.29.14. Da Budrio, *Commentarii*, 2, fo. 29v.

79. X.1.2.4. Da Budrio, *Commentarii*, 1, fos. 12v–13r.

80. Paolo Borgasio fathered the claim of necessity on Da Susa. *Tractatus de irregularitatibus, et impedimentis ordinum, officiorum, et beneficiorum ecclesiasticorum, et censuris ecclesiasticis, & dispensationibus super eis* (Venice: Guerra, 1574), p. 28.

81. "Obedientia vero consistit in tribus—in reverentia, iudicio, & praecepto. . . .Virtus autem sive efficacia praecepti est quod subditus tenetur obedire praecepto praelati sui ex necessitate, aliter peccat mortaliter immo ariolus & idolatria iudicatur. . . . sciendum quod intelligo cum superior praecipit licitum et honestum." Goffredo Da Trani, *Summa. . .in tit[ulis] decretalium* (Venice: ad candentis Salamandræ insigne [?Damiano Zenaro], 1564), 116.

82. "Item & si onerosum sit quod mandantur obediendum est . . . & si iniusta correctio sit tolleranda est . . . & quod dixi in dubio obediendum intelligo nisi dubitatio esset crassa & supina quae non excuseret ut si superior mandet aliquid quod sit contra articulos fidei, contra praecepta & prohibitiones, contra generale statutum ecclesiae. In talibus non excuseret dubitatio, quia nec ignorantia. . . . Unum non obmitto quod mandato superioris oneroso est parendum . . . & patientissime tolleranda est etiam iniusta correctio." Ibid., 116–17.

83. Raymond de Peñafort, *Summa de Poenitentia* (Rome: Giovanni Tallini, 1603), 381.

84. Sandeo, *Consilia*, fo. 118v.

85. Felino Sandeo, *Commentariorum [liber]*, 1, fo. 85v.

86. Da Budrio, admittedly not the most careful of jurists, is yet typical in treating on X.1.33.2 *praeceptum superioris*, *decretum*, *constitutio*, and *mandatum* as all more or less equivalent and Giovanni D'Andrea did much the same, both following Innocent IV's lead. Da Budrio, *Commentaria*, 2, fo. 85r–v; Giovanni D'Andrea, *In primum [-quintum] decretalium librum novella commentaria*, 5 vols. in 4 (Venice: Francesco Francesco, 1581), 1, fo. 263r; Innocent IV (Sinibaldo de' Fieschi), *In quinque libros decretalium, necnon in decretales per eundem Innocentium editas, quae modo in sexto earundem volumine sunt insertae. . .commentaria doctissima* (Venice: Giunta, 1578), fo. 66v.

87. Sandeo, *Commentariorum . . . Decretalium*, 1, fo. 17v. He might also have taken his lead from Da Susa who had distinguished on X.1.2.1 between "statuta, praecepta, vel prohibitiones continentia, nam consiliatoria non obligant" (1, fo. 7r–v).

88. E.g., Guido Da Baysio, *Super decreto* (1549), fo. 91r where he said that even the form of precept that everybody else thought the most obligatory had limits ("Precepta quae per modum statuti vel constitutionis proponuntur, non eodem modo obligant omnes, sed secundum quod requiritur ad finem, quem legislator intendit") or his correct etymology of praeceptum which he set in distinction to another possible but in his view incorrect meaning "quia preceptum obligat semper & ad semper," commenting on De consecratione, D.1.c.precepta.no.1.

89. X.1.11.5, *Ad aures, De temporibus ordinationum. Commentaria* (1570), fo. 63v; (1578), fo. 43r.

90. X.5.39.44, *Inquisitioni, De sententia excommunicationis.* Ibid. (1570), fos. 328v–29r (1578), fo. 229r.

91. "Nunquid tenet sententia lata a iudice, qui non secutus est consilium requisitum." X.1.29.3. *Si pro debilitate, De officio et potestate iudicis delegati.* Ibid. (1570), fo. 76r–v; (1578), fo. 52r.

92. Zabarella on X.1.11.5, *Ad aures, De temporibus ordinationum. Commentaria*, fos. 205v–6r. I have not located this passage in Innocent's commentaries.

93. Innocent IV on X.5.39.44, *Inquisitioni, De sententia excommunicationis. Commentaria* (1570), fos. 328v–29r; (1578), fo. 229r.

94. "Porro si non potest suam conscientiam praelati imperio conformare, sequatur conscientiam, nec obediat . . . etiam si conscientia erronea sit." X.1.11.5, *Ad aures, De temporibus ordinationum.* Da Susa, *Commentaria*, 1, fo. 99r–v.

95. "[I]n praecepto [the Gloss] distinguit, an spectet ad eius officium, vel non. Et primo casu subdistinguit, an sit iustum, vel iniustum, vel dubitetur. . . . ergo sufficere, quod subditus credat praeceptum iniustum . . . , quare excusetur [as in this case]. . . si potest suam conscientiam informare praelati praecepto. Nam si non obedierit, nec ostendit causam probabilem, punietur [Host.]" commenting on X.1.11.5 (D'Andrea, *Commentaria*, 1, fo. 156r–v); for obedience to the pope, see ibid., 5, fos. 144v–45r, discussion of X.5.39.44, *De sententia excommunicationis, Inquisitioni,* where any commentator would be likely to stress obedience.

96. X.1.2.4, *Nam concupiscentiam, De constitutionibus,* and X.1.3.5, *Si quando, De rescriptis.* De' Tudeschi, *Commentaria*, 1, fos. 20r–v and 46r–v.

97. Ibid., X.1.3.5, *Si quando, De rescriptis,* 1, fo. 46r–v.

98. 1570, unnumbered "Margarita" at the end of the volume interpreting Innocent's discussion of X.1.11.5, *Ad aures, De temporibus ordinationum* (see 1570, fo. 63v; 1578, fo. 43r).

99. Da Budrio, *Commentaria*, 1, fo. 46r–v. He hurried to conclude that a judge acting within the bounds of his office need not give reasons for his precept, but the damage had already been done.

100. Ibid., 1, fo. 173r.

101. X.1.11.5 *Ad aures, X, De temporibus ordinationum.* De' Tudeschi, *Commentaria*, 1, fo. 36r.

102. Fedele, "Precetti," 306n, cited the first in connection with the duration of precepts (*recte* sentences), oddly as if he held the majority view.

103. Prospero Fagnano, *Commentaria in primum [-quintum] librum decretalium*, 5 vols. (Venice: Typographia Balleoniana, 1742), 5, pp. 329–43, 332–33.

104. Federico Petrucci, *Consilia* (Venic: Francesco Zilettui, 1570), fo. 13v.

105. Cesare Beretta, "Jacopo Menochio giurista e politico," in *Bollettino della Società Pavese di Storia Patria* 91 (1991): 245–77, 266. Beretta could not take account of Menochio's troubles with the Inquisition since its archives were then closed. The article does have a careful discussion of his political context and the other difficulties Menochio encountered, including excommunication, which seems to have grieved him.

106. It must have begun at least in 1597, although the first surviving reference is from early 1598. ADCFSO:DSO 1597–98–99, p. 241; cf. 1598, fo. 217v. The last reference to it that I have found comes from just after Menochio's death on 10 August 1607. 1607, fo. 188v. Beretta, "Menochio giurista," 277. Federico Borromeo excommunicated him in 1596 over jurisdictional issues, but Clement VIII absolved him the following year. http://www .treccani.it/enciclopedia/giacomo-menochio_%28Dizionario-Biografico%29/, accessed 30 October 2013.

107. ADCFSO:DSO1598, fo. 222r; register copy in 1597–98–99, p. 250 and p. 739 for the congregation. It included Cardinals Camillo Borghese (the future Paul V), Pompeo Arrigoni (the Inquisition's secretary), and Roberto Bellarmino, along with two consultors, Anselmo Dandino (who usually gave long, careful opinions, e.g., 1600, p. 26) and the Dominican General Ippolito Beccaria. This was a blue-ribbon panel, much more so than Galileo's, which consisted only of consultors, one of whom did not leave much of a mark on the records. See Chapter 7 below.

108. The Inquisitors first ordered that case 421, about the ways in which a religious could transfer to another order, had to be amended to bring it into line with Rota decisions before eventually deciding that the whole thing had to go; later they also objected to how Menochio treated the seal of the confessional in case 414. ADCFSO:DSO 1597–98–99, p. 721 and 1601, fo. 100v. Eventually the pope backed down and allowed already printed copies to be sold, provided a marginal note was added to case 414. 1603, fo. 12v; slight damage supplied from Copia, fo. 13v). Menochio's printer did this, and he amended—but did not cut—case 421. For case 414, cf. *De arbitrariis iudicum* (Venice: ad Signum Con- cordiae, 1590), p. 9 to *De arbitrariis judicum* (1613), p. 755; and for 421 1590, pp. 39–42 vs. 1613, pp. 783–85. The 1624 Venice edition has nearly the same emended text of 414, but more variants relative to 1613 in case 421. The work's first edition appeared in 1569, but the offending cases were published for the first time apparently only in 1576, in which year at least two different editions appeared. The textual and publishing history is extraordinarily complicated. For the *consilia*, sec 1597–98–99, p. 729. The description of the problem spots in them is too vague to be able to identify them with certainty from the decree registers. Cardinal Bellarmino's censures cite them as numbers 948, 965, and 1000 (*Auctarium*, 502– 6; the originals are in BAV, Barb. lat. 1038, fo. 205rff.), but none of these appears conform to the Inquisition's description of the offensive content as concerning "occasione excom- municationis latae in Vicariam capitanei iustitiae Mediolani, et erectionis (?) Vicarii archi- episcopalis ac censuris ad illud"; both were in the tenth and final volume (ibid., 739 and

781). Peter Godman makes a start on Bellarmino's work for both Inquisition and Index in *The Saint as Censor: Robert Bellarmine Between Inquisition and Index* (Leiden: Brill, 2000); cf. the scathing review by Gigliola Fragnito in *Rivista storica italiana* 114 (2002): 584–600. A third work of Menochio also attracted critical attention, but I have not yet been able to identify it from the vague reference to it as dealing "in materias iuris dictionis et immunitatis ecclesiasticorum." 1598, fo. 222r; register copy in 1597–98–99, p. 250. This could describe just about any of Menochio's numerous works in the jurisdictional controversy between the governor of Milan, its archbishop, and Rome. For these, see Cesare Beretta, "Jacopo Menochio e la controversia giurisdizionale milanese degli anni 1596–1600," *Archivio Storico Lombardo* 3 (1977): 47–128. The decree register entry might just indicate his last work, *De iurisdictione imperio ac potestate ecclesiastica et saeculari* (Frankfurt: Daniel and David "Aubriorum," and Clement Schleichius, 1622; I have added the publisher), the fourth book of which did not appear until 1695, *De iurisdictione, imperio et potestate ecclesiastica ac seculari libri tres. Accessit liber quartus De immunitate Ecclesiae pro ad eam confugientibus* (Lyon: Cramer and Perachon, 1695; I have added the publisher), but how the Inquisitors would have known of either is a little hard to see. Beretta, "Menochio giurista," 274.

109. Bachelet says that Menochio's Venetian publisher posthumously cut the offending *consilium*, but I have not confirmed this. *Auctarium*, 511n. Bachelet's claim that the 1624 Venice edition of *De arbitrariis* omitted casus 421 appears untrue; at least it appears in the edition I consulted, Biblioteca Universitaria di Padova, 107.b.12, as well as in the Venice: Heirs of Girolamo Scoti, 1613 edition, which contains the inquisitor of Venice's imprimatur dated 8 June 1605.

110. Menochio, *De praesumptionibus . . . Commentaria* (Venice: Heirs of Girolamo Scotti, 1597), p. 168. See also, e.g, *Consilia*, 984/1, 3, 7; 10, pp. 322–3. Ruini had said "mandatum ex pacto non possit fieri irrevocabile. . . . hoc tamen operatur, quod mandatum non finiatur morte, nam finitur morte, non tanquam sit revocatum a domino, sed quia voluntas mandatis cessat per mortem. . . . Aliud est enim revocare, quia tunc ponitur voluntas contraria, & aliud est voluntatem cessare, quia tunc ponitur voluntatem non esse vel esse, sed cessare. Et propterea si quis delegat causam, donec duxerit revocandam, non expirat iurisdictio delegata per mortem mandantis." Carlo Ruini, *Consiliorum seu Responsorum [tomi I–VJ*, ed. Girolamo Zanchi (Venice: Felice Valgrisi, 1591), fo. 164v. Menochio, *De arbitrariis* (1613), p. 84. See also Menochio, *Consilia*, 1 no. 75 (1, fo. 6r).

111. His citation of Paolo Da Castro, *consilium* 438 (prob. *recte*, vol. 2, no. 48) is typically for Menochio not exactly to the point, or at least not in any obvious way.

112. X.1.3.19, *Constitutus, De rescriptis*. Da Susa, *Commentaria*, 1, fo. 17r.

113. Lapo da Castiglionchio, *Allegationes*, ed. Quintiliano Mandosio (Venice: Francesco Ziletti, 1571), pp. 64–65, alleg. 17.

114. I have not been able to identify this.

115. Not much is known of Scaccia's life beyond his law degree at Rome in 1584 and his service immediately thereafter as inquisitor of Malta. Later that would be a springboard to higher office, but this did not happen in his case. He spent the balance of his life as a species of itinerant justice. The first book of his most important work, *Tractatus de iudiciis*

was finished ca. 1593, published 1596, the second (also published separately as *Tractatus de sententia et re judicata*) by 1603, published 1604. His works were relatively frequently reprinted, his most popular *De appellationibus*, having twelve editions. Rodolfo de Laurentiis, "Sigismondo Scaccia (1564–1643). Fra pratica e teoria giuridica agli inizi dell'età moderna," *Rivista di storia del diritto italiano* 64 (1991): 233–339, 238–41, 279, 281; and Vincenzo Lavenia, "Scaccia, Sigismondo," *DSI* 3: 1389–1390. His *De commercio et cambio* (first ed. 1619) is now his best-known work.

116. Scaccia, *De iudiciis*, c. LVIII, pp. 149–54. He had earlier (p. 75) said the same thing, citing "Mars. in pract. crimin. para. constante, num 7–12 and Gail. in pract. observat. libr. 1 observat. 13 no. 4 and Observat. 16 no. 9," neither of which I have identified.

117. Ibid., pp. 154–57.

118. Sigismondo Scaccia, *Tractatus de sententia et re judicata* (Lyon: André, Jacques and Matthieu Prost, 1628), the second volume of *Tractatus de iudiciis*, 393–94 and 395.

119. It is difficult to count precepts and monitions with full precision because it is not always clear when older ones were being renewed, for example, together with the usual problems of damage to texts. The extrajudicial admonitions, sometimes more than one in each place, are found in ADCFSO:DSO1603 Copia, fos. 240r and 257v; 1604–1605 Copia, fos. 17r, 23r and p. 56; 1606–1607, fo. 28v and Copia, p. 129; 1607, fo. 229r; 1608, p. 299; 1609, p. 327; 1610–1611, fos. 101v, 133v and 135r; 1612, p. 381; 1618, p. 102; 1620, pp. 220 and 291; 1626, fo. 6v; 1627, fo. 134v; 1629, fo. 72v; and1630, fo. 175v.

120. Quintiliano Mandosio, *Tractatus de monitoriis* (Rome: Giorgio Ferrari, 1581), fos. 6r–v, 5r.

121. Sometimes penances were inserted between the *monitio* and precept, e.g., 29 October 1619. ADCFSO:DSO 1619, p. 393.

122. "[C]um monitione, ac praecepto, ne loquatur." ADCFSO:DSO 1608, p. 13.

123. "[F]acta ei monitione et praecepto iudiciali de non loquendo de causa sua." ADCFSO:DSO 1616, p. 367.

124. "[I]llos expediat cum acri monitione, et praecepto." ADCFSO:DSO 1618, p. 407.

125. "[C]um monitione, et praecepto." ADCFSO:DSO 1619, p. 260.

126. ADCFSO:DSO 1619, p. 393.

127. "[R]elaxari sub fideiussione, et monitione, ac praecepto, ut in futurum servent ordines praedictos." ADCFSO:DSO 1616, p. 88.

128. "[C]um monitione et pracecepto." ADCFSO:DSO 1619, p. 446.

129. 26 October 1569. BAV, Barb. lat. 1502, p. 35D.

130. The register of Inquisition out-letters in BAV, Barb. lat. 6334, fos. 12v, 10 January, 50r, 28 February, and 117r, 9 May, all 1626, contains at least three precepts not in the registers. I have found only one case in both places, that of Antonio Maggi, sentenced 9 June 1626 with the order passed on 13 June. ADCFSO:DSO 1626, fo. 96r and BAV, Barb. lat. 6334, fos. 153v–54r.

131. Tommaso Campanella, Apology attached to *De sensu rerum* (Paris: [Denis Bechet], 1637), 90. See Luigi Amabile, *Frà Tommaso Campanella e la sua congiura, i suoi processi e la sua pazzia*, 3 vols. (Naples: Morano, 1882), 1, 74–75.

132. 30 January 1603. ADCFSO, Decreta S.O. 1603, 26r.

133. 30 June 1599. ADCFSO, Decreta S.O. 1597–98–99, p. 699.

134. 15 July 1599. ADCFSO, Decreta S.O. 1597–98–99, pp. 721–22.

135. The case began 8 July with an order to find various letters, but nothing was then said about a precept. ADCFSO, Decreta S.O. 1597–98–99, p. 710. For his denunciation of Bruno, see *SI*, pp. 120 and 120n44.

136. 7 February 1609. ADCFSO:DSO 1609, p. 62.

137. 18 May 1627. ADCFSO:DSO 1627, fo. 83v.

138. ADCFSO:DSO 1630, fo. 171r.

139. 17 September. ADCFSO:DSO 1631, fo. 168v.

140. 4 June. ADCFSO:DSO 1620, p. 204

141. 11 August 1599, 6 April 1600, and 8 August 1602. ADCFSO, D.S.O. 1597–98–99, p. 753, 1600, fo. 43r and 1602, p. 404. For a precept to both generals in the dispute over grace, see 4 September 1602. 1602, p. 458.

142. 4 September 1608. ADCFSO:DSO 1608, p. 377.

143. 19 May 1602, nuncio–secretary of state. ASV, Seg. Stato, Nunz. Firenze, 14A, fo. 322r–v, undated precept on fo. 325r–v. Precept from Inquisition 19 September 1602. 1602, p. 507. See the last chapter.

144. ADCFSO:DSO 1610–1611, fo. 424r, 1614, p. 356 and 1618, p. 17.

145. Averoldo: 27 April 1604. Copia 1604–5, p. 167. Jesuit rector: 28 September 1605. Copia 1604–1605, p. 867.

146. 28 June 1605. 1604–1605 Copia, p. 718. The copy is illegible in key spots and the original version is destroyed. The author was Angelo Giustiniani da Chio, but I have not been able to identify his book.

147. 6 October 1605. Copia 1604–5, p. 884.

148. 9, 16, 23, and 30 January; and 4 and 13 February 1620. ADCFSO:DSO 1620, pp. 19, 27, 34, 42, 46, and 63.

149. 20 February 1620. ADCFSO:DSO 1620, p. 72.

150. 26 February 1620. ADCFSO:DSO 1620, p. 75; two marginal notes spoke of a warning. He was dismissed on 30 April. Ibid., p. 156.

151. It is first Maruo and then Marua in the index. ADCFSO:DSO 1610–1611, fos. 225v and 517v.

152. 18 December 1610. ADCFSO:DSO 1610–1611, fo. 225v. The book is called *Regole per una buona confessione* in Giovanni Vincenzo Patuzzi, *Lettere teologico-morali*, 5 (Trent: no publisher, 1754), 411, the only reference to it I have found.

153. 22 March 1611. ADCFSO:DSO 1610–1611, fo. 282v.

154. 4 May 1611. Ibid., fo. 306r.

155. 31 May 1611. Ibid., fo. 323v.

156. Ibid., fo. 326r.

157. Despite this precise detail, I have failed to identify this title. Roberti's book is *Vita con le apparitioni e miracoli della veneranda serua di Dio suor Francesca Vacchini di Viterbo, Monaca del terzo Ordine di san Domenico* (Tricarico: Giovanni Giacomo Carlino, 1613).

NOTES TO PAGES 103–104

158. 3 July. ADCFSO:DSO 1614, p. 325–26.

159. ADCFSO:DSO 1614, pp. 95, 325, and 331.

160. 18 December. ADCFSO:DSO 1624, fo. 198v.

161. ADCFSO:DSO 1603, fo. 176r–v/cf. Copia, fo, 182r–v.

162. 17 October 1612. ADCFSO:DSO 1612, p. 491.

163. For Gaetani, see José Ruysschaert, "Costantino Gaetano O.S.B. chasseur des manuscrits," in *Mélanges Eugène Tisserant*, 7 vols. (Vatican City: Biblioteca Apostolica Vaticana, 1964; Studi e Testi 237), 7: 261–326. For Alemanno or Alemanni († 1626), see Jeanne Bignami-Odier, *La Bibliothèque Vaticane de Sixte IV à Pie XI* (Città del Vaticano: Biblioteca Apostolica Vaticana, 1973; Studi e Testi, 272), 105. His prohibition probably applied to *De Lateranensibus Parietinis ab Franc. Card. Barberino restitutis Dissertatio historica* (Rome: Heirs of Bartolomeo Zanetti, 1625).

164. 28 August. ADCFSO:DSO 1625, fo. 146v.

165. For the Inquisition's actions via the nunciature in Cologne, see Peter Schmidt, "Inquisition und Zensur in der Kölner Nuntiatur," in *Die Aussenbeziehungen der römischen Kurie unter Paul V Borghese (1605–1621)*, ed. Alexander Koller (Tübingen: De Gruyter, 2008), 409–28.

166. The Inquisition's confusion in this case is understandable. The publishing history of Bzowski's work is complicated. It appears that volume 17 may already have been published by the time Rome had word of it, at least it came out in 1625, and there might not have been time to make the corrections demanded after the Inquisition finally settled the issue. Abraham Bzowski, *Annalium ecclesiasticorum post illustriss. et reverendiss. Caesarem Baronium [continuatio]*, 17 (Cologne: Boëtzer, 1625). BAV, Barb. lat. 3151, fos. 123r–32v contains censures on Bzowski's thirteenth volume. Cardinal Bellarmino's censures are in ARSI, Opp. NN 243.II, fos. 579r–87v.

167. His letter of 28 July was read in the congregation of 11 September. ADCFSO:DSO 1625, fo. 152v.

168. 3 February 1626. ADCFSO:DSO 1626, fo. 20v.

169. Ibid., fos. 28v–9r.

170. On 30 November 1628, Urban VIII ordered Inquisitor Desiderio Scaglia to talk to Bzowski about his reply to Paolo Sarpi; the inquisitor of Cologne reported that he could not find a copy nor of vol. 10 of Bzowski's *Annales*, which the archiepiscopal vicar of Cologne had told him treated the Council of Trent, as did volume 21, on the basis of Bzowski's letter to the prefect of printers (ADCFSO:DSO 1628, fo. 200v). On 3 January 1630, Urban ordered the suspension of printing, probably of volume 20, in Cologne because it dealt with the Council of Trent and refused Bzowski's request to have the ban lifted three months later. A month after that the censure of volume 20 was assigned to the Oratorian Orazio Giustiniani, soon to be made a consultor. 1630, fos. 7r, 67r, and 83r.

171. 6 May. ADCFSO:DSO 1626, fo. 75v.

172. 14 May. Ibid., fo. 80v.

173. 22 January 1631. ADCFSO:DSO 1631, fo. 14v.

174. For his case and the details not otherwise referenced here, see *SI*, chapter 4.

175. Antonino Poppi, *Cremonini, Galilei e gli Inquisitori del Santo a Padova* (Padua: Centro Studi Antoniani, 1993), no. VIII.

176. ADCFSO, Decreta, Copia 1604–5, p. 194; Leen Spruit, "Cremonini nelle carte del Sant'Uffizio Romano," in Ezio Riondato and Antonino Poppi, eds., *Cesare Cremonini. Aspetti del pensiero e scritti*, 2 vols. (Padua: Academia Galileiana, 2000), 1: 193–204, 194–95.

177. ADCFSO:DSO 1619, p. 207; Spruit, "Cremonini," 201.

178. 12 May 1604. Copia 1604–5, p. 188.

179. The reviser was also called Carlo Mordano, Cesare da Mordano, and Fra Cesare Lippi da Mondavio, all versions of Cesare Lippi da Mordano, vicar of the Paduan Inquisition. Poppi, *Cremonini*, 12. All the place names are hard to read.

180. 13 May 1604. ACDFSO:DSO, Copia 1604–5, p. 194.

181. 2 June 1604. Ibid., p. 217.

182. Ibid., p. 217.

183. Ibid., p. 256.

184. Ibid., p. 292.

185. Ibid., p. 300.

186. Ibid., p. 349.

187. Ibid., pp. 369 and 372.

188. Ibid., p. 373.

189. Ibid., p. 405.

190. Ibid., p. 415.

191. 15 February 1605. Ibid., p. 594. I have not been able to identify this edition.

192. Daniele Santarelli, ed., *La nunziatura di Venezia sotto il papato di Paolo IV: la corrispondenza di Filippo Archinto e Antonio Trivulzio (1555–1557)* (Rome: Aracne, 2010), 34–36. His abjuration calling him the son of Niccolò Vergerio of Capodistria is printed in Luigi Alberto Ferrai, *Studi storici* (Padua and Verona: Drucker, 1892), 204–5n2.

193. [Francesco Albizzi], *Risposta all'Historia della sacra Inquisitione, composta già dal r.p. Paolo Servita* (N.p.: N.p., n.d.), pp. 121–22, citing both the inquisitor's and the nuncio's correspondence. For this book, see Gaetano Melzi, *Dizionario di opere anonime e pseudonime di scrittori italiani*, 3 vols. (Milan: Pirola, 1848–1859), 2: 456–57, citing the catalogues of the press of Propaganda Fide under date 1678, http://dla.library.upenn.edu/dla/medren/record.html?id=MEDREN_2486514, accessed 14 December 2012, citing *NUC pre-1956*, 7: 341 guessing a publication date of 1646, and R. L. Bruni and D. W. Evans, *Italian Seventeenth-Century Books in Cambridge Libraries* (Florence: Olschki, 1997), n86, ca. 1678.

194. ACDSFSO:DSO 1597, fo. 432v.

195. Luigi Firpo, *Il processo di Giordano Bruno*, ed. Diego Quaglioni (Rome: Salerno, 1993), 216, 218, 222, 246.

196. ACDSFSO:DSO 1600–1601 copy, p. 50.

197. Ibid., pp. 233 and 312.

198. Ibid., p. 465.

199. Ibid., p. 696

200. ACDSFSO:DSO 1602, p. 103. The volume index puts this on fo. 319r.

201. Ibid., p. 402.

202. Ibid., pp. 554 (22 October 1602) and 658.

203. ACDSFSO:DSO 1624, fos. 169v and 188v.

204. ADCFSO:DSO 1624, fo. 185r.

205. 30 May and 6 July 1628 (ADCFSO:DSO 1628, fos. 94v and 113r) and 12 February 1632 (1632, fo. 31r).

206. 29 October 1619. ADCFSO:DSO 1619, p. 392.

207. 11 May 1627. ADCFSO:DSO 1627, fo. 81r–v.

208. 27 February 1629 and 5 October 1627 and 30 August 1629. ADCFSO:DSO 1627, fo. 172v, 1629, fo. 43r, and 1629, fo. 151v.

209. 26 October 1627. ADCFSO:DSO 1627, fo. 189r.

210. 6 June 1601. ADCFSO:DSO 1601, fo. 133r.

211. ADCFSO:DSO 1618, p. 36. The original precept has not been found.

212. 5 March 1625. ADCFSO:DSO 1625, fo. 43v.

213. 2 April 1625. Ibid., fo. 59r.

214. 9 May 1625. Ibid. fo. 82v.

215. Ibid., fo. 85v.

216. 16 September and 15 October 1625. Ibid., fos. 159r and 176v.

217. 1619–1629 (resigned). *HC* 4: 141. He may also have been bishop of Tropea 1615–1633 (†). *HC* 4: 347, when his name is given as Caracciolo Pisquizi of Naples, http://www.tropeamagazine.it/vescovivicarigeneralifrancescoadilardi/, accessed 15 December 2012.

218. For the frequency of such disputes, see *SI*, chapter 1.

219. ADCFSO:DSO 1625, fo. 124r.

220. 12 November 1625. Ibid., fo. 214v.

221. 5 March and 16 April 1626. ADCFSO:DSO 1626, fos. 39v and 63v.

222. 23 July 1626. Ibid., fo. 126v.

223. 19 November and 10 December 1626. Ibid., fos. 222v and 239v–40r.

224. 10 June 1627. "R.p.d. Fabritii Caraccioli episcopi Cathacensis retenti in Urbe cum praecepto verbali de non discedendo absque licentia Sanctissimi petentis gratiam ob necessitatem victus redeundi ad suam residentiam, lecto memoriali Sanctissimus auditis votis etc. fecit ei gratiam eundi Neapolim, facto illi praecepto iudicialiter, ne discedat e dicta Civitate absque licentia Sacrae Congregationis sub gravissimis poenis in eventum contraventionis." ADCFSO:DSO 1627, fo. 99r.

225. *HC* 4: 264.

226. An Observant Franciscan, Mongiogo was bishop of Minervino, 21 June 1596–resigned before 9 January 1606;archbishop of Lanciano, 27 January 1610, translated before 14 May 1618 to Pozzuoli, "ex dioec. Hydruntin. [Otranto] oriundus, aet. 60 an. summa cum laude suffragatus est archiepo. Valentin." *HC* 4: 243, 214, and 289. A brief life of Mongiogo written on the occasion of his imprisonment says he studied theology in Bologna before Gregory XIII called him to Rome to teach in the newly founded Collegio dei Greci. After being elected provincial he was sent by the same pope to visit Catholic parishes in Albania as part of the pope's plan for reunion with the Greeks. He acquired Habsburg patronage

and was in the service of the viceroy of Naples in the late sixteenth century. Under the patronage of Cardinals Enrico Caetani and Alessandro Peretti, nephew of Sixtus V, he became bishop of Minervino. After five years there, he was sent as suffragan of the archbishop of Salzburg. Two years later he went to Valladolid, his second trip to Spain, where Philip III refused a proposal for him to visit the grand priory of Castille and Leon. Instead, he served as suffragan bishop of Valencia for six years. He transferred to Lanciano under the patronage of the president of the Council of Italy, before finally moving to Pozzuoli at the behest of the duke of Lerma, viceroy of Naples. While bishop, he conducted many visitations, including of most of Lombardy. "Notorio della vita di F. Lorenzo Mongiò di S. Pietro in Galatina Frate Zoccolante e vescovo di Pozzuoli, fatta con l'occasione della sua carcerazione in Roma per conte di Santo Officio," Bibliothèque Nationale de France, MS Italien 733, pp. 27–32; formerly MS ital. 10496. Antonio Marsand, ed., *I manoscritti italiani della Regia biblioteca Parigina*, 1 (Paris: Stamperia reale, 1835), 533, his no. 478 with badly garbled title. See also "Il mecenatismo di Mons. Frate Lorenzo Mongiò di Galatina (1556–1630) e la Biblioteca Galatinese di S, Caterina secondo il 'Notamento' della Biblioteca Apostolica Vaticana (Cod. Vat. Lat. 11268, ff. 781r–797r) compilato nel 1600," in *La Regolare Osservanza Francescana nella Terra d'Otranto*, 1, *Il Divenire Storico-Legale 1391–1898* (Lecce: Congedo, 1992), 99–108.

227. ACDFSO, Decreta 1627, fo. 161r.

228. 14 October 1627. Ibid., fo. 181v.

229. 11 November 1627. Ibid., fo. 196v.

230. ACDFSO, Decreta 1628, fo. 26v.

231. 2 March 1628. Ibid., fo. 44r.

232. 16 March 1628. Ibid., fo. 50v.

233. Ibid., fo. 70r.

234. 27 April 1628. Ibid., fo. 77v.

235. 25 May 1628. Ibid., fo. 91r. The writings were ordered sent to Rome on 15 June. Ibid., fo. 103r.

236. Ibid., fo. 93r.

237. Ibid., fo. 114r.

238. Ibid., fo. 118v.

239. 27 July 1628. Ibid., fo. 128v.

240. BAV, Urb. lat. 1098 I, fos. 282r and 305v.

241. "R.P.D. Fr. Tedeschus [*sic*?] Laurentius Ord. Min. obs. Archip.us olim Lancianen., nunc Ep.us Puteolarum Constitutus, et genuflexus coram S.mo D. N. Papa p.to, tactis sacrosanctis Dei Evangelis coram (? Evangelicorum) positis manibus corporaliter tangens, abiuravit, maledixit et detestatus est haeresis de quibus vehementer suspectus iudicatus est etc, ac aliis prout latius in schedulis sententiae per abiuratonis etc prout in libro sententiarum." ADCFSO:DSO 1629, fo. 42r. If a correct reading, "Tedeschus" may be explained by the fact that Mongiogo had apparently acted as a suffragan bishop in Salzburg. Franz Ortner, "Mongiojo (Mongiogus), Laurentius Galatino (Galatinus) (OFM)," in *Die Bischöfe des Heiligen Römischen Reiches 1448 bis 1648. Ein Biographisches Lexikon*, ed. Erwin Gatz with the assistance of Clemens Brodkorb (Berlin: Duncker & Humblot, 1996), 488.

242. "Die 8 [prima Copia] Martii 1629 Adm. R. P. Com.rius gn.lis S. Officij retulit, SS.mum mandasse Epum Puteolarum relegari in Monasterio S.tae Praxedis Monachorum [aft. del. "Ordinis Vallis"] Vallis Umbrosae prope S. Mariae Majoris [both in accusative in Copia]. In cuius ordinis executionem [exequutionem Copia] idem adm. R. P. Com.rius unamecum [unà mecum Copia] Not.o etc p.tum Epum duxit ad p.tum Monasterium super Rheda, ibique coram me not.o, et Testibus infrascriptis eidem E.po notificavit ordinem S.mi, eique praecepto [but could be *praecipit* as in Copia as it should be grammatically], ne discedat [discederet Copia] a p.to Monasterio sub poenis arbitrio S. S.tis, successiveque illum commendavit Abbati eiusdem Monasterii. Super quibus etc Actum Romae in p.to Monasterio in mansionibus Palatii Illmi Card.llis titularis [Marcello Lante (*HC* 4: 48)], presentibus Angelo Finati Hidruntin. [Hidrumentin. copia], et Anello de Isanto [Sancto Copia] Pbro Puteolan. testibus." ADCFSO:DSO 1629, fo. 45r–v and Copia, unfoliated. Isanto or de Stanto was one of Mongiogio's servants, also imprisoned. 22 November 1629. 1628, fo. 193r.

243. *Avviso* by Alessandro Gualteruzzi of 10 March 1629 in BAV, Urb. lat. 1099 I, fos. 142v–43r.

244. 14 August 1629. ADCFSO:DSO 1629, fo. 141v. The release of the books had been ordered on 21 March. Ibid., fo. 56v.

245. The discussion in E. Rodocanachi, *Le Chateau Saint'Ange* (Paris: Hachette, 1909), 208, is largely erroneous. He says Mongiogo was brought to Rome at age twenty-four in 1628 on charges of coining and seeking treasure by magic and died in Castel Sant'Angelo on II February 1630, citing BAV, Urb. lat. 1089 (probably *recte* 1098, fo. 282r) and Ferdinando Ughelli, ed. Niccolò Coleti, *Italia sacra*, 7 vols. (Venice: Sebastiano Coleti, 1717), 6: col. 28, which states he died in the Castel, but his age and date of death are not found in either source. Ortner, "Mongiojo," says the bishop died before 7 April 1631. He is buried in the cathedral of Galatina to which he gave substantial donations; http://www.welcomesalento.it/index.php?option=com_content&task=view&id=49&Itemid=38&lang=en; and http://www.turismo.regione.puglia.it/at/10/luogosacro/732/en accessed 16 December 2012.

246. ADCFSO:DSO 1629, fo. 115r. The text is inserted after the end of the congregation of 27 June. Antonio Maria's precept was not found in the register for 1628.

247. Fedele, "Precetti," 278.

248. Fedele, "Precetti," 305–6.

249. ASV, Sec. Brev. Reg. 592, fos. 63r–v and 66r–v, expedited 1 June 1605, docketed in part as "S. V. ex iustis causis animum suum moventibus praeceptum d.i Praepositi generalis [Acquaviva] etiam eidem Ferdinando [de Mendoza, S.J.] intimatum, se non dum illi paruit, ad beneplacitum suum suspendit." See also the similar pairing of a precept to an offender with another annuling it involving a Dominican and the archbishop of Milan. S. L. Forte, "I Domenicani nel carteggio del card. Scipione Borghese, protettore dell'Ordine (1606–1633)," *Archivum fratrum praedicatorum* 30 (1960): 351–416, 372.

250. ASV, Sec. Brev. Reg. 595, fos. 346r–47r, 18 July 1608, docketed as "praeceptum extinguen. census" to the knights of St. James of Calatrava, unfol. sheet between 346 and 347 headed "Pro Rege Catholico Praeceptum extinguendi census;" Reg. 596, fo. 109r–v, another

similar text to the king of Spain with the same docketing; ibid., fo. 530r–v, 13 November 1609, refusing to allow the conversion of alms to other uses, the only one to contain the verb *praecipimus* in the text; and ibi. fos. 612r–15v, 27 December 1609, docketed as "praeceptum ut omnes fructus, et emolumenta quae ex illius officii, S. provenient in emptionem locorum montium non vacabilium," etc. to the pope's brother Marcoantonio Borghese.

251. *Dominorum de Rota decisiones novae, antiquae et antiquiores* (Cologne: Gymnich, 1581), 595–96.

252. See, e.g., ibid., p. 364, and Prospero Farinacci, ed., *Sacrae Rotae Romanae Decisionum recentiorum . . . pars prima*, etc., 19 vols. (Venice: Paolo Balleoni, 1716), 3: index, s.v. *praeceptum*, 4:1, p. 26 and 4:2, p. 178.

253. Nuncio–secretary of state, 19 May 1602. ASV, Seg. Stato, Nunz. Firenze, 14A, fo. 322r–v.

254. "Ill.mus et R.mus Dn.us Nuntius Apostolicus iustis et necessariis causis animum suum moventibus, et vigore cuiuscunque suae facultatis apostolicae, et omni meliori modo commisit fieri praeceptum. ¶ R.do Pri Fratri Niccolao de Lorinis ordinis praedicatorum, ad praesens in Conventu Divi Marci Florentiae degenti, nec non R.di Pri Antonio de Santarellis Lectori, ordinis seu societatis Jesuitarum ad presens [*sic*] Florentiae in Conventu, seu domo S.ti Joannis Evangelistae Jesuitarum degenti, quod in futurum quilibet ipsorum non audeat, nec aliquo modo praesumat tam in concionibus, quam in lectionibus, nec alias, discutere, vel alio modo tractare articulum pluries ab ipsis, diebus elapsis in controversiam concionando, deductum, An, scilicet, Confessio sacramentalis per scripturam, vel per nuncium fieri possit, sub poena excommunicationis latae sententiae, et hoc quam diù a S.mo D. N. aliud in casu huiusmodi fuerit ordinatum. ¶ Insuper idem Ill.mus D.nus Nuntius commisit praecipi R.do F.ri Mattheo de Bracceschis subpriori in praedicto Conventu S. Marci, nec non R.do P.ri Hyeronimo Costa Rectori in d.o Conventu seu societate Divi Joannis Evangelistae, et cuilibet ipsorum, quod in futurum in dictis eorum ecclesiis seu conventibus respective, tam in concionando, quam in legendo super articulo praedicto, neminem verba facere, permictant, sub poena suspensionis a divinis, et ab officio cuiuscunque eorum ipso facto incurrenda, et hoc quovisque a S.mo D. N. aliud ut supra fuerit mandatum, et hoc ne ullam alias," no date nor note of administration. ASV, Seg. Stato, Nunz. Firenze, 14A, fo. 325r–v.

255. 21 August 1602. ADCFSO:DSO 1602, pp. 427–28.

256. 28 November 1602. Ibid., p. 619.

257. ASV, Seg. Stato, Nunz. Firenze, 15B, fo. 16r.

258. Ibid., fo. 28r.

259. Judicial: ADCFSO:DSO 1616, pp. 285 and 367, and 1627, fo. 99r. Penal: 1604–1605 Copia, p. 867; 1617, p. 302; 1618, p. 93; 1624, fo. 52v; 1625, fo. 132v; 1626, fo. 145v and fos. 207v–8r; 1628, fo. 84r; 1629, fos. 29r and 95v; and 1630, fo. 146v.

260. BC MS 2631, fo. 300v; Cadène, "Collectio," 3: 459.

261. *SI*, chapter 10.

262. ACDFSO, St.St.L 3-e, fos. 599r–603r.

263. 10 January 1601. ADCFSO:DSO1600–1601, fo. 187v.

264. 31 January 1606. ADCFSO:DSO 1606–1607, fo. 21r. The case began before 4 August 1604, but a search of registers for 1602 and 1603 did not turn up the precept. 1604–1605, fo. 138r–v.

265. De' Tudeschi, *Commentaria*, 1, fos. 47r–48r, commenting on X.1.3.7.

266. Giovanni Francesco Da Ripa, *In primum Decretalium librum commentaria* (Venice: Giunti, 1586), fos. 30v–32v, also commenting on X.1.3.7.

267. It ordered the viceroy of Naples to free the Holy Office's notary there who had been condemned to the galleys. 16 September 1604. ADCFSO:DSO Copia 1604–5, p. 385.

268. See *SI*, chapter 6, whence the discussion here is compressed.

269. Borghese–Rivarola, 26 May 1618, in ASV, Arm. 36:29, fo. 16r–v.

270. See the account of Felice Contelori in ASV, Arm. 36:28, fos. 158r–73r.

271. The second breve to Rivarola ordered him "ut intimaret Roderico. . . . Quapropter Rodericus recessit a tractatu venditionis, & acquievit mandantis Sedis Apostolicae." ASV, Arm. 36:32, fo. 107r.

272. "Tibi per praesentes ininungimus, ut eidem Roderico auctoritate nostra praecipias, et mandes sub indignatione nostrae, ac S.tae Sedis apostolicae" not to sell without permission . . . "Dantes tibi plenam et liberam facultatem praefatum Rodericum monendi, ac illi ut praetur [abbrev.] praecipiendi et propter monitionis, seu praecepti affixionem ad valvas Palatii Curiae Ravennae, sive alterius loci Provinciae Romandiolae tibi benevisi, ita ut affixio monitionis seu praecepti huiusmodi eundem Rodericum arctet et afficiat proinde aesi illi personaliter intimata fuisset." ASV, Sec. Brevi 561, fos. 31r–34v.

273 ASV, Arm. 36:30, fo. 19r.

274. ASV, Arm. 36:29, fo. 22r.

275. It is not in the first edition of the *Vocabulario della Crusca* (Venice: Giovanni Alberti, 1612). There was still discussion in the nineteenth century about what the word meant and whether it belonged in an updated *Vocabulario*. Vincenzo Monti, et al., *Proposta di alcune correzioni ed aggiunte al Vocabolario della Crusca*, 3:1 (Milan: Dall'Imp. Regia stamperia, 1821), 105–6.

276. ASV, Arm. 36:29, fo. 31r. Cf. note on ASV, Sec. Brevi 561, fo. 32v.

277. ASV, Arm. 36:29, fo. 32r. It has not been found.

278. ASV, Arm. 36:30, fo. 34r.

279. ASV, Arm. 36:29, fo. 35r.

280. Ibid., fo. 105r–v, copy on 49r.

281. Ibid., fo. 47r.

282. Borghese–legate of Romagna, 20 April 1619. Ibid., fo. 55r.

283. See, e.g., BEM:RC, MS 'Y.O.4.25, fo. 1r and MS 'Y.O.4.24, fos. 97r/97v–8r. Some others are discussed in *SI*, chapters 5 and 6.

284. Decretum of 23 September 1632: "Relata serie totius facti circa impressionem libri a Galileo de Galileis Florentiae factam, nec non praecepto eidem ab hoc S. Officio anno 1616 facto, Sanctissimus mandavit Inquisitori Florentiae scribi, ut eidem Galileo, nomine Sanctae Congregationis, significet ut per totum mensem octobris proximum compareat in Urbe coram Comissario generali Sancti Officii, et recipiat ab eo promissionem de parendo

huic praecepto, quod eidem faciat coram testibus, qui, in casu quo illud admittere nolit et parere non promittat, possint id testificari, si opus fuerit." ACDFSO:DSO 1632, fo. 145r; *DV*, no. 130; *EN* 19: 279–80.

285. "[P]erò V. R. lo faccia chiamare in luogo dove siano presenti i testimonii et il Notaro, senza significare al detto Galilei per che fine li sudetti si trovino ivi presenti; et gli dirà che si contenti per tutto il mese di ottobre prossimo ritrovarsi in Roma. . .et accettando egli di venire, V. R. lo ricercherà a fargli fare fede di quanto ella gli ha fatto sapere, e di quanto egli ha promesso; e si ciò eseguirà, V. R. doppo la sua partenza farà che li testimonii, et il Notaro, che saranno stati presenti, faccino attestatione, essere stata scritta la sudetta fede et sottoscritta dal medesimo Galilei; ma s'egli ricuserà di fare quanto di è detto, in tal caso gli farà precetto coram Notario et testibus, quale si rogarà di questo atto, che comparisca in Roma." Antonio Barberini–inquisitor of Florence, 25 September 1632. Cioni, *Documenti*, 25.

286. I base this assertion on many years of experience reading such documents. Anyone who wishes to test its truth value can look at the numerous entries in the same volume as these two letters, the vast majority of which are nearly fair copies.

287. "Essendosi scoperte nell'opere del Gallileo [*sic*] alcune cose sospette N. S.re in riguardo del S.r Gran Duca *ha comesso [above] ad una congreg.ne particolare che [after deleted 'accio'] le esaminasse e vedesse se si poteva far di meno di non le portare nella S. Cong.ne del S.to Offitio, et essendosi quelli SS.ri congregati insieme per cinque volte, e considerato bene il tutto hanno risoluto che non poteva farsi di meno di non portar il negotio nella Congre.ne. Questa necessità è stata fatta rapresentare da S. B.ne al S.r Amb. re di S. A. *da Benessi [in margin] quale haveva supplicato la S.ta S. in nome della med.a A.za a non portar il negotio in Cong.ne accioche l'A. S. si sodisfacesse della buona volonta di S. B.ne verso il [altered from 'la'] *suo gusto [above deleted 'sua sodisfatione'; note in margin '(che fu il Benessi, di cui è questa minuta)']; quale replicò chi li portò l'Amb.ta che l'esser stato visto e passato il libro dal Maestro di Sacro Palazzo ['e passato' here deleted] faceva un poco di senso, ma li fu risposto che se effettivamente conteneva il libro errori, non dovevano in modo alcuno per questo rispetto lasciarsi correre. Tuto [*sic*] questo fù participato [*sic*] a S. E. con vincolo del segreto del S.to Offitio, li fu ben dato licenza di comunicarlo al S. Gran Duca sotto il med.o vincolo di segreto. Fu dunque portato il libro nella Cong.e del S.to Offitio e *dopo esser stato [above deleted 'fù'] considerato con ogni maturità il tutto fu risoluto di ordinare al P. Inquisitore di cotesta città che chiami il Galileo e che *d'ordine di S. S.ta li facci un precetto di presentarsi per tutto il prossimo mese di Ottobre avanti il P. Commissario del S.to Offitio, e si fare [?; *EN*: facci] prometter di obedire a detto precetto in presenza de testimonii accio ricusando di obedire e di accettarlo si possino in ogni caso esaminare [marg. replacing 'li dice che si contentti di essere in Roma per (ellipsis in original); following text (no. 1 in *EN* but misleadingly presented) deleted and replaced in margin, also deleted (no. 2; not in *EN*)]: 1) se egli prometerà di farlo non procede più oltre et se peraventura, o ricuserra di volerlo venire o lo difficoltasse che il Padre habbi pronto colà il notaro e {above} che la li facci precetto di presentarsi in Roma nel sudetto tempo'; 2) 'e che a cio l'esersi representandogli che (?) con la sua presenza haverebbe

riparato a molte cose e data e ricevuta sodisfatione'] Io do parte a V. S. di tuto [*sic*] questo per sua notitia solamente acciò che se le sarà parlato possa ella risponder con fondamento non dovendo ella da se parlarne ne molto ne poco. Intendo che non ostante che il Galileo sappi che in quella opera la Sacra Congregatione vi riconosce degli errori pensa con tutto ciò mandar in diverse parti del mondo li detti libri ad effetto di dispensargli, del che V. S. procuri di saper la verità ['e va dia re' (?) deleted] e trovando che si voglino inviare, avvisi il S.r Card.l Legato di Bologna e di Ferrara, acciocchè li faccino trattenere così ancora tutti gl'altri ministri e Vescovi [after deleted 'per'] o Inquisitori per dove potrebbeno passare e tenga mano di sapere in ogni modo quando doveranno muoversi questi libri di costà per reiterar l'avviso alli sudetti Em.mi et altri ministri, ma V. S. non confidi ciò [above] antecedentemente a' Vescovi et Inquisitori fuori dello Stato Ecc.co, bastando di avvisarlo allhora quando si moveranno li medesimi libri, parlo [after deleted 'e forse sarebbe meglio farlo che'] però di quelle balle che non doveranno necessariamente passare per Bologna o Ferrara o altro passo dello Stato Ecc.co, perchè per esse basta avisare gli Em.mi Legati e Governatori." Franceso Barberini–Giorgio Bolognetti, 25 September 1632, enciphered same day. BAV, Barb. lat. 7310, fos. 34r–35r; *EN* 14: no. 2311.

288. "Fu dunque portato il libro nella Congregatione del S.to Offitio, e dopo esser stato considerato con ogni maturità il tutto, fu risoluto di ordinare al P. Inquisitore di cotesta città che chiami il Galileo, e che d'ordine di S. S.tà li facci un precetto di presentarsi per tutto il prossimo mese di Ottobre avanti il P. Comissario del S.to Offitio, e si facci promettere di obedire a detto precetto in presenza de' testimoni, acciò, ricusando di obedire e di accettarlo, si possino in ogni caso esaminare." F. Barberini–Bolognetti, 25 September 1632. *EN* 14: no. 2311, from the register copy.

289. "Non ostante quello che io scrivo a V. S. del precetto da farsi al Gallileo [see last note], le soggiungo che N. S.re ha ordinato che si scriva all'Inquisitore che chiami il Gallileo [*sic* and below], et in presenza del notaro e testimoni, non però qualificati alla sua presenza per tali, gli dichi che la volontà della Congregatione è che egli per tutto Ottobre si trasferisca a Roma, e che lo esorti ad ubidire: se egli dirà di volerlo fare, che si facci far fede di sua mano che dall'Inquisitore gli è stato significato il senso della Congregatione e che lui haverebe ubidito; la qual fede, partito lui, doverà far riconoscer et autenticar dal notaro e testimonii che vi furono presenti: e se il Gallileo ricusasse di far la scrittura o di voler venire a Roma, che all'hora il Padre Inquisitore li facci il precetto in forma. Tutto si fa sapere a V. S. per sua notitia." F. Barberini–Bolognetti, 25 September 1632. *EN*, 14, no. 2312. For the apparent date of encipherment, see BAV, Barb. lat. 7310, fo. 37v (?).

290. "Mi valerò della notitia, che V. E.mza s'è degnata darmi [see last note?] nel particolare dell'opera del Galileo, mentre me ne sia parlato, come V. E.mza mi comanda, e se il med.mo Galileo havrà pensiero di mandar fuori di qua li libri stampati, eseguirò quanto V. Em.za mi ordina intorna a ciò." Giorgio Bolognetti–Francesco Barberini, 30 September 1632; BAV, Barb. lat. 7307, fo. 41r; *EN* 14: no. 2314 taken from the register copy of the nuncio's letter.

291. Beretta, "Menochio giurista," 274.

292. Maurice A. Finocchiaro's coinage in *Retrying Galileo, 1633–1992* (Berkeley:

University of California Press, 2005), 245. See my "The Status of the Inquisition's Precept to Galileo (1616) in Historical Perspective," *Nuncius* 24 (2009): 61–95.

293. Léon Garzend, *L'Inquisition et l'Hérésie: Distinction de l'Hérésie théologique et de l'Hérésie inquisitoriale: À propos de l'affaire Galilée* (Paris: Desclée, De Brower-G. Beauchesne, 1912), vii and 177.

294. Ibid., 294.

295. Ibid., 432–34.

296. Ibid., 475. Orio Giacchi, "Considerazioni giuridiche sui due processi contro Galileo," in Università Cattolica del Sacro Cuore, ed., *Nel terzo centenario della morte di Galileo Galilei* (Milan: Vita e Pensiero, 1942), 383–406, 402–3, and 405, adopted Garzend's theory wholesale.

297. Beretta, *Galilée*, 14 and 17, and Francesco Beretta, "L'affaire Galilée et l'impasse apologétique: Réponse à une censure," *Gregorianum* 84 (2003): 169–92, 173 and 183.

298. Bruno Neveu and Pierre-Noël Mayaud, "L'affaire Galilée et la tentation inflationiste: À propos des notions d'hérésie et de magistère impliquées dan l'affaire," *Gregorianum* 83 (2002): 287–311.

299. Adriano Prosperi, "L'inquisizione e Galileo," in Gian Mario Bravo, ed., *Il processo a Galileo Galilei e la questione galileiana* (Rome: Storia e Letteratura, 2010), 17–38, 31–33.

300. ADCFSO:DSO 1625, fo. 24r.

301. *SI*, 124–25.

302. Giacchi, "Considerazioni," 389.

303. Ibid., 393.

304. *DV*, no. 20. If we had the text in its full form it would read "monuit de errore supradictae opinionis, et ut illam deserat; et, successive, ac incontinenti, in mei [supradicti notarii praesentia] et testium [supradictorum et infradictorum praesentia], praesenti etiam adhuc eodem. . .cardinali, supradictus Pater commissarius praedicto Galileo adhuc ibidem praesenti et constituto, praecepit et ordinavit [nomine] . . . Papae" etc. I am grateful to H. A. Kelly for spelling this out.

305. Giacchi, "Considerazioni," 390.

CHAPTER 5. THE BEGINNING OF THE END

1. Michele Camerota, *Galileo Galilei e la cultura scientifica nell'età della Controriforma* (Rome: Salerno Editrice, 2004), 427–28.

2. His opinion is dated 2 February 1623. Ottavio Besomi and Mario Helbing, eds., *Galileo Galilei, Il Saggiatore* (Rome-Padua: Antenore, 2005), [86].

3. Castelli–Galileo, 9, 16, and 23 February 1630, Rome. *EN* 14: nos. 1984, 1986, and 1988.

4. Castelli-Galileo, 16 March 1630, Rome. *EN* 14: no. 1993.

5. *QE* 2:1: 503a, and Ambrogio Eszer, "Niccolò Riccardi, O.P., 'padre Mostro' (1585–1639)," *Angelicum* 60 (1983): 428–57, 429.

6. Eszer, "Riccardi," 435.

7. ADCFSO:DSO 1624, fos. 116v, 131v, 134v.

8. Ibid., 1625, fo. 124r and 1627, fo. 77v.

9. Ibid., 1632, fo. 95v; Copia, p. 314, and 1634, fo. 100v; Copia, p. 332.

10. ASMod:AE, 139, fasc. January 1633, unfoliated.

11. ADCFSO:DSO 1631, fo. 111v.

12. *QE.*

13. Riccardi acknowledged it on 28 May 1618. *EN* 12: no. 1327.

14. Eszer, "Riccardi," 429. I. Taurisano, "Series chronologica magistrorum sacri palatii Apostolici ab anno 1217 ad annum 1916," in *Hierarchi Ordinis Praedicatoru* (Rome, 1916), REF 56, dates the beginning of his regency to 1628, but he is documented in office as of 1626. ADCFSO:DSO 1626, fo. 184v.

15. *EN* 13: no. 1636.

16. Ibid., no. 1637. Eszer, "Riccardi," 432, infers that Galileo met Riccardi for the first time on this occasion through Virginio Cesarini. The first may be a reasonable inference, but the second is unsupported.

17. Bartolomeo Imperiali–Galileo, 27 February and 21 March 1626, Genoa. *EN* 14: nos. 1763 and 1770.

18. Castelli–Galileo, 26 February 1628, Rome. *EN* 13: no. 1856.

19. 7 January 1627 (Enrico Carusi, "Nuovi documenti sui processi di Tommaso Campanella," *Giornale Critico della Filosofia Italiana* 8 [1927]: 321–59, doc. 81, 354) and 15 November 1627 (Germana Ernst, "Cristianesimo e religione naturale: Le censure all'*Atheismus triumphatus* di Tommaso Campanella," *Nouvelles de la République des Lettres* 1–2 [1989]: 137–200, 172–200; see also Vito Angiuli, *Ragione moderna e verità del Cristianesimo: L'atheismus triumphatus di Tommaso Campanella* [Bari: Levante, 2000], 65). Riccardi's censures are in Ernst, "Cristianesimo," 199; Angiuli, *Ragione*, 224n; and A. Terminelli, ed., *Censure sopra il libro del Padre Mostro* (Rome: Monfortane, 1998), but cf. Ernst's strictures on this edition in *Tommaso Campanella: Il libro e il corpo della natura* (Rome: Laterza, 2002), 280n27. On Scaglia, see *RI*, 68–71.

20. Tommaso Campanella, *Lettere*, ed., Vincenzo Spampanato (Bari: Laterza, 1927), 248f and 230f and 282–95. Eszer, "Riccardi," 451–52n and 431, dates the anonymous "Censure sopra il libro del padre Mostro" in BAV, Barb. lat. 4602, fos. 250r–310r to November 1631 and assigns them to Campanella, as Pieralisi had not. Campanella's censures on Riccardi's sermons are in BAV, Barb. lat. 3150, fos. 396r–99v.

21. Eszer, "Riccardi," 431.

22. Ibid., 453, citing the authority of Luigi Firpo in support of Campanella's allegation.

23. Riccardi–Tommaso Campanella (according to a contemporary note at the head of the letter, 28 November 1638, Rome). BAV, Barb. lat. 3150, fos. 393r–4v.

24. *Concilii Tridentini synopsis* (Rome: Ludovico Grignani, 1629). The manuscript of the work may be in BAV, Barb. lat. 2938, "Adversus historiam concilii Tridentini Petri Suavis nomine inscriptam, 1. Synopsin eiusdem Historiae Emaculatae 2. Censuram authoris, et operis, 3 Vindicias Sacrosancta Synodi et 4. Apologiam pro sede apostolica una cum

necessaria defensione personarum Frater Nicholaus Riccardius ex ordine Praedicatorum elaboravit—Romae apud S. Petri Confessionem anno Sal. MDXXXVII," which is 91 folios long. The closure of the BAV during my last research period in Rome made it impossible to collate the book and the manuscript. The title of the rest of the manuscript is "Historiae Tridentinae a Petri Suavis calumniis vindicatae et restitutae." It is found in BAV, Barb. lat. 2934–40. Sante Pieralisi in his catalogue in the BAV thought BAV, Barb. lat. 862 "Historia Concilii Tridentini," dedicated to Urban VIII was also Riccardi's work, but an older catalogue assigned it to Terenzio Alciati, S.J. Hubert Jedin, *Der Quellenappart der Konzilsgeschichte Pallavicinos*, Miscellanea Historiae Pontificiae 4 (Rome: SALER, 1940), 12–16, which says nothing about the book's content.

25. "R.p.d. Assessor retulit S.mum concessisse, ut P.re Magro. Nicolao Riccardo S.ti Officii Qualificatori ad praesens scribenti contra damnatum librum, cui titulus, Historia del Concilio di Trento di Pietro [long blank; Sarpi] accomodentur libri praesentes in Archivio S.ti Officii, de quibus indiguerit." 9 June. ADCFSO:DSO 1627, fo. 98v.

26. BAV, Barb. lat. 2934, p. 4. See also pp. 88–89, 252, et passim.

27. "Credimus sacrae Genesis historiam, nec ambigitur de divino Bibliorum textu, scimusque verum esse aliquem unum ex sensibus qui circumferuntur, quamvis opinemur tantum hunc vel illum designate ubi infallibilis authoritas, vel indubitabilis significatio, non praevertunt opinandi libertatem." BAV, Barb. lat. 2934, pp. 256–57.

28. Ibid., p. 436.

29. Riccardi–Tommaso Campanella (according to a contemporary note at the head of the letter), 28 November 1638, Rome. BAV, Barb. lat. 3150, fos. 393r–4v.

30. ADCFSO:DSO 1629, fo. 100r.

31. See, e.g., his report on four books on the same day. Ibid. 1634, fos. 156v–57r; Copia, pp. 420–21, 6 September.

32. Melchior Inchofer, S.J., *Oratio funebris qua Rev.mo Patri Fr. Nicolai Riccardio Ordinis Praedicatorum . . . in aede S. Mariae ad Minervam primo die Iunii altero ab emortuali, praesente funere parentabat* (Rome: Lodovico Grignani, 1639).

33. Castelli–Galileo, 9 February 1630, Rome. *EN* 14: no. 1984.

34. Castelli–Galileo, 16 February 1630, Rome. Ibid.: no. 1986.

35. Francesco Niccolini–Andrea Cioli, 4 May 1630 May. Ibid.: no. 2004. For this visit, see William R. Shea and Mariano Artigas, *Galileo in Rome: The Rise and Fall of a Troublesome Genius* (Oxford: Oxford University Press, 2003), chap. 5.

36. Buonamici claimed that Urban "che di proprio pungno [*sic*] corresse alcuna cosa del titolo." Cited in "Rilettura di un documento celebre: redazione e diffusione della sentenza e abiura di Galileo," *Galilaeana* 1 (2004): 91–115, 98, from *EN* 19: 409 with an incorrect cross-reference to *EN* 15 (*recte* 14): no. 2294, 377, Francesco Niccolini saying Galileo gave the MS to the pope. Sante Pieralisi rejected this tale out of hand. *Urbano VIII e Galileo Galilei* (Rome: Propaganda Fide, 1875), 112. If Buonamici meant as soon as Galileo delivered the manuscript, he must be wrong, since Riccardi still gave it the original title on 24 May 1631. See below.

37. *Avvisi* of 4, 11 (2), and 18 May, all in ASMod:AE, 137, fasc. May 1630, unfoliated,

the first printed in Luigi Amabile, "L'Andata di Fra Tommaso Campanella a Roma dopo la lunga priogona a Napoli," *Atti dell'Accademia di Scienze Morali e Politiche di Napoli* 20, 8 (1886): 1–51, 38.

38. *Avviso* of 4 May 1630. ASMod:AE, 137, fasc. May 1630, unfoliated, printed in Amabile, "L'Andata," 38.

39. "Qua si trova il Galileo, ch'è famoso mathematico et astrologo, che tenta di stampare un libro nel qual impugna molte opinioni, che sono sostenute dalli Giesuiti. Egli si è lasciato intendere, che D. Anna partorirà un figliuolo maschio, che alla fine di Giugno havremo la pace in Italia, e che poco doppo morirà D. Thadeo et il Papa. L'ultimo punto viene comprovato dal [Giovanni Battista] Caracioli Napolitano, dal Padre Campanella, e da molti discorsi in scritto." Unsigned *avviso* of 18 May 1630 in ASMod:AE, 137, fasc. May 1630, unfoliated, in same hand as other *avvisi* signed by Antonio Badelli; printed with small errors of punctuation in *EN* 14: no. 2009 (and as certainly by Badelli), and Luigi Amabile, *Frà Tommaso Campanella e la sua congiura, i suoi processi e la sua pazzia*, 3 vols. (Naples: Morano, 1882), no. 203d, and "L'Andata," no. 9d. English translation in John Belden Scott, *Images of Nepotism. The Painted Ceilings of Palazzo Barberini* (Princeton, N.J.: Princeton University Press, 1991), 89. Virtually the same text appears in an 18 May dispatch from Rome by the Este resident. Giuseppe Campori, *Carteggio galileano inedito* (Modena: Società Tipografica, 1881), 593.

40. Brendan Dooley, *Morandi's Last Prophecy and the End of Renaissance Politics* (Princeton, N.J.: Princeton University Press, 2002). Dooley's claims "That the Morandi affair conditioned Urban's state of mind . . . seems to be the most likely explanation for what happened [to Galileo]" and that both trials "must have seemed much alike" while a little overstated point in a plausible interpretive direction. Brendan Dooley, "Astrology and the End of Science in Early Modern Italy," in *A Renaissance of Conflicts: Visions and Revisions of Law and Society in Italy and Spain*, ed. John A. Marino and Thomas Kuehn (Toronto: Centre for Reformation and Renaissance Studies, 2004), 395–420, 413. See also the expanded speculations and suggestions in the "Epilogue" to *Morandi*.

41. Orazio Morandi–Galileo, 24 May 1630, Rome. *EN* 14: no. 2016. Aside from his role in the *processo*, Morandi, and contacts with Galileo, not much is known of Visconti. The report of the particular congregation in late summer 1632 (see below) called him a "professor of mathematics." *DV*, 51. He does not appear in Federica Favino, "Matematiche e matematici alla 'Sapienza' romana (XVII–XVIII secolo)," *Mélanges de l'École Française de Rome: Italie et Méditerranée* 116 (2004): 423–69. Otherwise, a few scraps can be gleaned from his *processo*, including that he was a Roman, the son of one Agapito. AdS Roma, Governatore, Processi, sec XVII, b. 251, fo. 479r. On 21 February 1630, he sent an unknown person two copies of his astrological observations on Urban VIII's life and later gave Riccardi a copy. Ibid., fos. 484r–87v, 510r–12v, and 480v; Antonino Bertolotti, "Giornalisti astrololgi e negromanti in Roma nel secolo XVII," *Rivista europea* 5, 3 (1878): 466–514, 507–10 and 495. Dooley assigns him various titles from "employee" of the Inquisition, holder of an "administrative post" in the Congregation of the Index, "advisor to the Holy Office" to "secretary to the Master of the Sacred Palace and a chief censor for the Congregation on the Index."

Dooley, *Morandi*, 8–9, 70, 158, 162, and 181, drawing on the lending list of Morandi's library in AdS Roma, Governatore, Processi, sec XVII, b. 251, fos. 556r–62v. Visconti is last heard of writing Galileo from Florence on 1 October 1633. *EN* 15, no. 2734; cf. no. 2742. For Corbuzio, see *SI*, Chapter 5.

42. Campanella–Urban VIII, 9 April 1635, Paris. Campanella, *Lettere*, ed. Spampanato, 287. Campanella also claimed that the "colleggio" of astrologers at S.ta Prasede had promised the papacy in succession to Niccolò Ridolfi and Riccardi.

43. J. L. Heilbron, *Galileo* (Oxford: Oxford University Press, 2010), 90.

44. Michelangelo Buonarrotti the younger–Galileo, 3 June 1630, Rome. *EN* 14: no. 2022.

45. Dooley, "Epilogue" to *Morandi*.

46. Francesco Niccolini–Andrea Cioli, 19 May 1630, Rome. *EN* 14: no. 2010.

47. Filippo Niccolini–Galileo, 20 May 1630, Rome. Ibid.: no. 2011.

48. Orso d'Elci–Galileo, 3 June 1630, Florence. Ibid.: no. 2024. Galileo's letter of 1 June is missing.

49. Gino Bocchineri–Galileo, 10 June 1630, Florence. Ibid.: no. 2030.

50. Ibid.

51. This "frontispiece" is mysterious, since manuscripts technically speaking never have such. The frontispiece to the printed book would later cause serious problems.

52. Visconti–Galileo, 16 June 1630, Rome. Ibid.14: no. 2032. The letter becomes exhibit "H" in what has been taken as Galileo's draft defense but was probably really an effort to force Riccardi to issue the imprimatur. *DV*, doc. 114, and *EN* 19: 402.

53. Francesco Niccolini–Andrea Cioli, 29 June 1630, Rome. *EN* 14: no. 2034.

54. Information from *DBI* article (http://www.treccani.it/enciclopedia/francesco-niccolini_%28Dizionario-Biografico%29/, accessed 15 June 2013) as augmented.

55. Thomas F. Mayer, "An Interim Report on a Census of Galileo's Sunspot Letters," *History of Science* 50 (2012): 155–96, 175.

56. 7 June 1623 (ADCFSO:DSO 1623, pp. 194 and 195), renewed and enlarged 23 October 1624 (1624, fo. 165v).

57. Antonio Nibby, *Roma nell'anno MDCCCXXXVIII* (Rome: Tipografia delle Belle Arti, 1841), 2:2, 792.

58. Francesco Stelluti–[Galileo], Acquasparta, 2 August 1630. *EN* 14: no. 2042.

59. David Freedberg, *The Eye of the Lynx: Galileo, His Friends, and the Beginnings of Modern Natural History* (Chicago: University of Chicago Press, 2002), 74.

60. Galileo–Giovanni Battista Baliani [in Genoa], 6 August 1630, Florence. *EN* 14: no. 2043.

61. Castelli–Galileo, 24 August 1630, Rome. Ibid.: no. 2049.

62. Eszer, "Riccardi," 437.

63. Castelli–Galileo, 21 September 1630, Rome. *EN* 14: no. 2066. The same day Ciampoli wrote Galileo that he had given his letter to the pope and looked forward to Galileo's return to Rome. The letter probably concerned a dispensation for Galileo's daughters rather than the *Dialogue*. Ibid.: no. 2067.

64. AdS Roma, Governatore, Processi, sec XVII, b. 251, fos. 3r and 98r.

65. *Avviso* of 3 August 1630 II in ASMod:AE, 137, fasc. August 1630, unfoliated. The unidentified man was freed before 28 September. Ibid., fasc. September 1630, unfoliated.

66. *Avviso* of 20 July 1630 in ibid., 137, fasc. July 1630, unfoliated.

67. Luigi Tomassetti, Charles Cocquelines, Luigi Bilio, and Francesco Gaude, eds., *Magnum Bullarium Romanum*, 24 vols. (Turin: Sebastiano Franco and Enrico Dalmazzo, 1857–1872), 8: 646–50, 650.

68. ASR, Governatore, Processi, sec. XVII, b. 251, fos. 3r and 7r. Bertolotti, "Giornalisti," 479–81; reprinted in Antonino Bertolotti, *Martiri del libero pensiero e vittime della Santa inquisizione nei secoli XVI, XVII e XVIII* (Rome: Tip. delle Mantellate, 1891), 119. Bertolotti also printed another document of 17 July 1630 with very similar language to that on fo. 3r ordering Febei to join in the search of Morandi's rooms (as the text on fo. 3r does not), but I have not been able to find it in the *processo*. Dooley apparently did not find this document either; at least his only reference to Febei is to his appearance at Morandi's first interrogation. *Morandi*, 7. The closest text in the dossier is the protocol of the search of Morandi's rooms on 13 July by Fido and "Petrus Paulus Phoebeus Rev. Cam. Ap. Procurator fiscalis generalis." ASR, Governatore, Processi, sec. XVII, b. 251, fo. 9r.

69. The office went by various names. Properly it was "fiscal procurator of the apostolic chamber," and it "played the role of the intermediary between the different [Roman] courts." Laurie Nussdorfer, *Civic Politics in the Rome of Urban VIII* (Princeton, N.J.: Princeton University Press, 1992), 51; and Peter Blastenbrei, "Violence, Arms and Criminal Justice in Papal Rome, 1560–1600," *Renaissance Studies* 20, 1 (2006): 68–87, 69, citing Peter Blastenbrei, *Kriminalität in Rom 1560–1585* (Tübingen: Niemeyer, 1995), 13.

70. AdS Roma, Governatore, Processi, sec XVII, b. 251, fos. 115v–16v and 121r; Bertolotti, "Giornalisti," 438. For Bracciolini as Antonio Barberini, Sr.'s secretary, see *RI*, 54, and as subsecretary of the Roman Inquisition, see ADCFSO:DSO 1631, fo. 120r–v, 10 July. Benigno Bracciolini da Pistoia, a monk of S.ta Prassede, was his relative. Bertolotti, "Giornalisti," 484 and 488.

71. His was not the only name of a friend of Galileo to appear in the *processo*. It also contained three letters from Ilario Altobelli to Morandi, thanking him for help with his *Tabulae Regiae* [*Tabulae regiae divisionum duodecim partium coeli, et syderum obviationum, ad mentem Ptolemaei* (Macerata: Giovanni Battista Bonomi, 1628)]: 1, 22, and 29 June 1629 (AdS Roma, Governatore, Processi, sec XVII, b. 251, fos. 754r, 756r, and 755r). For Altobelli, see Thomas F. Mayer, "The Censoring of Galileo's *Sunspot Letters* and the First Phase of His Trial," *Studies in the History and Philosophy of Science, Part A* 42, 1 (2011): 1–10, 4.

72. AdS Roma, Governatore, Processi, sec XVII, b. 251, fo. 481v; Bertolotti, "Giornalisti," 496.

73. As Dooley also suggests in *Morandi*, 181–82.

74. *Avviso* of 27 July 1630 II in ASMod:AE, 137, fasc. July 1630, unfoliated.

75. *Avviso* of 5 October 1630 in ibid., fasc. October 1630, unfoliated, and dispatch of 12 October II in ASMOD, Cancelleria ducale, Ambasciatori Italia Roma, 227, fo. 403r.

76. *Avviso* of 23 November 1630 in ASMod, Cancelleria ducale, Avvisi dall'Estero, 137, fasc. November 1630, unfoliated.

77. Caterina Riccardi Niccolini–Galileo, 12 October 1630, Rome. *EN* 14: no. 2070.

78. Caterina Riccardi Niccolini–Galileo, 19 October 1630, Rome. Ibid.: no. 2073.

79. Professed at S. Marco ca. 1602 (in the dedication to *Aspirazioni di santa morte* [see below] Del Nente said he had been in the convent for almost forty years) where he apparently spent most of career, Del Nente took his *laurea* in 1622, made frequent retreats at a Servite hermitage. He became confessor to Grand Duchess Vittoria della Rovere and died in 1648. *QE* 2: 557–58. As lecturer in theology in S. Marco, "a nome del Santo Uffizio," he gave an opinion 17 March 1609 for Vincenzo Puccini, *Vita della Veneranda Madre Suor M. Maddalena de Pazzi Fiorentina* (Florence: Guinti, 1611), 364 and unpaginated and was involved in 1610 (?) in the authentication of the miracles of S.ta Maria Magdalena de' Pazzi with Cornelio Priatoni, inquisitor of Florence (*SI*, 154), Claudio Seripando, S.J. (*SI*, 185, 194–95), and Emanuele Ximenez, S.J. (see Chapter 2 above). Gottfried Henschenius and Daniel Papebroch, eds., *Acta sanctorum*, 68 vols., 19 (Paris and Rome: Victor Palmé, 1866), 240. Del Nente wrote or compiled *Vita et opere spirituali del beato Enrico Susone religioso estatico, e santissimo dell'ordine di S. Domenico* (Florence: Amadore Massi, 1642); *Breve modo di fare orazione mentale* (Florence: Francesco Onofri, 1677); *L'eremo interno del cuore* (Florence: n.p., 1711); *Novene di meditazioni esercizi brevi spirituali* (Florence: Luca Franceschini, 1648); *Solitudini di sacri e pietosi affetti intorno à misteri di Nostro Signore Gesù Cristo, e Maria Vergine* (Florence: Amadore Massi and Lorenzo Landi, 1643); *Della tranquillità dell'animo nel lume della natura, della fede, della sapienza, e del divino amore* (Florence: Filippo Papini, 1642); *Aspirazioni di santa morte* (Florence: Amadore Massi, 1643); *Stimoli di conversione a Dio. Solitudini di dolorosi affetti intorno all'ultime pene, e morte del peccatore* (Florence: Amadore Massi, 1646); *La tortore et il pellicano affetti pietosi sopra i gemiti, e le lacrime di Gesù Cristo nostro Redentore, e dell'anima penitente* (Florence: Amadore Massi, 1642, but written in 1634); *Vita, e costumi, et intelligenze spirituali, della gran serva di Dio, & veneranda madre suor Domenica dal Paradiso. Fondatrice del Monasterio dell Croce di Firenze; dell'Ordine di S. Domenico* (Venice: Michiel Miloco, 1664), about the spiritual leader of the Savonarolans, commissioned by Grand Duchess Vittoria. See also Tito S. Centi, "Il venerabile Ignazio del Nente nel quarto centenario della nascita," *Rassegna di Ascetica e Mistica* 23 (1972): 104–25. On unknown evidence, Eric Cochrane called Del Nente "none-too-intelligent" and claimed he thought of Galileo as another Epicurus as mentioned by Justus Lipsius, that is, a "pure speculator, one whose speculations served no other purpose than that of encouraging the young to strive for wisdom." *Florence in the Forgotten Centuries* (Chicago: University of Chicago Press, 1973), 211; the Bibliographical Note has no likely looking source. Del Nente is supposed to have edited Heinrich Suess, *Orologio della Sapienza* (Rome, 1663), according to Lynn T. White, "The Iconography of *Temperantia* and the Virtuousness of Technology," in *Medieval Religion and Technology: Collected Essays* (Berkeley: University of California Press, 1978), 181–204, 191. I have not been able to identify this edition, unless it is supposed to be part of the 1663 reprint of Del Nente's *Vita del beato Enrico Susone* (Rome: Niccolò Angelo Tinassi, 1663). The title may perhaps arise from confusion with "Dialogo d'amore tra l'Eterna Sapienza & il casto e divoto giovane Enrico Susone." White, *Medieval Religion*, 88–177.

80. Giacinto Stefani, O. P. (1577–7 February 1633, possibly a mistake) was a pupil of

Michele Arrighi in Spain at an unknown date, took his *laurea* at Perugia 1603, and, as of 20 November 1609, was in Venice at S.ti Giovanni e Paolo where he dedicated to a nephew of future Inquisitor Ottavio Bandini probably sermons intended for Dominicans in the form of *Delle pompe, o vero degli abusi del vestire* (Venice: Bernardo Giunta and Giovanni Battista Ciotti, 1610). He made submission after unknown trouble in 1614. Antonio Ricci-Riccardi, *Galileo Galilei e fra Tommaso Caccini: il processo del Galilei nel 1616 e l'abiura segreta rivelata dalle carte caccini* (Florence: Le Monnier, 1902), 132, citing a letter of Stefani's. He was a general preacher in 1615 and "accepted" in 1618. *MOPH* 11: 259, 303. Thereafter, he served as reader in Bible at the *studio* of Florence and for twenty years grand ducal preacher and consultor of Florentine Holy Office (*DV*, 71; other sources say to Christina of Lorraine). He possibly got a license to read prohibited books 7 June 1623. ADCFSO:DSO 1623, p. 195, renewed 23 Oct 1624 (1624, fo. 165v). He was his order's Roman provincial in 1626 and allegedly died in S.ta Maria Novella 7 February 1633, but this may be a mistake since "PP. Arrighi e Stefani" were said to be praying for Galileo as late as 26 March 1633. Mario Guiducci–Galileo, Florence; *EN* 15, no. 2454. I have not been able to consult the necrology in Archivio di S.ta Maria Novella, MS I.A.1, "Cronica fratrum Sancte Marie Novelle de Florentia," I (1225–1666). He may perhaps have been a relative of Urban VIII's *coppiere* Girolamo Stefani who allegedly took office at the beginning of Urban's reign. BAV, Barb. lat. 5340, fo. 35v. For Stefani as *coppiere*, see also the official biography of the pope by Andrea Nicoletti in BAV, Barb. lat. 4731, p. 94. The *DBI* entry for Angelo Giori says he held that office until 1629, but this is a mistake since both an *avviso* of 1 May 1632 and a letter from Francesco Barberini to the nuncio in Florence of 28 August 1632 say Giori had moved from *coppiere* to *maestro da camera*. BAV, Barb. lat. 6352, fo. 74r and Barb. lat. 7310, fo. 26r.

81. Filippo Magalotti–Mario Guiducci, Rome, 7 August 1632. *EN* 14: no. 2285; English translation in *TG*, no. 35. See also O. Besomi and M. Helbing, eds., Galileo, *Dialogo sopra i due massimi sistemi del mondo tolemaico et copernicano*, 2 vols. (Padua: Antenore, 1998), 1: 5 and 504. See their commentary 2: 125–26, and 899–902.

82. Caterina Riccardi Niccolini–Galileo, 17 November 1630, Rome. *EN* 14: no. 2083.

83. Dooley, *Morandi*, 1, and ACDFSO, S.O. Decreta 1630, fo. 178r.

84. ASMod:AE, 137, fasc. November 1630, unfoliated), fo. [4r–v]). For the *summarium* and discussion of charges, see *RI*, 196ff.

85. Castelli–Galileo, 30 November 1630, Rome. *EN* 14: no. 2085. Visconti's discussion of Urban's geniture is included in Morandi's processo and printed in Bertolotti, "Giornalisti," 507–10.

86. Raffaello Visconti–Pietro Paolo Febei, 30 November 1630, "casa." AdS Roma, Governatore, Processi, sec XVII, b. 251, fo. 530r, wrapper on 531v to "fiscale di Roma;" Bertolotti, "Giornalisti," 498 dated 36 [*sic*] November.

87. Castelli–Galileo, 29 March 1631, Rome. *EN* 14: no. 2132.

88. *Avviso* of 7 December 1630 in ASMod:AE, 137, fasc. December 1630, unfoliated, fo. [4r]. The bull was mentioned again without details on 21 December. BAV, Urb. Lat. 1100, fo. 811r. Although dated 1 April 1631, it was not made public until late May. *Avviso* of 28 May 1631 in AsMod:AE, 138, fasc. May 1631, unfoliated.

89. For the peace negotiations, see *avvisi* of 16 November and 6 December 1630 in BAV, Urb. Lat. 1100, fos. 726r and 770v. For Barberini family tensions, see *avvisi* of 6 December 1630 and 18 and 25 January 1631, in ibid., fo. 770v and BAV, Urb. lat. 1101, fos. 56r and 70r.

90. See *SI*, Chapter 1.

91. *Avviso* of 21 December 1630 in BAV, Urb. lat. 1101, fo. 12r; cf. virtually the same information in Camillo Molza–duke of Modena, 21 December 1630, Rome in ASMOD, Cancelleria ducale, Ambasciatori Italia Roma, 227, fo. 451r, printed in Amabile, *Congiura*, 2: 154, and, "L'Andata," no. 15, 44, and in ASMod:AE, 137, fasc. Dec 1630, unfoliated.

92. ADCFSO:DSO 1630, fo. 191v, 28 November. Borja was in attendance.

93. ASVe:SDR, f. 103, fo. 262r–v, 14 December.

94. *Avvisi* of 16 and 25 January 1631 in BAV, Barb. lat. 7301, fo. 33r.

95. Giacinto Ferri–Francesco Barberini, 1 February 1631, Florence. BAV, Barb. lat. 7301, fo. 37r.

96. Giacinto Ferri–Francesco Barberini, 15 February 1631, Florence. Ibid., fo. 39r–v.

97. Giacinto Ferri–Francesco Barberini, 22 February 1631, Florence. Ibid., fo. 41r.

98. Giacinto Ferri–Francesco Barberini, 5 April 1631, Florence, saying he had not yet announced the censures and would write Gessi. Ibid., fo. 53r.

99. Galileo–Andrea Cioli, 7 March 1631, Bellosguardo. *EN* 14: no. 2115. English translation in Finocchiaro, 206–9.

100. Geri Bocchineri–Galileo, 8 March 1631, Florence, and [Andrea Cioli]–Niccolini, 8 March 1631, Florence. *EN* 14: nos. 2116 and 2117.

101. Niccolini–Cioli, 16 March 1631, Rome. Ibid.: no. 2123. The letter went by ordinary courier and was received in Florence on 21 March. Ibid.: no. 2128. The telescope was finally dispatched on 23 April 1631. Ibid.: no. 2154.

102. Cioli–Niccolini, 29 March 1631, Florence. Ibid.: no. 2133.

103. For interim developments, see ibid.: no. 2138, 2145, 2147, and 2149.

104. Niccolini–Cioli, 19 April 1631, Rome. Ibid.: no. 2151.

105. Riccardi–Niccolini, 25 April 1631, Rome. Ibid.: no. 2156, autograph, marked "E" by Galileo in his resume of the imprimatur's tortured history. See *EN* 19: 401–2. English translation in Finocchiaro, 209–10.

106. Niccolini–Cioli, 27 April 1631, Rome. *EN* 14: no. 2160. Niccolini noted that "Io gliel'ho [Riccardi's letter] fatto metter in carta per mia maggior giustificatione."

107. Galileo misread the date of Riccardi's letter as 28 April. Favaro said it is easy to confuse Riccardi's 5 with an 8.

108. Galileo–Cioli, 3 May 1631, Bellosguardo. Ibid.: no. 2162; English translation in Finocchiaro, 210–11.

109. Niccolini–Cioli, 17 May 1631, Rome. Ibid.: no. 2165.

110. Niccolini–[Galileo], 25 May 1631, Rome. Ibid.: no. 2172.

111. *DV*, no. 25, 53; *EN* 19: 327; English translation in Finocchiaro, 212. Both this and Clemente Egidi's reply are known from the particular congregation's report in September 1632. *DV*, no. 25, 49. The file also contains a draft preface (see below) with some variants

from the printed version and a brief note of the conclusion. Besomi and Helbing, *Dialogo*, 929–30.

112. *DV*, 54; *EN* 19: 328.

113. *EN* 19: 401–2 from Bibl. Naz. Fir. Mss. Gal., Nuovi Acquisti, n.o 50., autograph. Favaro identifed this document as part of Galileo's defense, but the latest text cited is probably Riccardi's letter of 24 May 1631 (the summary does not make entirely clear which letter is meant). Since Galileo never used any of the evidence he collected at trial, the document is more likely to be a summary of the negotiations over the imprimatur designed to put pressure on Riccardi via the grand duke and may therefore date from about the beginning of May 1631. In addition to Riccardi's letter, the file contains copies of his of 17 November 1630 and 25 April 1631, Castelli's to Galileo of 24 August and 30 November 1630 and 19 April 1631, Niccolini's to Cioli of 19 April 1631, and Visconti's to Galileo of 16 June 1630.

114. Exchange between Niccolini and Cioli of 8 and 13 June. *EN* 14: nos. 2180 and 2183.

115. He did the same with *Sunspot Letters*. Mayer, "Interim Report."

116. Campanella had warned him of the book in April. *EN* 14: no. 2157. *Rosa Ursina* began printing in 1616 and was finished 13 June 1630 by Andrea Fei, then printer to Paolo Giordano Orsini in Bracciano. See the title page reproduced in Walter M. Mitchell, "The History of the Discovery of the Solar Spots," *Popular Astronomy* 24 (1916): 22–30, 82–96, 149–61, 201–17, 290–300, 341–53, 428–40, 488–99, and 562–70, pl. XIX between 344 and 345. Orsini was the grand duke's client and had to apologize to Galileo for having allowed the book to be printed. He made amends somewhat oddly by sending him a copy. Orsini–Galileo, 30 December 1631, Naples. *EN* 14: no. 2232.

117. Scheiner–Pierre Gassendi, Rome, 23 February 1633. *EN* 15: no. 2418.

118. Gabriel Naudé–Gassendi, Rome, [April 1633]. Ibid.: no. 2465. The date comes from Naudé's reference to Galileo having been in Rome for "more than fifty days."

119. Castelli–Galileo, 26 September 1631, Pesaro. *EN* 14: no. 2209.

120. Castelli–Galileo, 16 February 1632, Rome. Ibid.: no. 2243.

121. Galileo had asked Paolo Giordano Orsini for a copy, and Orsini ordered one sent to him. Orsini–Galileo, 9 September 1631, Posillipo. Ibid.: no. 2206. For the added section, see Besomi and Helbing, *Dialogo*, 2: 40.

122. Luca Bianchi, "'Mirabile e veramente angelica dottrina:' Galileo e l'argomento di Urbano VIII," in, eds., *Il "Caso Galileo": Una rilettura storica, filosofica, teologica: Atti del Convegno internazionale di studi (Firenze 26–30 maggio 2009)* , ed. Massimo Bucciantini, Michele Camerota and Franco Giudice (Florence: Olschki, 2011), 213–33, especially 224 and 230–31 for the speculation that Scheiner would not only have recognized the parody but could have pointed it out to Urban.

123. Besomi and Helbing, *Dialogo*, 2: 40, say printing began "almeno un mese" before Galileo announced in a letter to Cesare Marsili of 5 July 1631 that about six folios of fifty total were completed. *EN* 14: no. 2188.

124. Ibid.: no. 2185.

125. Castelli–Galileo, 14 June 1631, Rome. Ibid.: no. 2184. Castelli did not return to Rome until mid-October. Ibid.: no. 2213.

126. *DV*, 50, and *EN* 19: 324.

127. Niccolini–Cioli, 11 September 1632, Rome. *EN* 14: no. 2302; English translation in Finocchiaro, 232–34.

128. Niccolini–Galileo, 19 July 1631, Rome. *EN* 14: no. 2192, English translation in Finocchiaro, 213. Galileo made a copy. See *EN* 14: no. 2193. There are other instances of rebukes to masters for licensing books, but none specifically to Riccardi is known. See, e.g., ADCFSO:DSO 1606–1607, fo. 137r, 3 August 1606.

129. Niccolini–Galileo, 10 August 1631, Rome. *EN* 14: no. 2197, English translation in Finocchiaro, 214. See Ciampoli's complaint that he had no news from Galileo since Castelli left (in June). Ciampoli–Galileo, 23 August 1631. *EN* 14: no. 2200.

130. Galileo–Elio Diodati, 16 August 1631, Bellosguardo. Ibid.: no. 2199.

131. "Mi trovai allora presente in Roma; ebbi non solo udienze, ma ancora applausi de i piú eminenti prelati di quella Corte; né senza qualche mia antecedente informazione seguì poi la publicazione di quel decreto." Besomi and Helbing, *Dialogo*, 1: 5. They read "antecedente informazione" as a reference to Bellarmino's "monitio personale" (2: 2) or the "ammonizione precetto fatta a Galileo" (2: 124).

132. Francesco Beretta, "Melchior Inchofer et l'hérésie de Galilée: censure doctrinale et hiérarchie intellectuelle," *Journal of Modern European History* 3 (2005): 23–49; and Pietro Redondi, *Galileo Heretic*, trans. Raymond Rosenthal (Princeton, N.J.: Princeton University Press, 1987), passim (second Italian ed. with unchanged main text, Turin: Einaudi, 2004).

133. Giovanni Battista Landini and Galileo, both to Cesare Marsili, 21 and 22 February 1632. *EN* 14: nos. 2244 and 2245.

134. Cioli–Niccolini, 2 April 1632, Florence saying, "Io credo che il S.re Galilei habbia poi mandati i suoi libri con la venuta costà di Mons.re Arcivescovo di Fiorenza." Ibid.: no. 2255. Pietro Niccolini (1577–before 16 December 1652) was provided 7 June 1632 and consecrated 13 June 1632 by Antonio Barberini, Sr., secretary of the Roman Inquisition and head of the Congregation for Bishops and Regulars. *HC* 4: 188. An *avviso* of 10 April 1632 reported that he was staying with Ambassador Niccolini and had already been consecrated by Cardinal Barberini. BAV, Barb. lat. 6352, fos 60v, 91v and 92r. As vicar general of Florence, Niccolini gave an imprimatur dated 11 September 1630 for the *Dialogue*. Besomi and Helbing, *Dialogo*, 2: 922.

135. He received the book in July. Campanella–Galileo, 5 August 1632, Rome. *EN* 14: no. 2284.

136. Filippo Magalotti–Mario Guiducci, 7 August 1632, Rome. Ibid.: no. 2285; English translation in *TG*, no. 35.

137. Among the friends were Rafaello Masotti and Evangelista Torricelli. Ibid.: nos. 2269, 2275, and 2277.

138. Castelli–Galileo, 19 June 1632, Rome. Ibid.: no. 2277.

139. Ibid.

140. Magalotti–Mario Guiducci, 7 August 1632, Rome. *EN* 14: no. 2285; English translation in *TG*, no. 35.

141. R. A. Stradling, *Philip IV and the Government of Spain, 1621–1665* (Cambridge: Cambridge University Press, 1988), 143.

142. Auguste Leman, *Urbain VIII et la rivalité de la France et de la maison d'Austriche de 1631 à 1635* (Lille and Paris: R. Giard and É. Champion, 1920; Mémoires et Travaux publiés per des professeurs des facultés catholiques de Lille, fasc. 16), 119.

143. Leman, *Urbain*, 127. Leman's study, well grounded in archival sources, is nonetheless strongly biased in Urban's favor and his incessantly reiterated claim to act only as *pater communis* of all of Christendom. See, e.g, Leman's assertion on 11 that Urban never tired of trying to reconcile the Catholic powers or on 29 that he never abandoned strict neutrality.

144. Ibid., 130.

145. Ibid., 132. See the testimonial of 10 March 1632 by Francesco Adriano Ceva. BAV, Barb. lat. 8376, fo. 99r–v.

146. There are a number of accounts that agree tolerably well in details. They include the official papal version in a dispatch to Nuncio Monti in BAV, Barb. lat. 8376, fos. 85r–95r, printed in Ludwig von Pastor, *The History of the Popes from the Close of the Middle Ages*, 29, trans. and ed. Ernest Graf (London: Kegan Paul, Trench, Trübner, 1938), 560–64, and dated 8 March, although it seems rather to be dated the 16th together with a Latin account on fos. 96r–8v signed by Guido Bentivoglio, Scaglia, Zacchia, Berlinghiero Gessi, Giovanni Francesco Guidi di Bagno, Fabrizio Verospi, and Marzio Ginetti (all either then or later Inquisitors); a "Relatione" enclosed in an undated *avviso* and another account in an *avviso* of 13 March (which may well be the date of the "Relatione") both in ASMod:AE, 138, fasc. March 1632, unfoliated, both printed in Ferdinand Gregorovius, *Urban VIII. im Widerspruch zu Spanien und dem Kaiser: eine Episode des dreissig-jährigen Kriegs* (Stuttgart: J.G. Cotta, 1879), 135–38 and 132–34; a similar report in Vienna printed in ibid., 124–27; and an exceedingly anodyne Spanish account printed in Leman, *Urbain*, 560–63, followed by a text of the protest on 563–64, the nearest to the original that Leman could find in Simancas. Unfortunately, the Venetians had no representation in Rome at this time, having withdrawn their ambassador in the dispute over precedence occasioned by both the title of *eminenza* for cardinals and Taddeo Barberini's newly exalted status as prefect of Rome. Among many accounts in other European archives, there are supposed to be eight copies in the National Archives in London, PRO, SP For 85/7, fos. 51–55 and 270–76. Stradling, *Philip IV*, 140.

147. Leman, *Urbain*, 564. The text in Gregorovius, *Urban VIII*, 123–24, has the same reading.

148. "Relatione" in ASMod:AE, 138, fasc. March 1632, unfoliated.

149. "Relatione" and *avviso* of 13 March 1632 both in ASMod:AE, 138, fasc. March 1632, unfoliated. From the location of this information in the first text, it seems likely it came from Scaglia.

150. *Avviso* of 13 March 1632 in ibid.

151. "Relatione" and *avviso* of 13 March 1632 both in ibid.

152. *Avviso* of 6 June 1632 in ibid., fasc. June 1632, unfoliated.

153. For Borja's dissemination of his version, see the dispatch of 17 March 1632 in BAV, Barb. lat. 7306, fo. 18r; same content in ASV, Seg. Stato, Nunz. Firenze 20, fo. 26v.

154. BAV, Barb. lat. 8376, fos. 87r and 89v. The dispatch is probably dated 16 March,

although it may be as late as the 18th when the Latin version of the consistory was signed. The *congregazione* that debated the pope's diplomatic response met at Cardinal Spada's palace on 12 March. Leman, *Urbain*, 565–68.

155. For Urban's efforts to get Borja out of Rome, see *SI*, 13–19.

156. *Avviso* of 20 March 1632 in ASMod:AE, 138, fasc. March 1632, unfoliated and Giorgio Bolognetti–F. Barberini, Florence, 5 June 1632. BAV, Barb. lat. 7306, fos. 56r and 61r and ASV, Seg. Stato, Nunz. Firenze 20, fos. 41r and 43v.

157. *Avviso* of 27 March 1632 in ASMod:AE, 138, fasc. March 1632, unfoliated.

158. And in fact it was not. See *RI*, 33.

159. Niccolini–Cioli, 18 April 1632 Rome. Federica Favino, "'Quel petardo di mia fortuna.' Riconsiderando la 'caduta' di Giovan Battista Ciampoli," in José Montesinos and Carlos Solís Santos, eds., *Largo campo di filosofare: Eurosymposium Galileo 2001* (La Orotava, Spain: Fundación Canaria Orotava de Historia de la Ciencia, 2001), 863–82, 870n, not in *EN*.

160. David Marshall Miller, "The Thirty Years War and the Galileo Affair," *History of Science* 46 (2008): 49–74.

161. Favino, "Petardo," 868n. His tenure lasted until 31 December 1634. Christoph Weber, *Legati e governatori dello Stato Pontificio (1550–1809)* (Rome: Ministero per i beni culturali e ambientali, Ufficio centrale per i beni archivistici, 1994; Pubblicazioni degli archivi di Stato. Sussidi), 360.

162. He held the post in Avignon from May 1621 to March 1627. Weber, *Legati*, 188.

163. Christoph Weber, *Die Ältesten Päpstlichen Staatshandbücher: Elenchus Congregationum, Tribunalium et Collegiorum Urbis, 1629–1714* (Rome: Herder, 1991), 169, and *avviso* of 21 May 1630 in BAV, Urb. Lat. 1100, fo. 298r.

164. He was appointed 18 May 1630. *Avviso* of 21 May 1630 in ibid., fo. 298r, date confirmed from ADCFSO:DSO 1630, fo. 80r. See also Marian Surdacki, *Il brefotrofio dell'ospedale di Santo Spirito in Roma nel XVIII secolo* (Rome: Accademia polacca delle scienze, Biblioteca e centro di studi a Roma, 2002), 31. For Anselmi, also a consultor of the Inquisition, see *RI*, 103.

165. G. B. Beltrani, "Felice Contelori ed i sui studi negli archivi del Vaticano," *Archivio della Società Romana di Storia Patria* 2:2 (1878): 165–208, 2:3 (1879), 257–79, and 3:1 (1879), 1ff., 2: 279. In addition to Contelori, a key cog in Urban's administrative machine who had replaced Raccagna as general commissary of the Camera apostolica and one of Urban's experts in rewriting the record, one of the other two members was Francesco Barberini's auditor, Antonio Cerri.

166. *HC* 4: 152.

167. See *SI*, Chapter 1, for his biography.

168. Antonio Ricciulli, *Tractatus de iure personarum extra ecclesiae gremium existentium libris novem distinctus . . . ; annexus est alter Tractatus de neophytis* (Rome: Giovanni Angelo Ruffinelli and Angelo Manni, publishers, Andrea Fei, printer,1622), book 5, "De haereticis," 406. Ricciulli cited the Spanish Jesuit Juan de Rojas († 1577), *De haereticis* in *Singularia iuris* (Venice: Francesco Ziletti, 1583), part 1, no. 469 (fo. 52v), who in turn had cited Gratian's Decretum.

169. Antonio Cistellini, *San Filippo Neri: l'Oratorio e la congregazione oratoriana. Storia e spiritualità*, 3 vols. (Brescia: Morcelliana, 1989), 1: 162n; and Lothar Sickel, "Remarks on the Patronage of Caravaggio's 'Entombment of Christ'," *Burlington Magazine* 143, 1180 (July 2001): 426–29, 427. For Orsi, see Jolanta Wiendlocha, *Die Jugendgedichte Papst Urbans VIII. (1623–1644): Erstedition, Übersetzung, Kommentar und Nachwort* (Heidelberg: Universitätsverlag Winter, 2005), 222–24.

170. 11 September and 15 November 1624. ADCFSO:DSO 1624, fos. 143r and 179r.

171. ADCFSO:DSO 1627, fo. 58v.

172. *Avvisi* of 7 June and 11 October in AsMod:AE, 138, fasc. June and October 1631, unfoliated.

173. *Avviso* of 24 July in ibid., fasc. July 1632, unfoliated.

174. BAV, Barb. lat. 1794, frontispiece. See *SI*, 67. For his collection of Caravaggios, see Lothar Sickel, *Caravaggios Rom. Annäherungen an ein dissonantes Milieu* (Emsdetten/Berlin: Edition Imorde, 2003), 267.

175. ASMod:AE, 138, fasc. July 1632, unfoliated. For the rest of this paragraph, see *RI*, 133.

176. Francesco Beretta, "Urbain VIII Barberini Protagoniste de la Condamnation de Galilée," in Montesinos and Solís Santos, eds., *Largo campo*, 549–73; 566 links Vittrici, Febei, and Maculano and implicitly makes the change of personnel a function of the first's Spanish allegiance.

177. See *RI*, 33.

178. *Avvisi* of 28 and 31 July in AsMod:AE, 138, fasc. July 1632, unfoliated.

179. See *RI*, 133.

180. *Avvisi* of 28 and 31 August in ASMod:AE, 138, fasc. August 1632, unfoliated and BAV, Barb. lat. 6352, fo. 151r; 4 and 8 September in ASMod:AE, 138, fasc. September 1632, unfoliated; and 6 November ibid., fasc. November 1632, unfoliated.

181. Gaetano Moroni, *Dizionario di erudizione storico-ecclesiastica da S. Pietro sino ai nostri giorni* (Venezia: Tipografica Emiliana, 1846), 99, 141; Sickel, *Caravaggios Rom*, 267.

182. ADCFSO:DSO 1632, fo. 103v. For more on Boccabella, see *RI*, 134–36.

183. 13 and 28 July 1632. ADCFSO:DSO 1632, fos. 107r and 115r.

184. BAV, Barb. lat. 6352, fos. 98v–99r.

185. Two *avvisi* of 17 July in ASMod:AE, 138, fasc. July 1632, unfoliated, and another in BAV, Barb. lat. 6352, fos. 98v–99r. His formal nomination is dated 20 July. ASV, S. R. Rota, Miscellanea, 2, fo. 295r; cf. Hermann Hoberg, "Die Antrittsdaten der Rotarichter von 1566 bis 1675," *Römische Quartalschrift* 48 (1953): 211–24, 202; Emmanuele Cerchiari, *Capellani papae et apostolicas sedis; auditores causarum sacrii palatii apostolici seu Sacra Romana Rota ab origine ad diem usque 20 Septembris 1870. Relatio Historica-iuridica*, 4 vols. (Rome: Typis polyglottis vaticanis, 1870–1921), 2: 153.

186. *Avviso* of 17 July in ASMod:AE, 138, fasc. July 1632, unfoliated.

187. 2 October 1636 ADCFSO:DSO 1636, fos. 158v and 159r (assessor), 23 July 1636 ibid., fo. 118v (vice-assessor on his first appearance), and list of consultors at the front of 1637, fo. 1r (pro-assessor).

188. ADCFSO:DSO 1627, fos. 46r and 48r; 1629, fos. 18v and 28v.

189. ADCFSO:DSO 1624, fo. 184r and 1628, fo. 115v, 11 July 1628.

190. *RI*, 135.

191. *Avviso* of 15 February 1631 in AsMod:AE, 138, fasc. February 1631, unfoliated.

192. Domenico Ciampoli, "Monsignor Giovanni Ciampoli, un amico del Galileo," in *Nuovi studi letterari e bibliografici* (Rocca San Casciano: Licinio Cappelli, 1900), 5–170, 14.

193. Or perhaps Ciampoli told Pietro Aldobrandini. Nicoletti in BAV, Barb. lat. 4734, fo. 244r.

194. "Memorie intorno la Vita di PP. Urbano cavate dall'originale di Mon. Herrera al quale S. Ma. le dettava," BAV, Barb. lat. 4901, fo. 43r–v, and BAV, Barb. lat. 5340, fo. 34r, printed in Ciampoli, "Giovanni Ciampoli," 107; cf. Andreas Kraus, *Das päpstliche Staatssekretariat unter Urban VIII 1623–1644, Römischer Quartalschrift für christliche Altertumskunde and Kirchengeschichte*, Supplementheft 29 (Rome: Herder, 1964), 172n.

195. "Conclave dell'anno 1623 nel quale messa la prima volta in uso la Bolla della Elettione publicata da Gregorio XV. fu creato sommo Pontefice Il Card. Maffeo Barberino detto Urbano VIII." BAV, Barb. lat. 4724, fos. 7v–8r.

196. Ciampoli himself admitted the rumor that he had visited Borja. Ciampoli, "Giovanni Ciampoli," 77.

197. Nicoletti in BAV Barb. lat. 4734, fo. 243v.

198. Niccolini–Cioli, 25 April 1632, Rome in ASF:AMP, 3351, fo. 324v, quoted in translation in Richard S. Westfall, *Essays on the Trial of Galileo* (Vatican City: Vatican Observatory Publications, 1989), 96, not in *EN*, and Favino, "Petardo," 875 and passim. Nicoletti, BAV, Barb. lat. 4734, fo. 244v, cited a letter to the king of Persia.

199. Favino, "Petardo," 872. See also Federica Favino, "Ciampoli, Giovanni Battista," *DSI* 2:330–31.

200. Stefano Gradi, "De vita, et factis, dictisque Petri Benessae Ragusini, Commentarius a Stephano Gradio eius sororis filio conscriptus" in BAV, Vat. lat. 6095, fos. 1–121, fo. 29r–v; Kraus, *Staatssekretäriat*, 172n.

201. "Sopra la Corte di Roma" in ASV, Relationi di Roma, II, 150, 9, p. 123.

202. "Libro primo della politica Christiana." BAV, Ottob. 2440:3 (mistakenly numbered 2240 by Domenico Ciampoli), fos. 429r–508r, fo. 492v.

203. Favino, "Petardo," 863.

204. *Avvisi* of 1 and 15 May 1632 in ASMod:AE, 138, fasc. May 1632, unfoliated.

205. *Avviso* of 20 November 1632 in ibid., fasc. November 1632, unfoliated.

206. *Avviso* of 4 September 1632 in ibid., fasc. September 1632, unfoliated.

207. *Avviso* of 28 August 1632 in ibid., fasc. August 1632, unfoliated.

208. ASVe:SDR, f. 105, fo. 309v and *avvisi* of 20 and 27 November 1632 in BAV, Barb. lat. 6352, fo. 171r and ASMod:AE, 138, fasc. November 1632, unfoliated.

209. *Avviso* of 4 December 1632 ASMod:AE, 138, fasc. December 1632, unfoliated.

210. *Avviso* of 15 January 1633 in ASMod:AE, 139, fasc. January 1633, unfoliated.

211. First fragment of "Della filosofia naturale" in *Lettere di monsignor Giovanni Ciampoli* (Venice: Curti, 1676), 35.

212. Nicoletti, in BAV, Barb. lat. 4734, fo. 245r.

213. Ciampoli, "Giovanni Ciampoli," 60.

214. Riccardi–Clemente Egidi, 21 or 25 July 1632, Rome. Cioni, *Documenti*, no. XVII; dated 25? July in *EN* 20: no. 2283 bis.

215. Magalotti–Mario Guiducci, 7 August 1632, Rome. *EN* 14: no. 2285; English translation in *TG*, no. 35.

216. http://moro.imss.fi.it/lettura/LetturaWEB.DLL?AZIONE=UNITA&TESTO=Eb3 &PARAM= 1360-532883–47735&VOL=20&RADIO=B, accessed 20 March 2009. Among his dramatic works is *Il Gigante. Rapprensentazione fatta nel Seminario Romano, e altre poesie* (Rome: Francesco Corbelletti, 1632). See also Mirella Saulini, "Il Teatro gesuitico: il Gigante del p. Leone Santi," *Roma Moderna e Contemporanea* 3 (1995): 157–72.

217. "Da questo [discussion of Galileo's readiness to satisfy Riccardi had he been asked] trapassai a dire, e tirai come di pratica, che credeva di già che ne avessero scritto qualche cosa costà: a che egli mi rispose di sì, senza specificare nè che nè come, e questo perchè, come credo che ella ben sappia, non si può, sotto pena delle più gravi censure, rivelare alcuna, benchè minima, delle resoluzioni che si pigliano nel S.to Ufizio [*sic*]." Magalotti–Mario Guiducci, Rome, 7 August 1632. *EN* 14: no. 2285; English translation in *TG*, no. 35.

218. Ibid.

219. *EN* 20, no. 2285 bis; Cioni, *Documenti*, no. XX, dated 7 October 1632, corrected to 7 August on p. 12 and Fulgenzio Micanzio–Galileo, 14 August 1632, Venice. *EN* 14: no. 2286. Galileo's letter is missing.

CHAPTER 6. THE SECOND PHASE OF GALILEO'S TRIAL BEGINS

1. As usual, this moment has been garbled in many previous discussions. For example, Mariano Artigas, Rafael Martínez, and William R. Shea, "New Light on the Galileo Affair," in Ernan McMullin, ed., *The Church and Galileo* (Notre Dame, Ind.: University of Notre Dame Press, 2005), 213–33, 219, refer to it as a "Preparatory Commission." Thomas Cerbu labels it a "special commission." "Melchior Inchofer, 'un homme fin & rusé'," in José Montesinos and Carlos Solís Santos, eds., *Largo campo di filosofare: Eurosymposium Galileo 2001* (La Orotava, Spain: Fundación Canaria Orotava de Historia de la Ciencia, 2001), 587–611, 592. Francesco Beretta regards the particular congregation as a sham, saying it had "the air of being a diplomatic fiction" and calling it a "phantom commission." "'Magno Domino & Omnibus Christianae, Catholicaeque Philosophiae amantibus. D. D.' Beretta, *Le Tractatus syllepticus* du jésuite Melchior Inchofer, censeur de Galilée," *Freiburger Zeitschrift für Philosophie und Theologie* 48 (2001): 301–27, 310. Only one of the texts he cites is directly to the point, Filippo Magalotti's letter of 7 August 1632 (*EN* 14: no. 2285); it says the Inquisition was in charge from the first, which provides no evidence about how it exercised its control through the particular congregation.

2. Francesco Niccolini–Andrea Cioli, Rome. Excerpt in *EN* 14: no. 2287.

3. Tommaso Campanella–Galileo, 21 August 1632, Rome. *EN* 14: no. 2289.

4. *Avviso* of 21 August 1632 in BAV, Barb. lat. 6352, fo. 143r. Inquisitor Laudivio Zacchia substituted for the pope.

5. Niccolini–Cioli, 11 September 1632, Rome. *EN* 14: no. 2302. The facts that Campanella mentioned Theatine involvement and that Riccardi did not identify the Jesuit he suggested complicate the question of the congregation's membership. The first might indicate that Zaccaria Pasqualigo, the third consultor to pronounce on the *Dialogue* in 1633, also served on this congregation, as Cerbu suggests, but Riccardi's evidence seems to rule this out.

6. Francesco Beretta, "Melchior Inchofer et l'hérésie de Galilée: censure doctrinale et hiérarchie intellectuelle," *Journal of Modern European History* 3 (2005): 23–49, 34. Cerbu, "Inchofer," 593, makes Inchofer's participation in the particular congregation certain because of the reports he submitted during Galileo's *expeditio*. So does J. L. Heilbron, who also assumes his presence provided a conduit for Orazio Grassi and Christoph Scheiner to provide input. Without better documentation of the links between these three, this claim is incautious. Heilbron, *Galileo* (Oxford: Oxford University Press, 2010), 295. Both Shea and Richard Blackwell assume Inchofer served as Inquisition consultor because of his opinion on the *Dialogue*. William R. Shea, "Melchior Inchofer's 'Tractatus Syllepticus:' A Consultor of the Holy Office Answers Galileo," in *Novità celesti e crisi del sapere*, ed. P. Galluzzi (Florence: Giunti Barbèra, 1984), 283–92; and Richard J. Blackwell, *Behind the Scenes at Galileo's Trial* (Notre Dame, Ind.: Notre Dame University Press, 2006), 32.

7. See *RI*, 149–50 and passim.

8. For the papal dispensation to take orders granted to Inchofer, "born of heretic parents," see ACDFSO:DSO, 1605, fo. 452r; Copia, p. 995.

9. Cerbu, "Inchofer," 590–91, without much evidence for the link to Cardinal Francesco.

10. Ibid., 587. The document in ACDF, Index, Protocolli EE, fos. 301r–v, was independently discovered three times, first by Ugo Baldini and Leen Spruit in 1997 and then twice in 1999 by Cerbu and Artigas. Ugo Baldini and Leen Spruit, "Nuovi documenti galileiani degli archivi del Sant'Ufficio e dell'Indice," *Rivista di Storia della Filosofia* 56 (2001): 661–99, who published the text on 678–80; Cerbu, "Inchofer," 593–98, text on 608–9; and Artigas, Martínez, and Shea, "New Light," 213–33, text and English translation on 227–30. All three consider authorship and date and more or less agree on the second, and Cerbu and Artigas et al. on Inchofer's authorship. The suggestion of Artigas et al., 225, that Inchofer's opinion was discovered at the same time as the precept is extremely unlikely, not least because it is an Index record and, to judge from the present state of the volume containing it (which has no index of any kind), would have been extremely difficult to find, not least because Inchofer did not name Galileo in the text.

11. Baldini and Spruit, "Nuovi documenti," suggest a date between 1628 and 1630–31; Cerbu, "Inchofer," 597, implicitly about the time of the particular congregation; and Artigas et al., 221, give 1631–32 but not later than Galileo's first deposition.

12. As Cerbu, "Inchofer," 597, suggests. For "G3" see Pietro Redondi, *Galileo Heretic*, trans. Raymond Rosenthal (Princeton, N.J.: Princeton University Press, 1987; second Italian ed. with unchanged main text, Turin: Einaudi, 2004), chap. 5.

13. Niccolini–Cioli, 5 September 1632, Rome (*EN* 14: no. 2298; English translations in Finocchiaro, 229–32, and G. De Santillana, *The Crime of Galileo* [Chicago: University of Chicago Press, 1955], 204–5); Niccolini–[Cioli], 18 September 1632, Rome (*EN* 14: no. 2305; English translation in Finocchiaro, 234–37).

14. Magalotti–Galileo, 4 September 1632, Rome (*EN* 14: no. 2297); ibid. no. 2302; English translation in Finocchiaro, 232–34.

15. Niccolini–Cioli, 5 September 1632, Rome. *EN* 14: no. 2298; English translations in Finocchiaro, 229–32, and De Santillana, 204–5. Cerbu, "Inchofer," 591, claims links to Cardinal Francesco but documents them only thinly.

16. Cioli–Niccolini, 24 August 1632, [Florence]. *EN* 14: no. 2293.

17. F. Barberini–Giorgio Bolognetti, 28 August 1632, Rome. BAV, Barb. lat. 7310, fo. 26r.

18. Niccolini–Cioli, 28 August 1632, Rome. *EN* 14: no. 2294.

19. Magalotti–Guiducci, 4 September 1632, Rome, reporting a conversation of 31 August. Ibid.: no. 2296.

20. Magalotti–Galileo, 4 September 1632, Rome. Ibid.: no. 2297.

21. Niccolini–Cioli, 5 September 1632, Rome. Ibid.: no. 2298; English translations in Finocchiaro, 229–32, and De Santillana, 204–5.

22. For Alidosi's case, see *SI*, chapter 6.

23. Niccolini–Cioli, 11 September 1632, Rome. *EN* 14: no. 2302; English translation in Finocchiaro, 232–34.

24. For legal representation of defendants, see *RI*, 191–94. I am grateful to Christopher Black for the suggested translation of *diffidente*.

25. Jules Speller's notion (*Galileo's Inquisition Trial Revisited* [Bern: Peter Lang, 2008], 177) that an Inquisitor might himself have grubbed about in the archives and found the precept is bizarre and typifies his deep lack of understanding of how Rome worked. His book has been taken as a major contribution to the study of Galileo's trial. For an errantly positive review, see Maurice A. Finocchiaro in *Early Science and Medicine* 14 (2009): 576–78. Two more balanced reviews are Nick Wilding, in *Isis* 100, 4 (2009): 912–13), and W. R. Laird, in *Renaissance Quarterly* 62 (2009): 212–14. This evaluation holds up in one signal way (not pointed out by the reviewer). Speller offers a breakthrough interpretation of the trial as driven by two prosecutorial strategies, one based on the precept, the other on a charge of heresy. Unfortunately, his mistaken belief that the precept was either false or otherwise illegitimate damages his case, and his weak understanding of how the Inquisition worked causes a number of other problems. The book is also much more about the affair than the case; as Speller emphasizes in the Introduction, his object is to divine why Urban VIII insisted on Galileo's condemnation. Refusing out of hand a charge of "disobeying an official order" (Speller means the precept) as an "utterly inappropriate way of looking at the trial," he argues the unoriginal point that it was Galileo's rejection of Urban's insistence on unconstrained divine omnipotence that caused trouble for the *Dialogue* (29). To this point Speller adds a factional analysis, seeing rivalry between the pope and Cardinal Nephew Francesco Barberini as the engine of the trial's second phase: 45, a paragraph larded with

rhetorical phrases like "very probable" and "highly probable," and 167–71. Speller's assertion "that one breathes a liberal air around" Cardinal Francesco is nonsense, especially since
the cardinal raised several serious objections to Copernicus's ideas, one of which Speller immediately cites, and there is no reason to think he did not mean them seriously. In common
with other such analyses, Speller assigns Maculano, as Cardinal Francesco's catspaw, to the
side of the angels. The first claim is overdone, and the second two are impossible, as I shall
demonstrate. Putting a white hat on Maculano produces at least one notable deformation
of the evidence, which also wrecks an otherwise valuable observation about Galileo's first
interrogation. Usefully if imprecisely calling introduction of the precept into the questioning "the main conjuring trick," Speller goes on to blame it on "the Tribunal," instead of on
Maculano who conducted the session (210). Pressing the factional analysis farther than it
can safely be taken (if it has utility before that point), he claims "'Galileo's faction'" aimed
to prevent a formal trial, when the evidence indicates exactly the opposite (221).

Speller at least tries to put the trial into the context of Inquisition procedure, basing
himself almost entirely on manuals and to a much lesser degree some of Beretta's work.
A productive move to bring into prominence Prospero Farinacci's overlooked *De haeresi*,
which has a preface containing an implicit endorsement of the book by Inquisitor Bellarmino, is seriously undercut by the indiscriminate use of other manuals without any attempt
to establish their relative stature. Speller often misunderstands what the manuals say, for
example, translating *fustigatio* (a beating) as "castigation" or more seriously claiming they
put the Inquisition's assessor above the commissary or, worst of all, treating an Inquisitor as
a "minister" of the Inquisition (Speller's fondness for etymology might have stood him in
good stead here, since "minister" means "servant; 47, 133, 137). No matter which manuals
Speller used, he could not hope to establish how the Roman Inqusition did its business on
their basis alone. Nor can its practice be understood absent a grounding in its jurisprudence. For both points, see *RI*, passim. His notion that any "Congregation" can "su[e] the
crime of heresy" is bizarre (199). He speaks throughout of Galileo being sued (e.g., 221). He
does himself most damage by failing to grasp any part of the function of what, following
Maurice A. Finocchiaro, he calls the "Final Report," meaning the *summarium* of Galileo's
case. This, the only document the Inquisitors saw when proposing sentence, Speller instead
concludes "play[ed] a very limited role" (298). For the *summarium*, see *RI*, 113, 196–97. Similarly, Speller struggles and fails to understand the working of the Roman hierarchy, setting
a cardinal (*eminentissimo*) equivalent to a mere *prelato* and displaying almost no grasp of the
Vatican's bureaucracy (134). For example, he calls Giovanni Ciampoli Urban's "private secretary" (114) when his position as secretary of breves to princes much more nearly qualifies
as a public office and makes Pietro Benessa, effective head of the secretariat of state, "one
of Urban's secretaries" (149).

Most damaging to any advance his book might have made, Speller, vaguely following
Beretta, butchers the precept of 1616, alleging that Galileo received no more than a "charitativa monitio" (charitable warning) and that the precept was an illegitimate action taken
on his own authority by Commissary Seghizzi, before winding up in the certainly mistaken
"legal impropriety" school. The chapter in which Speller treats the precept is titled "Some

Kind of Legal Action in 1616." For the "admonitio" see 84 and for Seghizzi 106–7, an almost impossible argument to follow; see also 203ff. For legal impropriety, see 332. He also falsely claims Ambassador Francesco Niccolini never discussed the precept with Urban and incautiously endorses Pietro Redondi's claim that the particular congregation of summer 1632 was unusual, despite himself giving one piece of evidence that this is not the case (145, 161–62). Despite his commendable admonition that "one should therefore not overlook the theological and, above all, the legal grounds" of the congregation (162), Speller does just that.

The book depends on a number of close readings. While some provoke thought, many are tendentious or nearly unintelligible, given the author's fondness for parentheses and aversion to footnotes. (Contrariwise, there are a number of useless notes, including my favorite asserting that, since Cardinal Bonifacio Caetani had died in 1617, he could not have been alive in 1625; 78.) Instances of inappropriately close reading mar the argument, perhaps especially when trying to establish just what Galileo admitted about the precept in his first interrogation (213). Speller's close readings nonetheless offer the most help to further study, for example, the observation that the particular congregation's report "consists . . . of two distinct reports flung together" (172). This in turn leads him to get one crucial point precisely right. The congregation's report offered two lines of attack, a charge of disobedience to the precept or of "fraudulently" having concealed it when seeking permission to publish (or, of course, both at once, as Speller does not allow). "'Galileo's faction'" was well advised to choose the former, since that would make a charge of heresy more remote and thereby raise "the possibility of limiting the trial to an action ending very leniently," 221, 225, 229, 291). Speller's notion of what form that "ending," apparently meaning "sentence," might have taken is both garbled and unsubstantiated; of his three possibilities, only "spedire con monitioni e penitenze salutari" (to expedite with warnings and salutary penances)—an unattributed quotation—was a real option, although Speller has no idea what "spedire" means, as further demonstrated by his translation of "in ogni modo che si spedisca" as "in whatever way the case gets settled" (263). The first of the other two "endings," canonical purgation, had long since passed out of use and the other, a "retraction," is not an ending in the same sense, since that word can only refer to an abjuration. Speller compounds that mistake with another more serious one when he claims Galileo's abjuration was optional (334).

26. Niccolini–[Cioli], 18 September 1632, Rome. *EN* 14: no. 2305; English translation in Finocchiaro, 234–37.

27. *EN* 20: no. 2305 bis*; Cioni, *Documenti*, no. XIX, dated 28 September 1632, date let stand on p. 12*.

28. Minute by Benessa in BAV, Barb. lat. 7310, fos. 34r–5r, enciphered same day; *EN* 14: no. 2311; English translation in Finocchiaro, 222–23. Sergio Pagano dates the text "after February 1632" and does not connect it to the particular congregation and thinks the author was an official of the Holy Office. *DV*, no. 25 headnote; see also *EN* 19: 324–27. Finocchiaro (218) assumes the document to be the "special commission's" report but does not consider the question of authorship any farther.

29. *DV*, no. 44; *EN* 19: 348.

30. Beretta, "Censure doctrinale," 34. He compares the hand of ASV, Misc. Arm. X 204, fo. 52rff. to plate 48 in Andreas Kraus, *Das päpstliche Staatssekretariat unter Urban VIII 1623–1644*, *Römischer Quartalschrift für christliche Altertumskunde and Kirchengeschichte*, Supplementheft 29 (Rome: Herder, 1964). I doubt this identification. See also Beretta, "*Tractatus syllepticus*," 311–12.

31. "Octavus hodie dies agitur AA. quo ipse hoc eodem loco, hac eadem hora, Alexandro Boccabello Rotae Auditori, utrique nostrum amicissimo, sanus ac valens parentabat: non dubium quin tanti viri occasu, cui & virtus & fortuna aliis caeca, centum luminibus oculata praeluxerant ad summos honores, secum retractarit, quàm fragiles & vitreae sint humanarum rerum anchorae, quàm fugax spes bonorum, quae temporis precium non norunt." Melchior Inchofer, SJ, *Oratio funebris qua Rev.mo Patri Fr. Nicolai Riccardio Ordinis Praedicatorum . . . in aede S. Mariae ad Minervam primo die Iunii altero ab emortuali, praesente funere parentabat* (Rome: Luigi Grignani, 1639), sig. A5v. I am grateful to Tom Cerbu for sending me this reference.

32. Finocchiaro, 355n64, distinguished the report's parts by the watermarks in the paper, the most convincing evidence for the existence of two versions. Annibale Fantoli, *Galileo for Copernicanism and for the Church*, trans. George V. Coyne, 3rd English ed. (Vatican City: Vatican Observatory Publications, 2003), 526–27n27, repeated in compressed form in Annibale Fantoli, "The Disputed Injunction and Its Role in Galileo's Trial," in McMullin, ed., 117–49, 148, also divides the document in two but follows Beretta in thinking the first part in Boccabella's hand and excludes Riccardi and Oreggi as authors because of a trivial error in transcribing Visconti's name. Speller, *Inquisition Trial*, 172, writes of "two distinct reports flung together," although he later (199–200) almost accidentally works out the correct relation between them. He, too, makes much of variant spellings, an insignificant point.

33. *RI*, 211, *SI*, chap. 4 and Chapter 4 above for Paolo Beni.

34. *DV*, 53.

35. *DV*, 50, emphasis added.

36. We can be sure of this, since the Congregation quoted a title almost exactly like that of the report. ACDFSO:DSO 1632, fo. 145r; *EN* 19: 279–80; *DV*, no. 130.

37. ACDFSO:DSO 1632, fo. 145r; *EN* 19: 279–80; *DV*, no. 130; *DV*, 8–9; Finocchiaro, 283, quoting the *summarium*; pope's order quoted verbatim in Galileo's *processo* in *DV*, no. 26 and *EN* 19: 330.

38. For the citation, see Chapter 4 above. Giorgio De Santillana, *The Crime of Galileo* (Chicago: University of Chicago Press, 1955), 267–69. De Santillana's book is still the only one devoted to Galileo's trial. As the late dean of North American students of Galileo, Ernan McMullin, lamented in 1960, De Santillana perpetuated "the Galileo symbol one had hoped dead with the nineteenth century," *The Furrow* 11 (1960): 794ff, 796, quoted in Jerome L. Langford, *Galileo, Science and the Church*, 3rd ed. (Ann Arbor: University of Michigan Press, 1992), xiv. De Santillana's thesis was simplicity itself: the trial was a sham resting on a forged "injunction" concocted by Commissary Michelangelo Seghizzi,

a Dominican. Even more villainous were the Dominicans' rivals the Jesuits. Once Galileo published his *Dialogue* in 1632, "reason of state" drove the trial proper at the crisis of the Thirty Years War. De Santillana, *Crime*, 236. These two aspects of De Santillana's approach, faction and geopolitics, still have value. Despite his prejudices, De Santillana went through the trial carefully, highlighting both tension between orders and also faction among the Inquisitors. Finally, De Santillana got the precept's importance exactly right, even if his interpretation of its role in the second phase of Galileo's trial as designed to cover up the legal insufficiency of a case for heresy is wrong (225ff.).

De Santillana's book suffers from six weaknesses. First, he had a strong bias toward Galileo. Second, almost no one now defends the thesis of a forged "injunction." Third, De Santillana's broad-stroke factional argument blamed Galileo's downfall particularly on Inquisitor Roberto Bellarmino. De Santillana's notion of Bellarmino's role was strongly contested even in the 1950s, and neither his image of Bellarmino as intellectual creator of "the frame of a theological superstate" nor his final judgment of him as a man too timid to face Galileo's new reality who instead "fell back on the police" will do any longer in light of the work of Franco Motta, Peter Godman, and Stefania Tutino (85). See also De Santillana's hopelessly over-the-top claim that Bellarmino alone bears "the historic responsibility" for the events of 1616 (142). Fourth, De Santillana made an impressive number of mistakes in dates, citations, and quotations, some critical. The prize winner must be the unsupported claim that Urban struck a secret alliance with Gustav Adolf (198, 216–17). De Santillana suffered from a marked propensity to loose paraphrase made to look like quotation, which can make tracking his citations maddening (the book lacks source references). Fifth, he had little understanding of Roman bureaucracy and politics. For example, he appointed Bellarmino to the nonexistent post of "chief theologian of the Church" (28).

Finally and most serious, he knew no more than anyone else in the 1950s about the Roman Inquisition; this is the principal reason I have not given *The Crime of Galileo* more attention. For example, he summarized the Inquisition's institutionsl structure as consisting of six "Cardinal-Inquisitors" instead of ten; its assessor "functioned mainly as liaison with the Curia" instead of as chief legal officer; and cardinal-secretary was not a permanent post (125–26n). He also identified Bellarmino as "chief theologian as well as chief executive" (142), neither of which is true. His final description of the institution as "an emergency tribunal which had created its own administrative law" and whose "powers. . .were discretionary" (227) typifies De Santillana's half-right approach, the half-wrong side of which nearly always more than made up the balance in favor of a seriously misleading point. He (285) also claimed that Marzio Ginetti presided over the Inquisition in his capacity as "Cardinal-Vicar" [of Rome], which is nonsense. Thus De Santillana's account of procedure is completely unreliable.

39. François-Marie Appendini, *Notizie istorico-critiche sulle antichità, storia e letteratura de Ragusei*, 2 vols. (Dubrovnik: A. Martecchini, 1802), 1: 101–4, http://www.treccani.it/enciclopedia/pietro-benessa_%28Dizionario-Biografico%29/ and http://mathematica.sns.it/autori/1327/, both accessed 7 June 2013.

40. ASMod:AE, 138, fasc. November 1632, unfoliated. As Francesco Barberini's

number two in the secretariat of state, he wrote the unusually large number of 1,600 minutes, and about the same number again while interim head of the secretariat later.

41. Kraus, *Staatssekretariat*, 18, 84, and 85.

42. *RI*, chaps. 3 and 4.

43. Antonio Barberini–inquisitor of Florence, 25 September 1632. *EN* 20: no. 2309
bis*; Cioni, *Documenti*, 25. See the text in Chapter 4 above.

44. See Chapter 4 above.

45. *Decretum* of 11 November 1632 (ACDFSO:DSO, fo. 172r; *DV*, no. 131; *EN* 19:
280); Antonio Barberini–inquisitor of Florence, 13 November 1632 (Cioni, *Documenti*, 27);
decretum of 9 December 1632 (1632, fo. 188v; *DV*, no. 133; *EN* 19: 281); Antonio Barberini–
inquisitor of Florence, 11 December 1632 (Cioni, *Documenti*, 27); 30 December 1632 (1633,
fo. 4v; *DV*, no. no. 35; *EN* 19: 281. For the opening of Galileo's first interrogation, see *DV*,
66.

46. Antonio Barberini–inquisitor of Florence, 10 January 1633, *EN* 20: no. 2376bis and
Cioni, *Documenti*, 28–29, misdated 1 January.

47. Cioni, *Documenti*, no. XIX; *DV*, no. 27.

48. *EN* 20: 525. Favaro wisely cautioned against identifying this Rosati with the consultor to the Florentine Inquisition who signed Galileo's *fede* of 1 October 1632. *DV*, 59.

49. Cioni, *Documenti*, no. XX; *EN* 20: no. 2344bis.

50. See *RI*, 19, 39, 93–94, 109, and Chapter 4 passim. This issue will be further discussed in the Conclusion.

51. *DV*, no. 29.

52. Castelli–Galileo, Rome, 2 October 1632, *EN* 14: no. 2316.

53. Beretta ("*Tractatus syllepticus*," 316) speculates that Lanci had stated his opinion
already in September, but the source he cites (*EN* 14: no. 2297) does not contain the information Beretta alleges it does.

54. See the note to *EN* 14: no. 2316. Stillman Drake went so far as to make Lanci the
villain; he also quite incorrectly added that the engineer Maculano was "hardly a mathematician" and citing "some evidence, though at present tenuous" (which he never gave) that
Lucas Holstein meant Lanci when he blamed Galileo's downfall on the commissary. Stillman Drake, *Galileo at Work: His Scientific Biography* (Chicago: University of Chicago Press,
1981), 343 and 454. See also Vincenzo Ferrone and Massimo Firpo, "From Inquisitors to
Microhistorians: A Critique of Pietro Redondi's Galileo eretico," *Journal of Modern History*
58 (1986): 485–524, 503; and John Brooke, "Science and Religion: Lessons from History?"
Science 282, 5396 (11 December 1998): 1985–86, 1986. Beretta first corrected this major error.
See, e.g., "Urbain VIII Barberini protagoniste de la condamnation de Galilée," 566.

55. Note on *DV*, no. 27; *EN* 19: 330.

56. The entry in the decree register for this date also has an odd list of consultors, as if
more than one cat was playing in Urban's absence.

57. BAV, Barb. lat. 2819, fo. 110v, "Pauli Alaleonis diarium a die 20 Februarii 1630 ad
diem 31 Decembris 1637," and another slightly variant version in BAV, Barb. lat. 2415, fo.
62r.

58. Antonio does not appear in the decree registers between the coram of 30 September and the non-coram of 27 October. Riccardi said he had been away with the pope. Riccardi–Egidi, Rome, 6 November 1632 in *EN* 20: no. 2344 bis*; Cioni, *Documenti*, no. XVI, dated 6 March 1632, corrected to 6 November on p. 12*; English translation in *TG*, no. 45. Francesco's absence on at least several occasions is noted, e.g., in an *avviso* of 16 October (ASMod:AE, 138, fasc. October 1632, unfoliated) and in Niccolini's dispatch of 23 October (*EN* 14: no. 2333).

59. *DV*, no. 31; *EN* 19: 332–33 and 280; *DV*, no. 132, both incorrectly citing ACDFSO:DSO 1632, fo. 180r. The text is missing from the volume but must have been on fo. 181r, the recto of a leaf now removed. Pagano notes this absence and admits to having taken the section of the *decretum* referring to Galileo from Silvestro Gherardi, *Il processo Galileo riveduto sopra documenti di nuova fonte* (Florence: Tipografia dell'Associazione, 1870), 30, in its original publication in *Rivista Europea* in the same year, without page reference. Gherardi probably stole the document from the Inquisition archives in 1849. Thomas F. Mayer, "The Status of the Inquisition's Precept to Galileo (1616) in Historical Perspective," *Nuncius* 24 (2009): 61–95, 69. While claiming that he had taken only copies, Gherardi then made various ambiguous remarks that left open the possibility that he had the documents themselves, e.g., "Dieci erano i document, che io teneva in mano, fino dalla mia dimora di 13 [*sic*] mesi in Roma nel 1848–9," *Processo*, 4 and 11. For this and the two other missing texts cited in this chapter (see notes 78 and 96 below), see the attestation of 20 August 1875 by G. B. Storti, archivist of the Congregation of the Holy Office, that the commissary had summoned him that day and given him ACDFSO:DSO 1632, which Storti had known was missing since the archive moved "dalle stanze ove oggi è la segreteria [*sic*] degli affari ecclesiastici fu trasferito con indicibile fatico nel luogo dov'è oggi e dove già abitarono i pp. Domenicani del S. O. fino al 1858." The archivist immediately looked in the index for Galileo's name "e lo trovò registrato esattamente: onde corse subito in presenza dello stesso P. Commissario (con cui aveo [*sic*] parlato del Galileo pochi giorni prima per occasione di vedere certo scritto su quell'argumento redatto dall'ab. Prof. Pieralisi bibliotecario della barberiniana), a vedere i relative decreti agl'indicati fogli 173. 181. 189[,] ma si trovò ben deluso della sua curiosità, avendo trovato mancanti, cio'è strappati a forza tutti e singoli i tre indicati fogli. E tale cosa fu fatta notata nell'atto al P. Commissario: in mano a cui rimase il volume fino al giorno di ieri: in cui (?) l'ebbe il poscritto (?), che in questo momento parte dalla cancelleria nel palazzo del S. O. per andare a portarlo al suo luogo nella serie dei volumi dei decreti nell'archivio palatino del S. O." ACDFSO:DSO 1632, fo. 33r of front matter.

60. *EN* 14: no. 2318.

61. *EN* 14: nos. 2321, 2323, and 2325.

62. *EN* 14: no. 2324 from Galileo's autograph in BAV, Barb. Lat. 6480, among files of Cardinal Francesco Barberini's in-letters. See *TG*, no. 42, and David Wootton, *Galileo: Watcher of the Skies* (New Haven, Conn.: Yale University Press, 2010), 219.

63. Ludwig von Pastor, *History of the Popes from the Close of the Middle Ages*, 29, trans. and ed. Ernest Graf (London: Kegan Paul, Trench, Trübner, 1938), 161; James-Charles

Noonan, *The Church Visible: The Ceremonial Life and Protocol of the Roman Catholic Church* (New York: Viking, 1996), 5; and *avviso* of 19 June 1630 in BAV, Urb. Lat. 1100, fo. 365r.

64. *EN* 14: nos. 2333 (English translation in *TG*, no. 43) and 2334. In his reply Cioli substituted "great personage" (2335).

65. *EN* 14: no. 2327.

66. *EN* 14: no. 2328.

67. Niccolini–Galileo, 23 October, Rome. *EN* 14: no. 2333; English translation in *TG*, no. 43.

68. As of May 1637, Minutolo was Barberini's "segretario de' memoriali." Castelli–? [not Galileo, although taken from MSS Galileiani], Rome, 16 May 1637. Antonio Favaro, "Benedetto Castelli," in *Amici e correspondenti di Galileo* 21 (Venice: Ferrari, 1908), 118. There is no sign of other contact between Galileo and Minutolo about whom little else is known. He may perhaps be the same man ejected from the service of the cardinal of Lyon at Christmastime 1644. Lucas Holstein (Francesco Barberini's librarian)–Giovanni Battista Doni, Rome, 24 December 1644. Angelo Maria Bandini, *Commentariorum de vita et scriptis Ioannis Bapt. Doni patricii florentini olim sacri cardinalis collegii a secretis libri quinque* (Florence: Typis Cesarea, 1755), 172, and possibly the dedicatee of a medical consilium of Girolamo Mercuriale. *Consultationes et responsa medicinalia* (Venice: Giunta, 1624), 1, 128.

69. 24 October 1632. *EN* 14: no. 2334; English translation in Finocchiaro, 237–38.

70. 29 October 1632. *EN* 14: no. 2335.

71. 30 October 1632. *EN* 14: no. 2336.

72. *Avvisi* of 16 and 30 October in ASMod:AE, 138, fasc. October 1632, unfoliated.

73. BAV, Barb. lat. 2819, fo. 111v; Barb. lat. 2415, fo. 62v.

74. Castelli–Galileo, Rome, 6 November 1632. *EN* 14: no. 2340.

75. Riccardi–Egidi, Rome, 6 November 1632. *EN* 20: no. 2344 bis*; Cioni, *Documenti*, no. XVI, dated 6 March 1632, corrected to 6 November on 12*; English translation in *TG*, no. 45.

76. Niccolini–Cioli, and Niccolini–Galileo, 6 November 1632, Rome. *EN* 14: no. 2344; English translation in Finocchiaro, 238. Both letters contain nearly the same language.

77. For Mariano Alidosi's case, see *SI*, chap. 6.

78. *EN* 19: 280 from Gherardi's minute now in Florence; *DV*, no. 131 claiming from ACDFSO:DSO 1632, fo. 172r, apparently *recte* 173r, but it was not there already in 1875. This whole leaf was removed from the volume. See note 59 above. In its place is the stub of the sheet containing fo. 178r–v.

79. "Si è trattato di questo affare nell'ultima Cong.ne del S. Offitio: non occorre altra risposta; basta intender dall'Assessore se è stato eseguito l'ordinato in detta Cong.ne."

80. Cioni, *Documenti*, no. XXI; *EN* 20: no. 2347bis.

81. See *RI*, 86–89.

82. Castelli–Galileo, Rome, 13 November 1632. *EN* 14: no. 2345.

83. Niccolini–Galileo, Rome, 13 November 1632. *EN* 14: no. 2347; English translation in *TG*, no. 47.

84. E.g., Speller, *Galileo's Inquisition Trial.*

85. *EN* 14: no. 2348; English translation in Finocchiaro, 238–40.

86. See also the snippet of Niccolini–Cioli, Rome, 14 November 1632 in *EN* 14: no. 2349.

87. Egidi–Antonio Barberini, Florence, 20 November 1632. *EN* 19: 333; *DV*, no. 30.

88. The act is missing.

89. Niccolini–Galileo, Rome, 20 November 1632. *EN* 14: no. 2353.

90. Niccolini–Galileo, Rome, 21 November 1632. *EN* 14: no. 2355; English translation in *TG*, no. 49.

91. Castelli–Galileo, Rome, 20 November 1632. *EN* 14: no. 2351.

92. Ibid., no. 2362.

93. *Avviso* of 22 November 1632 in BAV, Barb. lat. 6352, fo. 183r.

94. http://www.treccani.it/enciclopedia/francesco-niccolini_%28Dizionario-Biografico%29/, accessed 23 May 2008.

95. BAV, Barb. lat. 6352, fo. 183r; ASVe:SDR, f. 106, fo. 3v, dispatch of 27 November 1632.

96. *EN* 19: 280–81 [*decretum*] and 334 [note in *processo*]; *DV*, no. 133 and headnote to no. 30, both incorrectly citing the whole text as on fo. 188v. It would have been on ACDFSO:DSO 1632, fo. 189r–v, which is missing. See note 59 above.

97. Cioni, *Documenti*, no. XXII; *EN* 20: no. 2363bis.

98. 11 December 1632. *EN* 14: no. 2365; English translation in Finocchiaro, 240.

99. 12 December 1632. *EN* 14: no. 2366.

100. ASVe:SDR, f. 106, fos. 60r–61r and 76r–v, dispatches of 11 and 18 December 1632. For more on this notorious episode, see Stephan Ehses, "Papst Urban VIII und Gustav-Adolf," *Historisches Jahrbuch* 16 (1895): 336–41, and Joseph Schnitzer, "Urbans VIII Verhalten bei der Nachricht vom Tode des Schwedenkönigs," in *Festschrift zum elfhundert-jährigen Jubiläum des deutschen Campo Santo in Rom*, ed. Stephan Ehses (Frieburg: Herder, 1897), 280–84.

101. *Avviso* of 25 December 1632 in ASMod:AE, 138, fasc. December 1632, unfoliated.

102. See David Marshall Miller, "The Thirty Years War and the Galileo Affair," *History of Science* 46 (2008): 49–74, esp. 65.

103. Ibid., 62. Miller dates Urban's severity to the moment when he ordered the threat of torture in June 1633 (see below), but this is much too late.

104. Castelli–Galileo, Rome, 4 December 1632. *EN* 14: no. 2360.

105. *Avvisi* of 18 February 1628 and 24 November 1629 in BAV, Urb. lat. 1098 I, fo. 90r–v and BAV, Urb. lat. 1099 II, fo. 763r.

106. *Avviso* of 17 July in ASMod:AE, 138, fasc. July 1632, unfoliated.

107. *Avviso* of 24 July in ibid., fasc. July 1632, unfoliated.

108. For the tangled story of Vittrici's end, see *RI*, 133–34.

109. *EN* 14: no. 2369.

110. *EN* 19: 334; *DV*, nos. 33 and 34 (the *fede*, dated 17 December). See *DV*, 64, for the physicians. Egidi's letter was received only on 28 December.

111. ACDFSO: 1632, fo. 195r.

112. See *RI*, 123–25.

113. Holstein–Nicholas Fabri de Pieresc, Rome, 7 March 1633. *EN* 15: no. 2436.

114. See Buonamici's "diary" entry of 2 May 1633; ibid., no. 2492; *TG*, no. 85.

115. Holstein–Nicholas Fabri de Pieresc, Rome, 7 March 1633. Ibid.: no. 2436.

116. *RI*, 128–29.

117. This interpretation descends from Domenico Berti. *Il processo originale di Galileo Galilei*, new and enlarged edition with "Avvertenza" (Rome: Carlo Voghera, 1878), 289.

118. *Avviso* of 13 November 1632; ASMod:AE, 138, fasc. November 1632, unfoliated.

119. For Maculano and Ridolfi's fraught relations, see *RI*, 128.

120. ASMod:AE, 138, fasc. December 1632, unfoliated.

121. *Avviso* of 1 January 1633; ibid., 139, fasc. January 1633, unfoliated.

122. *RI*, 117. This sketch of Maculano's career is compressed from 125–29.

123. In his letter to Galileo announcing that Carlo de' Medici had written as Galileo wished, Geri Bocchineri said both that "I understand" that Galileo had left and also asked for news of him, which seems to mean that Galileo had not written him directly. In his second letter, Bocchineri said he had written according to Galileo's "appuntamento." Geri Bocchineri–[Galileo], 24 and 27 January 1633, Pisa. *EN* 15: nos. 2394 ad 2395.

124. Bocchineri–Galileo, 27 January 1633; ibid., no. 2395. For Bocchineri, see http://moro.imss.fi.it/lettura/LetturaWEB.DLL?AZIONE=UNITA&TESTO=Eb3&PARAM=236-324894–29899&VOL=20&RADIO=B, accessed 13 June 2011.

125. *EN* 15: no. 2396.

126. G. Bocchineri–[Galileo], Florence, 14 April 1633. *EN* 15: no. 2463.

127. Andrea Maggioli and Pietro Maranesi, *Bartolomeo Barbieri da Castelvetro (1615–1697): un cappuccino alla scuola di San Bonaventura nell'Emilia del '600* (Rome: Istituto storico dei Cappuccini, 1998; Biblioteca Seraphico-cappucina, 55), 164, http://www.trec cani.it/enciclopedia/antonio-da-modena_%28Dizionario-Biografico%29/, accessed 13 June 2011.

128. "Collectio authentica ordinationum et decisionum capitulorum generalium," 29th chapter, historical notes, in *Analecta Ordinis Minorum Capuccinorum* [1890] 6: 68,136.

129. [Pasquale Da Marola], *Saggio della vita de' Cappuccini Liguri illustri in virtù, dottrina e santità* (Genoa: Delle Piane, 1822), 165–67. Michelangelo da Rossiglione and Bonifazio da Nizza, *Cenni biografici e ritratti di padri illustri dell'ordine capuccino: sublimati alle dignità ecclesiastiche dal 1581 al 1804*, 3 vols. (Rome: G. A. Bertinelli, 1850), 3: 55–57, repeat this entry verbatim.

130. *EN* 14: no. 2374; English translation in Finocchiaro, 240–41, and *TG*, no. 52.

131. 25 December 1632. *EN* 14: no. 2373.

132. Ibid.; Castelli–Galileo, Rome, 25 December 1632. Ibid.: no. 2372.

133. ACDFSO:DSO 1633, fo. 6r; *EN* 19: 281–82; *DV*, no. 134. There is a copy in Galileo's dossier, which Pagano appears to think is original. *DV*, no. 35.

134. *EN* 20: 2376 bis*, dated 10 January despite two indications of the correct date; Cioni, no. XXIV dated 1 January; Cioni, *Documenti*, no. XXIII; *EN* 20: 2376ter*, also dated 10 January.

135. *EN* 15: no. 2376. Cioli's letter is not in *EN*.

136. Nuncio Bolognetti–F. Barberini, Florence, 5 February 1633. BAV, Barb. lat. 7308, fo. 20r–22v; not in *EN* 15.

137. *EN* 19: 335; *DV*, no. 32; English translation in *TG*, no. 54.

138. ACDFSO:DSO 1633, fo. 16v, in Indice; *EN* 19: 282; *DV*, no. 135 and no. 32 head-note for receipt. For the intertwining of Alidosi's and Galileo's cases, see *SI*, chap. 6.

139. 9 January 1633. *EN* 15: no. 2381.

140. Niccolini–Cioli, Rome, 15 January 1633. *EN* 15: no. 2387; English translation in Finocchiaro, 241–42.

141. 11 January 1633. *EN* 15: no. 2382.

142. *EN* 15: no. 2382; English translation in Finocchiaro, 223–26; *EN* 15: no. 2385.

143. BAV, Barb. lat. 7308, fo. 12r; short extract in *EN* 15: no. 2386 from Arch. Vaticano. Cifre di Fiorenza, l'anno 1633, which may be the same volume.

144. Cioli–Niccolini, Pisa, 21 January 1633 in *EN* 15: no. 2390; and Egidi–Antonio Barberini, Florence, 22 January 1633, in *EN* 19: 336; *DV*, nos. 36 and 136.

145. *Avviso* of 22 January 1633 in BAV, Barb. lat. 6353, fos. 257v–58r. His next letter from Rome is dated 5 February. *EN* 15: no. 2405.

146. *Avviso* of 27 March 1632 in ASMod:AE, 138, fasc. March 1632, unfoliated. It also claimed that Febei covered himself by securing Francesco Barberini's intervention, but nevertheless had been disgraced and lost any chance at becoming governor of Rome.

147. ASR, Archivio Cartari–Febei, 141, fo. 206v for birth and death date of 3 August, versus his cenotaph in Santa Anastasia al Palatino, which gives the 4th. For Febei, see also *RI*, 136–39.

148. ASR, Archivio Cartari–Febei, 139, fo. 227v.

149. ASR, Archivio Cartari–Febei, 141, fo. 223r; 139, fo. 229r.

150. 29 September 1627–13 January 1629 according to BAV, Barb. lat. 9686, fo. 1r; ASR, Archivio Cartari–Febei, 139, fos. 228v and 229r.

151. It is in found in "Resolutiones Criminales Curiae Ferrariensis a die 16 Aprilis usque ad diem 28 Novembris 1627," which bears the first-person note that Febei left Ferrara on the last date. ASR, Archivio Cartari–Febei, 131, unfoliated.

152. BAV, Barb. lat. 9686, fo. 11r.

153. ASR, Archivio Cartari–Febei, 139, fo. 228v.

154. Cf. two letters of thanks in BAV, Barb. lat. 9686, fos. 1r, 2r.

155. ASR, Archivio Cartari–Febei, 141, fo. 220v.

156. ASR, Archivio Cartari–Febei, 139, fo. 229v.

157. *Tractatus de haeresi* (Lyon: Jacques Cardon and Pierre Cavellat, 1621).

158. *RI*, 138 and 139.

159. He was nominated by Urban's motu proprio of 20 July 1632. ASV, S. R. Rota, Miscellanea, 2, fo. 295r; cf. Hoberg, "Amtrittsdaten," 202 [*sic*]; E. Cerchiari, *Capellani papae et apostolicae sedis auditores causarum sacri palatii apostolici* (Roma: Typis Polyglottis Vaticanis, 1919), 2: 153.

160. See, e.g., 27 July. ACDFSO:DSO 1633, fo. 126v.

161. Ibid., fo. 163r. He was also several times incorrectly called dean of the Rota, even when the real dean also appeared in the list, e.g., 1 March (1635, fo. 40v).

162. Giacinto Gigli, *Diario di Roma*, ed. Manlio Barberito, 2 vols. (Rome: Carlo Colombo, 1994), 319.

163. ACDFSO:DSO 1633, fos. 42r, 46v, 47v, 51r.

164. See *RI*, 71–73, 67–71, and Chapter 3.

165. Niccolini–[Cioli], Rome 14 February 1633. *EN* 15: no. 2408; English translation in Finocchiaro, 242, and *TG*, no. 56. For the trip's length, see Galileo–[Cioli], Rome, 19 February 1633; Niccolini–Galileo, Rome, 5 February 1633. *EN* 15: nos. 2413 and 2405. It is unclear exactly how long Galileo's quarantine was. It normally lasted five days. Geri Bocchineri–Galileo, Florence, 3 February 1633. *EN* 15: no. 2402.

166. The syntax is tangled. "Si è rappresentato [which could mean "talk"] subito ancora, di suo [Boccabella's?] consenso, al nuovo Assessore, et ha [Boccabella? Febei?] procurato di far l'istesso al P. Commissario, ma non l'ha trovato."

167. Matti has not been identified. Titled only "Sig.," he cannot have been a Dominican. There is no entry for him in the Person Glossary to *EN*. He may perhaps have been the same man who was a clerk of the Apostolic Chamber in 1612 (BAV, Urb. lat. 1080, fo. 21v) and its dean in 1630 (*avviso* of 9 January in BAV, Urb. lat. 1100, fo. 16r). The name may be a mistake for Mattei, in which case he would have been the older brother and heir of Muzio Mattei of a wealthy Roman family. J. A. F. Orbaan, ed., *Documenti sul Barocco in Roma*, Miscellanea della R. Società di storia patria 6 (Rome: Biblioteca Vallicelliana, 1920), 259. This man was almost certainly related to the cardinal of the same name (1547–1603), probably his homonymous relative, later duke of Giove (1606–1676), whom Galileo met in Rome in 1624. http://www2.fiu .edu/~mirandas/bios1586.htm#Mattei and http://en.wikipedia.org/wiki/Girolamo_Mat tei,_Duca_di_Giove, both accessed 13 July 2011; Johannes Faber–Federico Cesi, Rome, 14 May 1624 ("Siamo stati insieme dal Sig. Gerolamo Mathei [*sic*], un vero compitissimo Cavalliere, il quale ha havuto gran gusto a conoscere il Sig.r Galilei, et di questo dice haver obligo a V.a Ecc.za; et viceversa il Sig.r Galilei restò molto sodisfatto di esso ancora"); and Galileo–Cesi, Rome, 8 June 1624. *EN* 13: nos. 1635 and 1637.

168. Niccolini–[Cioli], Rome, 16 February 1633. *EN* 15: no. 2409; English translation in Finocchiaro, 242–43, and *TG*, no. 57.

169. The attendance list does not bear out Niccolini's claim. Niccolini was right about F. Barberini's disinclination to attend Inquisition meetings. Most unusually for him, he came to ten of fourteen meetings between 17 February and 7 April before reverting to his usual pattern, appearing only twice more until 17 November and a total of only eight times for the rest of the year. All non-corams were held at Santa Maria sopra Minerva by Urban's order of 1628.

170. The Venetian ambassador reported on 5 February that Urban wanted the Inquisition to consider the dispensation and on 19 February that it still had the case. ASVe:SDR, f. 106, fos. 230v and 286r. It does not appear in the decree registers until 30 June 1633. ACDFSO:DSO 1633, fo. 116r. It may be that Bombino's correspondence is still to be found in the Archivio di Stato, Mantova, and might shed further light on Galileo's case. I have failed to find it, as have several friends with long experience in that rich archive.

171. *EN* 15: no. 2413; English translation in *TG*, no. 58.

172. Tommaso Rinuccini–Galileo, Rome, 20 July 1624. *EN* 13: no. 1652; see also nos. 1654 and 1657; cf. Redondi, *Heretic*, 184–85.

173. He was named vice-legate before 27 May 1628 and commissary in September 1628. BAV, Urb. lat. 1098 I, fo. 290r and 294v; BAV, Urb. lat. 1098 II, fo. 489v. For his degree, see *HC* 4: 166.

174. *Avvisi* of 18 May 1630 in BAV, Urb. Lat. 1100, fo. 283r, first item, but last in anonymous *avviso* on 308r, which looks as if it may be incomplete; ASMod:AE, 137, fasc. May 1630, unfoliated; BAV, Barb. lat. 6351, fo. 171v. For the end of his tenure as inquisitor, see *avviso* of 28 February 1632 in BAV, Barb. lat. 6352, fo. 53r.

175. *EN* 15: nos. 2416–17, 2419–21, and 2423.

176. Galileo–[G. Bocchineri], Rome, 5 March 1633. Ibid.: no. 2432.

177. *RI*, 47.

178. *EN* 15: no. 2424; English translation in *TG*, no. 59.

179. Galileo–[G. Bocchineri], Rome, 5 March 1633. Ibid.: no. 2432.

180. For all information not otherwise cited, see http://www.treccani.it/enciclopedia/ giovanni-francesco-buonamici_%28Dizionario-Biografico%29/, accessed 10 August 2010.

181. He probably arrived in December 1632. *Avviso* of 1 January 1633 in ASMod:AE, 139, fasc. January 1633, unfoliated, and see Galileo–G. Bocchineri, Rome, 12 March 1633. *EN* 15: no. 2437.

182. See, e.g., 15 January 1632 (ACDFSO 1632, fos. 12v and 13r), mentioning the duke's unnamed agent, and an *avviso* of 14 February 1632 in ASMod:AE, 138, fasc. February 1632, unfoliated.

183. Salvino Salvini, *Catalogo cronologico de' canonici della chiesa metropolitana fiorentina* (Florence: Gaetano Cambiagi, 1782), 126. The chronology of Gherardini's period in Rome is confused. He claimed to have met Galileo "not before 1633" during his trial in Rome. Niccolò Gherardini, "Vita di Galileo," *EN* 19: 634. Della Robbia was not provided until 6 August 1634, by which time Gherardini had by his own account left Rome. *HC* 4: 187.

184. Salvini, *Catalog*, taken over almost verbatim by Antonio Favaro, "Intorno ad un episodio non ancora chiarito del processo di Galileo," *Atti del Reale Istituto Veneto* ser. 5, 8 (1888): 213–31, 222–23.

185. Salvini, *Catalogo*, 126, and Gherardini, "Vita," 634 and 635.

186. "[E]t havendo io qualche famigliarità con uno de' principali ministri del S. Offizzio, offersi l'opera mia in suo aiuto, quale veramente non potea consistere in altro che in avvisarlo di qualche particolare avvertimento per suo governo. A far ciò fui animito dal medesimo Prelato, come quello che non solamente per l'efficaci raccomandazzioni che gli venivano fatte da chi proteggeva la causa e la persona del S.r Galileo, ma per far contrappeso ancora in parte alla maligna intenzione d'un altro personaggio che sosteneva grand'auttorità in quel Tribunale, inclinava di sottrarlo dall'imminente e troppo severa mortificazzione." Gherardini, "Vita," 634. For the date, see ibid., 633. De Santillana, *Crime*, 285, and Speller, *Inquisition Trial*, 132, give alternative translations, the second more accurate.

187. Favaro, "Episodio," 225, thought both men must have been cardinals, the first naturally Francesco Barberini; De Santillana, *Crime*, 285–86, guessed Gherardini's man might have been Bentivoglio or Francesco Barberini; Mario D'Addio, "Considerazioni sul processo di Galileo," *Rivisita di Storia della Chiesa in Italia* 37 (1983): 1–52; 38 (1984): 47–114, 79, threw out Zacchia's name; and Fantoli, although correctly observing on 533 that Gherardini could not have meant a cardinal, flung the door open to wild speculation about which one he meant on 538. Only Speller, *Inquisition Trial*, 132, restrains himself.

188. Niccolini–Cioli, Rome, 27 February 1633. *EN* 15: no. 2427; English translation in Finocchiaro, 244.

189. Niccolini–Cioli, Rome, 27 February 1633 II. *EN* 15: no. 2428; English translation in Finocchiaro, 245–46.

190. Auguste Leman, *Urbain VIII et la rivalité de la France et de la maison d'Austriche de 1631 à 1635* (Lille: R. Giard and É. Champion, 1920); Mémoires et travaux publiés per des professeurs des facultés catholiques de Lille, fasc. 16, 184–86; for the papal side, see the correspondence in BAV, Barb. lat. 7310.

191. Urban identified him as "son of Ferdinando," trying to make it appear that he was the duke's son. In fact, he was from the Gonzaga of Guastalla line, not the ducal house (ASVe:SDR, f. 99, fo. 152r), probably son of Ferrante II Gonzaga of Guastalla († 1670). He appears in the list of Ferrante's eight children in Giovanni Battista Benamati, *Istoria della città di Guastalla* (Parma: Mario Vigna, 1674), 94, but not of his nine on 109–10. He was tried among other charges for raping a nun. ASVe:SDR, f. 99, fo. 152r.

192. Galileo–G. Bocchineri and Galileo–Cioli, both Rome, 12 March 1633. *EN* 15: nos. 2437–38.

193. *RI*, 196–200, on *expeditio* as a technical procedure.

CHAPTER 7. THE END

1. *EN* 15: no. 2443; English translations in Finocchiaro, 246–48, and *TG*, no. 63; Giorgio De Santillana, *The Crime of Galileo* (Chicago: University of Chicago Press, 1955), 235–36.

2. Jules Speller, *Galileo's Inquisition Trial Revisited* (Frankfurt: Peter Lang, 2008), chaps. 5 and 17. See also Michele Camerota, *Galileo Galilei e la cultura scientifica nell'età della Controriforma* (Rome: Salerno Editrice, 2004), 406–17.

3. See below for Oreggi's treatment of the same theme, including an alleged conversation between Urban and Galileo about it.

4. Cioli–Niccolini, [Pisa], 17 March 1633. *EN* 15: no. 2444.

5. Alessandro Paoli, "La scuola di Galileo nella storia della filosofia," 1, *Annali delle Università Toscane* 22 (1899): i–cccxxvii, xi.

6. Galileo–[Cioli] and Niccolini–Cioli, both Rome, 19 March 1633. *EN* 15: nos. 2445 and 2449; English translation in Finocchiaro, 248.

7. *EN* 15: no. 2450.

8. Mario Guiducci–Galileo, Florence, 19 March 1633. *EN* 15: no. 2447; English translation in *TG*, no. 64.

9. Niccolò Cini–Galileo, Florence, 26 March 1633. *EN* 15: no. 2451.

10. Nerli's role raises some doubt about this lord's identity. Nerli was first Cardinal Roberto Ubaldini's auditor (1623–1627) and then Carlo de' Medici's; he was still in de' Medici's service in 1644. http://www.treccani.it/enciclopedia/nerli-francesco-senior_%28Dizionario-Biografico%29/, accessed 13 June 2013. Nor did Favaro put Dino Peri, whom Guiducci called "in casa sua servitore attuale," in Capponi's household in his biography, http://moro.imss.fi.it/lettura/LetturaWEB.DLL?AZIONE=UNITA&TESTO=Eb3&PARAM=1126-491729-44293&VOL=20&RADIO=B, accessed 11 July 2008.

11. *Avvisi* of 28 December 1630 and 11 January 1631. ASMod:AE, 137, fasc. December 1630, unfoliated, and 138, fasc. Jan 1631, unfoliated.

12. See, e.g., *avviso* of 5 June 1632 in BAV, Barb. lat. 7306, fos. 56r and 61r.

13. ASVe:SDR, f. 106, fo. 326v.

14. Guiducci–Galileo, Florence, 2 April 1633. *EN* 15: no. 2455.

15. Incidentally, he tried to free his brother from prison. See Castelli–Galileo, Brescia, 19 and 26 May and Rome, 23 July 1633. *EN*, 15 nos. 2512, 2520, and 2594.

16. G. Bocchineri–Galileo, Florence, 9 April 1633. *EN* 15: no. 2457.

17. Galileo–G. Bocchineri, Rome, 16 April 1633. *EN* 15: no. 2466.

18. Niccolini–Cioli, Rome, 9 April 1633. *EN* 15: no. 2461; English translation in Finocchiaro, 248–50

19. *EN* 19: 336–42; *DV*, no. 37; English translations in *TG*, no. 65 (from which I cite below), English translation in Finocchiaro, 256–62; Drake [*sic*], 344–48; and De Santillana, *Crime*, 238–42.

20. "Decreverunt [the Inquisitors] dictum librum recognoscendum [*Atheismus triumphatus*] a dicto Campanella." Enrico Carusi, "Nuovi documenti sui processi di Tommaso Campanella," *Giornale critico della filosofia italiana* 8 (1927): 321–59, doc. 87, p. 356.

21. See Chapter 2 above.

22. See Chapter 2 above.

23. See *RI*, 183.

24. Stillman Drake, for example, claimed that Galileo never admitted the precept. "On the Conflicting Documents of Galileo's Trial," in *Atti del simposium internazionale di storia, metodologia, logica e filosofia della scienza "Galileo Galilei nella storia e nella filosofia della scienza"* (1964), 55–65 reprinted in Drake, *Essays on Galileo in the History and Philosophy of Science*, ed. Neal Swerdlow and T. H. Levere, 3 vols. (Toronto: University of Toronto Press, 1999), 1: 142–52, 150. Francesco Beretta, "'Omnibus Christianae, Catholicaeque Philosophiae amantibus. D. D.'. *Le Tractatus syllepticus* du jésuite Melchior Inchofer, censeur de Galilée," *Freiburger Zeitschrift für Philosophie und Theologie* 48 (2001): 301–27, 312, properly stresses Maculano's concern with the precept ("la prescription").

25. There is a marginal pen stroke next to this word.

26. As Francesco Beretta also recognized without stressing the point sufficiently,

"Rilettura di un documento clebre: redazione e diffusione della sentenza e abiura di Galileo," *Galilaeana* I (2004): 91–115, 100.

27. Niccolini–Cioli, Rome, 16 April 1633. *EN* 15: no. 2471; English translations in *TG*, no. 66, and English translation in Finocchiaro, 250–51.

28. BAV, Barb. lat. 2819, fos. 132v–3r, the papal master of ceremonies noting both departure and return. For Urban's departure, cf. the Venetian ambassador's dispatch of 16 April. ASVe:SDR, f. 107, fo. 197r and an *avviso* in BAV Barb. lat. 2415, fo. 64v, saying he did leave on 16 April. For his return, see also *avviso* of 4 May in ASMod:AE, 139, fasc. May 1633, unfoliated.

29. ASVe:SDR, f. 107, fo. 233r, mistakenly dating the pope's return before 30 April.

30. Beretta, "*Tractatus syllepticus*," 315–16, offers one of the more careful studies of these opinions. He implicitly assumes the authors acted as consultors at the moment of expedition.

31. *EN* 19: 348; *DV*, no. 44; English translations in *TG*, no. 67a, and Finocchiaro, 262. The other two censures are in *EN* 19: 349–56 and 356–60; *DV*, nos. 45 and 46; English translations in *TG*, nos. 67b–c, and Finocchiaro, 262–70 and 271–76. Finocchiaro dates the other two from Oreggi's; and Ugo Baldini and Leen Spruit, "Nuovi documenti galileiani degli archivi del Sant'Ufficio e dell'Indice," *Rivista di Storia della Filosofia* 56 (2001): 661–99, 648n, suggest a terminus ad quem of 21 April.

32. Among his output are *Disputationes metaphysicae*, 2 vols. (Rome: Francesco Caballi, 1634–36); *Decisiones morales juxta principia theologica, & sacras atque civiles leges* (Verona: Bartolomeo Merlo, 1641), put on the Index in 1684; *Variarum Quaestionum Moralium Canonicarum Centuria I, II, III, IV* (Rome: Heirs of F. Corbelletti, 1647 and 1652); *Sacra speculativa doctrina de Deo*, etc., dedicated to Cardinal Capponi (Venice: Bertano, 1650); *Sacra moralis doctrina de statu supernaturali humanae naturae*, dedicated to Ginetti (Venice: N.p., 1650 and 1656), also placed on the Index; *Theoria & Praxis Magni Jubilei* (Rome: Corbelletti, 1650); *Praxis jejunii ecclesiastici* (Rome: Heirs of Francesco Corbelletti, 1644); *Singulares selectae quaestiones morales juridicae* (Rome: Heirs of Corbelletti, 1662); *De sacrificio novae legis quaestiones theologicae* (Lyon: Huguetan and Ravaud, 1662), ded to A7; *Theoria & Praxis, in qua iura, obligationes, & privilegia eorum, qui in periculo, aut articulo mortis constituuntur* (Rome: Ignazio Lazari, 1672); *Observationes ad controversias inter episcopos & regulares Laureti de Franchis Neapolitani . . .* (Rome: Biagio Reversin, 1656); *Prosperi Farinacii. . .Repertorium Judiciale*, ed. Pasqualigo (Lyon: Gabrielle Boissat and Laurent Anisson, 1639); and Farinacci, *Repertorium de Contractibus*, ed. Pasqualigo (Lyon, 1642). For these and his biography, see Antonio Francesco Vezzosi, *I scrittori de' cherici regolari*, 2 vols. (Rome: Sacra Congregazione di Propaganda Fide, 1780), 2: 156–61; and Giuseppe Silos, *Historiarum clericorum regularium* [*libri duo* in four parts] (Rome: Mascardi, 1650), 3: 658–59.

33. Francesco Beretta, "Melchior Inchofer et l'hérésie de Galilée: censure doctrinale et hiérarchie intellectuelle," *Journal of Modern European History* 3 (2005): 23–49.

34. Maculano–Francesco Barberini, Rome, 22 April 1633. ACDFSO, St. st. N 3–f, 1st fasc., [fo. 185r], part of St. st. N 3 e f g, Varie relative ai Gesuiti; *DV*, doc. 137; *TG*, no.

68. "Hieri mattina trattai con Mons.r Baffati, e gli rappresentai l'obligo nel quale era il S.r Alidosio di presentarsi prontamente in questo S. Off.o, così venne hieri sera detto Sig.re et lo ritenni in carcere assai buona; mi fece istanza, che gli concedessi un servitore massime dicendo egli di patire certa indispositione di palpitatione di cuore per la quale pensa essergli necessaria la continova assistenza di uno; non ho giudicato conveniente lasciargli il ser.re ma gl'ho assegnato per compagnia un carcerato de' spediti, e senza ordine di V. E. non farò altra mutatione. La notte passata il S.r Galileo è stato travagliato da' dolori che l'hanno assalito, e gridava anco questa mattina, vero è che havendolo io visitato due volte riceve il medicamento maggiore dal sentirsi dire che quanto prima si sbrigherà la sua causa, come veramente stimerei bene si facesse stando l'età grave di quest'huomo. Gia facessimo hieri la Congreg.ne sopra il libro, e fu risoluto che in esso si difenda, e s'insegni l'opinione riprovata, e dannata dalla Chiesa, et però che l'autore si renda sospetto anco di tenerla; stando questo si potrà più presto ridurre la causa in stato di speditione nella quale attenderò il senso di V. E. per obedire pontualmente." The document was originally published by Francesco Beretta on-line at a site now taken down but see Beretta, "Un nuovo documento sul processo di Galileo Galilei: La lettera di Vincenzo Maculano del 22 aprile 1633 al cardinale Francesco Barberini," *Nuncius* 16 (2001): 629–41.

35. Galileo–G. Bocchineri, Rome, 23 April 1633. *EN* 15: no. 2478.

36. Antonio Beltrán Marí, *Talento y Poder. Historia de las Relaciones entre Galileo y la Iglesia católica* (Pamplona: Laetoli, 2006), 469, mistranslates "spedirmi" as "liberarme" and rests his argument on the false claim that Galileo had been promised he would be freed. Annibale Fantoli, *Galileo for Copernicanism and for the Church*, trans. George V. Coyne (Vatican City: Vatican Observatory Publications, 2003; 3rd English ed.), 312, translates the key phrase as "a case to be handled expeditiously," which is grammatically impossible.

37. Beltrán Marí, *Talento*, 562, absolves Maculano of duplicity but still thinks he tricked Galileo unintentionally.

38. Agostino Borromeo, "A proposito del *Directorium inquisitorum* di Nicholas Eymerich e delle sue edizioni cinquecentesche," *Critica Storica* 20 (1983): 499–547.

39. Nicolau Eymeric, ed. Francisco Peña, *Directorium Inquisitorum* (Rome: In Aedibus Populi Romanorum, 1578), 292.

40. BAV, Barb. lat. 1502, 37A.

41. Niccolini–Cioli, Rome, 23 April 1633. *EN* 15: no. 2481; English translation in *TG*, no. 69, and Finocchiaro, 251–52.

42. Finocchiaro, 252n19, incorrectly makes him the elder Antonio Barberini, but he was known by and signed himself with his title of Sant'Onofrio.

43. Maculano–F. Barberini, Rome, 28 April 1633. *EN* 15: no. 2486; *DV*, no. 181; English translation in *TG*, no. 70; Finocchiaro, 276–77; De Santillana, *Crime*, 252–53; and Stillman Drake, *Galileo at Work: His Scientific Biography* (Chicago: University of Chicago Press, 1981), 349–50.

44. quando delatus de haeretica pravitate, processus meritis diligenter discussis cum bono consilio in iure peritorum, reperitur in haeresim deprehensus facti evidentia, seu testium productione legitima, non tamen confessione propria. . . . tamen ipse sic convictus

& deprehensus, persistit firmiter in negativa, & confitetur constanter catholicam sanctam fidem

45. Eymeric, *Directorium Inquisitorum*, 338.

46. Peña, *Scholion* 56 to part II, 185–86.

47. "Primum, quod sit convictus de vera & formali haeresi. . . . Alterum est, quod verba haereticalia, de quibus negativus convincitur, sint certa & clara. . . . Tertium est, quod reus convincatur de haeresi, quam negat, per testes legitimos & idoneos, seu omni exceptione maiores. . . . Quartum est, ut illud factum seu dictum haereticale. . .sit recens. . . . Postremum est, quod is negativus convincatur asseruisse se illa credere, & credenda aliis esse." Ibid., 187.

48. *De inconstantia in fide* in *De inconstantia in judiciciis tractatus* (Rome: Marcello Severolo, 1698), 82.

49. De Santillana, *Crime*, 293, translated this phrase badly as "enjoin him formally," reading "diffese" as "diffide," which he said meant a formal order to abstain. Others have mistranslated "give him" (*dargli*), e.g., Beltrán Marí, *Talento*, 480: "permitirle presentar su defensa"; "allow him to present a defense" (Finocchiaro, 277).

50. *RI*, 194–96.

51. Fantoli, *Galileo*, 316.

52. See *RI*, 123, 170, 191, 197, 200, and 210 (Vecchietti). For other instances, see, e.g., 3 July and 4 December (ACDFSO:DSO 1625, fos. 117r and 203r), 23 February and 4 October (1626, fos. 34v, 187r), and 18 and 23 February 1627 (1627, fos. 37v and 41v).

53. Franz Reusch, *Der Process Galilei's und die Jesuiten* (Bonn: Eduard Weber, 1879), 284, thought Urban's kindness was "undoubtedly" Maculano's "foundation." Cf. Fantoli, *Galileo*, 315.

54. *Avviso* of 28 April 1633 in BAV, Barb. lat. 6353, fo. 126v; of 23 April in ASMod:AE, 139, fasc. April 1633, unfoliated; dispatch of 30 April 1633 in ASVe:SDR, f. 107, fo. 222r.

55. Peter Rietbergen, *Power and Religion in Baroque Rome: Barberini Cultural Policies* (Boston: Brill, 2006), chap. 8.

56. Francesco Beretta, "Rilettura di un documento celebre: redazione e diffusione della sentenza e abiura di Galileo," *Galilaeana* 1 (2004): 91–115, 101, highlights Centini's absence.

57. ACDFSO:DSO 1633, fo. 73r and 1634, fo. 53v; Copia, p. 176.

58. *EN* 19: 342–3; *DV*, no. 38; English translation in *TG*, no. 71 (quotations from this source) and Finocchiaro, 277–79.

59. Emphasis in the original, as well as two pen strokes in the left margin and a single line against the whole page.

60. Riccardi–Egidi, Rome, 24 May 1631. *EN* 19: 327; *DV*, no. 25, p. 53; English translation in Finocchiaro, 212. See also Orso d'Elci–Galileo, Villa Imperiale, 3 June 1630. *EN* 14: no. 2024. D'Elci was referring to Galileo's missing letter of 1 June.

61. *EN* 19: 344; *DV*, no. 39; *TG*, no. 72.

62. Fantoli, *Galileo*, 537–38n72, and Speller, *Inquisition Trial*, 266, think Maculano had received authority from Urban earlier.

63. See, e.g., 23 July in ACDFSO:DSO 1625, fo. 126r, 8 March in 1627, fo. 49r or 14 February in 1629, fo. 35r.

64. 1 May 1633. *EN* 15: no. 2490; English translation in *TG*, no. 73, and Finocchiaro, 252–53.

65. Niccolini wrote "perchè questa causa si stiacci." *Stiacciare* (in standard Italian, *schiacciare*) means "to deform forcefully." "Put to an examination" seems the most likely alternative. Finocchiaro's translation of "have the trial expedited" is impossible.

66. 3 May 1633. *EN* 15: no. 2493; English translation in Finocchiaro, 253.

67. *Avvisi* of 30 April in BAV, Barb. lat. 6353, fo. 123r and ASMod:AE, 139, fasc. April 1633, unfoliated.

68. Second *avviso* of 30 April in ASMod:AE, 139, fasc. April 1633, unfoliated.

69. Cioli–Niccolini, [Florence], 4 and 6 May 1633. *EN* 15: nos. 2494 and 2495.

70. 4 and 19 May. ACDFSO:DSO 1633, fos. 75v and 82r.

71. *Avviso* of 4 May in ASMod:AE, 139, fasc. April 1633, unfoliated.

72. *EN* 19: 345; *DV*, no. 40; English translation in *TG*, no. 74, and Finocchiaro, 279.

73. The *fede* is *DV*, no. 41.

74. *EN* 19: 345–7; *DV*, no. 42; English translation in *TG*, no. 75, and Finocchiaro, 279–81.

75. Annibale Fantoli, "The Disputed Injunction and Its Role in Galileo's Trial," in *The Church and Galileo*, ed. Ernan McMullin (Notre Dame, Ind.: University of Notre Dame Press, 2005), 117–49, 127, typifies the usual position in asserting that Galileo "must have prepared his defense very carefully." He cites as evidence Galileo's reliance on Bellarmino's *fede*, a weak reed indeed as it turned out. There is no other evidence to support this allegation.

Both in this essay and in his *Galileo*, Fantoli confined himself to going once more through the corpus of evidence assembled in more or less the present form already in the 1870s. See Mayer, " Inquisition's Precept," passim. Fantoli's *Galileo* has been called "reader-friendly," a claim I find puzzling. Not only has each subsequent revision made the book more difficult to follow by piling up endnotes (there are now 203 pages of notes to a 373–page text), thereby producing a number of inconsistencies and mistaken cross-references, many of which must nonetheless be followed to get a complete argument, it is also shot through with errors. Fantoli inconsistently uses Beretta's important unpublished 1997 thesis on the legal dimensions of the case, but at least two problems vitiate his theory of it: making its end virtually automatic and treating Commissary Vincenzo Maculano as Galileo's friend. William Shea and Mariano Artigas's *Galileo in Rome* (Oxford: Oxford University Press, 2003) follows a line much like Fantoli's. Shea and Artigas take a step beyond him in the right direction by paying some attention to the canon law of the case.

76. *EN* 19: 401–2.

77. Niccolini–Cioli, Rome, 15 May 1633. *EN* 15: no. 2509; English translation in Finocchiaro, 253.

78. *Avviso* of 14 May 1633 in ASMod:AE, 139, fasc. May 1633, unfoliated.

79. Guiducci–Galileo, Florence, 21 May 1633. *EN* 15: no. 2517.

80. 22 May 1633. *EN* 15: no. 2518; English translation in *TG*, no. 76, and Finocchiaro, 253–54. The enclosures in which Niccolini demonstrated his diligence are missing.

81. "Eight" is a seriously mistaken number, unless the pope and his nephew were counting from the last coram.

82. For the expectations about the coram of 9 June, see G. Bocchineri and Guiducci–Galileo, Florence, 11 June 1633. *EN* 15: nos. 2540 and 2542.

83. Niccolini–Cioli, Rome, 29 May 1633. *EN* 15: no. 2527; English translation in Finocchiaro, 254.

84. Geri Bocchineri had it by 1 June. *EN* 15: no. 2530.

85. *RI*, 196. The *summarium* could also have been written by Camillo Giudici, long-time *summista* of the Inquisition. Antonio Beltrán Marí, "El 'caso Galileo,' sin final previsible (The "Galileo's [*sic*] case," no end in sight)," *Theoria: An International Journal for Theory, History and Foundations of Science* 20, 2 (May 2005): 125–41, assigns responsibility to Febei.

86. Beretta, "Rilettura," 98 and 102.

87. Ibid., 98.

88. *RI*, 15.

89. E.g., Beretta, "Rilettura," 102 or Beltrán Marí, *Talento*, 475. Speller, *Inquisition Trial*, 285, speaks of it as "disturbing to a point that it becomes difficult to make sense of it." He quotes other condemnations of it. As usual, he displays little understanding of either the document's status or function. His conclusion (298) that "the document does only play a very limited role" is certainly false.

90. *EN* 19: 293–7; *DV*, no. 1; English translation in *TG*, 77, and Finocchiaro, 281–86, "Final Report to the Pope."

91. *DV*, 14 and 5–6; *TG*, 179 and 62. Emphasis added.

92. *DV*, 6; *TG*, 180.

93. *DV*, no. 21; *TG*, 93.

94. *DV*, 8; *TG*, 181.

95. *DV* 9; *TG*, 181. This confession is watered down in Finocchiaro, 284, to "He admitted being given an injunction."

96. *DV*, 10; *TG*, 182.

97. "Galilei de Galileis Fiorentini, in hoc S. Officio carcerati, et [*EN* has comma here instead of after "carcerati"] ob eius adversam valetudinem ac senectutem, cum praecepto de non discedendo de domo electae habitationis in Urbe, [comma not in *EN*] ac de se representando toties quoties etc., sub poenis [paenis *EN*] arbitrio Sacrae Congregationis[, added in *EN*] habilitati, proposita [aft. del. S.mus; del. not in *EN*] causa, relato processu etc.[, added in *EN*] et auditis votis [; added in *EN* in place of ?&] S.mus decrevit [, added in *EN*] ipsum Galileum interrogandum esse super intentione, etiam comminata ei tortura[; in *EN* in place of comma] et si sustinuerit, praevia abiuratione de vehementi in plena [*EN* piena] Congregatione S. [Officii,] condemnandum ad carcerem arbitrio Sacrae Congregationis, iniuncto [e]i ne de [caetero; could be praefato, "p" is almost certain], scripto[, not in *EN*] vel verbo[, added in *EN*] tractet amplius quovis modo de mo[bili] tate terrae[, not in *EN*] nec de stabilitate solis [et] e contra, sub pena relapsus[; *EN* in place of .] librum vero ab eo conscriptum, cu[i titulus {has to have been an abbrev.}] est Dialogo di Galileo Galilei Linceo, prohibendum fore [Tra *Linceoe prohibendum* leggesi,

cancellato, *publice cremandum forte. EN* note 19 in online version only at http://moro.imss. fi.it/lettura/LetturaWEB.DLL?AZIONE=UNITA&TESTO=EaZ&PARAM=88-146565– 9795&VOL=19&RADIO=B#VediNota19, accessed 15 June 2013. These words are no longer visible]. Praeterea, ut haec omnibus innotescant, exemplaria sententiae desuper ferendae transmitti iussit ad omnes Nun[tios and following word damaged but still legible] Apostolicos et ad omnes haereticae pravitatis Inquisitores, ac praecipue ad Inquisitorem Florentiae [both words damaged; Favaro reads as *Inquisitorem Florentae* in online version (note 20) above.], qui eam sententiam in eius plena [piena *EN*] Congregatione [repeated as in *plena Cong.ne Cong.e accersitis* in online version (note 21)], accersitis etiam et coram plerisque mathematicae artis Professoribus, publice legatur [*legat* in *EN* text; note 22 has it right in online version]." ACDFSO:DSO 1633, fo. 102r, marked for insertion on fo. 101r, half fo. 102r blank, noted in Indice at front of volume; cf. Beretta, "Rilettura," 96. *EN* 19: 282–83; *DV*, no. 138; *TG*, no. 78. The version of the decree in Galileo's dossier has only "proposita causa," "the case having been proposed." *EN* 19: 360–61; *DV*, no. 47. For the necessity of the consultors' opinions on the *summarium*, see *RI*, 198.

98. Beretta, "Rilettura," 97. On 101 he corrected his mistake here in saying that this session included only the commissary and assessor, since the cardinals also attended. *RI*, 20.

99. Speller, *Inquisition Trial*, 307, accurately, if in typically convoluted fashion, defines *sustinere*, as Franz Reusch, *Process*, 314, had done much more lucidly more than a century earlier. It could also mean "persist."

100. See the covering letters in *DV*, nos. 113 and 143, and the forthcoming critical edition by Michel-Paul Lerner. There are also four copies in the AdS Modena, Archivi per materie, Astronomia e Astrologia, 1, nos. 37–38, fos. 38r–41r, originally from Inquisizione, b. 94 fasc. 1.

101. Niccolini–Cioli, Rome, 19 June 1633. *EN* 15: no. 2550; English translation in *TG*, no. 79, and Finocchiaro, 254–55.

102. Niccolini–Cioli, Rome, 26 June 1633. *EN* 15: no. 2558.

103. *EN* 19: 361–2; *DV*, no. 48; English translation in *TG*, no. 80, and Finocchiaro, 286–87.

104. Eliseo Masini, *Sacro arsenale, ovvero prattica dell'officio della S. Inquisizione ampliata* (Genoa: Giuseppe Pavoni, 1625), 131, 133, and 140–41 (Rome: Stamperia di S. Michele a Ripa, 1730): 264–65 and 270), and see the discussion in Speller, *Inquisition Trial*, 33–34.

105. Emil Wohlwill, *Ist Galilei gefoltert worden? Eine kritische studie* (Leipzig: Duncker and Humblot, 1877).

106. Speller, *Inquisition Trial*, 33, criticizing Fantoli ("reasons why he committed his error," 315), Drake, and De Santillana in particular.

107. Speller, *Inquisition Trial*, 38–44.

108. "Senes sexagenarii debiles arbitrio inquisitoris non sunt torquendi, possunt vero terreri, doctores refert." Francesco Bordoni, *Sacrum tribunal iudicum in causis sanctae fidei contra haereticos, et de haeresi suspectos* (Rome: Heirs of Corbelletti, 1648), no. 47, 576. Hartmann Grisar, *Galileistudien: Historisch-theologische Untersuchungen über die Urtheile der römischen Congregationen im Galileiprocess* (Regensburg, N.Y.: Friedrich Pustet, 1882;

originally published in *Zeitschrift für katholische Theologie* 2 [1878], 65–128 and 673–736, 90), followed by Ludwig von Pastor, *The History of the Popes from the Close of the Middle Ages*, 29, trans. and ed. Ernest Graf (London: Kegan Paul, Trench, Trübner, 1937), 58, also quoted this passage. Bordoni was never more than consultor of the Holy Office in Cremona, so the status of his work remains to be established.

109. "Et tandem non possunt torquere senes. Sed senectus non est annorum numero computanda [the only source Diana cited suggested sixty] sed valetudine, robore, qualitate delicti, & delinquentis Inquistorum arbitrio. Quando vero torqueri non possunt, posse terreri." Antonino Diana, *Summa Diana* (Lyon: Laurent Anisson and Jean Baptiste Deuenet, 1667), 341, no. 141. For Diana, see http://www.treccani.it/enciclopedia/antonino-diana_%28Dizionario-Biografico%29/, accessed 30 July 2013, and *DSI* 1:475.

110. Scholion 118 to *Directorium inquisitorum*, 652.

111. Philippe Gilbert, "La Condamnation de Galilée et les publications recentes," *Revue des questions scientifiques*, April 1877, no. 2, 353–98, and July 1877, no. 5, 130–94, 394. Girolamo Ferri beat Gilbert to it in 1785, but without documenting his claim. Maurice A. Finocchiaro, "Galileo as a 'Bad Theologian': A Formative Myth About Galileo's Trial," *Studies in History and Philosophy of Science, Part A* 33, 4 (December 2002): 753–91, 757.

112. Speller, *Inquisition Trial*, 32.

113. "é necessario per haverne la verità venir contro di lui al rigoroso essame: essendo stata a punto ritrovata la tortura per supplire al difetto de' testimonii, quando non possono intera prova apportare contro del Reo." Masini, *Sacro arsenale* (1625), 131; (1730), 263.

114. Ibid. (1730), 267.

115. Ibid. (1730), 270.

116. "Avvertimenti per formare le sentenze nel Tribunale del S. Offizio." BC, MS 2653, fos. 594r–608r, fo. 604r.

117. "Prattica per procedere nelle cause del Santo Uffitio," in Alfonso Mirto, "Un inedito del Seicento sull'Inquisizione," *Nouvelles de la république des lettres* 1 (1986): 99–138, 134.

118. Diana, *Summa*, 341, no. 136.

119. "Ut ergo reus torqueri possit, requiritur sufficientia testium deponentium vel immediate de ipso delicto, vel de confessione rei extraiudicali, vel de fama, vel de indicio proximo, & maxime inferente delictum, vel etiam de remotis. Ibid., 338, no. 109.

120. "Confessio extraiudicalis sufficit, ut Inquisitores reum torquere possint, quia non est credendum, aliquem sibi falso crimen imponere." Ibid., 340, no. 128.

121. "Quando delictum est vehementer indiciatum, & reus negat, non possunt Inquisitores eum punire aliqua poena extraordinaria, sed debent torquere, & veritatem elicere, ex *l. edictum ff. de qu.* In Tribunali maxime Inquisitionis; in quo non tam poena reorum, quam emendatio intenditur, quae obtinetur confessa veritate." Ibid., 340, no. 129.

122. Bordoni, *Sacrum tribunal*, no. 19, pp. 570–71; Cesare Carena, *Tractatus de officio sanctissimae inquisitionis, et modo de procedendi in causis fidei* (Bologna: Jacopo Monti, 1668), 293 ("Ex confessione extraiudicali Rei, regulariter oriri initium ad torturam tradiderunt"); Peña, *Scholion* 118 to part II, 656 and 657 ("Si vero indicium est propinquum,

urgens, vehemens, & (ut cum Eymerico loquar) violentum; tunc unicum sufficit ad tor-turam, ut unus bonus testis de visu, *vel confessio extra iudicium*" (emphasis added); "con-fessio delinquentis extraiudicialis sufficiens quoque indicium erit & probabile satis ad torturam;" "vocari poterit, & interrogari, & ubi expediens fuerit, iudicatum in carcerem mitti; & si negat, torqueri ob illam confessionem poterit. Ad haec, si factum vel dictum haereticale confiteatur, intentionem autem pravam haereticandi neget, torqueri poterit ut intentionem declaret."). Peña thought an extrajudicial confession also did not have to be ratified after the torture.

123. *Repertorium inquisitorum pravitatis haereticae* (Venetiis: apud Damianum Ze-narum, 1575), 765–75; "Postremo videndum est, An cum disputatur in hoc tribunali, num reus sit torquendus nec ne, debeat eius advocatus ad disputationem admitti, ut videatur num sufficientia sint indicia ex quibus est torquendus reus: & cum agatur de gravissimo de-linquentis preiudicio, ne indefensus videri possit, vocandum esse advocatum, ut reum iuste, si potest, tueatur. . . .hoc enim & naturalia & humana iura fieri iubent, & iurisconsulti uno ore fatetur." Peña, *Scholion* 118 to part II, 657.

124. Diana, *Summa*, 351, no. 236.

125. "Prattica," ed. Mirto, 110.

126. Orio Giacchi, "Considerazioni giuridiche sui due processi contro Galileo," in Università Cattolica del Sacro Cuore, ed., *Nel terzo centenario della morte di Galileo Galilei* (Milan: Vita e Pensiero, 1942), 383–406, 406.

127. *EN* 19: 402–6; Cioni, *Documenti*, no. XXVI, saying there were two identical copies in Florence; *DV*, no. 114; English translation in *TG*, no. 81, and Finocchiaro, 287–91; Beretta, "Rilettura," 108–13.

128. See *RI*, 200–201.

129. "Quando reus convictus torqueretus super intentione, et complicibus, tortura dari debet cum clausula *citra praeiudicium probatorum*: aliter si ipse persistet negativus, vel etiamsi cum dicta clausula interrogetur de delicto, ipse negativus manens purgabit omnes probationes. . . .Si vero torqueatur cum clausula, & nihil super delicto interrogetur, etiamsi negativus maneat, damnandus est ad poenam ordinariam; quia fisci ius acquisitum non laeditur." Diana, *Summa*, 353, no. 248.

130. Here the "Avvertimenti" took an old-fashioned position. Innocent III's original emphasis on *fama* had largely disappeared already in the fifteenth century. *RI*, 155–56 and 166–69.

131. *RI*, 201.

132. Bruno Neveu and Pierre-Noël Mayaud, "L'Affaire Galilée et la tentation infla-tioniste. À propos des notions d'hérésie et de magistère impliquées dan l'affaire," *Gregoria-num* 83 (2002): 287–311; and Francesco Beretta, "L'affaire Galilée et l'impasse apologétique: Réponse à une censure," *Gregorianum* 84 (2003): 169–92. See the preliminary remarks on the text in Michel-Pierre Lerner, "Pour un édition critique de la Sentence et Abjuration de Galilée," *Révue des Sciences Philosophiques et Théologiques* 82, 4 (October 1998): 607–29.

133. Beretta, "Rilettura," 96.

134. Léon Garzend, *L'Inquisition et l'Hérésie. Distinction de l'Hérésie théologique et de*

l'Hérésie inquisitoriale: à propos de l'affaire Galilée (Paris: Desclée, De Brower-G. Beauch-esne, 1912), 7, 430, 433–46.

135. Ibid., 475–76 and 480.

136. Mario D'Addio, "Considerazioni sul processo di Galileo," *Rivista di Storia della Chiesa in Italia* 37 (1983): 1–52, and 38 (1984): 47–114, 108; Neveu and Mayaud, "L'Affaire Galilée," passim; Speller, *Inquisition Trial*, 39 and chap. 14.

137. Maurice A. Finocchiaro, "Science, Religion, and the Historiography of the Galileo Affair: On the Undesirability of Oversimplification," *Osiris* 16 (2001): 114–32, 126, while criticizing the disciplinary interpretation for this reason, calls the sentence "an abuse of power." It is often said incorrectly that he was convicted of heresy tout court.

138. Francesco Beretta, "Le procès de Galilée et les Archives du Saint-Office: Aspects judiciaires et théologiques d'une condamnation célèbre," *Revue des sciences philosophiques et theologiques* 83 (1999): 441–90, 483.

139. Niccolini–Cioli, 26 June 1633, Rome. *EN* 15: no. 2558.

140. Agostino Oreggi, *De deo uno. Tractatus primus* (Rome: Rev. Camera Apostolica, 1629), 193–95, also cited in Galileo, *Dialogo sopra i due massimi sistemi del mondo tolemaico et copernicano*, ed. O. Besomi and M. Helbing, 2 vols. (Padua: Antenore, 1998), 2: 899–901.

141. Sante Pieralisi, *Urbano VIII e Galileo Galilei* (Rome: Propaganda Fide, 1875), 210.

142. Antonio Favaro, "Intorno ad un episodio non ancora chiarito del processo di Galileo," *Atti del Reale Istituto Veneto* ser. 5, 8 (1888): 213–31.

143. Beretta, "Rilettura," 104.

144. "È uscito un libro . . . col titolo come nell'accluso foglio [missing]. Mostra d'es-sere stampato in Bologna, ma la carta da sospetto che sia stampato altrove. In alcuni luoghi l'Autore inserisce delle maledicenze contro la Corona di Spagna, per la qual cosa Nostro Signore havea già ordinato al Ill. [S. Beretta; Sig. Pieralisi] Cardinal Legato che si riformasse [informasse Pieralisi] se veramente era stampato in Bologna e che vedesse perch'è stata data licenza di stamparlo contenendo le suddette cose. Un ordinario dopò è stato anche ordinato che si supprimase [supprimano Beretta Pieralisi] tutti gli esemplari. Dopò fatte queste diligenze venne [? Beretta] [è venuto Pieralisi] hieri [alli 22 Pieralisi] il [Sig. Beretta Pieralisi] Card. Borgia all'udienza di Nostro Signore et ha portato uno di questi esemplari dolendosi che si sia permessa in Bologna la stampa d'esso, e S. B. ha risposto che tiene ra-gione, e che [non Beretta Pieralisi] si doveva permettere ma che [missing Pieralisi] quelche si poteva fare già S. B. l'haveva [aveva Pieralisi] fatto, *ch'è de' [che è Pieralisi] dar ordine che si supprimase [supprimano Beretta Pieralisi] gli esemplari del che *l'Eminenza e restato sodisfatto [è stato sodisfatto il Sig. Cardinale Pieralisi]. Io ne dò parte a V. S. acciò se [ne Pieralisi] vagli di [not in Beretta] questa notizia nella meglior [meglio Pieralisi; miglior Beretta] maniera che le parera e perche non si meraviglia [maraviglino Pieralisi meraviglino Beretta] costà che alle volte per inavvertenza di chi ha cura di rivedere i libri da stamparsi, scappi qualche cosa indegna di stampa, si serva dell'esempio del Galileo il quale havendo composto un libro del moto della terra, fù ammesso alla stampa dal Maestro del Sacro Pala-zzo, e stampato. Nel quale sono stati poi trovati errori grave che hanno obligato la S. Cong. re del S. Uff.o non solo a supprimere i libri, ma a chiamar lo stesso Autore a [in Pieralisi]

Roma per disdirsi come ha fatto." F. Barberini–Nuncio Monti, 23 June 1633 in BAV, Barb. lat. 6228, fos. 91r–2v; printed in Pieralisi, *Urbano VIII*, 138–39, and as a discovery—because Pieralisi did not cite his source and made some small errors in his text—in Francesco Beretta, "Urbain VIII Barberini Protagoniste de la Condamnation de Galilée," in *Largo campo di filosofare: Eurosymposium Galileo 2001*, ed. José Montesinos and Carlos Solís Santos (La Orotava, Spain: Fundación Canaria Orotava de Historia de la Ciencia, 2001), 549–73, 572; cf. the extract of the undated minute in *EN* 15: no. 2561 from BAV, Barb. lat. 8370, fo. 107r; *DV*, no. 182. For the time of the audience, see Andrea Nicoletti's life of Urban in BAV, Barb. lat. 4731, p. 92, and Girolamo Lunadori, *Relazione della corte di Roma* (Rome: Rossi, 1728), 55. Pieralisi, *Urbano VIII*, 138, identified the book as *Le Soldat Svedois*, which has a tangled bibliography, but Sergio Pagano demonstrated that the offending title was Jacopo Gaufrido (born Jacques Godefroy, executed 1650, a councillor of the duke of Parma), *Protrita impietas sive odiorum in Francos extincta pernicies* (Bologna: Clemente Ferroni, 1633).

145. BAV, Barb. lat. 5628, fos. 278r–79v.

146. ACDFSO:DSO 1633, fos. 105v and 106r, virtually whole entry now destroyed!; *EN* 19: 284; *DV*, no. 141.

147. *RI*, 39.

148. (1) Absolution (*Scholion* 50, p. 161); (2) "solum diffamatus" ("De secundo modo finiendi processum in causa fidei per purgationem canonicam" according to *Scholion* 51, p. 162; cf. no. 7); (3) "quaestionibus & tormentis supponendus" (*Scholion* 53, p. 165); (4) "suspectus de haeresi leviter" (*Scholia* 55 and 56, pp. 169 and 173); (5) "vehementer" (Eymeric, *Directorium Inquisitorum*, 317–22; *Scholion* 57, p. 174); (6) "violenter" (*Scholion* 58, p. 175); (7) "diffamatus. . .& suspectus insimul" (*Scholion* 60, p. 177; cf. no. 2); (8) "confessus haeresim & paenitens, & non relapsus probabiliter (*Scholia* 61–62, pp. 178–81); (9) "sed relapsus veraciter" (*Scholion* 63, p. 181); (10) "impenitens sed non relapsus" (*Scholia* 51, p. 162, and 64, p. 183); (11) "confessus. . .impaenitens atque relapsus certitudinaliter" (*Scholion* 51, p. 162); (12) "non confessus, sed convictus" (*Scholia* 51, p. 162; 66, p. 185; 67, p. [on false witnesses]; and 68, p. 188); and (13) "convictus. . .sed fugitivus" (*Scholia* 51, p. 162, and 69, p. 190). These do not correspond exactly to the following discussion. Eymeric, *Directorium Inquisitorum*, 311–34. Masini, *Sacro arsenale* (1625), 183, and Carena, *Tractatus*, 304–6. See the long list of authorities cited in Peña, *Scholion* 55 to part 2, 595, among whom he singled out Juan de Rojas in the first article of his *Singularia iuris*, fos. 1rff. much of which Peña incorporated into his discussion.

149. See Masini, *Sacro arsenale* (1625), 183. It almost never appears in the decree registers.

150. Eymeric, *Directorium Inquisitorum*, 261.

151. Ibid., 258.

152. Peña, *Scholion* 55 to part 2, 596; Carena, *Tractatus*, 307.

153. Eymeric, *Directorium Inquisitorum*, 259.

154. "Summarium. 1) Vehementer suspectus de haeresi habendus est qui vocatus ad respondendum de fide, non comparet in tempore assignato: 2) Et quicunque scienter impedit sancte inquisitionis officium. 3) Item praestantes scienter consilium, auxilium, vel

favorem dictis impeditoribus. 4) Qui instruit haereticos citatos, ut veritatem subticeant, & dicant falsitatem. 5) Excommunicatus ex causa fidei quocunque modo. 6) Fautor, Defensor, Receptator scienter haereticorum. 7) Infamatus de haeresi ob familiaritatem cum his, quos haereticos esse cognovit. 8) Scienter deducens, visitans, receptans haereticos. 9) Convictus de periurio vel mendacio iudicialiter in causa fidei: 10) Et qui dixit vel fecit saepius aliquid contra fidem." Ibid., 260. These categories partially overlap, for example, numbers 1 and 5.

155. Peña, Scholion 62 to part II, question 56, 535.

156. Eymeric, *Directorium Inquisitorum* (1578), 259.

157. ACDFSO:DSO 1633, fos. 102v–103r; extract without names of consultors in *EN* 19: 283; Cioni, *Documenti*, no. XXVII; *DV*, no. 115; Beretta, "Rilettura," 113–15; English translation in *TG*, no. 82, and Finocchiaro, 292–93. An *avviso* of 25 June reported the abjuration. ASMod:AE, 139, fasc. June 1633, unfoliated, 2 copies; *EN* 19: no. 2556.

158. Scheiner–Athanasius Kircher, 16 July 1633, Rome. *EN* 15: no. 2588.

159. Decree of 14 September in ACDFSO:DSO 1628, fo. 156v; cf. BAV, Urb. lat. 1098 II, fo. 510r. See Beretta, *Galilée*, 230, for public abjurations at Santa Maria sopra Minerva. It is usually claimed that Galileo abjured in the present Biblioteca del Senato, but that room did not exist in 1633. See, e.g., the official site of the Camera dei deputati, saying "È probabile che il luogo prescelto dalla Congregazione del Santo Uffizio siano le sale attualmente denominate Galileo, arricchite da affreschi di Francesco Allegrini, il più importante dei quali rappresenta una vittoria delle forze cattoliche contro gli Albigesi, nella battaglia di Muret del 1213," http://legi6.camera.it/100?sede_camera_descrizione=10&sede_camera=3, accessed 8 July 2013, or Shea and Artigas, *Galileo in Rome*, caption to third last plate before 133.

160. Niccolò Riccardi, "Prodromos" to "Historiae Tridentinae a Petri Suavis calumniis vindicatae et restitutae," BAV, Barb. lat. 2934, p. 29.

161. Fulgenzio Manfredi's abjuration similarly did not follow his sentence proper, but instead tracked its narrative section almost exactly. *SI*, 94.

162. "supplicò li SS.ri Cardinali che, poiché si procedeva con lui in quella maniera, li facessero dire quanto a loro Eminenze piaceva, eccettuando solamente due cose egli non dovesse mai dire di non essere cattolico, perchè tale era et voleva morire, a onta e dispetto de' suoi malevoli; l'altro, che nè meno poteva dire di havere mai ingannato nessuno, et specialmente nella publicatione del suo libro, il quale haveva sottoposto alla censura ecclesiastica et, havutane legitimamente l'approvatione, fattolo stampare. *EN* 19: 411. Buonamici was in close touch with Galileo during much of the final phase of his trial. EN 15: nos. 2424, 2432, and 2437.

163. Beretta, "Censure doctrinale," 37.

164. ACDFSO:DSO 1633, fos. 105v and 106r, virtually the whole of which entry is now destroyed; *EN* 19: 284; *DV*, no. 141. See also Antonio Badelli's *avviso* of 2 July, excerpted in *EN* 15: no. 2565.

165. *Avviso* of 13 August in ASMod:AE, 139, fasc. August 1633, unfoliated.

166. Niccolini–Cioli, 3 July 1633, Rome. *EN* 15: no. 2568.

167. ACDFSO:DSO 1633, fos. 110v–10r, in Indice; *EN* 19: 284; *DV*, no. 49. The note of Niccolini's supplication in Galileo's dossier is *DV*, no. 51, misdated 30 instead of 29 June.

168. Niccolini–Cioli, 3 July 1633, Rome. *EN* 15: no. 2568.

169. For the vicars, see Paolo Vicari–Antonio Barberini, Sr., Bologna, 16 July 1633. *DV*, 107.

170. *SI*, 107 and 148. See also *RI*, 204.

171. Cioni, *Documenti*, 30n.

172. Francesco Beretta, "Orthodoxie philosophique et Inquisition romaine au 16e-17e siècles. Un essai d'interprétation," *Historia Philosophica* 3 (2005): 67–96; "Censure doctrinale," 26; "Condamnation," 48; and "Galileo, Urban VIII and the Prosecution of Natural Philosophers," in McMullin, ed., *The Church and Galileo*, 234–61.

173. Francesco Beretta, "Urbain VIII Barberini Protagoniste de la Condamnation de Galilée," in Montesinos and Solís Santos, eds., *Largo campo*, 549–73, 570; Beretta, *Galilée*, 227.

174. Neveu and Mayaud, "L'Affaire Galilée," 304.

175. Antonio Barberini–Clemente Egidi, Rome, 2 July 1633. *EN* 20: no. 2565bis and Cioni, *Documenti*, no. XXV.

176. *DV*, nos. 113 and 143.

177. E.g., nuncio to Venice Francesco Vitelli–Antonio Barberini, Sr., Venice, 6 August 1633, and nuncio to Vienna Ciriaco Rocci–Antonio Barberini, Sr., 20 August 1633. *DV*, nos. 60 and 65.

178. Paolo Delli Franci–Antonio Barberini, Sr., Naples, 14 September 1633; nuncio in France Alessandro Bichi–Antonio Barberini, Sr., Saint-Nicolas, 1 September 1633; *DV*, no. 81; and nuncio in Cologne Pier Luigi Carafa–Antonio Barberini, Sr., Liège, 11 September 1633; *DV*, nos. 74, 81, and 88.

179. Vincenzo Maria Pellegrini–Antonio Barberini, Sr., Perugia, 10 September 1633; *DV*. no. 68.

180. Galileo had "un particolare e speciale precetto fattoli in Roma dal Commissario, alla presenza del Card.le Bellarmino, di non tenere nè insegnare tal dottrina. . . avere con fraude [where did this come from?] estorto facultà di stamparlo, per non avere confessato di avere tal precetto." Guiducci–Galileo, Florence, 27 August. *EN* 15: 2661.

181. See Niccolini–Galileo (who had already moved to Villa Medici), 2 July, Rome, and Niccolini–Cioli, 3 July, Rome. *EN* 15: nos. 2564 and 2568.

182. *EN* 19: 363; *DV*, no. 50.

183. *EN* 19: 363–4ff.; Cioni, *Documenti*, no. XXV; *EN* 15: no. 2566; *DV*, nos. 52–99. Neither Egidi's nor Piccolomini's replies, noted as reported in congregations of 20 and 21 July, appear in the decree register.

184. Chancellor Stefano's attestation in Cioni, *Documenti*, 38; Egidi–Antonio Barberini, Sr., 27 August 1633, Florence (*EN*, 19, 369); and Guiducci–Galileo, 20 August 1633, Florence (*EN*, 15 no. 2661). See also *avviso* of 9 July in *EN* 15: no. 2573.

185. Decree of 24 August in ACDFSO:DSO 1633, fo. 143r; *EN* 19: 285, and *DV*, no. 144; *EN* 15: no. 2662; *EN* 19: 369 and 371–72, *DV*, nos. 63 and 67.

186. *EN* 15: no. 2670. Favaro identifed the copy as BNCF, Mss. Gal., P. I, T. III, fos. 6–9, but Lerner disagrees without argument. "Sentence," 610. For Galileo's return to Florence, see *EN* 15: no. 2695.

187. Decree of 23 March in ACDFSO:DSO 1634, fo. 59r–v; 1634, Copia, pp. 193–94; EN 19: 286. See Antonio Barberini, Sr.'s letter to Egidi of 25 March 1634 and Egidi's acknowledgment of 1 April. Cioni, *Documenti*, no. XXX; *EN* 20: no. 2909bis and *EN* 19: 394; *DV*, no. 103. For Galileo's previous appeals, see *EN* 15: nos. 2675, 2732, and *EN* 19: 389–90 (*DV*, no. 94), ACDFSO:DSO 1633, fo. 204r, entry now badly damaged (*EN* 19: 285–86; *DV*, no. 147), *EN* 19: 391 (*DV*, no. 98), and decree of 12 January 1634 in 1634, fo. 15v; 1634, Copia, p. 49 (*EN* 19: 286; *DV*, no. 148).

CONCLUSION

1. See *RI*, Chapter 5.

2. Thomas F. Mayer, "The Status of the Inquisition's Precept to Galileo (1616) in Historical Perspective," *Nuncius* 24 (2009): 61–95, 92–95.

3. See *RI*, 196.

4. For exceptions, see the cases of Antonio Ceparelli (two instances) (ACDFSO:DSO 1603, fo. 64r; cf. Copia, fo. 68r–v; 135r); Giacomo Antonio Marta (one, his own) (1610–1611, fo. 39v); Rodrigo Alidosi (*SI*, Chapter 5); and Christóbal Suárez de Figueroa (1630, fo. 121v and *SI*, 29 et seq.). For its use in Giordano Bruno's and Tommaso Campanella's cases without appearing in the registers, see *SI*, chapters 2 and 4. Perhaps significantly, all but Bruno had legal representation.

5. Guido Morpurgo-Tagliabue, *I processi di Galileo e l'epistemologia* (Milan: Edizioni di Comunità, 1963; Rome: Armando, 1981; originally published in *Rivista di storia della filosofia*, 1947 nn. 2, 3; 1948 n. 1), 126–27, noted that "Galileo's lack of legal expertise blinded him to the excellent strategy of attacking the precept." See Mayer, "Status," 85–86.

6. For Baffadi and Mariano Alidosi, see *SI*, Chapter 6.

7. *DV*, 7.

8. Rivka Feldhay, *Galileo and the Church: Political Inquisition or Critical Dialogue?* (Cambridge: Cambridge University Press, 1995).

9. Lorenzo Magalotti–Francesco Barberini, Rome, 3 April 1625. BAV, Barb. lat. 8729, fos. 15v and 17r.

10. See especially David Marshall Miller, "The Thirty Years War and the Galileo Affair," *History of Science* 46 (2008): 49–74.

11. Mario D'Addio probably pushes it hardest as a factor in Galieo's condemnation. "Considerazioni sul processo di Galileo," *Rivisita di Storia della Chiesa in Italia* 37 (1983): 1–52, 38; (1984): 47–114, 6, 79, 90, 104–5; published in book form as *Il caso Galilei, processo, scienza, verità* (Rome: Studium, 1993), English translation *The Galileo Case: Trial, Science, Truth* (Leominster: Gracewing, 2004).

12. Campanella–Galileo, Rome, 25 September 1632. *EN*, 14, no. 2309.

13. See Chapter 6, 187.

14. Jules Speller, *Galileo's Inquisition Trial Revisited* (Frankfurt: Peter Lang, 2008), 167.

15. Ibid., 170, repeated on 220.

16. *EN* 19: 344; *DV*, no. 39; *TG*, no. 72.

17. *SI*, Conclusion.

18. *EN* 15: no. 2449; English translation in Finocchiaro, 248.

19. *Memorie del Cardinale Bentivoglio* (Venice: Paolo Baglioni, 1648), 123. The article "un" before "luogo" has been universally omittted, giving Bentivoglio the nonexistent office of "Supreme Inquisitior General" or something similar.

20. *RI*, Chapter 3. D'Addio's ("Considerazioni," 79) suggestion that Zacchia might have been in Galileo's corner is not impossible since the cardinal was one of only a few willing to stand up to Urban, but there is no evidence of any kind of attitude to Galileo.

21. Niccolini–Cioli, Rome, 19 June 1633. *EN* 15: no. 2550; English translation in *TG*, no. 79, and Finocchiaro, 254–55.

SELECTED BIBLIOGRAPHY

MANUSCRIPTS

Dublin, Trinity College, MSS 1230–33
Modena, Archivio di Stato, Cancelleria Ducale
    Ambasciatori Italia Roma, 1629–32
    Avvisi dall'Estero, 137–39
Rome, Archivio di Stato
    Archivio Cartari-Febei, MSS 2, 19, 47, 57–58, 131, 139–41, 155
    Governatore, Processi, sec XVII, b. 251
Rome, Archivum Congregationis Doctrinae Fidei Sanctum Officium, Decreta Sancti Officii, 1597–1637
Rome, Archivum Romanum Societatis Iesu, MSS Rom. 55 and Opp. NN 241, 243.I, 246
Rome, Biblioteca Casanatense, MSS 2103–4, 2631, 2653
Vatican City, Archivio Segreto Vaticano
    Segretaria dei brevi, Reg. 337, 395–96, 446, 595, 667, 754, 789, 941, 948
    Segretaria di Stato, Venezia, 38; Nunz. Firenze, 14, 14A, 15B, 20
Vatican City, Biblioteca Apostolica Vaticana: MSS
    Barberiniani latini 862, 1038, 1093–94, 1107–10, 1123, 1367, 1502, 2415, 2819, 2934, 2938, 2941–56, 3105, 3150–51, 4602, 4676, 4731, 5628, 6228, 6334, 6344, 6351–53, 6480, 7301, 7306–8, 7310, 8370, 9686
    Urbinates latini 1079, 1083–84, 1098 I–II, 1099 I, 1100–1101
Venice, Archivio di Stato
    Senato Dispacci Roma, 99, 103, 105, 106

PRIMARY SOURCES

Albizzi, Francesco. *De inconstantia in fide in De inconstantia in judiciciis tractatus.* Rome: Marcello Severolo, 1698.
———. *De inconstantia in iure admittenda, vel non.* Amsterdam: Jean Antoine Huguetan, 1683.
D'Ancarano, Pietro. *In quinque Decretalium libros facundissima commentaria.* 5 vols. Bologna: apud Societatem Typographiae Bononiensis, 1581.

———. *Super Clementinas facundissima commentaria.* Bologna: apud Societatem Typographiae Bononiensis, 1580.

———. *Super sexto Decretalium acutissima commentaria.* Bologna: Societas Typographiae Bononiensis, 1583.

D'Andrea, Giovanni. *In primum [-quintum] decretalium librum novella commentaria.* 5 vols. in 4. Venice: Francesco Francesco, 1581.

———, attributed to. *Ordo iudiciarius.* Venice: Egidio Regazola, 1573.

Anon. *Repertorium inquisitorum pravitatis haereticae.* Quintiliano Mandosio and Pietro Vendramino, eds. Venice: Damiano Zenaro, 1575.

Anon. *Repetitionum in universas fere iuris canonici partes, materiasque sane frequentiores.* 6 vols. Venice: Luca Antonio Giunta, 1587.

Baldini, Ugo, and Leen Spruit. "Nuovi documenti galileiani degli archivi del Sant'Ufficio e dell'Indice." *Rivista di Storia della Filosofia* 56 (2001): 661–99.

Besold, Christoph. *Thesaurus Practicus.* Nürnberg: Wolfgang Endter, 1643.

Carena, Cesare. *Tractatus de officio Sanctissimae Inquisitionis, et modo de procedendi in causis fidei.* Bologna: Jacopo Monti, 1668.

Cioni, Michele. *I documenti galileiani del S. Uffizio di Firenze.* Florence: Giampiero Pagnini, 1996; reprint of Florence, 1908 ed.

Da Baysio, Guido. *Rosarium super decreto.* [Venice], 1494.

———. *Super decreto [liber].* Lyon: Ugo da Porte, 1549.

Da Budrio, Antonio. *Super librum primum-quintum Decretalium commentarii.* 4 vols. Venice: Giunta, 1578.

Da Castiglionchio, Lapo. *Allegationes*, ed. Quintiliano Mandosio. Venice: Francesco Ziletti, 1571.

Da Castro, Paolo. *Consiliorum . . . volumen primum [-tertium].* 3 vols. Venice: [Società dell'Aquila che si rinnova], 1580–1581.

———. *In Pandectarum, Iustinianeique Codicis, titulos commentaria.* 8 vols. Venice: Giunta, 1593–1594 [Venice: Giunta, 1592–1593].

Da Oriano, Lanfranco. *Repetitio on Quoniam contra [2]*, in *Repetitionum in universas fere Iuris canonici partes, materiasque sane frequentiores.* 6 vols. Venice: Luca Antonio Giunta, 1587.

Da San Gimignano, Domenico. *Super Decretorum volumine commentaria.* Venice: Giunta, 1578.

Da Sassoferrato, Bartolo. *Gemma legalis seu compendium aureum.* Venice: Giunta, 1596.

———. *Repertorium locupletissimum in omnes Bartoli a Saxo Ferrato lecturas.* Turin: Heirs of Niccolò Bevilacqua, 1577.

Da Susa (Hostiensis), Enrico. *In primum [-sextum] decretalium librum commentaria.* 7 vols. Venice: Giunta, 1581.

Da Trani, Goffredo. *Summa . . . in tit[ulis] decretalium.* Venice: ad candentis Salamandræ insigne [?Damiano Zenaro], 1564.

De Bohic, Henri. *In quinque Decretalium libros commentaria.* 5 vols. Venice: Heirs of Girolamo Scoti.

De Peñafort, Raymond. *Summa de poenitentia.* Rome: Giovanni Tallini, 1603.

De' Tudeschi, Niccolò. *Compendium aureum totius lecturae d. abbatis panormitani super decretalibus.* Venice: Michele Tramezino, 1564.

———. *Omnia quae extant commentaria, primae [-tertiae] partis, in primum [-quintum] Decretalium librum.* 9 vols. Venice: Giunta, 1588.

———. *Prima [-ultima] p[ar]s Abb. Panor. sup[er] primo [-quarto [et] q[ui]nto] Decre[talium].* [Lyon?]: Jean Petit, 1521–1522.

Del Maino, Giason. *In primam [-secundam] codicis partem commentaria.* 2 vols. Venice: Giunta, 1573.

Decio, Filippo. *In Decretalium volumen perspicua commentaria.* Venice: Giunta, 1593.

———. *Super decretalibus [libri].* Lyon: Mathieu Bernard and Étienne Servani, 1564.

———. *Super librum primum-quintum Decretalium commentarii.* 8 vols. in 5. Venice: Giunti, 1578.

Delle Colombe, Raffaele. *Delle prediche sopra tutto gli Evangeli dell'anno.* Florence: B. Sermartelli e fratelli, 1613.

———. *Dupplicato avvento di prediche.* Florence: Sermartelli, 1627.

———. *Prediche della quaresima.* Florence: B. Sermartelli e fratelli, 1622; first ed. 1615.

Durand, Guillaume. *Speculi pars prima [-tertia et quarta].* Lyon: no publisher, 1543.

Eymeric, Nicolau. *Directorium inquisitorum.* Francisco Peña, ed. Rome: Giorgio Ferrari, 1587.

———. *Directorium inquisitorum.* Rome: In Aedibus Populi Romanorum, 1578.

Farinacci, Prospero, *Tractatus de haeresi.* Rome: Andrea Fei, 1616; another ed., Lyon: Jacques Cardon and Pierre Cavellat, 1621.

Favaro, Antonio, ed. *Le opere di Galileo Galilei.* 20 vols. 1890–1909. Reprint Florence: G. Barberà, 1933.

Finocchiaro, Maurice A., ed. *The Galileo Affair: A Documentary History.* Berkeley: University of California Press, 1989.

Gauchat, Patrice, ed. *Hierarchia catholica medii et recentioris aevi.* 4 vols. Münster: Regensburger Bibliothek, 1935.

Gherardi, Silvestro. *Il processo Galileo riveduto sopra documenti di nuova fonte.* Florence: Tipografia dell'Associazione, 1870.

Innocent IV (Sinibaldo De' Fieschi). *In quinque decretalium libros, necnon in decretales per eundem Innocentium editas . . . commentaria doctissima.* Venice: Bernardino Maiorini, 1570 and Venice: Giunta, 1578.

Kahl, Johann. *Lexicon iuridicum iuris caesarei.* Geneva: Matthieu Berjon for the Societas Caldoriana, 1612.

L'Épinois, Henri. *Les pièces du procès de Galilée précédees d'un avant-propos.* Rome: Palme, 1877.

Lorini, Niccolò. *Elogii delle più principali sante donne del sagro calendario.* Florence: Zanobio Pignoni, 1617.

—. *Preparazione e frutto del Ss.mo natale di Cristo divisa in venti Prediche i Vangeli, e le Pistole, Sponenti delle Domeniche dell'Avvento, ove la sostanza del senso letteral dichiarata, tutto'l resto ne santi sentimenti morali si stende* . . . *predicata in Roma nella Chiesa di San Giovanni dell'illustrissima nazion fiorentina l'anno 1605 e 1606. All'illustrissimo & reverendissimo sig. il sig. cardinal Capponi legato di Bologna.* Florence: Giunti, 1615.

Mandosio, Quintiliano. *Tractatus de monitoriis.* Rome: Giorgio Ferrari, 1581.

Masini, Eliseo. *Sacro arsenale, ovvero prattica dell'officio della S. Inquisizione ampliata.* Genoa: Giuseppe Pavoni, 1625; also 1621, 1639.

———. *Sacro arsenale, ovvero prattica dell'officio della S. Inquisizione,* with additions by Tommaso Menghini and Giovanni Pasqualone. Rome: Nella Stamperia di S. Michele a Ripa, 1730.

Mayer, Thomas F., ed. *The Trial of Galileo, 1612–1633.* Toronto: University of Toronto Press, 2013.

Menochio, Giacomo. *De arbitrariis iudicum.* Venice: ad Signum Concordiae, 1590.

———. *De arbitrariis judicum quaestionibus et causis libri duo.* Venice: Heirs of Girolamo Scoti, 1613.

———. *De praesumptionibus . . . commentaria.* Venice: Heirs of Girolamo Scotti, 1597.

Nicoletti da Imola, Giovanni. *In primum [-tertium] decretalium commentaria.* 4 vols. Venice: Domenico Nicolini, 1575 [1574].

Pagano, Sergio M., ed. *I documenti vaticani del processo di Galileo Galilei (1611–1741).* 2nd ed. Collectanea Archivi Vaticani 69. Vatican City: Archivio Vaticano, 2009.

Peña, Francisco. *Scholia* to Nicolau Eymeric, *Directorium inquistorum.* Rome: In Aedibus Populi Romani, 1578.

Poppi, Antonino. *Cremonini, Galilei e gli inquisitori del Santo a Padova.* Padua: Centro Studi Antoniani, 1993.

Quétif, Jacques, and Jacques Échard. *Scriptores ordinis praedicatorum recensiti, notisque historicis et criticis illustrati.* 2 vols. Paris: Ballard and Simart, 1721.

Ricciulli, Antonio. *Tractatus de iure personarum extra ecclesiae gremium existentium libris novem distinctus . . .; annexus est alter tractatus de neophytis.* Rome: Giovanni Angelo Ruffinelli and Angelo Manni, publishers, Andrea Fei, printer,1622.

Ruini, Carlo. *Consiliorum seu responsorum [tomi I–V],* ed. Girolamo Zanchi. Venice: Felice Valgrisi, 1591.

Sandeo, Felino. *Commentariorum... ad quinque libros decretalium pars prima [-tertia] [libri].* 3 vols. Venice: Società dell'Aquila che si Rinnova, 1600–1601.

———. *Consilia Felini Sandei.* Venice: [Sub signo aquilae renovantis], 1601.

Scaccia, Sigismondo. *Tractatus de iudiciis causarum civilium, criminalium et haereticalium, liber primus.* Frankfurt: Officina Paltheniana, 1618.

———. *Tractatus de sententia et re judicata.* Lyon: André, Jacques and Matthieu Prost, 1628.

Schard, Simon. *Lexicon iuridicum.* Cologne: Johannes Gymnicus, 1616.

Socii Instituti Historici Fratrum Praedicatorum, ed. *Monumenta ordinis praedicatorum historica.* 30 vols. Rome: Institutum Historicum Ordinis Fratrum Praedicatorum, 1896–.

Spruit, Leen. "Cremonini nelle carte del Sant'Uffizio Romano." In *Cesare Cremonini: Aspetti del pensiero e scritti,* ed. Ezio Riondato and Antonino Poppi. 2 vols. Padua: Academia Galileiana, 2000. 1: 193–204.

Weber, Christoph. *Die Päpstlichen Referendare 1566–1809: Chronologie und prosopographie.* 3 vols. Stuttgart: Anton Hiersemann, 2003.

Zabarella, Francesco. *Super primo [-quinto] Decretalium subtilissima commentaria.* Venice: Luc'Antonio Giunta, [1602].

SECONDARY SOURCES

Amabile, Luigi. *Fra Tommaso Campanella e la sua congiura, i suoi processi e la sua pazzia.* 3 vols. Naples: Morano, 1882.

Beltrán Marí, Antonio. *Talento y Poder: Historia de las Relaciones entre Galileo y la Iglesia católica.* Pamplona: Laetoli, 2006.

Beretta, Cesare. "Jacopo Menochio e la controversia giurisdizionale milanese degli anni 1596–1600." *Archivio Storico Lombardo* 3 (1977): 47–128.

———. "Jacopo Menochio giurista e politico." *Bollettino della Società Pavese di Storia Patria* 91 (1991): 245–77.

Beretta, Francesco. "L'affaire Galilée et l'impasse apologétique: Réponse à une censure." *Gregorianum* 84 (2003): 169–92.

———. "Galileo, Urban VIII and the Prosecution of Natural Philosophers." In *The Church and Galileo*, ed. Ernan McMullin. Notre Dame, Ind.: University of Notre Dame Press, 2005, 234–61.

———. "'Magno Domino & Omnibus Christianae, Catholicaeque philosophiae amantibus: D. D.' Le *Tractatus syllepticus* du jésuite Melchior Inchofer, censeur de Galilée." *Freiburger Zeitschrift für Philosophie und Theologie* 48 (2001): 301–27.

———. "Melchior Inchofer et l'hérésie de Galilée: Censure doctrinale et hiérarchie intellectuelle." *Journal of Modern European History* 3 (2005): 23–49.

———. "Le procès de Galilée et les archives du Saint-Office: Aspects judiciaires et théologiques d'une condamnation célèbre." *Revue des Sciences Philosophiques et Théologiques* 83 (1999): 441–90.

———. "Le siège apostolique et l'affaire Galilée: Relectures romaines d'une condamnation célèbre." *Roma Moderna e Contemporanea* 7 (1999): 421–61.

———. "Rilettura di un documento celebre: Redazione e diffusione della sentenza e abiura di Galileo." *Galilaeana* 1 (2004): 91–115.

———. "Urbain VIII Barberini Protagoniste de la Condamnation de Galilée." In *Largo campo di filosofare: Eurosymposium Galileo 2001*, ed. José Montesinos and Carlos Solís Santos. La Orotava, Spain: Fundación Canaria Orotava de Historia de la Ciencia, 2001, 549–73.

Bianchi, Luca. "'Mirabile e veramente angelica dottrina': Galileo e l'argomento di Urbano VIII." In *Il "Caso Galileo": Una rilettura storica, filosofica, teologica: Atti del Convegno internazionale di studi (Firenze 26–30 maggio 2009)*, ed. Massimo Bucciantini, Michele Camerota, and Franco Giudice. Florence: Olschki, 2011, 213–33.

Boaga, Emanuele. "Annotazioni e documenti sulla vita e sulle opere di Paolo Antonio Foscarini, teologo 'copernicano'." *Carmelus* 37 (1990): 173–216.

Bucciantini, Massimo. *Contro Galileo. Alle origini dell'Affaire.* Florence: Olschki, 1995.

———. "Reazioni alla condanna di Copernico: Nuovi documenti e nuove ipotesi di ricerca." *Galilaeana* 1 (2004): 3–19.

Camerota, Michele. *Galileo Galilei e la cultura scientifica nell'età della Controriforma.* Rome: Salerno Editrice, 2004.

Cerbu, Thomas. "Melchior Inchofer, 'un homme fin & rusé'." In Montesinos and Solís Santos, eds., *Largo campo*, 587–611.

Ciampoli, Domenico. "Monsignor Giovanni Ciampoli, un amico del Galileo." In *Nuovi studi letterari e bibliografici.* Rocca San Casciano: Licinio Cappelli, 1900.

D'Addio, Mario. "Considerazioni sul processo di Galileo." *Rivisita di Storia della Chiesa in Italia* 37 (1983): 1–52; 38 (1984): 47–114.

Dooley, Brendan. *Morandi's Last Prophecy and the End of Renaissance Politics.* Princeton, N.J.: Princeton University Press, 2002.

Eszer, Ambrogio. "Niccolò Riccardi, O.P., 'padre Mostro' (1585–1639)." *Angelicum* 60 (1983): 428–57.

Fantoli, Annibale. "The Disputed Injunction and Its Role in Galileo's Trial." In McMullin, ed., *Church and Galileo*, 117–49.

———. *Galileo for Copernicanism and for the Church.* 3rd English ed. Trans. George V. Coyne. Vatican City: Vatican Observatory Publications, 2003.

Favaro, Antonio. "Intorno ad un episodio non ancora chiarito del processo di Galileo." *Atti del Reale Istituto Veneto* ser. 5, 8 (1888): 213–31.

Favino, Federica. "'Quel petardo di mia fortuna': Riconsiderando la 'caduta' di Giovan Battista Ciampoli." In Montesinos and Solís Santos, eds., *Largo campo*, 863–82.

Fedele, Pio. "Dei precetti ecclesiastici." In *Scritti giuridici in onore di Santi Romano.* 4 vols. Padua: CEDAM, 1940. 4: 267–310.

Finocchiaro, Maurice A. *Retrying Galileo, 1633–1992.* Berkeley: University of California Press, 2005.

Frajese, Vittorio. *Il processo a Galileo Galilei: Il falso e la sua prova.* Brescia: Morcelliana, 2010.

Freedberg, David. *The Eye of the Lynx: Galileo, His Friends, and the Beginnings of Modern Natural History.* Chicago: University of Chicago Press, 2002.

Galli, Giuseppe. "Il cardinale Vincenzo Maculano al processo di Galilei." *Memorie domenicane* (1965) fasc. I–III: 24–42, 65–101, 146–75.

Garzend, Léon. *L'Inquisition et l'Hérésie: Distinction de l'Hérésie théologique et de l'Hérésie inquisitoriale: à propos de l'affaire Galilée.* Paris: Desclée, De Brower-G. Beauchesne, 1912.

Von Gebler, Karl. *Galileo Galilei und die römische Kurie nach den authentischen Quellen.* [n.p.]: Emil Vollmer, [n.d.]; reprint of Phaidon edition itself reprint of Stuttgart: J.G. Cotta, 1876.

Ghisalberti, A. M., ed. *Dizionario biografico degli italiani.* Rome: Istituto dell'Enciclopedia italiana, 1960–; www.trecani.it.

Giacchi, Orio. "Considerazioni giuridiche sui due processi contro Galileo." In *Nel terzo centenario della morte di Galileo Galilei,* ed. Università Cattolica del Sacro Cuore. Milan: Vita e Pensiero, 1942, 383–406.

Gilbert, Philippe. "La Condamnation de Galilée et les publications recentes." *Revue des questions scientifiques* (April 1877): 353–98; (July 1877): 130–94.

Guerrini, Luigi. *Cosmologie in lotta: Le origini del processo di Galileo.* Florence: Polistampa (Mauro Pagliai), 2010.

———. *Galileo e la polemica anticopernicana a Firenze.* Florence: Polistampa, 2009.

Heilbron, J. L. *Galileo.* Oxford: Oxford University Press, 2010.

Jaitner, Klaus. "Der Hof Clemens VIII. (1592–1605): Eine Prosopographie." *Quellen und Forschungen aus italienischen Archiven and Bibliotheken* 84 (2004): 137–331.

Katterbach, Bruno. *Referendarii utriusque Signaturae a Martino V ad Clementem IX et Praelati Signaturae Supplicationum a Martino V ad Leonem XIII.* Studi e Testi 55. Città del Vaticano, 1931.

Kraus, Andreas. *Das päpstliche Staatssekretariat unter Urban VIII 1623–1644. Römischer Quartalschrift für christliche Altertumskunde and Kirchengeschichte, Supplementheft 29.* Rome: Herder, 1964.

De Laurentiis, Rodolfo. "Sigismondo Scaccia (1564–1643). Fra pratica e teoria giuridica agli inizi dell'età moderna." *Rivista di Storia del Diritto Italiano* 64 (1991): 233–339.

Leman, Auguste. *Urbain VIII et la rivalité de la France et de la maison d'Austriche de 1631 à 1635.* Mémoires et Travaux Publiés per des Professeurs des Facultés Catholiques de Lille 16. Lille: R. Giard and É. Champion, 1920.

McMullin, Ernan, ed. *The Church and Galileo.* Notre Dame, Ind.: University of Notre Dame Press, 2005.

Mayaud, Pierre-Noël. *La condamnation des livres coperniciens et sa révocation à la lumière de documents inédits des Congrégations de l'Index et de l'Inquisition.* Miscellanea Historiae Pontificiae 64. Rome: Editrice Pontificia Università Gregoriana, 1997.

Mayer, Thomas F. "The Censoring of Galileo's Sunspot Letters and the First Phase of His Trial." *Studies in the History and Philosophy of Science,* Part A 42, 1 (2011): 1–10.

———. "An Interim Report on a Census of Galileo's Sunspot letters." *History of Science* 50 (2012): 155–96.

———. *The Roman Inquisition: A Papal Bureaucracy and Its Laws in the Age of Galileo.* Philadelphia: University of Pennsylvania Press, 2013. (RI)

———. *The Roman Inquisition on the Stage of Italy, ca. 1590–1640.* Philadelphia: University of Pennsylvania Press, 2014. (SI)

———. "The Roman Inquisition's Precept to Galileo (1616)." *British Journal for the History of Science* 43, 3 (2010): 327–51.

Miller, David Marshall. "The Thirty Years War and the Galileo Affair." *History of Science* 46 (2008): 49–74.

Montini, G. Paolo. "I rimedi penali e le penitenze: un'alternative alla pene." In *Il processo penale canonico,* ed. Zbigniew Suchecki. Rome: Lateran University Press, 2003, 75–101.

Morpurgo-Tagliabue, Guido. *I processi di Galileo e l'epistemologia.* Rome: Armando

Armando, 1981, rev. ed.; 1st ed. Milan: Edizioni di Comunità, 1963; originally published in *Rivista di Storia della Filosofia* (1947), nn. 2, 3; (1948), n. 1.

Neveu, Bruno, and Pierre-Noël Mayaud. "L'Affaire Galilée et la tentation inflationiste: À propos des notions d'hérésie et de magistère impliquées dan l'affaire." *Gregorianum* 83 (2002): 287–311.

Onclin, Willy. *De territoriali vel personali legis indole*. Gembloux: J. Duculot, 1938. Dissertationes ad gradum magistri in Facultate Theologica vel in Facultate Iuris Canonici consequendum conscriptae, Universitas Catholica Lovaniensis ser. 2, vol. 31.

Pagano, Sergio. "Il precetto del Cardinale Bellarmino a Galileo: Un falso? con una parentesi sul radio, Madame Curie e i documenti Galileiani." *Galilaeana* 7 (2010): 143–203.

Pieralisi, Sante. *Urbano VIII e Galileo Galilei*. Rome: Propaganda Fide, 1875.

Reusch, Franz. *Der Process Galilei's und die Jesuiten*. Bonn: Eduard Weber, 1879.

Ricci-Riccardi, Antonio. *Galileo Galilei e fra Tommaso Caccini: Il processo del Galilei nel 1616 e l'abiura segreta rivelata dalle carte caccini*. Florence: Le Monnier, 1902.

De Santillana, Giorgio. *The Crime of Galileo*. Chicago: University of Chicago Press, 1955.

Shea, William R., and Mariano Artigas. *Galileo in Rome: The Rise and Fall of a Troublesome Genius*. Oxford: Oxford University Press, 2003.

Speller, Jules. *Galileo's Inquisition Trial Revisited*. Frankfurt: Peter Lang, 2008.

Westfall, Richard S. *Essays on the Trial of Galileo*. Vatican City: Vatican Observatory Publications, 1989.

Wieland, Christian. *Fürsten, Freunde, Diplomaten: Die römisch-florentinischen Beziehungen unter Paul V. (1605–1621)*. Norm und Struktur 20. Cologne: Böhlau, 2004.

Wilding, Nick. "Manuscripts in Motion: The Diffusion of Galilean Copernicanism." *Italian Studies* 66 (2011): 221–33.

Wohlwill, Emil. *Der inquisitionsprocess des Galileo Galilei: Eine prüfung seiner rechtlichen grundlage nach den acten der römischen inquisition*. Berlin: Robert Oppenheim, 1870.

———. *Ist Galilei gefoltert worden? Eine kritische Studie*. Leipzig: Duncker and Humblot, 1877.

INDEX

ACKNOWLEDGMENTS

This work began as a volume for the trade press. I thank all those who helped to whip the proposal into shape, Owen Gingerich (who also tried to attract his own publisher's attention), John Guy, Leanda De Lisle, Elaine Reiter, Suzanne Bozhkov, and John Thornton. In the early days, that book was to be written with my colleague David Hill, and I profited from numerous discussions with him. A large number of audiences helped me further refine my ideas, especially ones that reacted hostilely to my understanding of the Roman Inquisition, and I thank the host institutions and my sponsors: the Center for Medieval and Renaissance Studies at UCLA which honored me by making me its first Distinguished Visiting Fellow in its fiftieth year (Andy Kelly); University of the South (Brown Patterson); University of Mississippi (Joe Ward); Rhodes College (Lynn Zastoupil); University of California-Santa Barbara (Stefania Tutino and Anne Thaves); Trinity College, Hartford (Dario del Puppo and John Alcorn, the Barbieri Endowment); Wesleyan University (Marcello Simonetta, the Thomas and Catherine McMahon Memorial Fund); Yale University (Giuseppe Mazzotta); University of St. Thomas (Irving Kelter and Mary Katherine Sommers, Thomistic Institute); Texas A&M University, Melbern G. Glasscock Center for Humanities Research (director Jim Rosenheim, associate director Donnalee Dox and Cary Nederman for the original suggestion); Saint Louis University, Center for Medieval and Renaissance Studies (Thomas Madden, director, and Teresa Harvey); Università di Torino, Scuola di Dottorato in Studi Storici e Fondazione Luigi Firpo Centro di Studi sul Pensiero politico (Massimo Firpo); Scuola Normale Superiore, Pisa (Adriano Prosperi); Università di Roma 3 (Giorgio Caravale and Alberto Aubert); Institute for the History and Philosophy of Science and Technology, Department of Astronomy and Astrophysics, Victoria University and Department of Italian Studies, St. Michael's College, University of Toronto (Ken Bartlett, John Percy, Marga Vicedo and Domenico Pietropaolo); Duke University (John Martin); East Carolina University (Jonathan Reid); Davidson College (Robin Barnes); the

Webster Club, Adler Planetarium, Chicago (Voula Saridakis and Marv Bolt); Cornell University (John Najemy and William Kennedy, the Renaissance Colloquium); Hartwick College (Peter Wallace); LeMoyne College (Chris Warner); University of Notre Dame, John C. Reilly Center and Department of History (Brad Gregory and Katherine Brading); Indiana University, Renaissance Studies, History and Philosophy of Science, Religious Studies, History, and French and Italian (Constance Furey and Massimo Scalabrini); University of Oxford, Early Modern Seminar (Robin Briggs); University of Cambridge, Faculty of Divinity (Eamon Duffy); University of Warwick, Centre for Renaissance Studies and STUDIO (Peter Marshall); Northwestern University, Departments of French and Italian, History, and Friends of Italian Culture (Ed Muir); University of Minnesota, Center for Early Modern Studies, Program in the History of Science and Technology, and Studies in Early Modern Sovereignty (J. B. Shank); Iowa State University (Michael Bailey and David Wilson).

A half-dozen individuals made signal contributions to fostering my research, among them my publisher at Ashgate, John Smedly, who jiggered the publication schedule of *The Correspondence of Reginald Pole*; Eamon Duffy, who arranged a fellowship at Magdalene College, Cambridge, which allowed me to exploit the vast resources of Lord Acton's library in the Cambridge University Library; Jeff Abernathy, former dean of Augustana College, who encouraged my work, not least by providing time off; and Jerry Singerman, a model editor, along with his efficient staff at Penn who have made publishing this trilogy almost a pleasure. Finally, Chris Black and Andy Kelly read at least two thirds of the volumes for Penn. With impressive persistence, Chris read all three and offered unfailingly constructive criticism from the minute to the architectonic. Andy Kelly saved me from a number of blunders in both law and Latin. Our discussions of Galileo's trial while I was in residence at UCLA greatly improved this book.

Finally, a number of institutions facilitated my work, especially the American Academy in Rome, which provided a fellowship and congenial environment in which to work and exchange ideas (although this list is invidious, I have to single out Marina Lella, Paul Arpaia, Erik Gustafson, who also donated a copy of *DV*, Dylan Sailor, Alan Berger, Mark Danner, Daniel McReynolds and Jorie Woods). It would have taken much longer to write these three books without the resources of the Vatican Film Library at St. Louis University (Gregory Pass, Susan L'Engle and Barbara Chanel). The AV collection at the University of Iowa Law Library (Nancy Mashuda-Pohnl) similarly saved me time in more distant collections. The Interlibrary Loan staff at Augustana (Sherrie Herbst and Donna Hill) nearly always produced results, even in the case of obscure titles. Although founded in archival work, especially in the Archivio della Congregazione per la Dottrina della Fede Santo Uffizio whose staff (Alejandro Cifres, Daniel Ponziani, Fabrizio de Sibis) from top to bottom could not have been more accomodating, the Archivio Segreto Vaticano, and the Archivum Romanum Societatis Iesu (Tom McCoog, Jim Pratt, Elena and Stephen), many libraries provided almost as valuable resources, especially the Casanatense, the Fisher Rare Book Library, University of Toronto (Richard Landon), the Diamond Library, Columbia University School of Law (Whitney S. Bagnall) and the Houghton and Law School Rare Books Room at Harvard.

I dedicate this book to the memory of my grandfather, F. E. Mayer, whose *The Religious Bodies of North America*, first published in 1954, is still in print.

Tom Mayer died on 20 January 2014 at the age of sixty-two after a long struggle with cancer. His achievements are well known in the academy; and his meticulous scholarship has enriched our knowledge of the sixteenth and seventeenth centuries in a great many ways. His dedication to his work continued not only undiminished but more focused during the last eighteen months of his life. Once the seriousness of his illness was confirmed, Tom was committed to completing the third volume of his study of the Roman Inquisition. The first two books had emerged in 2013 and 2014 but he saw these as prologue to the third: *The Roman Inquisition: The Trial of Galileo*. Despite his failing health, Tom succeeded in finishing his manuscript, although he did not have the pleasure of seeing it through the press.

I had known Tom for more than thirty years. Our paths often crossed in North America and in Italy; and we shared a great number of interests both personal and scholarly. I learned of his cancer when he contacted me to say that we would not as planned meet in Italy in the summer of 2012 where we both expected to be teaching, he in Rome, I in Siena. That same year I became aware how serious his illness had become as Tom wrote to me in Italy and asked if I would take on the responsibility of ensuring that *The Trial of Galileo* saw print, should he not be able to finish the manuscript. I of course agreed. Fortunately for us all, Tom lived long enough to complete the text and submit the manuscript. My responsibility consequently became insignificant, little beyond completing some footnotes and bibliographical entries and reading the text closely to identify the few infelicities in Italian and Latin transcriptions. As usual, Tom's scholarly precision was evident in this his last work, which, I am delighted to say is altogether his.

The Roman Inquisition: Trying Galileo serves then as Tom's final contribution to knowledge. He is sorely missed by his wife, Jan, and daughter, Molly. And they are joined by a great many friends and colleagues on two continents who had expected his deep and insightful research to continue well into the new millennium. This fine book is a fitting memorial. Thomas F. Mayer *Ave atque vale.*

Kenneth Bartlett
Victoria College
University of Toronto